READINGS
IN
ETHNOMUSICOLOGY

Landmarks in Anthropology, a series of reprints in cultural anthropology
General Editor: Weston La Barre

READINGS

IN

ETHNOMUSICOLOGY

SELECTED AND WITH AN INTRODUCTION AND COMMENTS, BY

David P. McAllester

Professor of Anthropology and Music

Wesleyan University, Middletown, Connecticut

JOHNSON REPRINT CORPORATION

New York · London

1971

Library of Congress Catalog Card Number: 78-184042

Johnson Reprint Corporation
111 Fifth Avenue
New York, N.Y. 10003, U.S.A.

Johnson Reprint Company Ltd.
24/28 Oval Road
London, NW 7DD, England

PERMISSIONS

We gratefully acknowledge permissions received from authors and publishers to reprint the articles appearing in these volumes:

Bruno Nettl, "What is ethnomusicology?," reprinted from *Theory and Method in Ethnomusicology*, 1964, pp. 7-26, copyright © 1964 by The Free Press of Clencoe, a Division of The Macmillan Company; Kurt Reinhard, "The Berlin Phonogramm-Archiv," reprinted from *The Folklore and Folk Music Archivist*, V, 2, pp. 1-4; Charles Seeger, "Prescriptive and descriptive music writing," reprinted from *The Musical Quarterly*, XLIV, April (1958), pp. 184-195, by permission of the copyright holder, G. Schirmer, Inc.; Mantle Hood, "Slendro and Pelog redefined," reprinted from *Selected Reports*, I, 1 (1966), pp. 28-48; Linton C. Freeman and Alan P. Merriam, "Statistical classification in anthropology: an application to ethnomusicology," reprinted from *American Anthropologist*, 58 (1956), pp. 464-472; Samuel P. Bayard, "Prolegomena to a study of the principal melodic families of British-American folk song," reprinted from *Journal of American Folklore*, 63, 247 (1950), pp. 1-44; Paul Cullaer, "Cartography and ethnomusicology," reprinted from *Ethnomusicology*, II, 2 (1958), pp. 66-68; George Herzog, "Plains ghost dance and great basin music," reprinted from *American Anthropologist*, 37 (1935), pp. 403-419; Willard Rhodes, "A study of music diffusion based on the wandering of the opening Peyote song," reprinted from *Journal of the International Folk Music Council*, 10 (1958), pp. 42-49; Theodore C. Grame, "Bamboo and music: a new approach to organology," reprinted from *Ethnomusicology*, 6 (1962), pp. 8-14; Bruno Nettl, "Historical Aspects of Ethnomusicology," reprinted from *American Anthropologist*, 60, 3 (1958), pp. 518-532; Richard A. Waterman, "Music in Australian aboriginal culture — some sociological and psychological implications," reprinted from *Journal of Music Therapy*, V (1955), pp. 40-49; Edwin G. Burrows, "Music on Ifaluk Atoll in the Caroline Islands," reprinted from *Ethnomusicology*, volume 2 (1958), pp. 9-22; Harold C. Conklin and Jose Maceda, "Hanunou music from the Philippines," reprinted from Ethnic Folkways Library (1955), 20 pp.; David P. McAllester, *Indian Music in the Southwest*, Taylor Museum of the Colorado Springs Fine Arts Center, 1961, 15 pp.; Alan Lomax, Song structure and social structure," reprinted from *Ethnology*, 1 (1962), pp. 425-451; George List, "The boundaries of speech and song," reprinted from *Ethnomusicology*, 7 (1963), pp. 1-16; Leonard B. Meyer, "Universalism and relativism in the study of ethnic music," reprinted from *Ethnomusicology*, 4 (1960), pp. 49-54; Siegfried Nadel, "The origins of music" (translated by Theodore Baker), reprinted from *Musical Quarterly* XVI (1930), pp. 531-546, by permission of the copyright holder, G. Schirmer, Inc.; Robert E. Brown, "India's Music," *Chapters in Indian Civilization, Vol. II, British and Modern Period*, 1967, pp. 367-403 (ed. by Joseph W. Elder, Department of Indian Studies, University of Wisconsin, June, 1967); J. H. Nketia, "Modern trends in Ghana music," reprinted from *African Music*, I, 4 (1957), pp. 13-17; Lawrence Picken, "The music of Far Eastern Asia: 1. China," reprinted from *The New Oxford History of Music*, Oxford University Press, pp. 83-96, 130-134; William P. Malm, "Practical approaches to Japanese traditional music," reprinted from Center for Japanese Studies, *Occasional Papers*, no. 9, University of Michigan Press, 1965, pp. 95-104.

CONTENTS

FUNCTIONALISM

REGIONAL STUDIES

SELECTED AND ANNOTATED BIBLIOGRAPHY   367

INTRODUCTION

Present-day ethnomusicology was foreshadowed by such treatises as Amiot's *Mémoire sur la musique des Chinois, tant anciens que modernes*, in the late eighteenth century. Europeans were already developing a serious interest in non-European music, but it was the invention of the phonograph that led to the collection of actual sound recordings in archives and the possibility of systematic comparative study in the laboratory. The first such collection was the Berlin Phonogrammarchiv, started in 1900. It began as a repository for the early phonograph cylinders made by ethnologists in the German colonies but psychologists, physicists, musicologists, and others quickly became aware of the theoretical interest of tone systems, intonations, and melodies never before heard by Western ears.

Scholarly societies, especially those anthropological and musical, soon began to hear, at their meetings and in their publications, about the newly available musics, but the first organization with the focus on ethnomusicology as an independent field did not arise until 1930. The men who developed and made use of the Berlin archive established a society which eventually took the name Gesellschaft für Vergleichende Musikwissenschaft and in the same year an offshoot, the American Society for Comparative Musicology. was formed in New York. The American group had joint membership in the German society and received its journal, the *Zeitschrift für Vergleichende Musikwissenschaft*.

These promising beginnings were brought to a halt by the rise of the Nazi terror in Germany and by World War II. But after the war, in part because of the exposure of thousands of young people to new cultures all over the world and especially in the Orient, a very general interest in non-Western musics gave rise to a number of new organizations and publications. The International Folk Music Council, with international support through UNESCO, began publishing its proceedings in 1948. The Society for Ethnomusicology had its beginnings in 1952 and its formal organization took place at a meeting of the American Anthropological Association in 1955. In the same year the first Regional Music Conference of Southeast Asia was held in Manila under the sponsorship of the International Music Council and UNESCO. Public interest in folk music has become a mass phenomenon since the 1950's and there can be little doubt that this fact contributed importantly to the student support of the academic programs in folk music, folk lore, and ethnomusicology that have come into being since that time.

The rapid growth of journals and other publications can be seen in the selected bibliography at the end of this collection of readings. Also reflected there is the heterogeneity of the backgrounds of the scholars who are making contributions to the field. The presence in the societies of linguists, archivists, dance ethnographers, ethnologists, sociologists, psychologists, and others serves abundant notice that this is not a field for the music specialist alone.

As in the case of the anthropologists' interest in man, ethnomusicologists are concerned with music anywhere in the world and with almost as many approaches to this music as there are scholars. A comparative and relativistic view has led to a characteristic emphasis on the exotic but it is recognized in the field that the definitation of this term depends on the orientation of the speaker. As Gregory Corso's *haiku* puts it:

> In the Mexican zoo
> they have ordinary
> American cows.

The essays and selections gathered here represent an attempt to present characteristic examples of the various kinds and levels of writing in the field of ethnomusicology. Though many of these pieces defy any simple classification, they are grouped under five headings: definition of the field, notation and classification of material, historical interpretations, functional interpretations, and regional studies. These headings give a rough indication of the major emphases in ethnomusicological research to date.

I wish to thank the Editor, Weston La Barre, for his conception of this collection of readings and for the patient and painstaking help he and his staff have given in the long task of making such an assemblage. I am deeply grateful to my many colleagues who have generously given permission for the use of their work even though, in some cases, it has meant taking a section of a longer study out of the context for which it was written. My gratitude also goes to the various publishers whose kind consent has made this collection possible.

Any book such as this is bound to be plagued by its omissions. My apologies to any of my colleagues who would have chosen differently; all responsibility for inadequacies of any sort is mine alone.

COMMENTS ON THE SELECTIONS

A comprehensive introduction is provided by Nettl ("What is Ethnomusicology?"). The problems of collecting material and classifying it receive a large share of attention, as might be expected in a young discipline. Reinhard ("The Berlin Phonogramm-Archiv,") gives an account of the first collection of comparative music to be made available on phonograph records. Seeger ("Prescriptive and Descriptive Music Writing") points out the inadequacies of conventional music notation and discusses various kinds of electronic graphing devices which point the way to mechanical, and therefore objective, music writing in the future. The importance of electronic precision in acoustical measurement is demonstrated in Hood's reevaluation of the much-studied Javanese modes ("Sléndro and Pélog Redefined"; with a Note on Laboratory Methods by Max Harrell).

Linton and Merriam also make use of precise quantification ("Statistical Classification in Anthropology: An Ethnomusicological Illustration") in order to test the validity of a classificatory technique that focuses on just one aspect of melody: the comparative number of intervals of various degrees. Bayard ("Prolegomena to a Study of the Principal Melodic Families of British-American Folksong") comes to grips with the problem of identifying large numbers of melodies in enough detail to permit the recognition of similarities.

After they have been collected and classified, a major function of ethnomusicological data has been their use as evidence for historical connections between cultures. Collaer ("Cartography and Ethnomusicology") illustrates the interest of European scholars in this problem. Herzog ("Plains Ghost Dance and Great Basin Music") gives a classic example of a historical reconstruction based on an idiosyncracy of musical style. Rhodes ("A Study of Musical Diffusion Based on the Wandering of the Opening Peyote Song") does an even more particular study of the history of a single, widely known song. Grame ("Bamboo and Music: A New Approach to Organology") suggests the value of studying the materials from which instruments are made, as an aid to the understanding of history and development as well as classification. Nettl "'Historical Aspects of Ethnomusicology") gives a useful summary of this emphasis in the discipline.

By way of contrast, the functional approach of some of the American anthropologists in the field is represented in this collection of readings. Waterman ("Music in Australian Aboriginal Culture—Some Social and Psychological Implications") relates musical behavior to the culture seen as an organic whole. To varying degrees this is the theoretical emphasis in the descriptive essays on particular musical cultures by Burrows ("Music on Ifaluk Atoll in the Caroline Islands"), Conklin and Maceda (Hanunóo Music from the Philippines"), and

McAllester ("Indian Music in the Southwest"). The most ambitious program of research in the functional relationships between music and culture is the "canto-metrics" project of Alan Lomax and his associates ("Song Structure and Social Structure") which relates music on a worldwide scale to social and psychological orientations. List's article ("The Boundaries of Speech and Song") illustrates the promise of investigations in the relations between music and language. Such close relationships have been seen between music and the cultures in which they are found that there has been a tendency to close the door on any further discussion of the old hypothesis that music is in some sense a universal language. Meyer ("Universalism and Relativism in the Study of Ethnic Music") reopens this question at a sophisticated level. To remind us that functional explanations are neither new nor exclusively American, Nadel's essay ("The Origins of Music") has been included. Written nearly forty years ago, it presents a theory of music, and all art, that is both functional and structural.

Finally, to give more breadth to the regional coverage which is so much a part of the concern of ethnomusicologists, we include Brown ("India's Music"), Nketia ("Modern Trends in Ghana Music"), Picken ("Chinese Music"), and Malm (Practical Approaches to Japanese Traditional Music").

THE FIELD

"WHAT IS ETHNOMUSICOLOGY?"

Bruno Nettl

Some Approaches to Ethnomusicology

Like most young disciplines, ethnomusicology has engaged in a good deal of self-criticism and self-inspection. Since 1950, a number of articles have been written about the problems of defining the scope of ethnomusicology. While these give the impression of controversy, the authors do not argue so much about the outside limits of the field as about emphases within the field; with few exceptions, they agree on the scope of ethnomusicology. Most of them are prepared to include all cultures of the world, including Western civilization, but they recognize the greater importance to themselves of non-Western and folk music. Among the exceptions is Jaap Kunst (1959:1), who stresses the role of oral tradition as a distinguishing feature. Curt Sachs, in the subtitle of his general work on ethnomusicology (Sachs 1959), specifies that *Musik der Fremdkulturen* (music of foreign cultures) is the material to be studied in what he still calls *vergleichende Musikwissenschaft* (comparative musicology—the earlier term for ethnomusicology). The German Marius Schneider (1957:1) specifies non-European music, and emphasizes the importance, in defining the field, of comparative work. Rhodes (1956) tends to support the same position.

Kolinski (1957:1-2), however, points out that it is not so much the geographic area as the general approach which distinguishes our field. He believes that ethnomusicology has developed a point of view which results from the study of many and diverse cultures, but which should be applied also to Western art music. The notion that the subject matter should be limited geographically, i.e., include only the non-Western world, has been the object of widespread objection and criticism. But in spite of the acceptance by many scholars of the desirability of including Western art music, it is taken for granted that only in studying a culture foreign to himself can a scholar muster sufficient objectivity. By studying his own culture, he may be conditioned to too many prejudices and personal associations to be properly objective—so many ethnomusicologists believe. Thus one may envision Western music being investigated in ethnomusicological fashion by African or Asian scholars, while Westerners could continue to specialize in non-Western cultures.

Going even further in this direction, (Merriam (1960) stresses the need for universal use of ethnomusicological methods. Indeed, Seeger ("Whither Ethnomusicology?", p. 101) believes that historians of Western art music have usurped the name "musicology," which should really be reserved for those now called ethnomusicologists; the mentioned historians would then be considered special-

3

ists within the broader field, coeval with, say, historians of Chinese music. While a case can be made for the justice of this proposal, there is not much point in urging its acceptance on the scholars involved. Finally, Chase (1958:7) defines ethnomusicology as the "musical study of contemporary man," including Western man; but he seems to omit from his definition the historical study of oriental cultivated music which is usually included, as well as the use of archeological evidence in nonliterate cultures.

In the matter of emphasis, most ethnomusicologists agree that the structure of music and its cultural context are equally to be studied, and that both must be known in order for an investigation to be really adequate. In the research done before 1930, analysis and description of the music itself outweighed the other approaches. Since 1950, on the other hand, the American ethno-musicologists coming from anthropology seem to have favored the study of musical culture over detailed work with the music itself. Merriam (1960:109-10) lists six main areas to which a student of one musical culture should give his attention, in addition to the music itself: 1) instruments; 2) words of songs; 3) native typology and classification of music; 4) role and status of musicians; 5) function of music in relation to other aspects of the culture; and 6) music as creative activity. Merriam also stresses the importance of field work, that is, of the need for the ethnomusicologist, in order to work effectively, to collect his raw material himself, and to observe it in its "live" state. Again, probably no one would deny the importance of field work. Before about 1940, however, it was taken for granted that some scholars would not or could not go into the field, and that they would do comparative work in the laboratory. It was also assumed that those who did field work would occasionally spend time at home working on music collected by others—general anthropologists perhaps—who could make recordings but could not analyze the music. These "armchair ethnomusicologists," according to Merriam (1960:113), are gradually decreasing in importance. Now, it may be argued that the basic field work can be replaced by the collecting and descriptive study on the part of native scholars in underdeveloped countries, for instance that the American field worker in the Congo can be replaced by the Congolese working in his own backwoods. Also, it may be said that an ethnomusicologist devoting himself entirely to a field study of one culture can hardly engage in comparative work. And if he is replaced by the native field worker, what will his function be? It may be argued that, in addition to field work, the armchair approach, broad and comparative, is a very essential contribution of ethnomusicology. According to Seeger ("Whither Ethnomusicology?", p. 104), "who will digest the results? It is the Hornbostels who will do so with great and lofty objectivity, and together the two techniques (field and comparative) will give us the music of mankind." On the other hand, few would seriously object to Merriam's statement that the primary understanding of music depends on an understanding of the people's culture (Merriam 1960:113).

Since 1953, a group of American ethnomusicologists has tried to achieve the kind of understanding envisioned by Merriam by immersing itself into foreign cultures as active musicians. The basic assumption of this group, whose leader is

Mantle Hood, equates the musical style of a culture to some extent with a language, so that by long contact with a given musical culture, an ethnomusicologist can become the equivalent of a native musician. Just as it takes a great deal of learning and practice to learn a second language beyond one's native tongue, and thus to become bilingual, it requires time and frequent contact with another musical culture to become bi-musical (Hood, 1960). Some ethnomusicologists have become proficient as Siamese, Indian, and Japanese musicians, having studied with native masters. A member of such a group becomes a specialist on only one or two foreign musical cultures. This approach has been a great success, but it seems to exclude the possibility of the broad comparative approach, since a Westerner can no more become proficient in many musical cultures than he can learn to speak many languages perfectly. The concept of bi-musicality has also been used by ethnomusicologists in non-Western nations whose aim is not only the objective study of their music but the shaping of a musical culture in which Western and native elements are combined. This approach could perhaps be called "applied ethnomusicology," in a fashion analogous to "applied anthropology," whose function is to help non-Western groups through the process of acculturation with Western civilization. A much more comprehensive statement of Hood's position was published in 1963. (Hood 1963). Here Hood also surveys the history of ethnomusicology in America.

We see, then, that the field of ethnomusicology has a core of subject matter—the music of nonliterate cultures, the music of advanced oriental societies, and the folk music of Western and oriental civilizations—which is generally accepted as its field of competence, and that disagreements exist only in defining the outer limits of the field and in determining emphasis and approach. We can summarize the consensus in stating that ethnomusicology is, in fact as well as theory, the field which pursues knowledge of the world's music, with emphasis on that music outside the researcher's own culture, from a descriptive and comparative viewpoint. Field work and laboratory analysis, structure of music and cultural background, broad comparison and the narrower specialization associated with developing bi-musicality, synchronic and diachronic study—all are relevant and important. Needless to say, in all approaches, objectivity, avoidance of value judgments based on the investigator's own cultural background, and the acceptance of music as a part of culture are essential.

Finally, we may ask again whether ethnomusicologists should concern themselves with the music of the Western high culture; and if they did this, how they would be distinguished from the "ordinary" historians of Western music. My personal answer to the first question is a not-too-emphatic "yes." The second question will be answered, in part, in this book. In summary, this answer is that historians of Western music have concentrated on a few aspects of musical culture, and that they have sometimes taken things for granted which should not have been taken for granted. An ethnomusicological approach to Western music would take into account the role of music in culture, the problems of performance practice, those of descriptive versus prescriptive notation, the procedures and methods of describing music (which have barely been touched in

Western music). The difficulties of studying foreign musical cultures have forced ethnomusicologists to develop methods which try to assure objectivity and criticism of evidence. The historian of Western music, being a member of the culture which he is studying, has not always had to be so concerned with objectivity, and the approach of the critic rather than the scholar is still felt in many of his publications. The ethnomusicologist's main potential contribution to the study of Western music is, then, the techniques which he has developed in the study of other musical cultures.

Trends in the History of Ethnomusicology

A definitive history can hardly be written for a field, such as ethnomusicology, which is so new that the majority of its exponents are still living and active. Several brief surveys of the history of ethnomusicology have appeared; those by Sachs (1962:5-32), Kunst (1959), and Nettl (1956:26-44) may be mentioned here. This history is actually the subject of our book and appears in its various aspects in each chapter. Our task here is to summarize the ideological trends in the history of ethnomusicology, something which is not easy to do because so many of the scholars are of the present rather than the past: their total contributions as well as their predominant points of view can hardly be evalu-superseded by still more significant ones. Many trends can be felt in different countries at various times, and the emergence of individual scholars has occasionally wrought sudden changes in these trends because the field is so sparsely populated. Nevertheless, certain tendencies have been manifested, and the alternating influence of various disciplines has caused an alternation of emphasis and interest which is worth noting.

As a field concerned with the music of non-Western cultures, ethnomusicology is an old area of interest; but as a field with modern methods and equipment and with a name, it is relatively new. In some ways it goes back to the composers of the later Middle Ages and the Renaissance who used folk music and even some Asian material, which would have been considered very exotic, as elements in some of their compositions. The Renaissance humanists and the eighteenth-century rationalists were surely the spiritual predecessors of the modern interest in all aspects of man's behavior, and in the ways of men outside one's own culture. To the history of ethnomusicology belongs Jean-Jacques Rousseau, whose famous encyclopedia of music, first published in 1767, contains samples of folk, Chinese, and American Indian music. Descriptions of oriental music were written by missionaries in the late eighteenth and early nineteenth-centuries. And an interest in European folk music has been conspicuous in the world of scholarship in early nineteenth-century Europe, particularly England and Germany.

Perhaps we can consider the descriptions of Chinese music by French missionaries (du Halde, Amiot) and the collecting of German folk songs by philosophers and philologists (such as Herder and the brothers Grimm) as part of the same cultural tradition. Different as were the backgrounds of these two groups of students, both were evidently motivated by a regard for the value of musical material foreign to themselves. It is curious to find missionaries, whose aim was to present Western culture and religion to the Orient, doing also the opposite, bringing oriental music to the West. But it was to be expected that the poets of Romanticism would take an interest in the songs of the rural population. The collections of individuals such as Herder (see Pulikowski 1933) and the theoretical treatises on folklore by what Dorson (1955) calls the first group of English folklorists were eventually to have considerable impact on the development of ethnomusicology. But there is actually not much connection between, on the one hand the nineteenth-century collectors of folk song, the missionaries such as Amiot, and the historians of Western music who also delved into the Oreint, such as Kiesewetter, and on the other hand, the founders of the discipline of ethnomusicology.

Whereas ethnomusicology is usually, by implication, considered much younger than historical musicology, the two areas, in the modern senses of their names, originated in the same decade. Musicology is usually considered to have started in 1855 with the publication of the *Vierteljahrschrift für Musikwissenschaft*, whose founders were Philipp Spitta, Friedrich Chrysander, and Guido Adler. These scholars distinguised between music history and the presumably more scholarly and in some ways scientific approach of musicology, which was to embrace not only Western music history but also the various aspects of "systematic musicology"—music theory, acoustics, psychology of music, and the synchronic study of the music of non-Western cultures. The second volume of the *Vierteljahrschrift für Musikwissenschaft* did indeed contain a milestone in ethnomusicology: Carl Stumpf's study of Bella Coola Indian songs (Stumpf 1886), which is considered by some as the first really ethnomusicological publication since it is a study of the musical style of a single tribe with emphasis on the structure of scale and melody.

Jaap Kunst (1959:2-3) does not consider Stumpf as the first *bona fide* ethnomusicologist, but prefers to place A. J. Ellis in this honored spot. Ellis's major work (Ellis 1885) is close in time to Stumpf's and again shows the proximity in time of origin between historical musicology and ethnomusicology. Kunst considers Ellis important because of his contributions to methodology—the so-called cents system of measuring intervals was devised by him—rather than because of his investigation of any individual musical style or culture. Whichever of these scholars is considered the real founder of our field, its beginnings belong properly in the 1880's, the time in which historical musicology also began.

Ethnomusicology was not the outgrowth of a single field; rather, representatives of several disciplines converged, roughly at the same time, but probably not by coincidence, on the music of the non-Western cultures. Carl Stumpf can perhaps be considered a representative of the field of psychology, which was one of the subjects on which he published widely, and both he and the outstanding Erich M. von Hornbostel were employed in the "psychological institute" of the

University of Berlin. A. J. Ellis was a philologist and mathematician. Walter Fewkes was an anthropologist; while Franz Boas, the anthropologist who had such a great impact on American ethnomusicologists, brought to his field the methods of his first areas of study, geography and physics. The historians of Western music who were prominent at the time of the first ethnomusicological publications—Adler, Spitta, Chrysander—had an interest in and a respect for this new branch of their discipline, but their own contributions to it and their influence on it were relatively minor. In later times, and even during the 1940's and 1950's, ethnomusicologists seem to have been recruited less from the ranks of music historians than from those of folklorists and anthropologists, and when the field of music did contribute a scholar to the field, it was perhaps more likely to be a practicing musician or composer than a historian.

The large number of disciplines which have contributed personnel has made ethnomusicology a field with little centralized methodology. We cannot say that any single tradition led to our methods. A field which has the broad goal of understanding all of the world's music in its cultural context has of necessity had to draw on the experience of many fields of study. The diversity of our origins has been more of an asset than a liability, even though it has at times obstructed clear communication. But in the early days of ethnomusicology, the importance of psychologically and mathematically oriented scholars had far-reaching consequences. Characteristically, the recognition by Ellis, that intervals must be measured objectively, and his invention of the cents system according to which each halftone is divided into 100 equal parts (the cents) gave impetus to the objective description of scales.

The importance of the invention of sound recording to the development of ethnomusicology cannot be overestimated. Right from the time of the earliest recordings, students of non-Western music began using this marvelous method of preserving the sound of a performance of music, as a way of collecting their raw material and as an aid to its analysis. It is generally believed that the first recordings of non-Western music were made by Walter Fewkes, who made Edison cylinders of Zuni and Passamaquoddy Indian songs in 1889. The phonographic recording of ethnic music was taken up by other American scholars, such as Frances Densmore, and shortly after Fewkes' beginning, the German pioneer Carl Stumpf also published a study of Indian music (Stumpf 1892) based on recorded material. The need for using recordings in the study of non-Western music was immediately obvious to the student. He was, after all, confronted by a kind of sound which may have seemed chaotic, which made no musical sense to his Western-oriented ear, and he needed repeated hearings in order to enable him to reduce this mass of strangeness to something which his mind could perceive as a system. In the area of folk music, the need for studies based on recordings was not generally accepted quite as early. Here the student thought himself to be faced by a kind of music with whose style he was already familiar through his acquaintance with Western cultivated music, and because folk songs had already been written down and published in collections for decades. It was not until the highly prestigious Béla Bartók (whose notations, based on recordings, differ so greatly from those presented in commercial folk song collections) showed that ethnomusicological methods of notating music produced a page of music which looked quite different from the pages of older folk song collections, and began to publish his scientific studies of Hungarian and other Eastern European folk music, that European folk song began routinely to partake of the processes of field recording and transcription.

After the practice of recording became established at the turn of the nineteenth century, many individuals not primarily or particularly interested in music began to make recordings of the music of cultures near which they happened to be. It became evident that the processes of colonization and Westernization of all peoples was about to work changes in the musical cultures of the world, and that many musical styles would soon disappear. This applied also to Europe and North America, whose rapid urbanization and industrialization threatened to cause the traditional folk music styles to disappear. Anthropologists and folklorists therefore took up the cause of music recording, and since they required no special knowledge of music in order to make these recordings, great numbers of cylinders, and later, of disks, were produced and given to the ethnomusicologists, who worked at home in the laboratory, for transcription and analysis. Indeed, the bulk of the material collected was too great for the small sprinkling of ethnomusicologists to handle, so that the establishment of organized archives became essential.

The idea of having archives for storing, processing, classifying, and cataloging ethnomusicological recordings has become basic in the field and has led to the development of a special area of knowledge and skill within ethnomusicology. Archives are, in a sense, equivalent to libraries in other disciplines insofar as their importance in research is concerned.

The most famous of the European archives is the Phonogramm archiv in Berlin, founded in 1900 by Carl Stumpf and Otto Abraham mainly for storing cylinders brought by German ethnologists. It functioned for several decades as the model for archives established elsewhere, especially in the United States, where a former assistant in the Berlin archive, George Herzog, was later to build at Columbia University a similar collection which moved, in 1948, to Indiana University. Since World War II, the leading role among archives has been taken over by Herzog's institution, called the Archives of Folk and Primitive Music (and which in 1954 came under the direction of George List), and by the Library of Congress's Archive of Folk Song. For histories of the various European archives, see issues of the *Folklore and Folk Music Archivist*, also the works of Kunst (1959), Herzog (1936) and Hornbostel (1933). The history of archives is a fascinating one to which an entire volume should be devoted: we can mention only the most important individual institutions.

Most of the archives have recordings as their primary interest; background information of all sorts (see Chapter 3) is included, but notations are not usually part of the collections, although the Indiana University archive as well as the Berlin-Phonogrammarchiv have issued lists of publications based on their recorded holdings. Some of the European folk song archives, however, have consisted largely of transcriptions, and only lately have begun adding recordings to their holdings. Possibly the most prominent of these archives is the Deutsches Volksliedarchiv in Freiburg-im-Bresgau. Here are stored collected versions of the words and music of German folk songs in manuscript as well as on recordings. The disadvantages of manuscript collections compared to recorded ones, if not self-evident, are discussed in Chapter 4. But an archive such as that in Freiburg has the advantage of making possible a much more thorough indexing and cataloging of its material than does a collection consisting only of recordings. The Freiburg archive has a number of catalogues and indexes, making it possible to identify songs according to type, place collected, first phrase of the tunes, related tunes in European folk music outside Germany, inclusion in printed sources, etc. This type of cataloguing has not had a great impact on the archives which concentrate on non-Western music, but it should become, increasingly, an aspect of all ethnomusicological archiving. In summary, we should stress that the development of archives has been tremendously important. In the 1960's, national archives in many nations, regional ones in large countries such as the United States, and more modest institutional ones abound; and one of the future tasks of ethnomusicology will be to centralize the information regarding the holdings of all of these collections. The work of many ethnomusicologists has been oriented toward the individual piece of music, rather than—as some would wish—toward the musical behavior of cultures. And this fact has as its background the development of archives and their emphasis on identifying and creating approaches to the specific work of music. The fact that archives have, to a degree, neglected the cultural context of music is perhaps a factor in the relative neglect, until very recently, of this important phase of ethnomusicology.

Ethnomusicology in the United States

In the United States, ethnomusicology since 1900 has occupied a position of relatively greater prominence than it has in Europe. We have mentioned the early recording activities of Walter Fewkes, who was later to become the director of the Bureau of American Ethnology in Washington (an institution which was, throughout this century, to sponsor a great deal of research on Indian music including the tremendous recording activity of Frances Densmore). American students of non-Western culture soon began to realize that music is an aspect of human behavior worth including in any picture of culture; but their European counterparts, with few exceptions, have shown less interest in music beyond making field recordings—which is in itself, of course, a valuable contribution. In the United States, some of the anthropologists became active in the study of these recordings, in transcription, analysis, and so forth. And anthropological institutions were the ones which supported scholars working in non-Western music. This is probably due to the attitude of Franz Boas, the German immigrant who is generally considered the leader of the distinctively American approach to anthropology which emphasizes field work, the description of whole cultures, and an interest in psychology. Boas himself made field recordings on the northwest coast of the United States and Canada, and did a certain amount of transcribing. And he trained a number of investigators who were to become scholars of great prominence (among them George Herzog), and who were to emphasize the role of the arts in their work. This tradition of anthropological background in American ethnomusicology (in contrast to the prevailingly musicological background in Europe) continued into the 1950's. Of course the statement of this tradition should not be taken too literally, for it indicates only a tendency; exceptions abound, and many individual scholars cannot be classified as being on either side of this not-too-distinct fence. In his relationship to other scholars, the ethnomusicologist (according to Sachs 1962:15) "sits on the fence between musicology and ethnology." But this is in a way only due to the coincidences which caused the field to be populated by individuals who began in one of the two main disciplines and then found the other attractive and necessary.

The American ethnomusicologists who approached their field as anthropologists did, indeed, frequently get into anthropology from the field of music. Some were practicing musicians (especially jazz musicians) who wished to delve into the folk and non-Western roots of their art. Others were students of Western music history who discovered the music of other cultures more or less by academic coincidences such as being required to take a cognate course in "comparative musicology." Some were students of anthropology who, hearing examples of African music, were motivated by the piano lessons taken in their youth to explore the exotic music further. Characteristically, it was the musician who in his student days was stimulated by anthropology, but who then returned to approach the field of ethnomusicology as an anthropologist. It has been rare for a student of culture to begin, as a graduate student, to show an interest in music, and to start from scratch to develop the knowledge of music needed for detailed ethnomusicological work. Perhaps the musical skill required for transcription and analysis must be acquired early in life, or at least cannot be gleaned from books but requires hours of laboratory training. At any rate, until recently, the American anthropologist who did not have a musical background of sorts was sometimes discouraged from making studies of music beyond simply collecting recordings in the field. Thus, while they have recognized the importance of music in culture and have encouraged the ethnomusicologists in their ranks, American anthropologists have not been very active in describing musical behavior themselves. But again, exceptions must be noted, and this is only a tendency. Since the 1940's, there have been efforts, especially on the part of Melville J. Herskovits, Alan P. Merriam, Richard A. Waterman, and others, to encourage anthropologists without a music background to study directly at least certain aspects of musical behavior which do not involve the technical analysis of music (see Merriam 1960).

Similar trends can be noted in European institutions in the 1950's. But in most cases, European scholars have been completely trained musicologists who later moved into ethnomusicology and digested the anthropological information which they needed when they were already mature scholars. Being historians of music, they frequently turned to the art music of the Asian nations, although they showed an interest also in the nonliterate cultures. Up to the 1950's, the American ethnomusicologists were mainly students of what they themselves called "primitive and folk music."

Since the early 1950's three important trends in American ethnomusicology have changed its image. Perhaps the most evident of these is the concept of bi-musicality as a way of scholarly presentation of the music of other cultures, and of active performance and even composition in the idiom of another culture as a way of learning the essentials of its musical style and behavior. This concept, fostered primarily by Mantle Hood at the University of California at Los Angeles, has had a great impact on the musicians in the United States and has taken the field of ethnomusicology to a degree out of the hands of anthropology departments in the universities and placed it in the music departments, many of which had previously been quite neglectful of it. Students of this new school of thought go into the field not so much as ethnological investigators but as pupils, and their desire is among other things to find competent native teachers who would teach them, as they would teach native pupils, the musical arts of their countries. Of course this approach is simplest in those cultures which have a way of talking about music, a system of music theory, and a tradition of music instruction. Thus it has been followed most frequently in the Asian high cultures. Pupils of Mantle Hood have begun teaching ethnomusicology at a number of American colleges, the result being that oriental music has begun to play a much greater role in ethnomusicology as it is practiced in this country. The more traditional, anthropological approach continues side-by-side with this new one, but even anthropologists, such as David P. McAllester, have been profoundly influenced by the idea that active performance, as well as passive observation, is of great use in studying a musical culture outside one's own background. We should add that while the performance or bi-musicality approach is obviously a great help, a student who has simply become accepted as a native Indian or Japanese musician has not yet, by virtue of this fact, become an ethnomusicologist, for at that point he has not yet made a contribution to our knowledge of world music: he has simply helped to prepare himself for making such a contribution in the future.

A second trend of the 1950's was the increasing concern of the ethnomusicologist with the contemporary music of other cultures. The tendency to look for "pure" or "authentic" material which had never undergone any influence from Western music has gradually given way to an attitude according to which musical material available in a culture is the object to be studied, and its presumed age or the degree to which it has been influenced by other musical cultures, while interesting, is not a criterion for inclusion in ethnomusicological study. An interest in the processes whereby the musical influence of the West is being brought to bear on non-Western musics, and, ultimately, in the ethnomusicological study of Western high culture, is becoming increasingly evident. Here ethnomusicology has followed the trend in American anthropology, according to whose views the anthropological methods must be used to study not only the cultures outside the investigator's background, but also his own culture. Since World War II, anthropologists in the United States have devoted increasing energy to studies of the American culture (see for example a special issue of *American Anthropologist*, vol. 57, no. 6, 1955), and investigators native to other cultures have worked in their own backgrounds. The emergence of musical scholars in those countries inhabited by some of the nonliterate societies has made it possible to accept the idea that the student of ethnomusicology can work in his own culture. Just as anthropologists have, in following this kind of an interest, collided with sociologists, historians, psychologists, etc., the ethnomusicologists may be stepping on the toes of their brother historians of contemporary Western music, of psychologists of music, etc. But many ethnomusicologists in the United States feel strongly that the methods and approaches which they learned in dealing with music outside their own culture can usefully be applied to Western art music, and that these methods can show things which the methods of musicologists at large cannot. Whether they are right remains to be seen; but especially in the area of comparison and in studies involving music as a universal concept can their point of view be useful. Just as some of the early ethnomusicologists came to the study of foreign cultures because of their desire to find out about man's musical behavior at large, which could not be determined on the basis of their own culture alone, the modern ethnomusicologist, who still wants to study man's musical culture, feels that he must include also the most complex culture of all along with the non-Western and folk cultures traditionally part of his discipline.

A third trend is the investigation of musical culture without the analysis and description of musical style, but through field work in which the role of music and of the individual's musical activity is researched. The impact of anthropology on this attitude has been mentioned above. We should indicate also another factor, the sudden growth of the recording industry, which has made available vast numbers of commercial records of non-Western and folk music, much of it of excellent research quality. One result of this sudden mushrooming of available sound has been a feeling of frustration on the part of the ethnomusicologist who must spend hours making a notation of one song, and a feeling that it is possible to analyze a considerable portion of musical behavior without the use of notation. Thus the emergence of mass recordings has tended to discourage the kind of detailed study of individual pieces which was formerly characteristic, and to reinforce the tendency, already present in anthropology, to describe musical behavior rather than musical style. It is to be hoped that the very laudable stress on the cultural context of music will not cause a substantial decrease in the technical study of the music itself.

The three tendencies mentioned here as being important during the 1950's and early 1960's are most evident in North America. The European ethnomusicologists have continued, largely, to work in solid traditions developed in the 1920's; and their contributions have been great. An interest in the typology of music, in the relationship of folk to art music, and in the geographic distribution of musical style have been among the noticeable emphases in European ethnomusicology since World War II. But since 1955, the amount of contact and the interdependence of European and American scholars so far as theory and method are concerned have steadily grown.

Bibliography

Chase, Gilbert, 1958, "A dialectical approach to music history," *Ethnomusicology* 2:1-8.

Dorson, Richard M., 1955, "The first group of British folklorists," *Journal of American Folklore* 68:1-8, 333-340.

Ellis, Alexander J., 1885, "On the musical scales of various nations," *Journal of the Society of Arts* 1885.

Herzog, George, 1936, *Research in Primitive and Folk Music in the United States, a survey.* Washington: American Council of Learned Societies, Bulletin 24.

Hood, Mantle, 1957, "Training and research methods in ethnomusicology," *Ethnomusicology Newsletter* 11:2-8.

Hood, Mantle, 1960, "The challenge of bi-musicality," *Ethnomusicology* 4:55-59.

Hornbostel, Erich M. von, 1933, "Das berliner Phonogrammarchiv," *Zeitschrift für vergleichende Musikwissenschaft* 1:40-47.

Kolinski, Mieczyslaw, 1957, "Ethnomusicology, its problems and methods," *Ethnomusicology Newsletter* 10:1-7.

Kunst, Jaap, 1959, *Ethnomusicology*, 3rd edition. The Hague: M. Nijhoff. Suggested reading, pp. 1-66.

Merriam, Alan P., 1955, "The use of music in the study of a problem in acculturation," *American Anthropologist* 57:28-34.

Merriam, Alan P., 1960, "Ethnomusicology, discussion and definition of the field," *Ethnomusicology* 4:107-114.

Merriam, Alan P., and Linton C. Freeman, 1956, "Statistical classification in anthropology . . . ," *American Anthropologist* 58:464-72.

Nettl, Bruno, 1956, *Music in Primitive Culture*. Cambridge: Harvard University Press. Suggested reading, Chapter 1.

Nettl, Bruno, 1961, *Reference Materials in Ethnomusicology*. Detroit: Information Service.

Pulikowski, Julian von, 1933, *Geschichte des Begriffes Volkslied im musikalischen Schrifttum*. Heidelberg: C. Winter.

Rhodes, WIllard, 1956, "Toward a definition of ethnomusicology," *American Anthropologist* 58:457-63.

Sachs, Curt, 1959, *Vergleichende Musikwissenschaft, Musik der Fremdkulturen,* 2nd edition, Heidelberg: Quelle und Meyer.

Sachs, Curt, 1962, *The Wellsprings of Music.* The Hague: M. Nijhoff. Suggested reading pp. 1-16.

Schneider, Marius, 1957, "Primitive music," in Egon Wellesz, ed., *Ancient and Oriental Music.* London: Oxford University Press (New Oxford History of Music, Vol. I), pp. 1-82.

Seeger, Charles, 1961, "Semantic, logical, and political considerations bearing upon research in ethnomusicology," *Ethnomusicology* 5:77-81.

Stumpf, Carl, 1886, "Lieder der Bellakula Indianer," *Vierteljahrschrift für Musikwissenschaft* 2:405-426.

Stumpf, Carl, 1892, "Phonographierte Indianermelodien," *Vierteljahrschrift für Musikwissenschaft* 8:127-144.

Wachsmann, Klaus P., 1961, "Criteria for acculturation," in International Musicological Society, *Report of the 8th Congress, New York 1961.* Kassel: Baerenreiter, p. 139-149.

"Whither ethnomusicology?", 1959, Panel discussion. *Ethnomusicology* 3:99-105.

NOTATION
AND
CLASSIFICATION

THE BERLIN PHONOGRAMM-ARCHIV
Kurt Reinhard

Shortly after the invention of the phonograph, Felix von Luschan, who later became Director of the Berliner Museum für Völkerkunde (Berlin Museum for Anthropology), suspected that this new type of equipment might someday be an important aid to anthropological research. However, he soon gave up the practical experiments which he had started in the mid-eighties, mostly because others convinced him that such a thing belonged in a public fair and not in the Museum. Thus Berlin lost the distinction of being the first to make scholarly recordings with a phonograph. Nevertheless, contact was soon established with the pioneer ethnomusicological field recordings in America: Carl Stumpf wrote a commentary on the recordings which Fewkes had made in 1889 among the Zuni Indians, and which Gilman had analyzed. Carl Stumpf began making his own phonograms only in 1900, when the Siamese court orchestra visited Berlin for a guest concert. He deposited these cylinders at the University of Berlin, in the Psychological Institute, of which he was Director. In effect, he laid the foundation for the Berlin Phonogramm-Archiv, although it was not given that name until a few years later.

Then two of his assistants, Otto Abraham and Erich Moritz von Hornbostel, also began to take an interest in comparative musicology, a field which Stumpf had founded only incidentally. They made their own recordings in Berlin, and analyzed these phonograms as well as those which ethnologists, at Stumpf's suggestion, brought back from their expeditions. In the meantime the Archiv had grown so rapidly that in 1905 von Hornbostel was officially appointed its Director. Von Hornbostel was, of course, one of the leading figures in the field of comparative musicology and the real center of the "Berlin school." We need not add anything here concerning his importance. Stumpf also did independent research in the new field, and in 1911, for example, published *Die Anfänge der Musik* (The Beginnings of Music) as his first comprehensive work. He always held his protective and influential hand over the new institution, but in actuality the Berlin Phonogramm-Archiv became the lifework of Erich von Hornbostel. Otto Abraham soon withdrew from the circle of scholars, but around von Hornbostel gathered many other scholars, whose chief fields lay mostly outside the Archiv, like Curt Sachs, Robert Lachmann, and George Herzog.

Another group of students grew up later, in connection with von Hornbostel's teaching activity at the University of Berlin. From these came the assistants, who worked mostly without pay, like M. Kolinski, F. Bose, and M. Schneider, who directed the Phonogramm-Archiv after von Hornbostel's emigration in 1934 and into the Second World War.

17

The Director of the Berlin Phonogramm-Archiv, Kurt Reinhard. In the background is a portrait of Carl Stumpf, the founder of the Archiv, by the noted German impressionist Max Slevogt, 1925 (on loan from the National Gallery).

An international exchange of phonograms had been set up very early. This exchange was considerably strengthened when the Institute—the first to do so—shortly after 1906 began producing copper negatives from the original cylinders, from which as many copies as desired could be cast. The financial situation of the Archiv was always very strained, and an appeal by Carl Stumpf which appeared in 1908 in many newspapers had attracted only a few private donors. Yet it was possible, thanks mostly to the personal sacrifice of von Hornbostel, to equip almost all German expeditions with recording equipment and blank cylinders. Many of the collections brought back were fairly well documented, since von Hornbostel made as many travellers as possible acquainted with the technique of recording and the data to be noted, or at least placed at their disposal a copy of the chapter "Musik" from the *Anleitungen für ethnologische Beobachtungen und Sammlungen* (Instructions for Ethnological Observations and Collections), published by the Museum für Völkerkunde in 1908.

In 1906 there were already more than 1000 recordings. These were augmented so greatly that at the beginning of the Second World War they numbered about 11,000. Among these was the collection of over 1000 recordings made in the First World War prisoner-of-war camps, particularly by Georg Schünemann. In order to make the best recordings in the Archiv available also to outsiders, in the early twenties von Hornbostel put together a "Demonstrationssammlung"

(Demonstration Collection) of 120 cylinders, which anyone interested could purchase.

The Phonogramm-Archiv remained in the Berliner Schloss until 1934, in the same quarters as the Psychological Institute. But in 1922 its administration was taken over by the Senate, and for no logical reason it was attached to the Hochschule für Musik. A really significant change came only in 1934, when it was united with the Museum für Völkerkunde; at that time it moved to Berlin-Dahlem. In the meantime seventy publications had appeared; these contained the earliest transcriptions of recordings in the Archiv.

The most valuable holdings were transferred in order to protect them from air raids; nevertheless, a certain percentage of the recordings in and outside of Berlin were lost. The greatest part survived intact, but these recordings are no longer in Western hands. Through the kind deposit of tape and cylinder copies, however, the originals of which are missing from the Archiv, it has been possible to acquire about twenty percent of the old holdings. Among the persons and institutes which in this matter were helpful to the Archiv in such an unselfish way are the following: Frau Koch-Grünberg (50 cylinders), Museum für Völkerkunde München (369 cylinders), Institut für Völkerkunde der Universität Tübingen (56 cylinders), and the Research Center in Anthropology, Folklore, and Linguistics (about 170 cylinders).

Since the last director of the Phonogramm-Archiv was no longer in Berlin after the war, the Institute was not taken into consideration when the Berlin Museum für Völkerkunde was rebuilt. From the very beginning it did not appear in the budget of the city of Berlin, and this, too, had an arresting effect on the work of the Archiv for many years. The author, who was appointed Ethnomusicologist at the newly-founded Freie Universität in 1948, was able to transfer the few holdings of the Archiv left in Berlin, as well as a part of the library, to the University's Musikwissenschaftliches Institut (Institute of Musicology). Because of technical administrative reasons, however, the Phonogramm-Archiv in 1950 had to be incorporated into the Ehemals Staatlichen Museen association; this, however, was of no immediate help in building up the Archiv again. Only some years later did it succeed in acquiring the tape recorders and tape it needed, as well as a small basic collection of commercial discs.

At the same time, the exchange of recordings with other institutions was arranged. Numerous German and foreign scholars allowed the Phonogramm-Archiv to copy their tape recordings, and in recent years it has even been possible to equip ethnologists closely connected with the Archiv with portable tape recorders, tapes and questionnaires. In this way the holdings of the Archiv have again reached considerable stature. To be sure, the number of recordings does not correspond to that of the earlier cylinders. On the other hand, the newer tape recordings offer greater advantages for research because of their better technical quality, and even more, because each musical item is now recorded in its entire length, and not interrupted or broken off after two minutes, as was the case with cylinder recordings. The areas of collection could not be systematically chosen. Although much had to be left to chance, the

Archiv today again possesses recordings from the entire world. The folkloristically interesting areas in Europe are now much more strongly represented than before. Through trips by people connected with the Archiv, a few areas of specialization have been built up, in which the Institute is superior both quantitatively and qualitatively to many other collections. To these belong Turkey (recordings by Reinhard), the Lapps (Laade, Christensen, Munser, and Seipoldy), Corsica (Laade), Kurdistan (Christensen), and the Ellice Islands (Koch).

The most important task of the Archiv is still scholarly research and teaching. The publications of the Archiv now number 94. The association with the University has become especially close through the personal contact of the author, who is both Director of the Archiv and Professor of Ethnomusicology at the Freie Universität. The Archiv offers the students rich possibilities for work. Various seminars are held in the Archiv itself. So far, five students have graduated with ethnomusicology as their major, and seventeen with ethnomusicology as their minor. Besides that, six dissertations are currently in process.

Because of lack of room, in 1959 the Phonogramm-Archiv was transferred to the storage building annexed to the Museum für Völkerkunde (Berlin-Lichterfelde, Gardeschützenweg 71-101). Here enough room is available that a long-held wish could be translated into reality: the compiling of a representative selection from the holdings of musical instruments of the individual divisions of the museum. This study collection, which is housed in three rooms, is at the disposal of the student and can be visited by those with special interests. For the first time, a scholarly catalog which will include all the musical instruments of the museum has been started. Dr. Dieter Christensen, the research assistant of the Phonogramm-Archiv, has taken on the bulk of this work.

The holdings on sound recordings are represented in three card indexes. The main card index is arranged geographically with respect to cultures and tribes. Each musical item is represented by a card, and the original recording medium (cylinder, disc, or tape) is recognizable through various colors of cards. These cards (size Din A 6) contain indications of place, group, title of the piece, function, performance (singers, instruments), and source (collector, record company and so on). In addition to the exact label there are indications of the length of the pieces and sometimes a note about the speed of the discs or tapes. All further documentation for the recordings, such as texts and expedition reports, is found in special files, which bear the same label as the cylinders, discs, or tapes. Besides this main card file, there are two slip catalogues (size Din A 7), on which the necessary notes are transferred from the main card file. The first is arranged according to presentation, that is, singers and instruments; the second is arranged according to genre, for instance, "love song" or "mask dance."

Questionnaires are given to all scholars who are willing to place copies of their recordings or the originals in the Archiv. These consist of a folded sheet (size Din A 3). Two of the four pages are blank; here the texts or descriptions of the gestures and dances are to be written. The two remaining sides contain all the questions which it is necessary to answer if the recordings are to be used for scholarly purposes. These questions have to do with place and date, type of musical item, title, function, source and age, and beyond that, with the singers or else the instrumentalists (name, age, sex, tribe, education, musicality, and so forth) and the instruments used. These questionnaires have the special advantage that the collector gets everything pre-planned and ready for his use, and does not have to stop and mull over the directions given to him, or perhaps make up his own diary.

The following publications give information about the publications to date:

Marius Schneider: "Das Phonogramm-Archiv des Museums für Völkerkunde," *Archiv für Vergleichende Phonetik*, Erste Abtl., Bd. II, 1938.

Dear Sir,

Allow me to introduce myself to you. I am Professor at the Royal Hungarian Music Academy in Budapest, and in my free time occupy myself very much with folk music, that is, as a collector. Up to now I have handed in nearly 1000 phonograph cylinder recordings to the Ethnographic Museum in Budapest. Several of my countrymen have spoken to me concerning your studies, among them Dr. Solymossy, who also gave me your publications.

Now I am turning to you on behalf of the Director of our Ethnographic Museum, Mr. V. Semayer.

As we know, your Phonogramm-Archiv prepares copies of phonograph recordings, which it uses in exchange with other institutes. Our museum would likewise like to enter into such a kind of exchange agreement with some institutes. We do not know, however, how and where such copies can be prepared, and how high the cost of the process might be.

Now we request that you be so kind as to send me information about it.

Or instead of that, might I perhaps visit you the 19th, 20th, or 21st of June, and get information in person, since at this time I will be in Berlin?

Respectfully yours,
(signed) Béla Bartók

My address is: Rákoskeresztur (Hungary)

Kurt Reinhard: "Das Berliner Phonogramm-Archiv," *Die Musikforschung* 6, 1953.

Kurt Reinhard: "Das Berliner Phonogramm-Archiv," *Baessler-Archiv*, Neue Folge 9, 1961.

In the last of these articles there is also a detailed survey of the holdings on sound recordings. Here, instead of that degree of detail, only a few figures can be given concerning the situation as of October 15, 1961.[1]

The annual budget, from which only special business expenditures of the Archiv are paid, amounts to 5000 DM ($1,250) for 1962. This does not cover personal expenses, office equipment, stationery, rent, or royalties for copies. In 1962, 3000 DM ($750) was also available for special purchases, phonograph records in particular. In 1963 an additional 18,000 DM ($4,500) will be available for the purchase of tape recorders.

The equipment inventory appears as follows:

Phonographs, for recording and playback	6	
Turntables, commercial, mostly portable	4	} 5
Turntables, studio models	1	
Disc-cutting machine	1	
Tape recorders, battery operated	4	
Tape recorders, electrically run, mostly portable	9	} 15
Tape recorders, electrically run, studio models	2	

Besides the Director, the Archiv has as permanent staff members a research assistant and a technical assistant (sound technician). Beyond that, a typist and several workers are available as needed. Moreover, it was possible to carry through the extensive work of building up the Phonogramm-Archiv only because since 1953 from one to three workers have been provided on the basis of the relief program financed in part by the government of the United States. Finally, thanks are due to a group of students who have unselfishly helped out in the Archiv, some for years.

In spite of the other losses, the Phonogramm-Archiv retained the card catalogs and the expedition reports for all the earlier recordings. The same holds true for the correspondence since 1900, included in which are valuable letters from well-known scholars (for instance, the Bartók letter of which a facsimile is given here). The small library also suffered some losses, which so far it has not succeeded in replacing. But what is not to be found there, despite some new acquisitions, is for the most part available to the staff and students in the general library of the Museum für Völkerkunde or in the University.

In addition to loaning tape recordings to radio stations, film companies, schools, societies, and so forth, the Phonogramm-Archiv is very interested in an active exchange with other scholarly institutes. The equipment at its disposal makes it possible to produce copies at any desired speed. Recordings deposited with us are always protected in writing, with the assurance that they will be used "only for scholarly and not for commercial purposes." The index cards for these recordings are marked with a corresponding restriction. Likewise, assurance is given that no scholarly study will be published without the permission of the collector.

[1] Distribution of holdings in the Phonogramm-Archiv:

	Europe	Near East	Africa	Asia	Oceania	America	Total
on cylinders	243	358	839	435	410	128	2413
on tapes (originals)	2502	1612	71	141	226	80	4632
total of Archiv's own recordings	2745	1970	910	576	636	208	7045
on discs	821	549	619	911	167	569	3636
on tapes (copies)	714	348	499	297	742	330	2930
total of recordings from elsewhere	1535	897	1118	1208	909	899	6566
grand total	4280	2867	2028	1784	1545	1107	13611

PRESCRIPTIVE AND DESCRIPTIVE MUSIC WRITING
Charles Seeger

Three hazards are inherent in our practices of writing music. The first lies in an assumption that the full auditory parameter of music is or can be represented by a partial visual parameter, i.e., by one with only two dimensions, as upon a flat surface. The second lies in ignoring the historical lag of music-writing behind speech-writing, and the consequent traditional interposition of the art of speech in the matching of auditory and visual signals in music-writing. The third lies in our having failed to distinguish between prescriptive and descriptive uses of music-writing, which is to say, between a blue-print of how a specific piece of music shall be made to sound and a report of how a specific performance of it actually did sound.

I shall deal here with the writing of only the simplest kind of music—unaccompanied melody. All three hazards have combined to render probable that speech conceptions of melody have played an important part not only in the development of the technique of writing but also in the composition and performance of melodies in writing. And the conditions of the musicological juncture, in which we attempt to communicate in the art of speech relative to the nature of the art of music and what it communicates, render certain that speech-conceptions of melody may sometimes outweigh music-conceptions of it, particularly in any discussion of the problem of music-writing. We cannot, therefore, dismiss with a wave of the hand the questions 1) to what extent do our speech-conceptions of melody correspond to our music-conceptions of it, and 2) to what extend does the visual representation of melody condition both conceptions of it?While it is risky to think we can answer these questions definitively, we can at least bear them in mind and set ourselves seriously to consideration of ways and means of evading or offsetting the hazards of the task. I shall refer only briefly to the problem of multidimensional visual representation of melody. For technological advance, upon which we must depend for aid in this respect, has not yet overcome the difficulties in the visual representation of the composite melodic functions of tone-quality and accentuation. And since we cannot conceivably escape from the limitations of the musicological juncture, I shall single out two speech concepts of melody, not as comprehending the total range of the problem, but as underlying the two methods of music-writing now available to·us—the one prescriptive and subjective, the other descriptive and objective.

On the one hand, let us agree, melody may be conceived (verbally, it must be remembered) as a succession of separate sounds, on the other, as a single continuum of sound—as a chain or as a stream. Conception as a chain tends to emphasize structure and entities that move; conception as a stream, function and movement itself. Neither, of course, tells the whole story as the musician knows it. Both distort this knowledge to extents we cannot precisely gauge. For many of the links of the chain may be fused together; and the stream may run through successions of comparatively stable levels. And there may be breaks in both. Like so many speech constructions, these verbal constructions are not mutually exclusive opposites, but can be shown to have possibilities of serving as complements to each other. And the truth may lie somewhere between them.

Visual representation of melody as a chain is comparatively easily done by a chain of symbols; as a stream, by a curving line. Symbolization inevitably results in sharp distinction between music space (tone) and music time (rhythm) as separate, independent factors; lineation, in non-separation of the two, as overlapping, interdependent factors. Within the incomplete frame of the two-dimensional page, both symbolization and lineation depend upon certain graphic conventions of obscure origin. One, identification of elapse of time with occurrence from left to right on the page, possibly borrowed from speech-writing, underlies both factors. Another, identification of height in pitch with height on the page underlies some symbolic and all linear music-writing. Uniform vertical coordinates for elapse of time (indicating tempo) and uniform horizontal coordinates for height of pitch form the basic chart for the most recent developments of linear music-writing known as "graphing."

The history of the European fine art of music shows that our conventional music-writing was first a predominantly symbolic, second a predominantly linear, and third a mixed symbolic-linear notation. The Greek tradition, as made known to us most clearly by Alypius, was based upon the convention of representing elapse of time from left to right. Separate symbols for pitches of tones and for meter were placed accordingly. The accents and neumes of the early Christian era added the convention of identifying height of pitch with height on the page, but were linear in character, expressing movement rather than the points moved to and moved from. They seem first to have come into use to describe an existing practice of recitation. The notation became, however, more and more used for prescriptive purposes. First, ecclesiastical authorities and, later, composers began to specify exactly from where and to where movement was to go, and how long it was to take to do so. Addition of the lines of the staff and of the stems and barlines (prototypes respectively of the horizontal and vertical coordinates of the graph chart) were major steps towards the graph; standardization of the note-head and the metrical flags and beams was a reversion to symbolism.

As we find it today, our conventional notation is still a mixed symbolic-linear music-writing in which the symbolic element is the more highly organized and therefore dominates. It is practically entirely prescriptive in character. Emphasis is upon structures—principally of pitch and meter. It does not tell us much about the connection of the structures. It does not tell us as much about how music sounds as how to make it sound. Yet no one can make it sound as the writer of the notation intended unless in addition to a knowledge of the tradition of writing he has also a knowledge of the oral (or, better, aural) tradition associated with it—i.e., a tradition learned by the ear of the student, partly from his elders in general but especially from the precepts of his teachers. For to this aural tradition is customarily left most of the knowledge of "what happens between the notes"—i.e., between the links in the chain and the comparatively stable levels in the stream.

In employing this mainly prescriptive notation as a descriptive sound-writing of any music other than the Occidental fine and popular arts of music we do two things, both thoroughly unscientific. First, we single out what appear to us to be structures in the other music that resemble structures familiar to us in the notation of the Occidental art and write these down, ignoring everything else for which we have no symbols. Second, we expect the resulting notation to be read by people who *do not carry the tradition of the other music.* The result, as read, can only be a conglomeration of structures part European, part non-European, connected by a movement 100% European. To such a riot of subjectivity it is presumptuous indeed to ascribe the designation "scientific."

There are three ways out of the dilemma, for that is what it is, so rare is the carriage by any one person of more than one music tradition and so difficult the correction of the bias typical of that one.[1] On the one hand, we may increase the already heavy over-load of symbols in the notation, with a resulting increase of difficulty in reading and but little, if any, gain in accuracy or objectivity. On the other hand, we may dispense with many of the symbols and extend the graphic potentialities of the notation. The hand-made graph based upon the notation has its uses. But for purposes of formal description—our main concern here—the objectivity of the electronic reduction of the oscillographic curve, especially of the sound-track of high-fidelity sound-recording, is vastly superior. As Bartók has rightly said, "The only true notations" (music-writing is what he might have said) "are the sound-tracks on the record itself."[2] These, unfortunately, are legible only through laborious mathematical calculation. For when large enough to be seen in detail by the human eye they are several feet long per second. Electronic analysis can reduce or compress them automatically, as desired. Compression within a range of about 2.5 to 25mm per second produces a graph legible by anyone who can read conventional notation and is willing to do a little practice.

The time has not yet come, of course, for abandonment of our conventional notation. It has come, I aver, for development of the graph. Structure and function are equally important methodological concepts. Prescriptive and descriptive uses of music-writing are equally necessary and not necessarily incompatible. Musics surely differ from one another in their adaptability to one or the other kind of music-writing. But surely, also, we may hope, they resemble each other in this respect. The important thing for study is to know objectively

---

[1] E. von Hornbostel, *Fuegian Songs,* in *American Anthropologist,* XXXVIII (July-Sept., 1936), 357, note.

[2] Béla Bartók and Albert B. Lord, *Serbo-Croatian Folk Songs,* New York, 1951, p. 3.

wherein they differ and resemble, regardless of their being written one way or another. Furthermore, as a means of communication among people, music must be expected to have its subjective aspects. The least we should expect of the scholar is that he will not be a party to the passing off of his own subjectivity as someone else's or that he will fail to report objectively upon the subjectivity of that someone else. My recommendation for the foreseeable future, then, is to employ the notation and the graph concurrently.

Correlation of the graph and the notation depends in great measure upon recognition of their relative capacities and limitations. Both are based upon the conventions of identifying elapse of time with left to right on the page and height in pitch with height upon it. They differ in that spacing is irregular in the notation, but uniform in the graph. The comparative efficiency of the two methods of writing in handling the six principal functions of the single melody may be summarized as follows:

TONAL FUNCTIONS. 1) *Pitch* is only roughly indicated, i.e., within a half tone by the notation. The attempt to increase accuracy by superscription of additional symbols such as cents numerals, arrows, plus and minus signs, modifications of accidentals, etc., found in many ethnomusicological works is severely limited by the decrease in legibility. My present fundamental frequency analyzer, which is a mere Model T in the way of graphing devices, has a top discrimination of about 1/14 tone.[3] 2) *Amplitude* (dynamics) is only roughly indicated by the notation. My present amplitude graphs show changes in dynamics far beyond what the ear can detect. 3) *Tone-quality* cannot be shown at present by either method of writing. Ample acoustic research has been completed and engineering applications are already in use permitting rough but meaningful graphs of tone-quality. A practical device is still to be designed and manufactured.

RHYTHMIC FUNCTIONS. 4) *Tempo* is only roughly indicated in the notation, even with the aid of the metronome. It is very accurately indicated upon the chart in both frequency and amplitude graphs by the analyzer I am using. The margin of error seems to be about 1/100 second. 5) *Proportion* is easy to read in the notation, but difficult, in the graph. 6) *Accentuation*, for the present, is problematic in both notation and graph—in the notation, because of the multiplicity of symbols; in the graph because of its representation of stress solely in terms of amplitude. The notation can lay down an unheard basic pulse, certainly as prerequisite to the perception as to the performance of some musics. This the graph can do only by manual superscription of notational symbols, as, for example, of meters, bars, etc. But it can show, with surprising accuracy, the fluctuation of a basic pulse so symbolized. And this, the notation cannot do.

On the whole, the student will find the pitch and the beat more accurately shown in the graph than in the notation, but less independently delimited. As conceptions of verbal thinking, he will find both becoming less rigid and

[3] Charles Seeger, *Toward a Universal Music Sound-Writing for Musicology*, in *Journal of the International Folk Music Council*, IX (1957), 63.

absolute. Also, he will find the gross formal aspects of melody more readily perceivable in the graph. But he will have some difficulty in fitting conventional terminology with what he sees in the graph. The problem is most clearly presented in all its complexity in the sung melody. For it is there that the tonal factor of vibrato meets the rhythmic factor of rubato head-on, in the most diverse and subtle manners.

First, let us consider the sung melody as a chain. From this viewpoint, vibrato and rubato are separate, unrelated factors.

Surely, all students of Occidental music know that the actual variance of the vibrato is an alternation of adjacent pitch frequencies customarily perceived, i.e., musically thought of, by us as one salient deviation from the mean of the variance.[4] (Variance of loudness and of tone-quality in the vibrato are secondary and need not detain us for the moment.) It is this mean, not the actual, variance that we identify as a "note" and relate to a norm of our music theory such as a degree of a scale and, so, as a link in the chain.

Surely, also, all students of this music know that the actual variance of the rubato is an alternation of anticipation and delay (or delay and anticipation) of successive beats customarily perceived by us as one salient deviation from the mean of the variance, or tempo. (Variance of accentuation need not detain us for the moment.)

Operation of the vibrato is mostly below the threshold of deliberate control. That is, it is largely automatic, customarily thought of as a characteristic of voice-production, as, for example, of the single note or link in the chain. It can be modified—even acquired—by conscious effort, but not so much in terms of its actual as of its mean variance. Once acquired, it is set in its pattern and persists throughout the process of rendition, regardless of changes of pitch or loudness. The singer does not, and perhaps cannot, change its rate, span, or regularity as we are accustomed to change the rate or regularity of divisions of a beat, by deliberate control.

Operation of the rubato, on the other hand, is mostly above the threshold of deliberate control. It is thought of as a characteristic of the sequence of notes or links in the chain. While factors of which we are largely unconscious are constantly deflecting it in minute ways, our deliberate control of it is mainly in terms of its actual variance with respect to whole beats and, in slow tempos, of divisions of beats. As to its mean variance, the Grand Tradition, as I received it from my most admired teachers, requires that it be 1) continuous in all but very strict tempos and 2) compensatory, for "the music should come out with the metronome at the end"—a quaint, but tenaciously held bit of musical folklore. The notation does not even attempt to show this; but the graph can submit it to an acid test. It can also show any unevenness in vibrato or rubato that is musically significant.

Now, the attack upon the next succeeding note in any melodic process, the more so if it is accented, long held, dissonant, or unusual in some respect, is very much a matter of deliberate attention and control on the part of the

[4] Carl E. Seashore, ed., *The Vibrato*, Iowa City, n.d., p. 369.

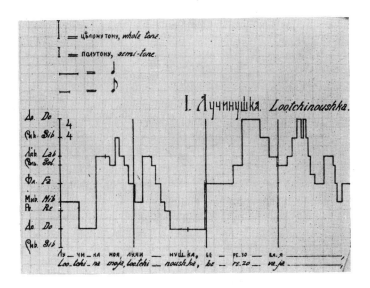

Hand Graph, made by ear from phonograph recording. Excerpt of Diagram 1, in *The Peasant Songs of Great Russia*, by Eugenia Eduardovna (Paprik) Lineva. Moscow, 1912. The vertical lines are music bars. Rectangular chart, in color, not reproducible.

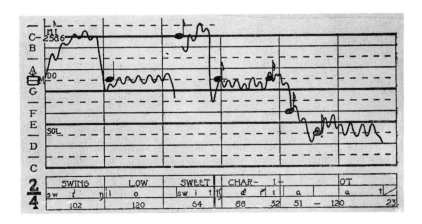

Hand Graph, made by mathematic reduction of a "sound wave photograph." Fig. 29, in *Phonophotography in Folk Music*, by Milton Metfessel. Copyright 1928 by the University of North Carolina Press. Reprinted by permission. The light vertical lines are seconds; the heavy one, a music bar.

Plate I

executant. But according to the Iowa and other students of the vibrato, we customarily vastly underestimate 1) the extent of its actual variance, which may be commonly 40-200 cents, i.e., from one-fifth to a whole tone, 2) its rate, which may be 4-10 per second, and 3) its irregularity in both respects. Such variances might be expected to modify the expectations of the singer, automatic as they are and occupied as he may be with the mean variance of the tone he is producing with the intention of arriving within the mean variance of beat required in the rendition of the melody he is carrying. Seashore and others have pointed out that singers—even the best—habitually over- or under-shoot both upward and downward melodic progression. The fundamental frequency analyzer that I have been using shows this also. I would like, therefore, to advance the hypothesis that when the phase of the actual vibrato is in the direction of the melodic progression the establishment of the mean variance of the new note upon the beat expected is more likely to occur, whereas if it is contrary the new note may not be established until after the beat, a slide being interposed.

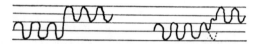

Schematic diagram of vibrato and upward melodic progression, in phase (left) and out of phase (right)

If the slide, which is typical of legato singing, is fairly slow or covers a wide interval, the graph may show little jagged points where the continuation of the vibrato may have forced an interruption of the progression. Over- and undershooting may also involve or be involved in difference in phase and progression. Thus rubato may be influenced by vibrato.

Conversely, if the attack upon a higher or lower note is anticipated or delayed by rubato, a vibrato that might have facilitated a decisive attack may be upset. A slide or over- or under-shooting may result. Thus, vibrato may be influenced by rubato.

It is not only in the attack or release of substantial notes (links in the chain) that vibrato and rubato may meet head-on. A very common complication seems to result within the beat when the rate of actual variance of the vibrato and a division of the beat by articulated notes are within the 4-10 alternations of the vibrato and the 2-16 (approximately) of the beat division. For example, a vibrato of five actual variances per second will produce a very different rendition of a group of four sixteenth notes at a quarter = 60 from that of a vibrato of seven per second.

Next let us consider the melody as a stream, broken only by the necessity to take breath, as at the end of a phrase, or by the briefer closures of the vocal apparatus in enunciation of certain consonants, or the making of exceptional effects such as staccato, etc. From this viewpoint, vibrato and rubato are closely related factors in a continuum. For here, melody is not viewed as a jagged rising and falling but as a sinuous flowing along a course. In what may be the vast majority of cases, the glide between levels, their over- and under-shooting, and

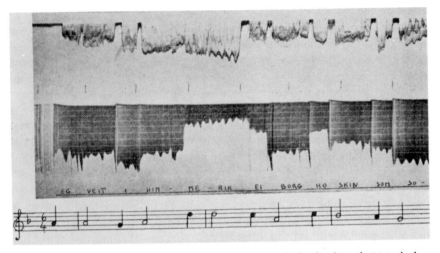

Automatic Graph (oscillogram) made by electronic-mechanical reduction, photographed on film, of Norwegian folksong, sung by woman's voice. Excerpt of Fig. 2, in *Photography as an Aid in Folk Music Research*, by Olav Gurvin, in *Norveg*, III (1953), 181-96. Reprinted with permission. Upper, shaded, outline shows intensity (amplitude); lower, white, outline, pitch (fundamental frequency) upon ruled, semitonal staff, with seconds marked by timer. (Enlarged?)

Plate II

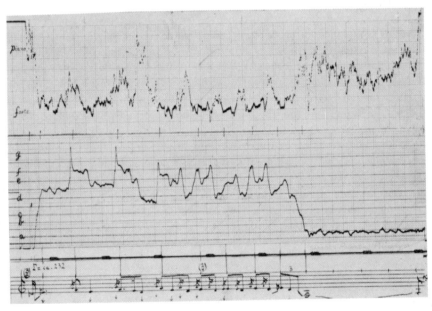

Automatic Graph (oscillogram) made by electronic-mechanical reduction written directly on paper (see footnote 3), of Abatusi Traditional Song, sung by man's voice. Excerpt of Band 16, in *Voice of the Congo, Riverside World Folk Music Series,* RLP 4002, recorded in Ruanda by Alan P. and Barbara W. Merriam, 1951-52. Upper, broken, line shows amplitude; lower, continuous, line, fundamental frequency, upon rectangular millimeter chart (green) with ruled, semitonal staff, and with seconds marked by timer. (Reduced)

Plate III

the various inflections given them are not exceptions to theoretical norms but integrated characteristics of the stream, intentional and cultivated. Except in the most strict *tempo giusto* and marcato, which are rare in singing, the manner of proceeding between levels and of modifying the levels themselves are, then, often quite as important data for the student as are the levels themselves.

In instrumental performance, the collision (in the chain) or interplay (in the stream) of vibrato and rubato is modified or even broken variously by movements of the fingers, changes in bowing or embouchure, etc., peculiar to each technique. Approximation of many of the devices of singing style above mentioned can, however, be noted in instrumental playing—as on the vina and sitar, the ch'in and koto, and even in our own banjo and guitar playing—where slide-fretting, pressing down on strings and pulling them sidewise are common, as are tightening, relaxing, and shaping the embouchure on the trumpet, clarinet, and other wind instruments in our jazz bands. The almost infinite variety of this interplay between and within beats defines more closely the fault so often found with the unskilled performer: that he rendered the notes correctly but "left out what should have come between them," which is to say, he did not connect them in accordance with the appropriate aural tradition. Each of the many music traditions in the world probably has its own distinctive ways of connecting or "putting in what should come between the notes." Conventional notation can give no more than a general direction as to what these ways are, as, for example, by the words and signs for portamento, legato, détaché, staccato, spiccato, crescendo, diminuendo, accelerando, rallentando, etc. In the graph they are all there for anyone to see, in clear detail. If it causes us some trouble to find out just what the notational equivalents are, we must not complain that the performer did not render notes. Rather, we should be glad that instead of rendering notes he rendered music, and that we may set ourselves with greater assurance to the task of finding out what he did sing, without preconceptions that he meant to, or should, have sung notes.

At this point it is necessary to say a word of warning about the fetish of extreme accuracy in the writing of music. Physics can determine and engineering can reproduce incredibly small difference of pitch and time. Psychology (and rare musical experience) can prove that human beings—not necessarily with talent or training in music—can perceive differences beyond 1/100 of a tone or of a second.[5] But the great music traditions, their practice by those who have carried them, and the phenomenological and axiological norms[6] incorporated in

[5] See, for example, one of the most valiant attempts at descriptive accuracy using conventional notation (Bartók-Lord, *op. cit.*), in many of whose transcriptions there are passages in which it is difficult or impossible to decide to what extent the notes represent 1) unequal articulated divisions of a beat sung in strict time, 2) equal articulated divisions sung with rubato, 3) either of these with written out or partly written out vibrato, 4) an uneven vibrato, or 5) a vibrato that a less sensitive ear would hear as a single tone, i.e., whose mean, instead of actual, variance would be the musical fact.

[6] The elasticity with which our notational norms are actually made to sound by competent professionals has recently been measured with great accuracy by Charles R. Shackford in his doctoral dissertation (Harvard, 1954), *Intonation in Ensemble String Performance—An Objective Study.*

them were not determined by the exceptional human being. He contributes to them. We may never cease the controversy how much. The same is true of our notation, which is, *par excellence*, a matter of norms determined by the vast aggregate of practice and codified by generations of workers. The graph, on the other hand, shows individual performance. Each graph, whether of the exceptional performer or the merest tyro, is unique. Norms can be arrived at by comparative studies of large numbers of graphs. But these norms may differ in many important respects from the norms embodied in the notation. Or they may confirm them. In any event, where the individual notation may give too much norm and too little detail, the individual graph may easily give too little norm and too much detail. It is well, therefore, especially in these pioneer stages of the development of the graph not to look for too much detail or, better, detail too far beyond the norms of general practice, except for most carefully considered ends. For the present, I am inclined to set 1/10 of a tone (20 cents) and 1/10 of a second as fair margins of accuracy for general musicological use. Detailed study may go beyond these at the discretion of the student.

As a strictly musicological tool, the graphing apparatus brings to our existing notational techniques the needed complement to show "what happens between the notes" and what any departures from their theoretical norms really are in terms of actual hearing—and what these norms should be in terms of musicological thinking. For lexicographical and many classificatory uses, the pitch-time graph will probably be the most useful. Used side by side with the amplitude-time graph, a beginning can be made in the all-important exact study of performance style, especially of singing-style, without which the infant discipline of comparative melodic research cannot hope to do more than half a job. But as yet, this can be only a beginning. For its full study, graphing of tone-quality and "visible speech," both now in advanced stages of development, will be necessary.

We are, then, at last nearing the time when scientific definition of the world's musics and comparative studies of them can, and should, begin in earnest. Extrinsic contributions in terms of culture history, of geographic extent, and of social depth are being made by anthropology, sociology, psychology, physiology, physics, and other non- or extra-musical disciplines. Musicology is hardly ready yet to attack the necessary definition and comparative study in intrinsic terms. We have not more than coined a word when we speak of the concept "music" or even "a music." We do not even know whether our basic categories of music "idiom"—fine, folk, popular, and primitive arts of music—hold everywhere outside of the Occidental culture community.

The volume of data now already at hand shows that in the near future we shall be compelled to adopt statistical techniques such as those being developed by anthropology.[7] These will increasingly employ the kind of thinking and operating that depends upon precise visual representation of the most detailed observation as well as of the most generalized synopsis or synthesis. Musicolo-

[7] Linton G. Freeman and Alan P. Merriam, *Statistical Classification in Anthropology: An Application to Ethnomusicology*, in *American Anthropologist*, LVIII (June, 1956), 464-72.

gists will have to learn to read the graphs of non-musical sciences. And it is not impossible that non-musical scientists might learn to read the music-graph more readily than the conventional Occidental notation.

As a descriptive science, musicology is going to have to develop a descriptive music-writing that can be written and read with maximum objectivity. I believe that the graphing devices and techniques, above referred to, show the way towards such an end. But it must be remembered that technological aids of this sort report only upon the physical stimulus to the outer ear. At present, too, it is possible to put into visual form only fractioned aspects of this, such as pitch and time, amplitude and time, etc. One can conceive, though scarcely imagine, an automatic music-writing that would comprehend the total physical stimulus in a single, continuous process of writing or reading. But even if this present impossibility were to be realized, we would still have to take pains lest the visual representation of the stimulus were mistaken for the full sensory and perceptual reaction of a person conditioned by the particular music-cultural tradition of which the stimulus were a product. For perception does not accept sensation without change. Put bluntly, "we do not hear what we think we hear." Just what is the nature of the change is one of the things we most want to know. For culturally unconditioned listening to music, unless by "wolfboys," congenital idiots, or the like, is not known to us. If the stimulus is a product of the particular music tradition that we carry, we perceive it as such. If it is a product of a tradition we do not carry, we perceive it as we would a product of the one we do carry, making such changes as we are accustomed to. Therefore, automatic music-writing by such aids as those referred to must no more be taken for what we think we hear than most conventional notation. But even in its present pioneer stage of development, such writing must be accepted by us as a far truer visual portrayal of what we actually hear than is the notation. By comparing the two, we may achieve several useful ends: 1) we may learn more about the divergence of sensation and perception in our own music; 2) we may take steps towards the discovery of how a music other than our own sounds to those who carry its tradition; 3) we may begin to correct our misperception of other musics than our own by cultivating "bi-musicality"—surely, one would think, a prerequisite for musicological work. For the automatic graph can serve as a bridge between musics—a common denominator, as it were. The physical stimulus constituted by a product of any musical tradition is identical to those who carry the tradition and to those who carry another. It is the perceptions of it by the respective carriers that are different. Is there not a clue here to the vexing problem of form and content in music, and perhaps an indispensable guide to the present almost abandoned effort to develop a world-wide philosophy of music upon a rational rather than a mystical base?

SLÉNDRO AND PÉLOG REDEFINED

Mantle Hood

In March, 1962, the Royal Anthropological Institute of Great Britain and Ireland held a three-day symposium in London devoted to an interdisciplinary discussion under the broad heading "Music and History." Subjects chosen from Africa and Asia were presented by scholars representing the various disciplines that make up the Institute, including history, archaeology, anthropology, linguistics, and musicology. The free exchange of ideas among scholars from these different disciplines and the speculations and intellectual stimulation provoked by the postulation of connections between Africa and Asia made this symposium a memorable occasion. The principal papers were distributed in advance so that a full hour-and-a-half discussion could be allowed for each. Given this generous amount of time, I decided to present the first of a series of related studies under the general title of a long-range research program "The Effects of Medieval Technology on Musical Style in the Orient."[1] Several months later I was extended the privilege of presenting a second aspect of this subject at the annual meeting of the British Association for the Advancement of Science.[2] The third phase of the project, presented in the following, is a progress report of a study based on the discovery of what appears to be an essential and complex refinement underlying tuning systems in Indonesia.[3]

As studies in musicology progress from year to year and from decade to decade, the quantity of information, the number of composers and their works, and the list of specific musical terms increase at an alarming rate. In addition to the quantity of information appearing in journals and music encyclopedias pertaining to the European art tradition, more and more information is becoming available about the musical cultures of the non-Western world. Perhaps it is safe to speculate that most students of musicology have heard not only of the classical Greek concept of *nomoi* and Byzantine *hirmoi* but also of the Indian *raga*, the Javanese *paṭet*, the Sundanese *papaṭet*, the Arabic *maquam*, the Turkish *maqam*, the Persian *dastgah*, and the Russian *popievki*. However, in view of the fact that even our familiar term "mode" is variously defined, and the

---

[1] *Essays on Music and History in Africa and Asia* (K. P. Wachsmann, Editor), published by the Royal Anthropological Institute for Great Britain and Northern Ireland (London, in press).

[2] August, 1962, Manchester.

[3] This report is based on a joint paper read for the Annual Meeting of the American Musicological Society held at Columbus, Ohio, December 27-30, 1962. I was assisted in all of the original laboratory measurements by Mr. Max Harrell, and it was he who first called attention to the possibility of the presence of an "errant tone."

terms "tuning" and "scale" are not always clear in their application, we may assume that relatively few Western scholars understand these foreign concepts. The already overburdened scholar in musicology might reasonably question the need for adding a long list of non-Western ideas to his present store of knowledge. But if our musical heritage indeed derives from the East, is it not likely that surviving musical practices in the East may be indispensable in filling in the details of musical style in the West? The coexistence of ancient and modern musical ensembles in the Orient might be described as a vast laboratory in which the living specimens of the old and the new, side by side, offer a great potential in establishing historical depth in the subtleties and complexities of musical style. Musical style as adumbrated in the manuscript or printed score of Western music, by comparison, is in some ways more tangible, but at the same time, inaudible. It may be argued that a musical manuscript is supported by theoretical writings of the time, as well as studies in organology. But the apt student of musicology is aware of the distance and difficulty in communication—even in his own day—between the theorist and practitioner. He should also be aware that the ability to hear the musical score as it was written in earlier times is hardly the same as being able to hear the musical score as it was actually performed.

For some years two non-Western musical terms, *sléndro* and *pélog*, have traveled beyond the borders of their native Java and Bali and by now have appeared in significant music encyclopedias throughout the world. Recently *sléndro* became the center of a controversy among specialists of various disciplines in West African studies.[4] *Pélog* has been used in comparison with Japanese tunings and scales.[5] Both terms have occupied the attention of Sir Stamford Raffles,[6] A. J. Ellis,[7] Erich von Hornbostel,[8] Jaap Kunst,[9] Kurt Sachs,[10] and Manfred Bukofzer,[11] and others. Between the time of Ellis' measurements of Javanese gamelan in 1884 and the appearance of Kunst's second edition of *Music*

---

[4] In connection with the communication read by the Reverend Doctor A. M. Jones at the Symposium of the Royal Anthropological Institute, London, March 19-21, 1962; in his recent book, *Africa and Indonesia: The Evidence of the Xylophone and Other Musical and Cultural Factors,* both *sléndro* and *pélog* are terms of primary concern; but also see my review in *Man,* July-August, 1965.

[5] See, for example, the program notes of *Music of the Orient,* Parlophone Records, copyright 1934, pp. 11-13.

[6] *The History of Java* (London: Black, Parbury and Allen, 1817), 469 ff.

[7] "Tonometrical Observations on Some Existing Non-Harmonic Musical Scales," *Proceedings* of the Royal Society [London: 1884], 374 ff.

[8] The author of the program notes referred to in Footnote 5.

[9] For a list of Kunst's publications complete up to 1949, see Vol. II of his *Music in Java.*

[10] *Passim* in the following works: *The History of Musical Instruments* [New York: W. W. Norton, 1940]; *Die Musikinstrumente Indiens und Indonesiens* [Zweite Auflage, Berlin: Walter de Gruyter, 1923]; *Real-Lexikon der Musikinstrumente* [Berlin: Julius Bard, 1913]; *The Rise of Music in the Ancient World, East and West* [New York: W. W. Norton, 1943]; etc.

[11] "The Evolution of Javanese Tone-Systems," *Papers* read at the International Congress of Musicology, held at New York, September 11-16, 1939, published New York, 1944, pp. 241-50.

in Java in 1949, a completely distorted meaning of *sléndro* and *pélog* proved once again the distance and difficulty in communication between the theorist and the practitioner. Studies in organology should have prevented some of the misconceptions, but unfortunately these studies were limited to physical description and therefore missed important features related to musical style.

In oversimplified terms, *sléndro* has been described as a five-tone system and *pélog* as a seven-tone system. Ellis, and for a long time Kunst also, maintained that *sléndro* was tending toward a structure of equidistant intervals of 240 cents. Finally it was shown that in actual practice all gamelan *sléndro* tunings are non-equidistant.[12] *Pélog*, on the other hand, has always been recognized as non-equidistant, probably because the size between small and large intervals is more marked.[13] Various five-tone modes are formed in each system.[14]

The Sundanese (living in West Java), the Balinese and the Javanese (in Central and East Java) each have utilized both *sléndro* and *pélog* in a particular way. For the sake of brief comparison, the Sundanese practice will be mentioned only in passing, the Balinese in connection with a particular principle of tuning, and the rest of our attention will be devoted to four Javanese gamelan—two *sléndro* and two *pélog*—housed in the collection at UCLA.

In West Java, the Sundanese use both *sléndro* and *pélog* as the basis of a well-defined system of modes, (*papatet*), and "submodes" (*surupan*). Although Kunst has made an elaborate theoretical presentation of this material,[15] the present study will indicate that more specific information about musical practice and tuning is needed before this complicated system can be fully understood.

In Bali, there are at least thirteen types of gamelan extant.[16] A few archaic ensembles are tuned to a complete seven-tone *pélog* derived originally from Java, a few to a six-tone *pélog* and many to different versions of a five-tone *pélog*.[17] The four-tone *gamelan angklung* need not concern us in this discussion.[18] No two gamelan are tuned precisely alike, and even within any one of these several systems, deviations are great.[19]

Most Balinese gamelan as well as *gendèr wajang* quartets are constructed on a principle that might be termed "paired tuning."[20] The keyed instruments of the ensemble, consisting of bronze slabs suspended over bamboo resonators, are

---

[12] Mantle Hood, *The Nuclear Theme as a Determinant of Patet in Javanese Music* [Groningen: 1954], Chapter VII, *passim.*

[13] Mantle Hood, *op. cit.,* p. 11, 12.

[14] Mantle Hood, *op cit., passim.*

[15] *Music in Java* [2nd Edition, the Hague: Martinus Nijhoff, 1949], pp. 51-70.

[16] According to an oral communication from Colin McPhee in 1962.

[17] Colin McPhee, "Music in Bali," *Publication* of the Festival of Oriental Music and the Related Arts, UCLA May 8-22, 1960, page 14.

[18] See further: Colin McPhee, "Angkloeng Gamelan in Bali," *Djawa* XVII [1937], pp. 322-66.

[19] Colin McPhee, "Music in Bali," *Publication* of the Festival of Oriental Music and the Related Arts, UCLA, p. 15.

[20] An exception would be the gamelan *gambuh*, a small ensemble made up of several *gambuh* (end-blown flutes), a *rebab*, several gongs, and drums.

built and tuned in pairs, so that one is tuned slightly higher (*pengisep*) than the other (*pengumbang*). When corresponding keys of this pair of instruments are sounded, the slight difference in pitch results in a musical beat. This tuning principle applied throughout the compass of the ensemble produces a "shimmering" effect, for which Balinese music is justly famous. Stroboconn measurements of all the keys of the *gamelan gong kebyar* housed at UCLA in the Institute of Ethnomusicology, and known by the proper name "Gamelan Gong Sekar Anjar" ("New Flower"), and of my own *gendèr wajang* quartet, "Pemungkah"[21] indicate that a constant factor in the tuning of these ensembles is a difference of six to seven cycles per second between corresponding keys of all paired instruments throughout the entire range of gamelan and quartet. The example used to illustrate this principle (Fig. 1) is the lowest-pitched pair of melodic instruments in the gamelan, the *djegogan*. The difference between corresponding keys of the two instruments is expressed in beats per second and cents.

According to the composer and gamelan leader Tjokorda Mas of Ubud, Bali,[22] the musical beats heard as the result of *pengisep* (high) and *pengumbang* (low) corresponding keys of paired instruments sounding together are referred to as the *penjorog*. The size of the *penjorog*, that is, the number of beats per second, is a matter of taste and varies from one gamelan to another. It so happens that the famous gamelan gong of Pliatan, Bali,[23] has the same *penjorog* as that of the UCLA gamelan.[24] Gamelan and *gendèr wajang* quartets in other villages may have a greater or lesser number of musical beats as a constant factor in their preferred tuning. The size of the *penjorog* characteristic of a particular gamelan, therefore, is one of the important distinguishing factors that must be taken into account in considering the tuning practices and musical style of Balinese ensembles.

Tjokorda Mas also speaks of the *penjorog,* regardless of its size, in connection with another important aspect of tuning—"stretched or compressed octaves." He explains that the first octave of the *panjatiah*, an instrument voiced in the third and fourth octaves of the five-octave range of the melodic instruments, is considered a "central octave," and that each successive octave higher is tuned a whole or a half *penjorog* sharper and each successive octave lower a whole or a half *penjorog* flatter. The degree of stretching and compressing of octaves can be determined from either *pengisep* or *pengumbang* instruments because the difference (*penjorog*) between high and low keys of paired instruments throughout all octaves is a constant factor.

[21] A recording of these two ensembles can be heard on *The Exotic Sounds of Bali* (Columbia Masterworks, Stereo MS 6445, Monaural ML 5845).

[22] In residence at the Institute of Ethnomusicology, UCLA, 1960-62, 1964-65.

[23] A recording of this ensemble can be heard on *Dancers of Bali*, Columbia Masterworks Record, ML 4618.

[24] At the time the Balinese gamelan was purchased in 1958 in Bali, musicians of the gamelan gong in Pliatan told me that this new gamelan was tuned the same as theirs. Recently, Harrison Parker of USAID at the suggestion of the Institute of Ethnomusicology has been making stroboconn measurements in Indonesia. His measurements of the Pliatan gamelan confirm the fact that this ensemble and the UCLA gamelan have the same *penjorog* and reaffirm the principle of "stretched and compressed octaves," to be discussed presently.

In summary, an accurate description of the tuning of a Balinese gamelan must include: (1) the size of the *penjorog* expressed in musical beats or cycles per second; (2) the amount of the *penjorog* by which octaves are stretched and compressed; (3) the intervallic structure of each octave of the ensemble, including gongs lying below the range of the melodic instruments.

In 1958 UCLA acquired from Java a very fine gamelan *sapangkon*, that is, a double set of instruments, a complete gamelan *sléndro* and a complete gamelan *pélog* with one pitch in common (*tumbuk*). The proper name of the double gamelan is "Khjai Mendung" ("Venerable Dark Cloud"), and at the time of purchase it was documented as being 120 years old. This gamelan was tuned by a professional Javanese tuner and approved by leading musicians of the cities of Djogjakarta and Surakarta just before it was shipped to the United States. Immediately upon arrival the pitches of all keys, bronze kettles, and gongs were measured by a stroboconn. In 1961 the University of California was presented with another Javanese gamelan *sapangkon* by the Indonesian government. It, too, was measured with a stroboconn. In December, 1962, both gamelan *sapangkon* were measured again, and it was found that the bronze keys yielded the same readings within ±2 cents, a reassuring testimony not only to the stability of aged bronze[25] but also to the accuracy of stroboconn and technician.

A fine gamelan becomes famous for its distinctive quality of sound, and very often it will be given a proper name. The *sléndro* and *pélog* halves of the gamelan *sapangkon* may have individual but related names or may have one name in common. Sometimes exceptionally fine large gongs are also given proper names. This evidence of great sensitivity to sound itself is not uncommon in the Orient and must inevitably be taken into account as an important element of musical style.

In the second volume of *Music in Java*, Kunst gives the frequencies and intervallic structure in cents of 46 gamelan *sléndro* and 39 gamelan *pélog* measured with the monochord.[26] Forgetting for the moment the relative inaccuracy of the monochord, we should bear in mind that these measurements represent only one octave of the six octave compass of the gamelan. (See Figs. 2 and 3). It should also be noted that the instrument upon which Kunst based these determinations (the *saron demung*) lies in the fourth octave of the gamelan, and that only the *saron demung* in *sléndro* has a closed octave, that is, has six or sometimes seven keys giving the five tones of *sléndro* plus the octave of pitch 1, or sometimes also the lower octave of pitch 6. The *saron demung* in *pélog* has seven keys for the seven pitches of *pélog*; therefore the octave of pitch 1 given by Kunst is an extrapolation in the ratio of two to one cycles per second.

Kunst makes the interesting comment that ". . . in olden times, some tones

---

[25] Javanese musicians claim that it takes ten to thirty years for new bronze to "settle." Metallurgists have confirmed that it takes approximately this length of time, depending on the amount of "work" the metal receives, for the crystalline structure to stabilize.

[26] Pp. 572-74; also see Vol. I, p. 251.

(? only the *barang* [pitch 1] tones) were not tuned exactly alike through all octaves, but slightly sharper for each higher octave. The sound of the gamelan thereby became what is called *silir* (= out of tune), but gained in penetration. Any unintentional, more marked or irregular falseness in a gamelan is called *geseh*. . . . At present the corresponding intervals are tuned perfectly alike through all octaves [*sic*]. . . ."[27]

Stroboconn readings of the two double gamelan housed at the Institute have been plotted according to deviations from the perfect octave (Figs. 4, 6, 8, 10) and summarized to show an "eyeball curve" or approximate mean deviation of pitches along with the one or more pitches that contradict this pattern (Figs. 5, 7, 9, 11). The five pitches of *sléndro* are numbered according to the Javanese cipher notation 1, 2, 3, 5, 6, and the pitches of *pélog* correspondingly, 1, 2, 3, 4, 5, 6, 7. All bronze keys, kettles, and gongs in each of the four ensembles were measured. Reference to Figs. 2 and 3, showing the range of the different instruments of the gamelan, will reveal that the greatest number of duplicated pitches from instrument to instrument occurs in octaves III, IV, V, and VI. Octaves I and II, representing the pitches of the larger gongs, usually have no pitch duplicated and not all the pitches of either *sléndro* or *pélog* are represented. The two large gongs in gamelan *sléndro* 1 and gamelan *pélog* 1 ("Khjai Mendung"), representing respectively pitches 3 and 2, according to Javanese informants were constructed as part of the original gamelan and maintained in tune. Nothing is known about the origin of the large gongs found in gamelan 2. Sometimes through the bilateral kinship system of Javanese inheritance, sets of gamelan are dispersed among two or more heirs. This kind of fragmentation of sets, or accidental breakage of a large gong, or the collection of different instruments of various age and origin to make up a complete gamelan will require the purchase of an old gong to complete a set. Selection is guided in the first place by pitch, and in the second place by the quality of the instrument. There is insufficient evidence at this time to indicate to what extent the ear of the keen Javanese musician may be guided by the factor of *tuning pattern*, as we shall define it presently. At any rate, we may say that there is a high degree if reliability in the measurements representing octaves III through VI, and at best tentative reliability of measurements covering octaves I and II.

In the majority of instances keys, kettles, and gongs making up different sets of instruments and representing the same piches in octaves III through VI were not more than 3 or 4 cents apart, and sometimes they were identical in pitch. In a few instances, a single key or kettle deviating 6 cents or more from others of the same pitch was considered unreliable. The five families of instruments which yield reliable statistics in this study and extend from the upper part of octave II through octave VI are: the small gongs suspended vertically, known as *kempul*, the large horizontal gongs known as *kenong*, the smaller *keṭuk, kempyang, engkok,* and *kemong,* the complete family of *gendèr,* the three *bonang,* and the three *saron.* The wooden xylophone (*gambang*), the plucked zither (*tjelempung*), and the bowed lute (*rebab*) were, of course, not included.

[27] *Music in Java*, p. 251.

The details of Figs. 4 through 11 can be most easily understood by referring to Fig. 12, a diagrammatic representation of the 14 keys of the *gendèr barung* and the *gendèr panerus*. It is important to note at this time that the professional gamelan tuner in Central Java uses the *gendèr* as a standard. The suitability of such a standard will be understood as our exposition of tuning pattern continues.[28] The lowest key of the *gendèr barung*, pitch 6, is the highest pitch of octave II in *sléndro*, shown in Fig. 4. In Fig. 12, the distance between low pitch 6 of the *gendèr barung* and its octave is shown to be 1206 cents. In Fig. 4, the location of pitch 6 as the highest pitch of octave II shows that the average octave of all instruments in gamelan *sléndro* 1 having this range is 1210 cents. The next point of pitch-line 6 in Fig. 4 shows that the average is 1202 cents, and the next octave shown in Fig. 12 indicates that the *gendèr barung* and *gendèr panerus* have an octave of 1203 cents. In other words, each point in Fig. 4 represents the deviation in ± cents from a perfect octave, indicated by the heavy line at 0 cents.

The mean deviation of gamelan *sléndro* 1 (Fig. 5) indicates that the lower two octaves are compressed, and the middle and upper octaves stretched, with one errant tone, pitch 2, contradicting the pattern. The mean deviation for gamelan *pélog* 1 (Fig. 7) creates a different but related pattern with the errant tone 7 contradicting the pattern. The comparison of the mean deviation of gamelan *sléndro* 1 (Fig. 5) with the mean deviation of gamelan *sléndro* 2 (Fig. 9) indicates considerable contrast in their basic tuning patterns, although in each of these gamelan *sléndro* pitch 2 is the errant tone. The mean deviation of gamelan *pélog* 2 (Fig. 11) shows two contradictory patterns, one made up of the pitches 2, 3, and 6, and the other, pitches 1, 4, 5, and 7, Figs. 5 and 7 indicate a general similarity in the tuning pattern between the *sléndro* and *pélog* halves of gamelan 1. Figs. 9 and 11 show some similarity in tuning pattern between the two halves of gamelan 2, but less than is characteristic of gamelan 1.

Members of the Institute have performed the same orchestral pieces for full Javanese gamelan, first on gamelan *sléndro* 1, then on gamelan *sléndro* 2, then on gamelan *pélog* 1, then on gamelan *pélog* 2. Both double sets of gamelan are Solonese in style (i.e., come from the principality of Surakarta), have an absolute pitch that is almost identical (determined from the common tone or *tumbuk*, pitch 6), and are both of sufficient age so that the bronze has stabilized. The remarkably different character of sound perceived when the same piece is played on the two *sléndro* sets and the two *pélog* sets can be explained in terms of the tuning patterns illustrated in Figs. 4 through 11 and the resulting intervallic differences discussed below.

Kunst indicates different species of *sléndro* and *pélog* according to their absolute pitch and according to the size of the interval between pitches 1 and 2.[29] There are three recognized pitch standards: medium, low, and high, and three sizes of initial intervals: in *sléndro*—average or *rata*, 240 cents, small or

---

[28] Kunst apparently misunderstood the *saron demung* to be the "standard" of the gamelan; although this instrument has a particularly responsible role in relation to mode (see Mantle Hood, *The Nuclear Theme as a Determinant of Patet, passim*), the instrument used as a *tuning* standard is a *gendèr*.

[29] *Music in Java*, p. 252.

luruh, 220 cents or less, and large or *sigrak*, 260 cents or more; in *pélog*–average, 120 cents, small, 100 cents or less, large, 140 cents or more. Therefore, the Javanese recognize in all, 18 different species of *sléndro* and *pélog*.

A summary of the first intervals (between pitches 1 and 2) of octaves III through VI of the four gamelan measured are presented in Figs. 13 and 14. The letter S (*sigrak*, large), R (*rata*, medium) or L (*luruh*, small) appears to the left of each chart for each octave, indicating the size of the first interval. Only gamelan *sléndro* 2 (Fig. 14) is consistently *sigrak* in all four octaves. S or L appearing *after* the intervallic size expressed in cents in both of the gamelan *sléndro* charts indicates either small (less than 240 cents) or large (more than 240) *sléndro* intervals. Note how the sequence of small and large intervals changes from octave to octave in both of these charts[30] so that it becomes impossible to describe a *particular* gamelan *sléndro* tuning as being S L S S L or L S L S L, or any other single arrangement of small or large intervals. From this we may deduce that only a complete representation of tuning pattern is adequate to describe the intervallic structure of a particular gamelan *sléndro*.

It has been shown elsewhere that in each *paṭet* or mode of both *sléndro* and *pélog*, two of the five tones form a principal interval of the (*sléndro* or *pélog*) fifth, which in turn serves as the basis of modal melodies and cadential patterns. These principal intervals of the fifth are shown covering octaves III through VI for each *paṭet* in both tuning systems in Figs. 15 and 16. The pitches of the principal fifth are shown below the name of each *paṭet*, the size of the interval is given for each octave, a schematic diagram represents the increase or decrease in the size of the interval through the four octaves, and the range of interval size is given for each *paṭet*, and in summary for each system, with the amount of variation expressed in cents.

The following conclusions are presented in summary form:

1. The tuning of Javanese gamelan *sléndro* and *pélog* is based on distinct patterns of compressed and stretched octaves with one or more errant tones establishing a contradictory pattern.

2. The multi-octave *gendèr* (Fig. 12), used as a standard by the professional gamalan tuner in Java, is a reliable guide to the tuning pattern of the individual gamelan; however, the complete pattern, that is the true character of the gamelan, should include octaves I and II not represented on the two *gendèr*.

3. The 18 recognized species of *sléndro-pélog* tunings are distinguished firstly, by their absolute pitch (average, high, low) and secondly, not by the relative size of the first interval in Octave IV as suggested by Kunst, but by the total tuning pattern.

---

[30] In this connection an awareness of the tuning pattern as it affects the various octaves of the gamelan might have avoided the faulty speculations by Kunst and others in relation to the intervallic structure of *sléndro* (see further, Mantle Hood, *The Nuclear Theme as a Determinant of Paṭet*, Chapter VII).

4. The measurements of 46 gamelan *sléndro* and 39 gamelan *pélog* of Volume II of Kunst's *Music in Java* limited as they are to a one-octave sample of a six-octave compass, give no indication of the tuning pattern of Javanese gamelan nor can they be considered as representative of the intervallic structure of specific gamelan.

5. The intervallic structure of a specific gamelan must be stated in terms of a tuning pattern covering six octaves.

6. The size of the principal fifth interval in each *paṭet* or mode varies throughout the compass of octaves III through VI; and on the basis of the four gamelan measured, the size of the principal fifths in the *sléndro* modes varies from 708 to 772 cents and the size of the principal fifths in the *pélog* modes varies from 635 to 720 cents.

7. Average or idealized or normalized or actual single-octave representations of *sléndro* and *pélog* tunings are unreliable for purposes of either comparative or anlytical method.

8. The quality of bronze itself and the detailed shapes of keys, kettles, and gongs are two additional important factors in the consideration of musical style as a basis for comparative studies of various gong-chime cultures.

In conclusion, it may be stated that stroboconn measurements of all bronze instruments in a large sampling of gamelan of sufficient age to have stabilized and which are judged in tune by Javanese musicians will indicate the extent to which tuning pattern as illustrated above may provide an index to the recognized 18 species of *sléndro-pélog* tunings; and, further, that a sufficient quantity of detailed tuning patterns should form a number of stereotypes that may be useful in regional and cross-cultural comparative studies. Were such information available now, for example, it might help settle the current controversy centered on the hypothesis that many centuries ago West Africa was colonized by Indonesians.[31]

A Note on Laboratory Methods

Max Harrell

The cents-table of Hornbostel for the conversion to cents of the ratio between two pitches expressed in cycles per second begins with the figure 340 cycles per second represented by zero and extends to 809 cps represented by 1500.[32] The standard of the stroboconn is A-440 cps, represented on the table by the figure 446. The other eleven pitches in the Western equal-tempered

---

[31] One side of the controversy has been presented by Doctor Jones (see Footnote 4).

[32] See further, Jaap Kunst, *Ethnomusicology* (3rd ed.) (The Hague: 1959), p. 232.

tuning are successively greater or smaller by 100 cents and are represented on the Hornbostel table by the following figures: A sharp = 546; B = 646; C = 746; G sharp = 346; G = 246, and so on. As a simplified procedure, plus or minus readings on the stroboconn were simply added or subtracted from these figures representing the pitches of equal temperament, and the results recorded, preceded by numbers indicating the octave band, that is, A-440 in the 4th band, A-220 in the 3rd band, A-880 in the 5th band, and so on.

In Figure 17, the lefthand column refers to the pitches of the slendro tuning system by octave (cf. Fig. 2). Measurements of the individual keys of each instrument are listed in the following 13 columns under their appropriate instrumental names. The first digit refers to the octave band of the stroboconn and the digits that follow represent the computation made from the Hornbostel table explained above, for example, the highest pitch of the *Saron Peking*, column 2, 7-859, equals octave band 7 and a pitch represented on the Hornbostel table by 859, whose nearest equivalent is 559 cps. In column 5 the highest pitch of the *Bonang Panerus* is represented by the same pitch as that of the *Saron Peking*. In column 3, the highest pitch of the *Saron Barung* is given as 6-138; the corresponding key of the *Saron Peking* (column 2) is given as 6-141, that of the *Bonang Panerus* (column 5) is given as 6-143, that of the *Gender Panerus* (column 7) is given as 6-137, with an average (column 14) of 6-140 or, expressed to the nearest cps integer, 369 cps. If the measurements of all keys representing the same pitch showed a spread greater than 6 cents, the key or keys farthest from the median of the majority were rejected—unless other over-riding reasons such as clarity of tone or "reliability" (established by instrumental type) had to be taken into account. An example of comparative reliability is the greater stability of the keys of the gender family as compared with the kettles of the bonang. Two of the *Saron Barung* readings were rejected, one of the *Saron Demung*, one of the *Bonang Panerus*, two of the *Bonang Barung*. One of the *Gender Barung* readings was rejected, one of the kenong readings and two (of three) of the *Kempul* readings; both of the *Engkok Kemong* readings were rejected and the single *Ketuck* reading. Thus of a total of 92 readings, 13 were rejected. In the table of data, Fig. 17, those readings rejected are in small figures.

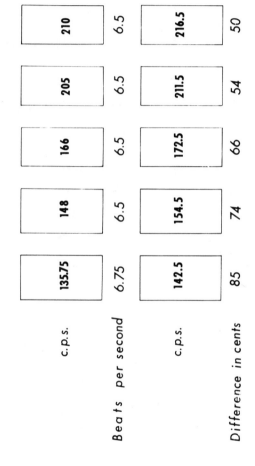

Fig. 1 The *penjorog* of the *djegogan*.

Fig. 2*

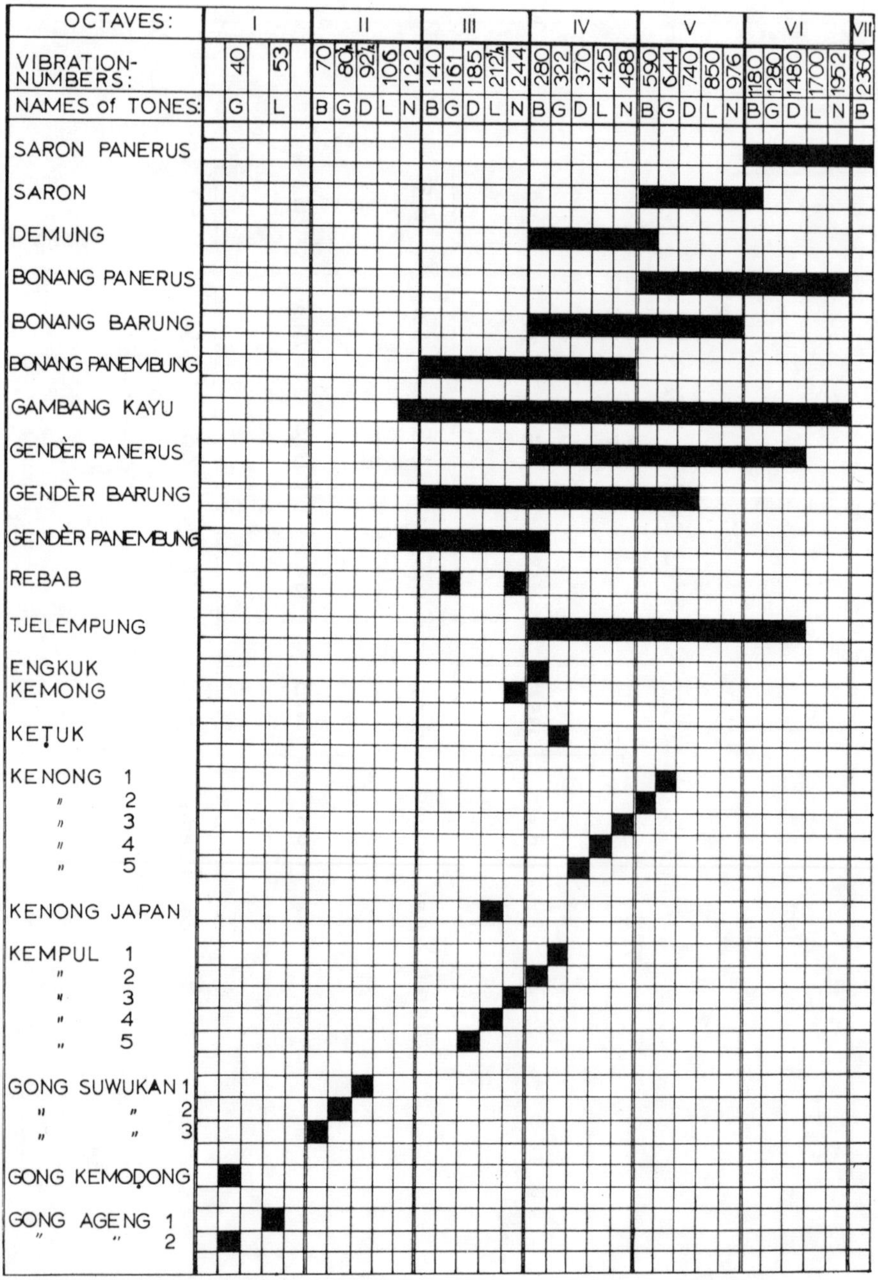

*From Kunst's *Music in Java* (2nd. ed.), by permission of the publisher.

Fig. 3 *

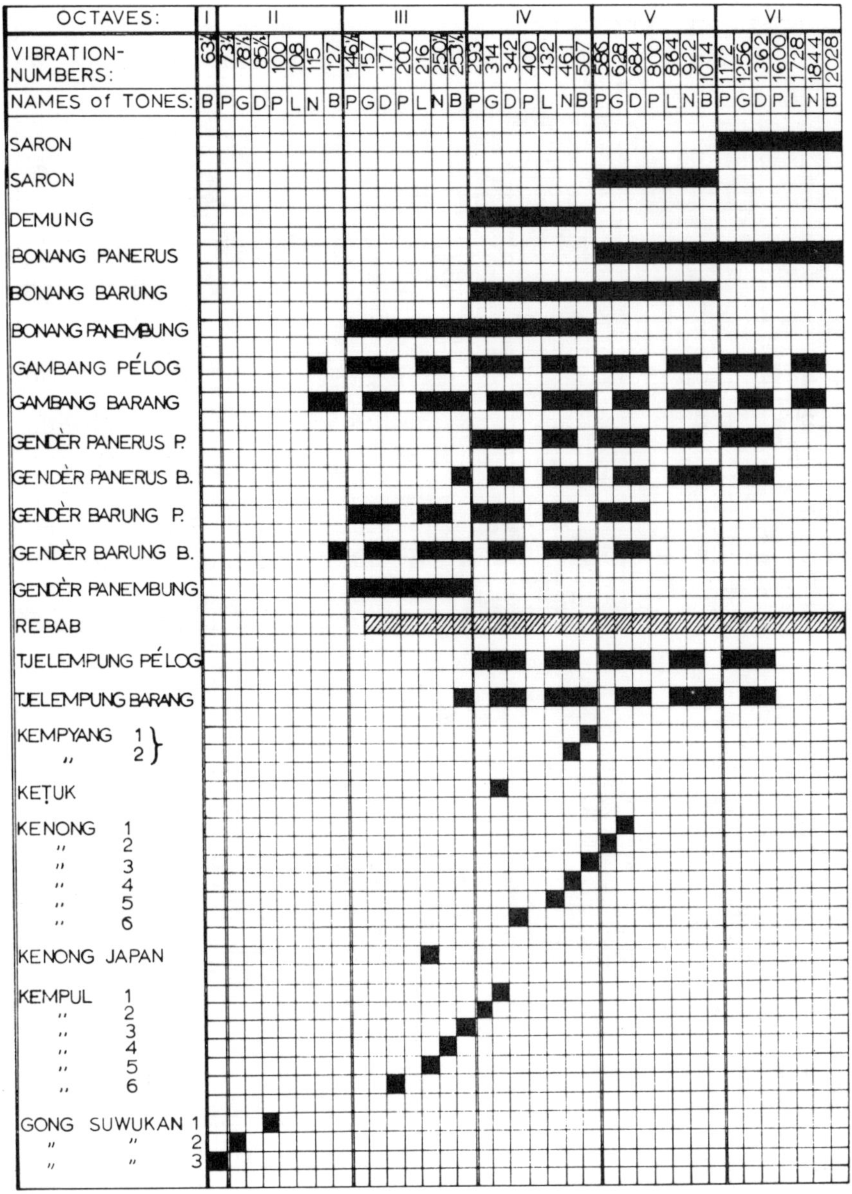

*From Kunst's *Music in Java* (2nd. ed.), by permission of the publisher.

Fig. 4

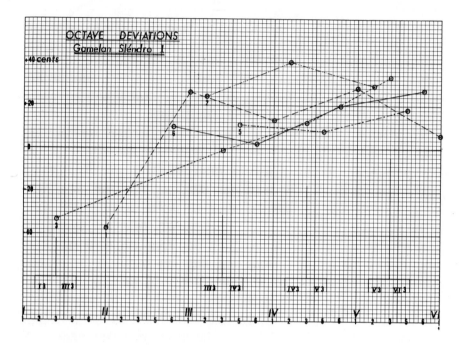

Fig. 5

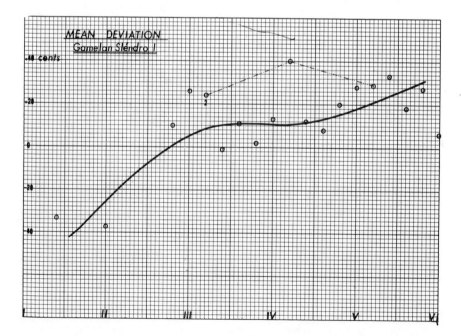

Fig. 6

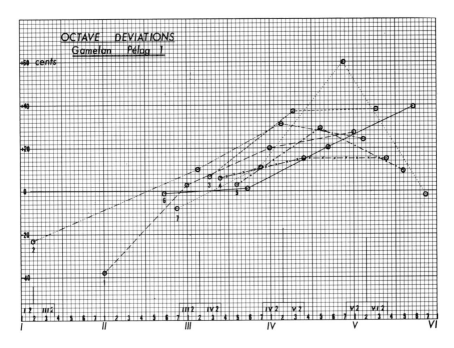

Fig. 7

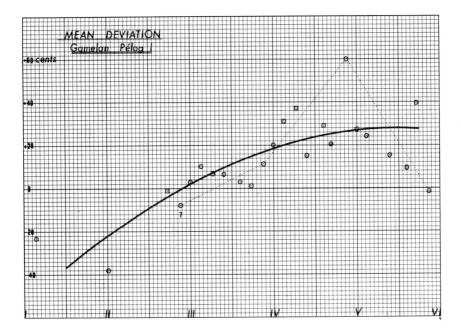

Fig. 8

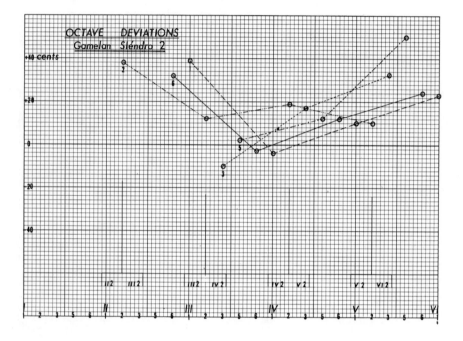

Fig. 9

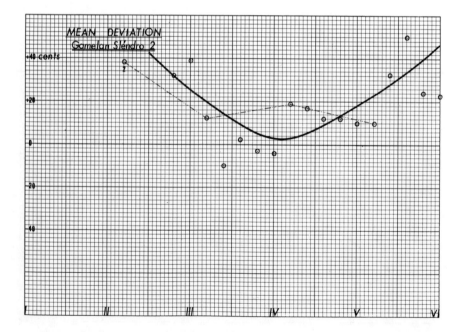

Fig. 10

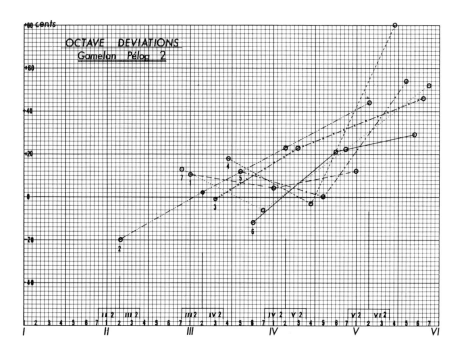

Fig. 11

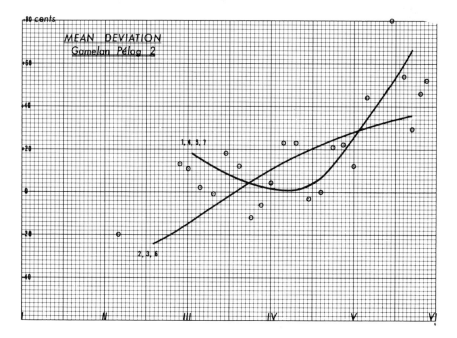

Fig. 12

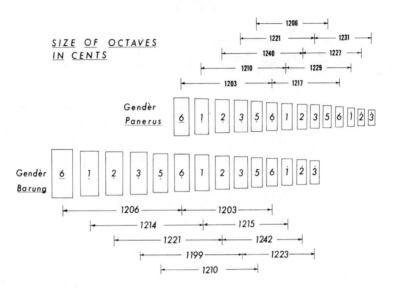

Fig. 13

SLÉNDRO INTERVALS GAMELAN №1

octave	1	2	3	5	6	1
vi	R 246 L	241 L	219 S	254 L	246 L	
v	R 245 L	237 S	234 S	245 L	267 L	
iv	L 218 S	255 L	248 L	233 S	259 L	
iii	L 220 S	280 L	236 S	242 L	248 L	

PÉLOG INTERVALS GAMELAN №1

octave	1	2	3	4	5	6	7	1
vi	S 131	163	252	126	131	173	—	
v	S 140	143	275	127	116	204	222	
iv	R 125	141	297	113	124	165	255	
iii	R 120	144	297	117	126	155	246	

S ~ Sigrak   sl. 260,   pl. 140   S ~ small sléndro interval
R ~ Rata   sl. 240,   pl. 120   L ~ large sléndro interval
L ~ Luruh   sl. 220,   pl. 100

Fig. 14

SLÉNDRO INTERVALS GAMELAN Nº2

octave	1	2	3	5	6	1
vi	$\underline{S}$ 254 L	249 L	257 L	203 S	260 L	
v	$\underline{S}$ 254 L	226 S	246 L	229 S	261 L	
iv	$\underline{S}$ 274 L	228 S	245 L	229 S	263 L	
iii	$\underline{S}$ 258 L	250 L	233 S	234 S	264 L	

PÉLOG INTERVALS GAMELAN Nº2

octave	1	2	3	4	5	6	7	1
vi	$\underline{S}$ 167	137	316	102	115	164	—	
v	$\underline{S}$ 135	134	283	128	140	141	251	
iv	$\underline{R}$ 116	134	309	125	119	140	261	
iii	$\underline{R}$ 125	137	290	131	143	134	251	

$\underline{S}$ ~ Sigrak sl. 260, pl. 140   S ~ small slendro interval
$\underline{R}$ ~ Rata sl. 240, pl. 120   L ~ large slendro interval
$\underline{L}$ ~ Luruh sl. 220, pl. 100

Fig. 15

PRINCIPAL FIFTHS OF PATET
Gamelan Nº1

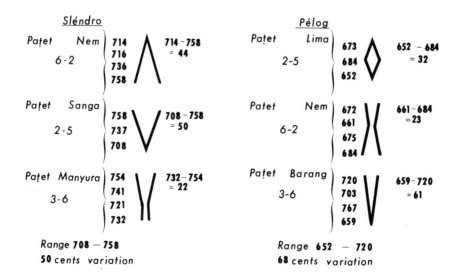

Sléndro

Patet Nem
6-2
714
716
736
758
714−758 = 44

Patet Sanga
2-5
758
737
708
708−758 = 50

Patet Manyura
3-6
754
741
721
732
732−754 = 22

Range 708 − 758
50 cents variation

Pélog

Patet Lima
2-5
673
684
652
652 − 684 = 32

Patet Nem
6-2
672
661
675
684
661−684 = 23

Patet Barang
3-6
720
703
767
659
659−720 = 61

Range 652 − 720
68 cents variation

Fig. 16

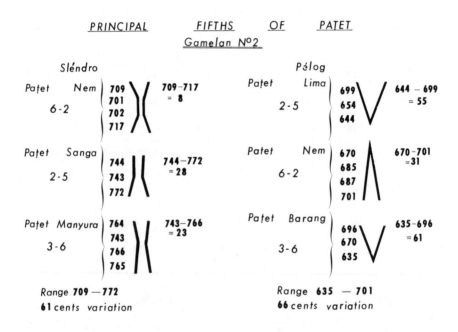

PRINCIPAL   FIFTHS   OF   PATET

Gamelan N°2

Sléndro

Paṭet   Nem   709   709–717
6-2   701   = 8
702
717

Paṭet   Sanga   744   744–772
2-5   743   = 28
772

Paṭet Manyura   764   743–766
3-6   743   = 23
766
765

Range 709 — 772
61 cents variation

Pélog

Paṭet   Lima   699   644 — 699
2-5   654   = 55
644

Paṭet   Nem   670   670–701
6-2   685   =31
687
701

Paṭet   Barang   696   635–696
3-6   670   = 61
635

Range 635 — 701
66 cents variation

Fig. 17 Laboratory Data

Instrument	VI/6	VI/5	VI/3	VI/2	VI/1	V/6	V/5	V/3	V/2	V/1	IV/6	IV/5	IV/3	IV/2	IV/1	III/6	III/5	III/3	III/2	III/1	II/6	II/5	II/3	II/2	II/1	I/6	I/5	I/3
Average	7-859	6-613	6-359	6-140	6-1099	6-853	5-856	5-341	5-107	5-1070	5-825	4-566	4-333	4-1285	4-1030	4-812	3-564	3-322	3-1286	3-1006	3-786							
Gong																						2-823						1-119
Keṭuk															4-1028													
Engkok Kemong											5-812	5-557																
Kempul																4-811	3-576	3-301										
Kenong											5-829	5-566	4-337	4-1289	4-1039													
Slentem																4-812	3-565	3-322	3-1286	3-1003	3-786	2-550						
Gènder Barung									5-108	5-1071	5-825	4-566	4-332	4-1285	4-1029	4-810	3-563	3-322	3-1286	3-1008	3-796	2-557						
Gènder Panerus				6-137	6-1096	6-851	5-582	5-338	5-106	5-1069	5-822	4-565	4-332	4-1285	4-1029	4-812	3-562											
Bonang Barung					6-1100	6-853	5-585	5-344	5-106	5-1070	5-808	4-565	4-326	4-1283	4-1030	4-812												
Bonang Panerus	7-859	6-613	6-359	6-143	6-1099	6-851	5-586	5-342	5-107	5-1057	5-819																	
Saron Demung											5-829	4-566	4-332	4-1285	4-1030	4-824	3-566											
Saron Barung				6-138	6-1101	6-853	5-588	5-334	5-107	5-1057	5-824	4-566																
Saron Peking	7-859	6-613	6-359	6-141	6-1102	6-853	5-588																					
Pitch No.	6	5	3	2	1	6	5	3	2	1	6	5	3	2	1	6	5	3	2	1	6	5	3	2	1	6	5	3
Octave	VI					V					IV					III					II					I		

(Row group label: INSTRUMENTS)

STATISTICAL CLASSIFICATION IN ANTHROPOLOGY: AN APPLICATION TO ETHNOMUSICOLOGY

Linton C. Freeman and Alan P. Merriam

While a growing interest in the application of statistics to cultural anthropology is indicated by the current literature (Driver 1953; Clements 1954), it is only relatively recently that such processes have received any widespread attention from cultural anthropologists. The earliest application was made by Tylor (1889), but Driver and Kroeber (1932) with their trait-element list were the forerunners of the current trend which has culminated in Murdock's extensive study of the interrelationships among various aspects of social structure (1949). With the development of the Cross Cultural Survey at Yale as well as the Human Relations Area Files, statistical treatment of cultural materials has become relatively common (Anon. 1954a); the importance of the trend is perhaps best indicated by the fact that an entire section of the 1954 meeting of the American Statistical Association was devoted to "The Use of Statistics in Anthropological Studies" (Anon. 1954b).

Most statistical studies in cultural anthropology have been relational. They have attempted to determine the degree of association which exists between two or more cultural variables through application of the techniques of correlation. However, correlational techniques may be extended to deal with problems of classification. It is with problems of this latter sort that the present paper is concerned.

Classification is one of the central problems of cultural anthropology. Types are established and distinctions are made among them, but for the most part both the classifications and the distinctions are intuitively established. Even when mathematical techniques are used, they are usually restricted to simple frequency counts and comparisons of percentages. At best, such procedures afford only crude generalizations and comparisons. The present report is designed primarily as a demonstration of the power of statistical techniques in classifying and comparing.

Statistical techniques provide the investigator with precise estimates of the homogeneity of objects classified together. Furthermore, one may determine the exact degree to which differences obtain between two or more classifications. Comparisons made by statistical means need no longer be based on intuitive judgment nor subject to revision on the basis of "expert" opinion. Accurate statements of probability describe the confidence with which statistical generalizations may be held. In short, statistical techniques can provide system and precision in constructing and comparing classificatory types.

Among those aspects of culture which seem particularly susceptible to statistical analysis, music is perhaps outstanding (Herskovits 1949:573–74). This is partly due to the nature of the way in which materials can be gathered in the field, and partly due to the structure of music itself. With reference only to music as a structure, it may be said that laboratory control is more closely approximated in ethnomusicological studies than in most anthropological methodology. Through the use of a recording device a specific cultural activity can be mirrored in process; the activity may be examined over and over again without change, and the element of subjectivity which enters into observational method can be excluded to a considerable degree. Thus in field work itself, a high degree of control over the materials is achieved with a minimum of effort. Music is also particularly susceptible to objective analysis once collection has been made; through study of its actual structure the investigator can define a musical style without recourse to subjective characteristics based either upon his own preconceptions of what music should be structurally or upon qualities of music which cannot be objectified. Thus in a specific rendition of a song, such qualities as pitch, tonal range, tonal duration, interval usage, modal structure, and others, can not only be isolated, counted, computed, and analyzed, but can be objectified in terms of the fact that in the rendition at hand they do not change. This does not indicate, of course, that variation should not be taken into account, but it does suggest that if a song A has a variant B, the structure of each can be objectively isolated from a number of rigorous standpoints and then compared in like terms. These characteristics of music, which in the sense discussed above are analogous to those of language, make it a potentially rich area for inquiry by methods of statistics.

So far as is known to the present authors, no statistical applications as such have been made in the field of comparative musicology. Various trigonometric calculations have been used in the study of tonometrics (Hornbostel 1921; Kunst 1950), but these are not statistical in the sense used here. Arithmetical counts and percentages have also figured in comparative musicology, as in the work of Densmore (1929), and these have been extended by Kolinski (1936), for example, until they form the basis for at least one method of research inquiry. The set of problems treated here is derived from the Kolinski method.

One of the techniques used by Kolinski, as well as by other students, is the interval count and the resulting percentages of specific intervals used in a particular body of music; this is usually broken down into ascending intervals, descending intervals, and total intervals. Thus in a brief study made by one of the present authors (Merriam 1949, 1950) of Cheyenne music, it was found that in a group of songs 33 percent of the total intervals were major seconds, 27 percent minor thirds, 15 percent perfect fourths, and so on; similar percentages expressed the relative use of specific ascending and descending intervals. The purpose of such analysis is to express in objective terms a particular musical measure which will differentiate between groups of songs. Thus it is hopefully assumed that by comparing interval counts, as well as other characteristics, a differentiation could be made between Cheyenne and Iroquois songs, for example; or conversely, that if the percentage of major seconds used in an unknown body of song is 32.66 percent, it has a far greater probability of being Cheyenne than anything else. This is, of course, reducing the problem in the extreme; a single interval count would probably not give such an indication. However, there is a possibility that a group of interval counts might do so, and it is this possibility which is investigated here. The question, then, is whether interval count will actually differentiate between two bodies of music; the problem is to find a statistical procedure which will indicate both the plausibility of the use of intervals or other measures to differentiate bodies of song, and the extent to which it is reliable.

If music can be classified into various types, and distinction made among these types by statistical methods, several problems in comparative musicology can be attacked with considerably greater precision than has heretofore been possible. Restricting ourselves to the interval count as an example, we have already pointed out this method might be used to differentiate between two groups of songs; more specifically, interest lies in whether or not certain groups of percentages in interval usage can be used as a criterion of identifying a body of song. In extension, if the measure proves valid, it should also be possible to trace musical influences which have played upon a specific group or tribe. Further, if it is established that specific interval usages and other structural forms characterize specific cultures or subcultures, a clearer picture of the relationship between music and other elements of culture is obtained, and the individuality of esthetic expression as it is shaped by the customs of a particular group is more sharply established. The present paper does not hope to answer these problems, but rather to suggest the possibilities which may be assayed through the use of statistics. It must also be emphasized that the interval count alone, or for that matter ethnomusicology itself, cannot be expected to indicate past contact or derivations with finality without corroboration from other investigations. The normal precautions taken by anthropologists when postulating contact are equally valid in ethnomusicology; in this sense the study of music is simply contributory as an added technique of anthropological investigations.

The problem of classifying into types and distinguishing among them is not peculiar to the field of ethnomusicology. In any science the investigator is frequently faced with the necessity of differentiating between two groups of objects on the basis of measurements of several characteristics of each. The procedure is simple in those cases in which the measures yield very different values for the two groups, but where the measured values are fairly similar for objects in the two groups there may be considerable overlap in the distribution of any single measure; thus differentiation on the basis of any one of the measurements may be impossible.

The process of distinguishing among classes of objects on the basis of a set of measurements of their properties calls for a specialized statistical technique. Such a technique, the discriminant function, has been developed by R. A.

Fisher (1936). This function enables the investigator to make a linear combination of several variables in such a manner that scores on the resulting combined index will possess a minimum of distributional overlap. Thus the possibility of grouping the objects into their proper classes is increased, and the chance of error in any single classification is reduced. In short, the discriminant function provides a technique of weighting scores so that a maximum separation for differentiation between groups is accomplished.

In practice, Fisher's technique may be applied to any multiple measurements on two or more groups. Weights are computed and the original measurements converted into index scores. A critical value of the index is determined, and all cases which fall above it are classed as members of one group while those falling below it belong to the other. New cases may then be transferred into the index classification and assigned to their proper groups with a high degree of success.

Anthropological applications of the discriminant function need not, of course, be limited to studies of ethnomusicology; they may be made wherever successive measures are taken on any object of interest. The technique has been employed at least once in craniometry (Barnard 1935) to describe a progressive trend for a dated series of skulls. It has also been used recently in classifying teeth (Bronowski and Long 1952). Applications are possible in any area of anthropometry, in linguistics, or in almost any study of material culture. Pottery, for example, might be classified, compared, and related through use of the discriminant function. Empirical types could be established and these might be contrasted and their derivations traced in terms of their overall differences. Music was chosen for the present illustrative report, but any of the objects noted above upon which suitable data were available might also have been used.

The music selected for the present study represents New World Negro material derived from Africa—the two groups are the Ketu cult of Bahia, Brazil, and the Rada cult of Trinidad. Ceremony, including music, in the Ketu groups is derived from the religious practices of the Yoruba people of Nigeria (Bascom 1944; Carneiro 1936; Ramos 1943), while that of the Rada stems from Dahomey (Herskovits 1938; Carr 1953). The Ketu songs were recorded by M. J. and F. S. Herskovits in 1941–42 in Bahia (M. J. and F. S. Herskovits 1943), the Rada songs by Andrew Carr in Trinidad in 1953; both groups of songs were analyzed by one of the present writers (Merriam 1951; Merriam, Whinery and Fred 1954). The selection of these materials is based on the special interest in attempting to differentiate between two derived variants of what has been classed as a regional style (Waterman 1952).

It was clear from the outset that a random sample of these song-groups would be impossible to obtain, since the universe of songs in any group was necessarily unknown. While without sampling, statistical results could not be generalized to all of the music of the societies in question, such sampling was considered unnecessary in view of the fact that this application was designed primarily to suggest a technique of analysis.

Considerations of economy, availability of materials, and potential productivity led to the selection of three measures of interval use; these are song length measured in intervals, the proportionate use of major seconds, and the proportionate use of minor thirds. Proportion of use was chosen in order to avoid any systematic bias resulting from differential song length, since one very long or very short song might have completely changed the results.

Twenty songs of each of the two musical forms were selected. Interval counts were made, and the frequencies of use of major seconds, minor thirds, and total intervals were determined for each song. The frequencies of major seconds and minor thirds were divided by their song length, and the resulting proportions were tabulated. Means were computed for each form and differences were calculated. These means and differences are reported in Table 1.

TABLE 1. MEANS AND DIFFERENCES OF UNCORRECTED MEASURES FOR RADA
AND KETU

	Major Seconds	Minor Thirds	Total Intervals
Radu	.2335	.4081	148.9
Ketu	.4240	.2086	134.2
Difference	− .1905	.1995	14.7

A glance at this table indicates that differences between means do obtain on each of the three measures. "Student's" *t*-test was employed in order to evaluate the significance of these differences.[1] Table 2 shows that the mean differences for major seconds and minor thirds were each significant beyond the one percent level of confidence, while the value for totals was not significant at that level.

TABLE 2. SIGNIFICANCE OF DIFFERENCES IN UNCORRECTED MEASURES FOR
RADA AND KETU

	Difference	S.E.	t	P
Major Seconds	− .1905	.0297	6.41	< .01
Minor Thirds	.1995	.0307	6.50	< .01
Total Intervals	14.7	17.5779	.836	> .01

In other words, the measured differences between Rada and Ketu may be evaluated as reflecting a real difference in proportionate use of major seconds and of minor thirds. Differences as great as those observed would have arisen by chance in a sample of songs less than one time in a hundred. Total interval use, however, presents a less well-defined result. A difference as great as the one observed would arise through the operation of chance factors alone more than one time in one hundred. It must therefore be concluded that no significant difference in total interval use has been demonstrated.

The results of the *t*-tests indicate the possibility of accurate discrimination between samples of the music of Rada and Ketu either on the basis of use of major seconds or use of minor thirds. There is, however, a large amount of overlap in the distributions of each measure. Any attempt to classify a single song on the basis of either of these intervals would be subject to a high probability of error. Even the distribution of minor thirds, which is the best index of discrimination, contains this wide area of overlap in which it is impossible to distinguish between music of Rada and Ketu. Table 3 illustrates that any song which involves use of minor thirds in a range from .20 to .49

TABLE 3. DISTRIBUTIONS OF MINOR THIRDS FOR RADA AND KETU

Score	Rada	Ketu	
.50–.59	4		
.40–.49	7	2	Area
.30–.39	6	2	of
.20–.29	3	5	overlap
.10–.19		9	
. 0–.09		2	

cannot be classified on the basis of this measure. Twenty-five of the forty songs fall into this area of overlap, and it is likely that half of these (12.5) would be misclassified. Thus, thirty-one percent of all the songs in the sample would be incorrectly categorized if use of minor thirds was employed as the only classifying instrument. It therefore seemed inadvisable to compute a discriminate function on all three of these measures in order to maximize their ability to differentiate.

In employing the discriminant function, maximum differentiation is achieved by computing a set of lambda (λ) scores which are used to weight the various measurements.[2] These scores result from the solution of the following three simultaneous equations in three unknowns:

$$\lambda_2 \sum x_2{}^2 + \lambda_3 \sum x_2 x_3 + \lambda_T \sum x_2 x_T = d_2$$

$$\lambda_2 \sum x_2 x_3 + \lambda_3 \sum x_3{}^2 + \lambda_T \sum x_3 x_T = d_3$$

$$\lambda_2 \sum x_2 x_T + \lambda_3 \sum x_3 x_T + \lambda_T \sum x_T{}^2 = d_T$$

These equations may be solved by substituting the known values and solving for three unknowns.[3] Solving for the three lambdas yielded the following results:

$$\lambda_2 = -\ .49069$$

$$\lambda_3 = \quad .47958$$

$$\lambda_T = \quad .00045$$

The final step involved computation of the mean weighted score for each group and the point of discrimination between the groups. For this operation the following equations were employed: For the Ketu,

$$D_K = \lambda_2\overline{X}_{2K} + \lambda_3\overline{X}_{3K} + \lambda_T\overline{X}_{TK}$$

For the Rada,

$$D_R = \lambda_2\overline{X}_{2R} + \lambda_3\overline{X}_{3R} + \lambda_T\overline{X}_{TR}$$

and for the point of discrimination,

$$D = \lambda_2\overline{X}_2 + \lambda_3\overline{X}_3 + \lambda_T\overline{X}_T$$

Substituting means and λ's, the following results were obtained:

$D_K = (-.49069)(.4240) + (.47958)(.2086) + (.00045)(134.2) = -.0476$

$D_R = (-.49069)(.2335) + (.47958)(.4081) + (.00045)(148.9) = .1481$

$D = (-.49069)(.3288) + (.47958)(.3084) + (.00045)(141.55) = .0503$

Thus the mean weighted score for Rada was .1481 while that for Ketu was −.0476. The point of discrimination halfway between these values was .0503. Any weighted score falling above .0503 would be classified as Rada and any falling below as Ketu.

The difference in means of weighted scores was .19576. The average variance of the two musical forms was estimated by dividing this value by the degree of freedom for the two groups (36). This yielded a variance of .005438, the variance of the difference between two means of twenty songs each. For this mean difference the standard error is .0233.

Dividing the mean difference (.19576) by its standard error (.0233) produced a t value of 8.39 which was significant well above the one percent level of confidence. This t value is greater than any of those obtained from differences in individual measurements. Use of the discriminant function, then, has reduced the probability of error in classifying samples of songs.

Here a question may be raised concerning the possible improvement in classifying a single song through application of the discriminant function. An estimate of the proportion of error in classifying single songs is provided by dividing one-half of the difference between means (.09788) by the standard deviation. The variance is .005438, which yields a standard deviation of .0737. The ratio of this number to one-half the mean difference is 1.33. A table of areas of the normal curve indicated that only 9 percent of the cases in a distribution will fall beyond this point. Such cases will be misclassified. When this error of 9 percent is compared with 31 percent, the estimated minimum error before combining scores, a substantial improvement is seen. It is reasonable to believe that further reduction in error may be accomplished merely by adding more variables. In the final analysis it should be possible to reduce error in classification to less than one in one hundred.

The present report has outlined a statistical device which might prove useful in meeting the problem of classifying data in cultural anthropology. As an example, a preliminary application of Fisher's discriminant function was made to data from the field of comparative musicology. Songs of Trinidad Rada and of Brazilian Ketu were compared with respect to use of major seconds, minor thirds and total intervals. Although it was possible to differentiate significantly between music of these societies on the basis of some of the frequencies of interval use, application of the discriminant function markedly enhanced the probability of correct classification. After combining weighted scores, the probability of misclassifying a single song was reduced from about .31 to about .09.

This study has demonstrated that classification may be systematized and improved through application of a statistical technique. Further studies must employ larger samples and more variables, and in so doing significant measures may be isolated and classificatory problems solved. In this manner errors may be further reduced and questions of relatedness and derivation may be systematically attacked.

NOTES

[1] Descriptions of the *t*-test are available in any standard introductory statistics text. (*t* is not to be confused with T, which symbolizes total interval use in the present report.)

[2] Computational procedures for the discriminant function may be found in Fisher (1946), Garrett (1943), Hoel (1947), and Moroney (1953).

[3] A discussion of the solution of simultaneous equations may be found in any text in college algebra.

Bibliography

Anonymous, 1954a, Function and scope of the Human Relations Area Files, Inc. New Haven, Human Relations Area Files.

Anonymous, 1954b, 114th Annual Meeting of the American Statistical Association. American Statistician 8:32.

Barnard, Mildred M, 1935, The secular variations of skull characteristics in four series of Egyptian skulls. Annals of Eugenics 6:352-71.

Bascom, William R., 1944, The sociological role of the Yoruba cult-group. Menasha, American Anthropological Association Memoir 63.

Boas, Franz, 1927, Anthropology and statistics. *In* W. F. Ogburn and A. A. Goldenweiser, The social sciences and their interrelations. Boston, Houghton & Mifflin Co.

Bronowski, J. and W. M. Long, 1952, Statistics of classification in anthropology. American Journal of Physical Anthropology 10 n.s.:385-94.

Carneiro, Edison, 1936, Religioes Negras. Rio de Janeiro, Civilizacao Brasileira.

Carr, Andrew, 1953, A Rada community in Trinidad. Caribbean Quarterly 3:35-54.

Clements, Forrest E., 1954, Use of cluster analysis with anthropological data. American Anthropologist 56:180-99.

Densmore, Frances, 1929, Papago music. Washington Bureau of American Ethnology Bulletin 90.

Driver, H. E., 1953, Statistics in Anthropology. American Anthropologist 55:42-57.

Driver, H. E. and A. L. Kroeber, 1932, Quantitative expression of cultural relationships. University of California Publications in American Archaeology and Ethnology 31:211-56.

Fisher, R. A., 1936, The use of multiple measurements in taxonomic problems. Annals of Eugenics 7:179-88.

Fisher, R. A., 1946, Statistical methods for research workers. New York, Hafner Publishing Company.

Garrett, Henry A., 1943, The discriminant function and its use in psychology. Psychometrika 8:65-79.

Herskovits, Melville J., 1938, Dahomey. New York. J. J. Augustin. 2 vols.

Herskovits, Melville J., 1949, Man and his works. New York, Alfred A. Knopf.

Herskovits, Melville J. and Frances S. Herskovits, 1943, The Negroes of Brazil. Yale Review 32:263-79.

Hoel, Paul G., 1947, Introduction to mathematical statistics. New York, John Wiley and Sons.

Hornbostel, Erich M. von, 1921, Eine Tafel zur logarithmischen Darstellung von Zahlenverhaltnissen. Zeitschrift für Physik 6:29-34.

Kolinski, Mieczyslaw, 1936, Suriname music. *In* Melville J. Heskovits and Frances S. Herskovits, Suriname folklore. New York, Columbia Contributions to Anthropology, Vol. 27, pp. 491-760.

Kunst, Jaap, 1950, Musicologica. Amsterdam. Koninklijke Vereeniging Indisch Instituut.

Merriam, Alan P., 1949, A transcription and analysis of Cheyenne Indian music. Unpublished MS.

Merriam, Alan P., 1950, Notes on Cheyenne songs. Journal of the American Musicological Society 3:289-90.

Merriam, Alan P., 1951, Songs of the Afro-Bahian cults: An ethnomusicological analysis. Unpublished Doctoral Dissertation, Northwestern University.

Merriam, Alan P., Sarah Whinery, and Benhart Fred, 1954, Music of a Rada cult group. (Forthcoming in Anthropos).

Moroney, M. M., 1953, Facts from figures. Melbourne, Pneguin Books.

Murdock, George Peter, 1949, Social structure. New York, Macmillan.

Ramos, Arthur, 1943, Introducao a antropologia Brasileira. Rio de Janeiro, Colecao Estudos Brasileiros.

Tylor, E. B., 1889, On a method of investigating the development of institutions, applied to laws of marriage and descent. Journal of the Royal Anthropological Institute 18:245-69.

Waterman, Richard A., 1952, African influence on the music of the Americas. *In* Sol Tax, Acculturation in the Americas. Chicago, University of Chicago Press.

PROLEGOMENA TO A STUDY OF THE PRINCIPAL
MELODIC FAMILIES OF BRITISH-AMERICAN FOLKSONG

Samuel P. Bayard

The present essay is intended to serve as a prelude to studies that may be described as efforts directed principally at melodic identification; i.e., the distinguishing of variant forms of different individual folk tunes in tradition. The objects of study will be those tunes which appear to be the ones most commonly associated with folk poems sung in the British Isles and (by speakers of English) in North America. Our natural starting point, of course, is with tunes sung to songs in English; but it is impossible to confine attention to the traditions of any one British language. The tune-families to be considered are apparently broadcast over the British Isles, and are often sung to songs in Gaelic, Welsh and Manx, while some of their versions will be found still farther afield in Europe.

Our discussion cannot be historical, strictly speaking, because the data are fragmentary for the present and recent past, and are entirely lacking for the remoter past. That is, there do not seem to be any versions of these melodies which are traceable definitely to the Middle Ages, or which were recorded in times so distant. However, the discussion will try to set forth a number of considerations which were borne in upon the writer from a rather long study of the musical material; and will endeavor to clarify the meanings of certain terms used throughout. Thus, this essay will be concerned with what might be called "background" considerations applying to the material studied, the conditions under which it is studied, and the methods of approach. The national melodic traditions involved will be characterized roughly and their important overall features set forth to the best of the writer's ability. Records of the observations of various collectors will explain the impetus of this study, and the bases for some of the assumptions under which it was begun. The writer's own experiences and observations as a collector—which correspond rather closely with those of others—will naturally be drawn upon also.

Collectors and editors of folk music in the British Isles, from the earliest to the latest, have testified to their perception of tunes widely current in whatever localities they explored, and known in more than one variant form. So, for instance, with certain eighteenth-century Scottish collectors such as the Gows[1]

---

[1] In the *Journal of the Folk Song Society* (hereinafter called *JFSS*), 2 (1906), 261, Miss Anne G. Gilchrist notes that Neil Gow and Sons, in publishing the second part of their *Repository of Original Scotch Tunes*, stated that they had never heard *"Two Professional Musicans* who play the same notes of *any* tune"—hence, they propose a "standard" setting of each tune in their publication. Miss Gilchrist remarks that the statement "points to a large number of then existent variants of the best known tunes, in actual performance. . . ."

and Patrick McDonald[2]; and nineteenth- and twentieth-century students such as William Chappell,[3] Alexander Campbell,[4] Simon Fraser,[5] G. Farquhar Graham,[6] John Glen,[7] George Petrie,[8] W. P. Joyce,[9] Gavin Greig,[10] Father Henebry,[11] and Cecil J. Sharp,[12] to name only some of the more prominent ones. So also, apparently, the Irish collectors Pigott and Forde[13] —and, in fact, all the eminent

[2] This is implied throughout the preface to his rare *A Collection of Highland Vocal Airs* (c. 1784), and definitely stated on page 4 of that valuable dissertation.

[3] Throughout his well-known *Popular Music of the Olden Time* (1855-1859), Chappell discusses his material as composed of individual airs, and points out occasionally the occurrences of what look like variant forms of some of them.

[4] See, for instance, the notes at the foot of page 92 of the second volume of his *Albyn's Anthology* (1818); and again, the note, p. 96 of the same volume, where he speaks of variant manifestations as striking examples of "the commutability of our National Melodies, without any violence to their original beauty."

[5] See his *Airs and Melodies Peculiar to the Highlands of Scotland and the Isles* (1815), p. 3, where he falls afoul of McDonald for what he thinks is bad notation of certain widespread tunes; also pp. 105, 106 (where he again accuses McDonald of "murdering" tunes), note to No. 7; p. 107, note to No. 31; etc. Fraser is apparently obsessed by the idea of the need for a "standard" version, as were the Gows: cf. his note to No. 19 (p. 107), and to Nos. 70 (p. 110), 85 (p. 111), and 150 (p. 115), where Fraser gives an air which he has treated traditionally himself. He says that this air was "very imperfect, but constantly dwelt upon his mind until modelled into its present shape." Other notes testify to his recognition of variant forms of certain tunes.

[6] See his introduction to *The Popular Songs and Melodies of Scotland*, Balmoral Edition (London & Glasgow, 1908), p. viii; and *passim* in his notes to the several melodies throughout the work.

[7] Of course, the whole of John Glen's *Early Scottish Melodies* (Edinburgh, 1900) is written from the point of view that distinct individual airs are found in several variant forms; the writer gives a number of comparative tables of these forms in the course of his valuable notes on the earliest Scots melodies and those in the *Scots Musical Museum*.

[8] Petrie gives the most explicit statement of his view that tunes may often be found in quite diverse forms in the introduction to his *Ancient Music of Ireland*; see this introduction reprinted in C. V. Stanford's *Complete Petrie Collection of Ancient Irish Music* (London: Boosey & Co., cop. 1902), p. x.

[9] Dr. Joyce has made particularly valuable observations (supported by examples) of how tunes vary in tradition in his *Ancient Irish Music* (Dublin: M. H. Gill; London: Longmans, Green & Co., 1872, or re-issue of 1912). See especially his notes to No. 21 in that volume. Joyce's *Old Irish Folk Music and Songs* (London: Longmans, Green & Co., 1909 contains notices of the same sort.

[10] According to Alexander Keith, his editor, in *Last Leaves of Traditional Ballads and Ballad Airs* (Aberdeen: The Buchan Club, 1925), pp. xli-xliii, Greig thought that the total number of folk song airs in the northeast of Scotland was under 300. Keith concurs, and in the pages just cited, mentions the frequent occurrence of an air to different pieces and in many variant forms.

[11] See his *Handbook of Irish Music* (posthumous; London: Longmans, Green & Co., 1928), pp. 190, 191, especially. On page 192 Father Henebry makes what looks like an exceedingly daring statement. Commenting on the "ballad" airs, he says "They are all four-strain, or ABBA tunes . . . and appear to have . . . a common ground scheme . . . which is always recognizable through an infinity of changes. The early prototype from which they are all undoubtedly descended has been the most prolific tune in Irish music. . . ." In the course of the present article I shall try to show why these words cannot be accepted in their entirety for British folk-tune versions.

[12] See especially his *English Folk-Song: Some Conclusions* (London: Novello & Co., 1907), p. 122.

[13] See P. W. Joyce, *Old Irish Folk Music and Songs*, pp. ix, x.

collectors with the sole exception of Edward Bunting,[14] whose views are the more unaccountable inasmuch as his experiences must have closely paralleled those of the others. the list of students who have recognized the presence of cognate versions of melodies occurring in British tradition could be enlarged; but these names will perhaps suffice.

The testimony of these writers agrees remarkably in substance. Sometimes a tune has been easily perceptible in many forms, widely scattered, and seemingly well known. Sometimes, on the other hand, differences in versions have so obscured the relationship that it went unobserved for a time, but suddenly became apparent when the student had learned more tunes and had gotten their outlines better fixed in his mind.[15] The fact that substantial agreement existed between students and collectors about the power of survival of some tunes in tradition, and the circumstance that my own observations so often agreed with theirs, were my initial warrants for assuming that in this British-American material we have strong individual persistence of tunes. In studying a collection of English folk songs with their music, which I had gathered in southwestern Pennsylvania and northern West Virginia, I attempted to pay some adequate attention to the music as well as the words, and to such special aspects as had rarely been accorded attention before: namely, the diffusion, textual associations, and different forms of individual tunes in their aggregate of variant settings. Only Phillips Barry and Grieg-Keith had gone much into these aspects.[16] My own musical discoveries were such as to make me realize that the study of our folk tunes was neither short nor simple; nor was it bound up, necessarily, in an inseparable manner, with the study of our folk texts. Indeed, it became increasingly apparent that, in some way, the melodies would have to be considered first independently of their text-associations; and that their intrinsic nature and interrelations, so therefore their identities, would have to be better determined, before it would become possible fruitfully to study the folk songs as text-tune complexes with both their elements, verbal and musical, taken together in a balanced consideration. As a result of my deciding thus, my attention became concentrated especially on the melodies, whose manifestations proved exceedingly complicated when subjected to a closer scrutiny.

Stated as curtly as possible, the broad result of some years' study of British-American folk song melodies has been my eventual belief that the number of distinctly different folk melodies in circulation among our modern folk singers is somewhat smaller than I had at first believed; that the groups of variants, versions, and otherwise closely related airs are correspondingly more

---

[14] Bunting's assertions regarding tune-variation are quoted at length, and criticized, by J. F. Graham and by Petrie, in the introductions referred to in notes 6 and 8.

[15] So also says Petrie, in effect, on page x of the introduction referred to in note 8.

[16] Nothing could exceed the justice of Keith's remarks in the work cited in note 10, above. Barry's penetrating study of many tune-versions is apparent in all his works, and shows with particular clearness in his *British Ballads from Maine*, with F. H. Eckstorm and M. Smyth (New Haven: Yale University Press, 1929) and in the volumes of the *Bulletin of the Folk-Song Society of the Northeast* (Cambridge, Mass: Powell Printing Co., 1930-1937), to which he was the major contributor of critical and historical notes.

inclusive; and that these derivative forms, with relatively few exceptions, are current wherever folk songs in English are sung. I believe that it is possible to indicate cognate relationship between groups of tunes not before suspected of such affinities; and if this belief seems warranted by what follows, the conclusions to be drawn from such a fact should be highly interesting to all who study the phenomena of folk memory and the processes of creation in oral folk arts.

My concentration on music has revealed, I think, that it is perfectly possible, by studying the song tunes apart from their texts, to throw light ultimately on the entire composite tradition of folk song. For these tunes to all appearances have a very real life independent of text-associations. They are capable of travelling about, of being varied, of undergoing influences and attractions from other music, and of being elaborated or simplified by various performers no matter what their textual associations may be. And despite what has been said about the "inseparability" of air and words in a folk singer's mind, it is perfectly evident that tunes have been carried in the minds of musical folk without reference to any words, and that many folk singers can and do separate words and air with ease.[17] Perhaps, then, the study of tunes in at least partial divorcement from their texts will be found to have some justification. In their mass, as well as individually, they seem to have had a development along lines which have, strictly speaking, no complete correlation with the occurrence and diffusion of individual folk song text-versions, insofar as can be observed.

In attempting, then, to identify specific melodies in as many of their variant forms as possible, I have proceeded along lines already laid out by previous investigators. But in trying to go as far as possible along one path, I trust that I have not failed to appreciate the value of other approaches to knowledge of our folk music tradition. This particular method of attack seemed capable of casting sufficient light on that subject to justify the effort expended upon it. It appears to be a worthy partner of tune-indexing efforts; a logical precursor and accompanier of melodic-variation studies, analyses of musical style, inquiries into the migrations and history of songs, and studies in the relations of melodies and words. It may also possibly illuminate that elusive quality called "national style" in folk music, and those thus far mysterious categories known as "types" of melody in our traditional song.

The results of my inquiries must be presented with full realization of the uncertainties of the subject and the liabilities of error. Hence, statements which may sound arbitrary are not really intended to be so; to make them straightforwardly is the only way of insuring that what is erroneous about my conclusions will in time be corrected by someone with deeper insight than mine. An attempt such as this at analyzing a folk music tradition has to be based on a

---

[17] Keith, *op. cit.*, p. xlii, criticizes C. J. Sharp's statement that the singer is "more or less unconscious of his melody" and cites instances of singers' using tunes as aids to recalling words, and singing more than one tune to a single song. Sharp, however, speaks of finding singers in the American Appalachian area who could "mentally separate the tune from the text. . . ." See C. J. Sharp, *English Folk Songs from the Southern Appalachians*, ed. Maud Karpeles (London: Oxford University Press, 1932), I, xxvii. My own observation of folk singers' practices is expressed exactly in the words to which this note appends.

working theory. Mine is that, by and large, our folk songs are (and perhaps always have been) sung to a limited number of tunes whose variant forms— apparently originating in oral transmission and re-creation—may be found all over the area where these folk songs are sung, and in some parts of the world where they are not.

Having done with this *apologia*, let us pass on to some considerations of the character of our folk song melodies as a whole. These considerations embrace such matters as (1) the nature of our information about the individual melodic items, and the evidence we have to work with in making conclusions about their affinities; (2) the nature of the melodic alterations that always confront a student of folk music, and are, of course, abundant in our own melodies; and (3) the general aspect of the tune-repertories known in the British Isles and in this country.

To begin with, it is apparent that an examination of folk tunes must be primarily descriptive. We cannot speak with exactness about stages in the development of any tune, for our records are still too incomplete and too recent; and back of every folk-melodic item lies a history of transmission and cultivation that remains quite unknown. Besides, we are all aware of the fact that the time when any folk-tune variant is recorded has no reference to the real age of the variant. So far as I have been able to discover at present, none of the important (i.e. widespread, much-used) tunes of our folk singers' repertories can be traced back beyond the early sixteenth century; most of them seem untraceable beyond the eighteenth. Again, we must always realize that our record of collectanea is rather uneven. Some regions have had careful collecting done in them, whereas others have been comparatively neglected. I shall not pause here to discuss the accuracy with which folk music records have been made in the past.[18]

About the history of individual melodic items we generally know nothing that is really helpful. When, in present-day collecting, we can trace a tune-variant at all, it is usually for only a generation or two back, and in some family line or restricted locality. The development of that variant, its time and place and cause of branching-off from some widely known air of which it may be a form, its routes of transmission and diffusion, its alterations from singer to singer and generation to generation—these are data with which the singers cannot supply us. We can often see what look like links between widely divergent forms of the same tune; what may *seem* to be stages of development between those forms, and illustrations of the steps by which one version gradually became transformed into another. The links are certainly there; but when we see them, we have to remember that they are actually not *stages* in the formal development of the tunes, so far as we really know. They cannot be regarded as such, because we

[18] Sharp (*English Folk-Songs: Some Conclusions*, pp. 112-114) regards the early nota-tions of folk tunes as worthless. They were doubtless inaccurate as regards correct notation of modal features; but that defect is not necessarily a hindrance to melodic identification, since, as Barry justly observes, "Nothing in folk music is more evanescent than modality ..." (*Southern Folklore Quarterly* [Southeastern Folklore Society: Gainesville, Fla.], I, No. 2, 1937, p. 39).

have no idea of the time element involved in their creation, nor have we any starting point from which to calculate the order in which they might have appeared. Each tune-item is presumably an end product of variation, with its own partially independent line of evolution behind it. We have no record, consequently no idea, of either the course or the rate of development for these items; hence, we cannot tell by what exact steps they evolved into the forms we know. One version or group of variants may be older than another; but we have yet no way of telling which is which. One form of a tune may have evolved and become widespread before another appeared; but at the present day we cannot safely distinguish between them in this respect. There is every opportunity for older tunes to be remodeled in accordance with the requirements of a later musical influence, and for newer tunes to be re-created along lines (or after fashions) of melodizing that go rather far back. So far as we are concerned, then, these folk melodies are *parallel*, not successive, as they occur and are noted down from tradition. And the fact that batches of them have been collected at various times, in different regions, and without specialized inquiry, hence, doubtless, without proportional representation, does not help to clear up our ignorance about the stages of their growth and change.

We are thus for the most part thrown back on the tune-records alone, and our evidence about their kinship must be almost purely internal. The witnesses to their relationship must therefore consist of those resemblances in structural and melodic features which have survived a period of continuous re-creation by countless anonymous singers of an unknown number of generations. There can be no doubt about the fact of oral re-creation; neither can there be a doubt that resemblances of the sort just indicated do exist. But there is really no logical place to start in our analysis of the versions of any air; we simply make a beginning with some perceptible variant-group and thence proceed to others, being careful not to assume that one version is derived in direct line of descent from another.

The sorts of resemblances we look for, to guide us in disentangling separate tunes one from another, are those of tonal range; of rhythm; of melodic progression, or melodic line; of order (or recurrence) of corresponding musical phrases; and of order (or recurrence) of stressed notes or tones. These various kinds of resemblances are not of equal importance or dependability. Preeminent among them are the correspondences in melodic line and in the place and succession of the stressed tones throughout the compass and course of individual melodies. Range, rhythm, and phrase-order are all variable, and less dependable than similar melodic lines and the presence of corresponding stressed tones. If these latter two are relatively constant per phrase, we can be comparatively well assured that we are dealing with a group of cognate or closely related melodic items. But though these features may be enumerated and roughly evaluated, they cannot be looked for one by one, or taken into account separately in the endeavor to identify tune-versions. They must all be considered together. And before such phenomena can be used most beneficially, the investigator must, by immersing himself in the tunes, have impressed on his mind the identifying features of various members of perhaps many different tune-families. Thus, the business of recognizing tune-versions is bound to be gradual and cumulative. The obvious members of a version-group will be perceived at once and easily. Later, when the salient and relatively persistent features of the basic tune are firmly fixed in mind, the identity of the less apparent forms will dawn on the student's comprehension. Folk-tune investigations are full of these sudden discoveries of hitherto unsuspected affinities. Ordinarily, the more often a student re-reads a good-sized collection of folk airs in our tradition, the more members of cognate version-groups he will discover. I have no doubt, therefore, that many versions of familiar, widespread melodies have passed under my eye undetected—especially when I have been able to examine a collection of tunes only once.[19]

The identifier of tunes is really up against a somewhat harder task than the identifier of folk song text-variants. The former does not have recurrent corresponding stanzas, or runs of stanzas, a correspondence or identity of situation and thought, and a perceptible story to guide him, as the textual critic has. Instead, he is confronted by a multitude of fluid and variable melodies, usually much shorter than the song texts to which they are set, and presumably not bound to follow any special lines in the course of their inevitable variation. Among these brief and ever-changing little artistic creations, he tries to confirm what seem to him to be relations of a genetic sort. In order to accomplish this, he has to take into account whatever he can find out about the ways in which the tunes vary: this in order to ascertain, if possible, whether the resemblances which meet his eye are the products of chance or the actual manifestations of some fundamental individual design that endures throughout repeated alterations.

One of the inevitable results of oral cultivation in any folk tradition, whether of texts or music, is the development of a number of congenial idiomatic expressions which are at once functional and artistic in their purpose and use. These are the verbal and melodic formulae—long known in folk poetry by such names as "the ballad tags" or "the ballad commonplaces," and clearly perceived also in the folk tunes, though not designated by any special names. I call them "congenial" because they suit the people who evolved them, and harmonize with other similar manifestations in the folk songs. They are "idiomatic" because their incessant use and continual recurrence confirm them as the regular, accepted idiom—musical or textual—of the folk-song art. They are "artistic" because to their users they are evocative and expressive, and constitute the proper and formally (or conventionally) fitting special means of utterance in verse or melody. They are "functional" in that they are employed in verse to outline situations, designate actions, indicate feelings, provide transitions, and fill structural or formal gaps. In music the formulae serve similar purposes. They are used to start a melody; to end it; to progress from one point to another, according to conventional practices associated with the various scales (which

---

[19] For other short discussions of these manifestations of tunes in oral tradition see my brief papers "Aspects of Melodic Kinship and Variation in British-American Folk-Tunes," *Papers Read at the Internationl Congress of Musicology*, 1939 (New York: Music Educators' National Conference, for the American Musicological Socety, cop. 1944), pp. 122-129; and "Ballad Tunes and the Hustvedt Indexing Method," *JAF* 55 (1942), 248-254.

practices also dictate largely the ways in which ascent to, or descent from, a given point in the melody is to be managed); and to provide, as it were, a carrying-on matter between two especially expressive or artistically valuable points in a melody. In short, if, as Professor Entwistle says, "ballad language is formula,"[20] then we may also say "ballad music is formula"—and with the same reservations that we should expect to be applied to the verse. For neither folk songs nor tunes are simply chance collections of formulae; and like the ballads, the several separate folk melodies are distinguished by strongly imprinted features. They are, in fact, quite individual musical creations, with varying content and message, just as folk ballads are individual poems telling different stories. But in the case of poems and airs alike, the messages are conveyed to a great extent by the help of formulae. And formulae can best be recognized as those features which tend to recur, as occasion arises for their use, in any piece of traditional verse or music, despite incalculable variations.

The fact is worth emphasizing that most of our folk tunes cannot be regarded primarily as bundles of formulae combined momentarily or on occasion in a semi-extemporaneous way. The presence of numerous cognate tune-versions in our tradition closes the door on that possibility. But neither must we allow ourselves to assume that formulae have a sort of fixed order of recurrence in single tunes, so that, for instance, if an air commenced with formula A, then formulae B, C, and D would inevitably follow in that order, and the tune would be promptly identifiable by its opening notes. This assumption is not borne out by the features of tune-versions. Such an assumption would also necessarily include the idea that the melodic formulae are clearly definable and isolable—which, in fact, they are not. In folk tunes, as in other works of art, the parts are subordinate to the whole, and the formulae are in all cases inseparable components of the entire melody. They are welded together; they merge with one another to build up the coherent and organized musical composition (however brief and simple); and though they may be seen to recur, it is a mistake to suppose that they can have boundaries set to them. Even when they evidently interchange in different tune-versions, they are so naturally woven in that the exact limits of the interchange cannot be definitely set. No one can take a musical formula in folk song and set it apart as one can a formulaic line of folk verse such as "An angry man was he," or "An ill deid mat he die," and say "Here, for all time and for all purposes, is the formula." If anyone disbelieves this, let him take any ordinary folk melody and try to draw a circle around every formulaic element he sees—*setting thereby its limits*, in the tune or out of it. The logical end result of an effort of this sort will be that the formula definer will have at last a series of isolated single notes which mean and reveal nothing. Folk melodies are living musical form and movement—not mechanical compilations of musical odds and ends.

[20] W. J. Entwistle, *European Balladry* (Oxford: Clarendon Press, 1939), p. 27. Motherwell speaks of textual formulae as "certain common-places which seem an integrant portion of the original mechanism of all our ancient ballads." See his *Minstrelsy Ancient and Modern*, New Edition (Paisley, 1873), p. v. In like manner, the musical formulae may be regarded as "integrant portions of the mechanism" of our tunes—but whether of these tunes' *original* mechanism or not is impossible to tell.

The reason why so much must be made of formulae is that formulaic resemblances among folk tunes have played an important part in previous attempts to identify or classify—or index—the tunes. In being turned to these uses, I think, such resemblances have been given an importance beyond their due. Sooner or later we must face the fact that our folk-musical tradition is pervaded not only by unmistakably formulaic details in the tunes, but also by versions of quite individualized melodies. The outlines of these melodies are strongly ingrained and persistent. Formulaic variation does not easily, or ordinarily, derange them. On the other hand, the interchange and alteration of formulae can easily derange the outlook of a student who gives them paramount importance in his examination of the folk music, and who fails to look beyond them, so to speak, and take into his view the folk-music items in their entirety. In doing so, he at once deprives himself of any fixed point from which he may contemplate our folk music in its broader aspects.[21]

I realize that the remarks in the foregoing paragraph can be made only under the assumption that the more persistent tunes discernible in our tradition are the logical starting place for an examination of the nature and content of our folk-tune stock, and for a study of the processes of its oral re-creation. As it happens, however, under present circumstances, this assumption—whether immediately justifiable or not—is the inevitable, and in fact the only possible one. It gives us our sole attainable point of reference in dealing with the really significant elements in this music as a part of the larger tradition that includes the folk poems and their melodies together. At the present time, our folk music, because of its complicated and unravelled tangles, has to be used with the greatest caution in attempting to extend knowledge about the traditional history of our folk songs. All work with any folk song version and its tune is at present inhibited by our lack of a broad view which takes in, on the one hand, the occurrences and other uses of the tune, and on the other the associations of other versions of the text with different tunes. Of course it is possible—such is the fundamental ambiguity of folk-music records—that even after we have learned much about the manifestations of the tunes in version-groups over a wide area, we might find the music of only limited usefulness in solving folk song problems. However, we continue to hope otherwise.

A mention of the involvement of melodic formulae in efforts to classify folk tunes brings to mind at once the word "type," one of the most ambiguous, loosely used, and generally troublesome terms in the English language, as applied to traditional melodies. During the years when the priceless volumes of the *English Folk Song Society Journal* were appearing, the musical notes furnished

---

[21] In this way alone can I account for the strange observations on page 58 of J. W. Gendren's otherwise valuable *Study of Ballad Rhythm with Special Reference to Ballad Music* (Princeton: Princeton University Press, 1936). The remarks in question are: "Tunes, we may summarize, do not generally survive long distances. We find locally related groups, but no truly *national* tunes. Very few melodies are recorded in this country which have also been recorded in England or Scotland." It is safe to say that the truth is better expressed by statements precisely the opposite of these; except, of course, that we do, also, find locally related groups.

by the editors were necessarily inspired by data which were growing too fast for leisurely study. There was no time for elaborate folk-music investigations, nor would they have been very beneficial in that stage of the work of recovering the material. As a natural result, in their efforts to draw attention to tune-records which seemed worthy of comparison, the editors overused and misused the word "type." It was a term easily employed—though not so easily defined.[22] Later students have not been overcareful, either, to define this vague word so that only one meaning could be taken from its use. Hence, no one can be sure now whether the word "type," when used, refers to the function of a version; to rhythmic pattern; design (order, arrangement) of phrases or themes; melodic range or contour; cadential or other formulaic resemblances; modality; "national" stylistic features; or to any combination of any of these traits in a tune, or in tune-groups.

Thus, the confusion is complete; for it is not certain that any two folk-music investigators employing the word "type" have ever had in mind approximately the same meaning. The use of this term in relation to folk tunes has been quite on a par with its use in reference to folk texts: e.g., in the expression "ballads of the Child type"—a phrase of which the meaning is unknown.[23] Because of these circumstances, I have tried to avoid altogether the use of "type" in my remarks and—in keeping with my fundamental aim of distinguishing versions of individual melodies—have preferred to use the word "tune," or even better, the term "tune family," as being more expressive, less ambiguous, and altogether more accurate. A definition of the term "tune family," however, will have to wait until we have considered further aspects of our musical tradition in these remarks.

The word "style" is another dangerous one for investigators of British-American folk music to use in connection with groups of similar airs, since it can be so employed that it can hardly be distinguished in meaning from any of the possible meanings of "type." The late eminent scholar Béla Bartók some time ago made this pronouncement about styles in Hungarian folk music: "At the time when a certain style is in full bloom, a great number of tunes identical in build crop up; each one shows one or several stereotyped features of a certain kind. . . . An abundance of very similar tunes supplies the

---

[22] See the editorial notes in *JFSS, passim.* I may perhaps be excused from giving specific examples from that journal for the reason that the editors' references are to items of collectanea under local titles, and would be incomprehensible without long and detailed explanation. However, a thoroughly representative example of the sort of editorial note under discussion may be drawn from the pages of the *Journal of the Welsh Folk Song Society*, in which the same vagueness may be found. In that journal, Vol. I, Pt. ii (1910), pp. 85, 86 are notes about tune No. 13, to "White Rose of Summer." Miss Broadwood, on page 85, says "This and No. 15 are very Danish in type." On page 86, however, Frank Kidson asserts that the same tune "strongly suggests the Gaelic type of melody"—as if there were actually known to be only one type so called. The tune in question (along with Nos. 14 and 15 following it) is in reality a rhythmically recast version of the (?Irish) air of "The Boyne Water," which is certainly one of the best-known tunes in Anglo-American tradition.

[23] Professor Thelma James demonstrates the truth of this latter statement in her article "The English and Scottish Ballads of Francis James Child," *JAF* 46 (1933), 51-68. See especially pp. 56-59.

decisive proof that we are confronting a fully mature style. . . ." As a footnote to this, Bartók adds: "When we have to deal with a very great mass of tunes similar in character, it is sometimes difficult to determine whether one is a variant of another or should be considered independent. One is led to one of two extremes: either to consider all these tunes as forming one group of variants, or to treat them as independent tunes that differ from one another only in a few of their curves." And later in the same work: "During the heyday of a style of peasant music a great number of tunes closely resembling one another (and indeed almost impossible to differentiate) arise. . . . That every one of these, differing from the remainder only in a few melodic details, should ever have been . . . inseparable from one . . . text, is . . . impossible."[24]

These words of Bartók express with unsurpassed accuracy one of the immediate major difficulties besetting a folk-music student. The problem Bartók sees and states is also our problem. It is true that in discussing music, one's language is always bound to be rather vague: musical examples alone are adequate to reveal and illustrate the phenomena under discussion. However, it is surely not out of place to point out that this language about "styles" of music could also be understood to refer to "types" of melodies; and in English our confusion is great enough without the addition of any such new troubling element. Nevertheless, the alternatives Bartók presents call for a fundamental decision one way or the other by every student of every folk music, according to the facts observed in the particular musical tradition under study. The features which Bartók enumerates as characterizing a mature and fully developed style we also observed in British-American folk tunes. And they at once pose for us the question: Do we have here a large number of tunes composed independently along very similar lines, or a large number of versions, variants, and forms otherwise derivative of some original fundamental melodies?

It is obvious, of course, that if the phenomena of our own folk music be interpreted as the independent outgrowth of the influence of various musical styles, each producing its crop of closely similar, yet genetically unrelated melodies in multiple parallel production, we must bid farewell to the effort to identify and trace any individual tunes by means of their variant forms. Instead we must concentrate on an effort to find out how the styles (? types) arose. However, when we apply this attitude, suggested by the language of Bartók, to our own folk-tune records, we encounter what appear to me to be serious difficulties—which I wish to review at once.

First, if we subscribe to this view, we must then assume that the testimony of practically every eminent folk-tune collector in the British Isles is all wrong in one respect: that they treated their material as consisting in large part of versions of individual melodies, of which they were accustomed to hear various sets in tradition. This blanket indictment applies not only to those who

---

[24] Béla Bartók, *Hungarian Folk Music*, transl. M. D. Calvocoressi (London: Oxford University Press, 1931), pp. 8, 36. Compare Bartók's statements with those of Fr. Henebry, quoted in note 11.

had grown up among folk-music traditions and inherited them naturally (e.g. Patrick McDonald, Simon Fraser, W. P. Joyce), but likewise to those other collectors, from George Petrie down to Miss Anne Gilchrist, whose observations are no less valuable because they approached the musical tradition from the outside, as conscious investigators. From the utterances of those named (and others) we may infer that they have never dreamed of such a thing as a succession of musical styles impressing themselves upon the peasantry and producing each in its turn a crop of inseparably similar melodies. Rather, they saw in their traditions a number of separate tunes—sharing alike the traits of a common musical idiom which they were apt to call the national style of their folk music, and showing structural similarities which made their students endeavor to classify them roughly into various "types."

Second, we are decidedly conscious of the presence in our traditional music of "stereotyped features"—they are perhaps most prominent in opening and cadential passages. However, these features are common not only among the members of certain closely resembling tune-groups, but in practically all the folk melodies. I take such features to be *formulae*—as they certainly interchange, and generally appear to have no decisive effect on the prominent melodic outlines of members of the closely resembling tune-groups.

Third, those clusters of airs in our tradition whose resemblances suggest relationship have in common (as I have already pointed out) a close correspondence of melodic outline or contour; of melodic intervals; and of recurrent accented tones. These correspondences persist across differences of rhythmic pattern and of mode. Thus, if these tunes exemplify the growth and spread of a "style" of music, then each of the folk-musical styles we know must have arisen and developed in complete independence of modal and rhythmic characteristics; and we must infer that such characteristics cannot be taken into account as features of any style of music found in British cultivation. This would be difficult to explain.

Fourth, it is exceedingly hard to see how the features enumerated in the preceding paragraph as possessed in common by closely similar tune-groups can be parts of any style, unless that style is underlain by—and has its foundation in—one archetypal, individual *tune*, of which all the members of the groups would then be variants or derivatives. If a style having these melodic characteristics were *not* derived ultimately from a single tune, then, in order to account for such persistent features, we should have to believe in simultaneous identical inspiration among the folk on a wide scale (in fact, internationally), but applying only to *tone-interval steps* in the construction of melodies, and having no reference to the part that rhythmic and modal patterns might play locally in the formation of any melodic style. Here we should have a dark mystery indeed.

Fifth, whereas similarities in tone interval (*i.e.*, melodic) outline enable us to see groups of airs that resemble each other strongly, *differences* of the same sort likewise make perceptible other and different groups of airs. Each of these various groups shows strong interresemblance among its component melodies. All these groups share certain stereotyped and idiomatic features in common, but are otherwise quite diverse. If, then, these separate groups of tunes stand for "styles," we have not only two or three of them to deal with: at the very lowest count, and making all the allowances of which I am capable at the moment for traditional divergence, I reckon that no fewer than thirty-five of these "styles" must at various times have had their heyday in British folk music.

If that be the case, the observed distribution of the tune-items themselves is puzzling. One would naturally expect, I believe, that a style of music would normally have a single starting place, or region of beginning development, and thence would spread abroad. Accordingly, one would also expect to see certain styles especially prominent in certain regions, and to find more scattered examples of their products penetrating into the music of other regions. Also, one might expect to find one or more styles predominant and universal, while others, giving evidence of greater antiquity, would appear to be dying out—would be surviving, for example, in peripheral areas or especially remote or backward parts of the country, preserved in the minds of relatively few people, and fast being forgotten. Phenomena of this sort were certainly detected by Bartók in the regions where Hungarian folk music was cultivated.

But this is emphatically not the state of affairs we note in connection with our well-known clusters of similar tunes in British-American folk-music cultivation. Here, on the contrary, we find members of the well-known different clusters of interresembling tunes mingled together everywhere. Furthermore, in most regions, we find these clusters well represented, by the currency of rather diversified forms of their members. If they stand for styles which arose in any successive way among the British peoples, we must conclude that the styles spread without ousting one another, or without popularity at one another's expense; that they were all accommodated side by side in the folk-tune repertories of the singing people. In short, if these groups of melodies are "styles," we have no evidence whatever of the order in which they spread, or the routes they took in their diffusion. There is nothing associated with these groups of airs *as* closely resembling groups, which would in any way connect them each with the spread of a separate popular style of folk music.

Another observation regarding style-characteristics may be made in connection with the foregoing paragraph. In British-American folk music, our tunes are nearly all divided into parts of exactly or approximately equal length, and these parts generally differ, or contrast in some way one with another. Most commonly in our tunes, these parts are only two in number, and could be labelled A and B (variant renderings and internal subdivisions of both in any tune-item are of course to be expected). Without trying to exhaust the possibilities, we may say that the most common tune-patterns among our folk songs, with reference to the ways in which these parts alternate, are the following: AABA, AABB, ABAB, ABBA. Perhaps to be regarded as traditional derivatives of these, among the closely resembling tune-groups, are the phrase-

orders AAAB, and the apparent reversals, BBAA and BBBA, *inter alia.* Now
the point is that, among the aforesaid clusters of closely resembling melodies—
which have in common their strong accented-tone and melodic-interval similarities per phrase or per section—we can observe the variant orders of parts
just outlined. Their alternations do nothing to lessen the interresemblances
between the tunes; they merely change now and then the succession of the
phrases. So, for instance, among these groups there will be some examples in
which part A corresponds to the first and second tune-lines (or phrases), and
others in which part A will be the first and fourth of these lines. Thus, one
member of such a group will have the order AABA; another, ABBA. This
means that if we are inclined to take the pattern of phrase-recurrence in a
tune-item as showing a trait of any specific musical *style,* we cannot apply
that particular stylistic criterion to version-groups among our traditional melodies either. The mutual interresemblances of tune-groups override the order in
which tune-phrases may occur. Thus, another feature, in addition to rhythm
and modality, would have to be discounted in our efforts to connect styles of
music with each of these tune-groups; and, in fact, our definitions would have
to be very narrowly circumscribed if we wished to identify these melodic
clusters each with a particular musical style.

The sixth, and final, objection to the identification of closely resembling
tune-groups with special styles is this: There remains to be answered the
question of how to regard tunes occurring *outside* British tradition (especially
in the folk music of the Scandinavian peoples) which are still seemingly or
manifestly members of these British groups. These scattered airs themselves
are apparently merged into closely related local groups of tunes. How shall we
account for their presence or their features? Are they cases of accidental
convergence, in whole or in part? Are they remnants of older styles once
widespread, but now scantily represented (perhaps largely displaced) in Scandinavia, yet still flourishing in the British Isles? Or are they "wandering
melodies"—much more genuinely so than Tappert's[25]—which have migrated

---

[25] The title of Wilhelm Tappert's curious book *Wandernde Melodien* (2nd ed.; Leipzig,
1890) is a misnomer. The work should rather be called "Wandernde Motive" or
"Wandernde melodische Bruchstücke," for nearly all its entries are mere fragments; there
are few complete melodies or organized tunes in it. Tappert's original contention, in
attempting to show the "all-mählige Entwicklung" of the folk tunes (a sort of evolutionary theory attaching to the development of popular melody), was correct: that the
tunes were not spontaneous creations of a people, starting from nothing, independent of
outside influence, and forming under the stimulus of moving circumstances or the fire of
genius—but were groupings and re-groupings of melodic formulae common to a widespread musical culture over perhaps a long period of time. Where his theory falls down,
however, is in his contention that these formulae, since they are found in the works of
the "masters" as well as in folk airs, were all taken directly by the folk from the works
of these masters. His lists of variant strains (which are simply strains or motifs, not
"melodies") are sometimes partly from anonymous art-compositions. And it must be
pointed out that the tracing of such a motif through many pieces of music over perhaps
several centuries of time is not discovering the origin of any piece of music containing
that motif; nor is it indicating the source of that motif itself—in the works of the
"masters" or anywhere else. These strains are, in fact, just what Tappert himself calls one
of them: "herrenloses Gut" (p. 62). And in his earnest contentions that "the folk cannot

from their homeland? If so, which way have they migrated, and where is the homeland of the styles they represent? Did an air migrate from Scandinavia to Britain, there to become the nucleus of a new folk style? If we decide thus, we put ourselves in the position of assenting to the fourth point raised above: that such styles are derivatives of a single melody. Or, perhaps, has the style spread from Britain to Scandinavia, but never become universally popular there? In that case, what should we call these Scandinavian melodies— examples of a style, or members of groups of versions, cognate, in their northern homes, with widespread British airs? In short, the "style" approach to these groups of basically similar airs in our tradition raises more un- answerable questions than does the approach which assumes that these airs are descendants of single melodies which have doubtless had their rise in certain musical styles, but which do not necessarily owe the preservation of their marked and salient special traits to the integrity or the preservation of such styles. I shall therefore continue to talk about tunes, tune-versions, and tune- families, in these remarks, and shall treat the material discussed as consisting of groups of melodies which are derived ultimately from single originals. There is apparently no time on record when the British folk-music traditions have not consisted essentially of individual tunes living in many variant forms.

My own opinion regarding national and regional musical styles is that there certainly are such things in the British tradition; and that sometimes these styles are quite noticeable. Such common national and local idiomatic features as deserve the name of "musical style" affect, but do not obscure the identity of, the numerous members of the tune-version groups that are common to the folk music of different British nationalities. Though these styles remain largely unanalyzed, it is plain that the individual melodies, wherever they are found, naturally bear the imprint of the prevalent local musical idiom. However, no local musical idiom can be said certainly to have affected the currency of the individual melodies. The tunes do not regulate the regional styles in the Brit- ish Islands; instead, they are adapted to the styles, for the greater part. Nor are the tune-versions, to all appearances, instantaneously translated from one stylistic idiom into another as soon as they are transported from one nation or region into another. On the contrary, in their free movement from person to person and locality to locality, they seem occasionally to have carried what may sometimes be regarded as the stylistic characteristics of one region into another area—thus confusing still more the already vague enough picture of developed regional musical idiomatic features. In short, national tune-repertory is not found to coincide with what can be recognized as national melodic

compose—it merely selects," Tappert goes to some pains to show that members of the folk can *recompose* ("Die Umbildung hat keine Ende," etc., p. 6); that they can use, choose, vary, annex, accommodate, the musical material (p. 38). The distinction between melodic selection and rearrangement on the part of the folk singer and melodic selection and rearrangement on the part of the artistic (or formally trained) composer seems to be clear to him; but it is not so to me. I prefer to believe with Joseph Bedier that "recréer et créer sont termes exactement synonymes" (*Les Légendes Épiques* [3rd ed.; Paris, Champion, 1929], III, 447).

style in British tradition; hence we infer that the styles in themselves neither conserve the identity nor restrict the diffusion of a folk tune in this area.

I guess that we shall ultimately ascertain the regional musical styles of British folk song cultivation to be based upon inherited mannerisms of melodizing—stocks of little *motifs* or successions of tones of the same character as the tetrachord a—g-sharp—f—e, which is so much heard in oriental music—mannerisms that have been developed or adopted and become habitual among the British singers. Doubtless these have been exchanged among groups of people; but some would probably tend to become especially favored by one group and relatively little used by another. Favorite scales and formulae used habitually among Irish singers, for example, would be those singers' ordinary way of making music; and what would be more natural than that these formulae and these modal characters should slip into versions of airs learned from some other people and received into traditional currency among the Irish? As examples of such formulae, let me cite a few progressions commonly found in Irish folk music, and apparently much esteemed. With a tonic of G, in order to progress to the D a fifth above, Irish tunes quite often use the succession G-A-C-D; and so also in reverse to descend. When rising from A or B (with the same tonic assumed) to G, numerous Irish melodic versions go thus: B-D-E-F sharp-G; whereas in order to descend in the same compass, it is quite common practice to slide down by means of G-F (sharp, natural or neutral)-D-C, and so to B or A. These little conventional mannerisms, while not entirely confined to Irish tunes in British music, are still exceedingly popular among Irish singers. It is such details as these which seem to me to furnish the best guide to detection of folk-singing styles in this tradition; not the currency of organized tunes which may be internationally known, and may sound English in England, Irish in Ireland, and Hebridean Scottish when they have penetrated into the northern Highlands and Isles.[26]

There is also a seeming preference for, and especially common use of, one or another diatonic scale among these British nationalities. The English singers, for instance, would appear to be particularly fond of what we call the Dorian mode (D to D), since they have used it so incessantly and artistically. On the other hand, we observe what seems to be a similar decided fondness among Irish singers for the so-called Mixolydian mode (G to G, with neutral F); while Hebrid Gaels and American Appalachian mountaineers are often well satisfied with scales of five or six tones, presenting gaps at one place or another.[27] Our internationally known tune-versions, accordingly, are found in forms modified by all these differing musical preferences: they may be detected in Dorian, Aeolian, Ionian (or Major), Mixolydian guise; pentatonic, hexatonic and heptatonic scales alternate in their variant manifestations; and all without des-

---

[26] Some tentative listings of formulae in an effort to indicate features of national melodic style may be seen in C. J. Sharp's *English Folk-Song: Some Conclusions*, pp. 83-86. Compare also Chappell, *Popular Music of the Olden Time*, II, 792-794, and Chappell, *National English Airs* (1840), II, 185, 186.

[27] See the modal table provided by Miss Gilchrist to classify her Highland Gaelic tunes, *JFSS*, 4 (1910), facing page 152; and the modification of it used by C. J. Sharp in his *English Folk Songs from the Southern Appalachians*, I, xxxii.

troying the fundamental successions that make the basic air discernible.

I realize that the foregoing remarks about style comprise a mere glance at matters of much complexity, and are in part expressions of personal opinion. However, it seems that they are borne out by what may readily be seen among versions of widely known folk tunes in British repertories. I take it to be inevitable that folk artists will alter tunes learned and transmitted by ear in the direction of the idiosyncrasies of music-making most habitual and familiar to their ears and congenial to their acquired artistic tastes. And there seems to be good testimony to this in the diversified forms assumed among different peoples of the British Isles by the tunes current internationally.

But in order to be varied in tradition, a tune, needless to say, does not have to be borrowed by one people from another. Slight variations—minute changes, or exchanges, or formulae—go on, of course, all the time. It might be that if we really could isolate the formulaic passages, we should find that each of them, likewise, was one of a little cluster of variants. We actually do not know what proportion of this variation is unconscious or involuntary, and how much is conscious or intentional. In some folk singers we seem to see mere repeaters, unaware of their few slight variations, and to some degree mechanical; in others we apparently are face to face with artists playing with their material, and expending upon it all the resources of their inherited traditional knowledge and aptitude. However, it seems as though certain rather important recurring types of melodic variation can be perceived; of which all may entail still further variation in the melodic formulae found in tune-versions. Thus, these types of variation may seemingly also be in themselves causes of variation, at times, and of some very important after effects. I take the types in question to be at least eight in number, as follows:

First: An unusually long melodic jump up or down. This generally necessitates some re-arrangement of the melodic line immediately following, and is likely to be compensated by another jump, or a progression, in the opposite direction. But sometimes, also, the skip can be perfectly accommodated without significant additional alterations of the melodic line.

Second: A strong alteration in the tempo or pace of a tune. This is ordinarily caused by the adaptation of the tune to a quite different text, or to a different function. There is apparently no inevitable correlation, however, between the function of a tune-version and its relative degree of ornateness or simplicity. A fast dance-version may be ornate; a quick song-or-game-version may be simple. Slow versions may be furnished with many decorative graces or passing-tones, but these do not necessarily obscure the basic formulae. Rhythmic changes may accompany alterations in pace (e.g. between 3/4, 3/2, 6/4, 4/4, 6/8, etc.), being also associated to some extent with function, and probably also bringing along melodic-line variation. To all appearances, these alterations in pace may be brought about either deliberately or involuntarily.

Third: A marked alteration in rhythm, and a contraction or prolongation of tune-line or phrase (see the preceding point, which overlaps this). Tune-lines may be altered to suit the varying number of syllables or main accents in lines of verse; and may thus present the appearance of having been either "drawn out" or "telescoped."

Fourth: The translation of a tune-version from one mode into another. That this has happened often among our traditional airs there is no doubt whatever. And, as Cecil Sharp pointed out long ago, the change is in the nature of a "free translation":[28] i.e., the formulae most suitable to (or habitually associated with) the mode into which the version is being altered will tend to appear in the recast version, which thus will not be entirely or purely an interval-for-interval transposition. The use of neutral or quarter-tones in our folk scales would seem to facilitate this modal exchange. Although the demonstrated presence of these neutral tones in our folk music[29] may somewhat confuse the picture for the student of modality, it does nothing to obscure the main outlines of the various individual tunes.

Fifth: The influence of other melodies contemporarily current in tradition. Very probably, all melodies in oral tradition side by side exert some influence on each other; but such influence (?contamination) is hard to talk about, since it so often cannot be definitely traced or proved. However, there are cases—which one might call examples of melodic "attraction"—where it seems perfectly clear that a strain of one well-known, strongly individual tune has had a pronounced effect on a strain of another. To this, also, we may perhaps attribute some of the instances in which the first half of a melodic item will belong unmistakably to versions of one large tune-family, while the second half pertains just as clearly to another. Such cases are confusingly frequent in our folk dance music; somewhat less often encountered among song-tune versions. There are also even more perplexing cases of seeming fusion in some tune-sets, where one may be puzzled about whether to account for the facts by means of "attraction" or to consider that the versions one sees are examples of older melodies out of which (by traditional divergence) have emerged two or more distinct tunes. Cases of this kind I shall presently discuss further.

Sixth: Repetitiveness—I call it this for lack of a better term. The presence of this feature can be convincingly attested only by the detailed comparison of a number of variants of a tune. Its special interest seems to me to lie in its apparent close analogy to the repetition of phrase, line, couplet, or stanza which is such a notable feature in traditional song texts. By means of what I call "repetitiveness," a formula characteristic of one place or point in a folk melody may be repeated in another place (sometimes the corresponding point in another phrase, sometimes immediately before or after the regular or expected occurrence of the formula), with the consequent displacing and discarding of the formula otherwise normally occurring in that second place. This repetition-with-replacement may alter only a few notes of an air; or it may affect whole phrases or lines. Perhaps it has been the cause of a good many of

---

[28] *English Folk-Song: Some Conclusions*, p. 26.

[29] For a discussion, see Annabel Morris Buchanan, "Modal and Melodic Structure in Anglo-American Folk Music. A Neutral Mode," in *Papers Read at the International Congress of Musicology*, 1939, pp. 84-111.

the alternating-formula examples we see among various versions. On the other hand, it is not to be confounded with such features of tune-structure as the repetition of a phrase with differing cadential formulae, or the occurrence of two differing phrases, one following the other, but both furnished with the same ending notes. The occurrence of variants in which a short passage common to other variants is omitted, with the "gap" filled in by repeated material, is sporadic on the whole; and it is this fact which leads me to surmise that this type of variation is caused by "repetitiveness." If such features were not merely occasional, we should have no way of guessing whether the repeated bits were original features in the variants, or later developments. As they occur, however, they have the air of being not ordinary, organic phrase-repetitions, but the intrusive repetition of material worked into the phrase from somewhere else in the tune.[29a]

Seventh: The transposition of tune-phrases or strains, already discussed above.

Eighth: Corrupt rendition, the result of faulty learning and bad performance of a tune. Corruption we can actually see only when it thoroughly upsets the balance and coherence of a tune. But it may also give occasion for redeeming re-creation. In a process like that, however, any tune may conceivably be varied so much that its original features may be lost, and another tune evolved. I suggest that some of our folk tunes may possibly have arisen from just such processes—which by their very postulated nature would of course, be impossible to trace.

Perhaps under the heading of "corruption" might go the phenomenon which Barry called "wearing down."[30] The expression refers to a progressive loss of content by a melody in tradition, so that eventually some versions will appear shortened and lacking in variety—sometimes both monotonized and unbalanced; at other times, simply abbreviated, with no loss of organization. The theory of this occurrence is easy to set down on paper; but the actual process itself is often hard to demonstrate, because we cannot by any means always tell when a melody has been "worn down" and when it has been "built up." Presumably, in oral transmission, a tune can be either augmented or curtailed; but the sort of evidence we have for both procedures is far from satisfactory, and editors have varied greatly in their attitudes toward melodies which have been recorded sometimes in a longer, sometimes in a shorter form. Dean Christie, for example, was so certain that every tune should properly consist of two "strains," and was originally so composed, that he set himself to provide second strains for all the tunes he conceived lacking them in his

---

[29a]What Barry calls the "law of anticipatory iteration" seems to be an aspect of this type of variation (see *Bulletin of the Folk-Song Society of the Northeast*, No. 12 [1937], p. 3, col. 1). However, it seems that the repetition is not always anticipatory—it could sometimes even be called "reminiscent"; hence my attempt at coining a term to indicate the phenomenon.

[30] See, for discussion of the phenomenon, *British Ballads from Maine*, pp. 193, 194, where Barry examines a group of tunes sung to Child No. 81.

own and his father's collection.[31] Keith, on the other hand, was convinced
that the "one-strain" versions of his ballad tunes were the correct older or
original forms, and that second strains had been supplied by unknown revisers
after the tunes had circulated awhile in tradition.[32]

The actual condition of our orally cultivated tunes three or four hundred
years ago, naturally, is unknown—even assuming that most of the ones we
now encounter were in existence at that time, a speculation that may as well
be dismissed, because there is no evidence either for or against it. The original
form of any widespread folk tune of our acquaintance is also unknown. Tunes
of varying lengths are current in present-day singers' repertories, as also tunes
which at one time we hear in a longer form, at another time in a shorter. We
therefore are in no position to maintain offhand that any one (not to mention
the bulk) of our folk airs was or was not originally composed of two complementary strains of equal length.

These "strains," as normally written down in our folk music, would ordinarily amount to about eight bars each, covering the two lines of a rhyming
or assonating couplet (four bars to a line). Some exceptions are furnished by
tunes in 9/8 time; by tunes whose phrase-ends are curtailed, or which are
otherwise rhythmically disturbed; by tunes that accommodate lengthy refrains;
and by a group of melodies adapted to songs which make their lines only
three bars long, with their "strains" (halves) becoming consequently six bars
in length.[33] Aside from these, however, the two-strain or one-strain tune, with
eight bars to a strain, is normal, and holds for association with folk song texts
whether the texts are set down in stanza-form as two-line couplets, as four-
line couplets (with or without refrains), or as four lines with two couplets side
by side.[34] This means that under ordinary circumstances it is not always
possible to tell by the verse form of our folk poem texts whether their
accompanying melodies did (or should) consist of two of these "strains" or of
only one.

Sometimes we meet with a four-line, two-couplet stanza sung to only one
strain of music, which is repeated in order to cover both couplets. These cases
are often made perceptible by the practice of ending each stanza pointedly

[31] See W. Christie, *Traditional Ballad Airs* (Edinburgh, 1876-1881), I, 8, 9. Christie's
representation is that he has rejoined strains which properly belong together, yet which
were found apart in the memories of different traditional singers. It is only just to
remark, however, that some of his second strains are set to airs which never appear
elsewhere with them or any other additional matter; and that these added strains appear
nowhere else outside the Christie edition.

[32] See Grieg-Keith, *Last Leaves of Traditional Ballads and Ballad Airs*, p. xliii

[33] This is a feature especially characteristic of Irish folk music; where the strains of the
same air may sometimes be found written out in six bars of 3/4 time, or in only two
bars of 9/8 time. Irish airs—and Irish versions of internationally current melodies—also
show tune-lines of five bars' length; hence strains of ten bars each.

[34] My language here may be considered strange; but it is unavoidable when considering
the character of the musical settings to folk song words. Since (as implied in note 33) the
melodies are adaptable to songs in varied meters, and appear in forms so adapted, metrical considerations do not necessarily fix the form and rhythm of a folk tune perma-
nently. Hence, they do not apply to studies directed toward melodic identification.

with the same or a similar line, or with the same phrase[35] —a textual feature that sometimes lets us know when lines of a song-version have been lost in transmission, but which tells us nothing, necessarily, about the proper form of its tune. Sometimes, on the contrary, to a song customarily written down in stanzas of four lines and one couplet, we find a two-strain air joined; and the presence of an uneven number of these couplet-stanzas is then apt to cause the singer simply to ignore and drop one strain of his tune somewhere in the course of the song. The same may be said for songs in four-line, two-couplet stanzas: here, half a stanza may be missing somewhere, hence half the tune is also dropped for the nonce. The so-called "common ballad stanza" (four lines, one couplet) is very apt to be sung to a melody which covers it exactly, and is repeated with variations for every such stanza in a folk poem so written down. In other words, the common ballad stanza generally goes to a one-strain melody, of which it may be impossible to tell whether the recorded form was previously longer (two-strain) or not. Where, then, are our bases for assuming such a phenomenon as the "wearing down" of a folk melody? Or for saying, as I did above, that some tune-versions, worn down, will be monot-onized and unbalanced, and others simply abbreviated?

To answer these questions, we must explain some conditions not always easy to describe. I shall commence with the simplest and most explicit sort of record. Vaughan Williams testifies that when singers grow old, they often "sing only the second half of a tune." They commence a song set to a two-strain air; but after singing awhile, they abandon the first strain and continue the song to the second only.[36] I also have seen this occurrence, and so, doubtless, have other collectors. Often repeated, this sort of performance would tend to fix a worn-down, one-strain version of the tune on popular memory locally, and start such a version out on a line of traditional culti-vation.

Again: a tune design lending itself easily to such modification is one in which the two main phrases, A and B (see above) are organized as follows: AcBd, A'cBd—that is, with variant cadential closes, or variant half-phrases at the end of each separate phrase, and an additional variation of the A-phrase. The two strains, being rather close in resemblance, can become simplified into one, and that one repeated for all couplets of the verse; so that such tunes just as often appear as AcBd alone, or A'cBd alone—or also as AcBc and AdBd. The next observed occurrence that we shall consider will explain why we sometimes feel justified in saying that the longer form of a folk air does not present a lengthened or elaborated rendering of the shorter.

Suppose that we have two different folk songs, X and Y, both being often—perhaps usually—sung to versions of the same air; and suppose, in addi-

[35] See, for example, the late ballad "Walter Lesly" (Child No. 296), with its recurrent stanza-ending line about going "to Conland, this winter-time to lye." The practice was a favorite one with broadside ballad writers.

[36] *Journal of the English Folk Dance and Song Society*, 5, No. I (Dec., 1946), 22. The air which called forth this note was correctly characterized as being obviously only half a tune.

tion, that the air has the phrase-design ABB′ A (for tunes of such phrase-design often have a variation of the B-phrase on its repetition, amounting to a sort of climax). Versions of X and Y will be found scattered about over the English folk-singing world. Depending on how thorough the collecting has been in any region, we may expect to find some texts of X and Y recorded often in some regions, but scantily represented in others. As to musical records, we may expect to see only a fraction of the recorded texts accompanied by recorded tunes; but most of these tune-sets will be recognizable as versions of ABB′A. Among the texts for which our tune (with its ABB′A form) has been re-corded, some will show association with the full air; and this association is likely to be observed wherever the poems have been found. But right along with those forms of X and Y will be found other variants which are not set to our tune ABB′A in its entirety; on the contrary, they will be joined to melodies which, when compared with ABB′ A, will reveal themselves as con-sisting of such combinations as the following: AAAA, BBB′ A; AB; B′ A, etc. The tune-phrases will be unmistakably the same as those making up the air ABB′ A as it occurs with other versions of X and Y; but in some cases a phrase will be lost; in other cases, the arrangement will be altered so that the balancing occurrence of the phrases, and their peculiar alternation-pattern will be sacrificed; and in still others, what will be recognized as only the first or second half of the tune will occur—so that a whole stanza of X or Y will now be set not to ABB′A, but to AB *plus* AB or B′A *plus* B′A. It may happen, too, that versions of X and Y will get taken down differently by different recorders, so that some appear in stanzas of two couplets apiece, others in stanzas of only one couplet. In the latter case, the tune-versions AB or B′ A will constitute the whole recorded melody.

In circumstances such as these, and taking into account what has been observed of the strain-dropping tendencies of some folk singers, we may often be correct in inferring that sets of a tune which have lost some of their regular design-features and perhaps their melodic balance and variety, are *worn-down* sets of the air which may elsewhere be noted in a fuller and more highly organized condition. But we may not feel safe in assuming this wear-ing-down in every case we meet of the seeming occurrence of full-tunes beside half-tunes. All possible factors connected with the continuing association of versions of one tune with versions of a certain text, *plus* the use of that tune in various sets along with other texts, have to be weighed before we may unhesitatingly say that any tune-version is present in a worn-down form. There is no external evidence to tell us whether the very first, original, set of a melody had one or another of the several recurring melodic phrase-patterns now broadcast among our traditional tune-versions, or was originally longer or shorter than we find its sets to be at present.[37]

[37] Just how uncertain these matters can be, a number of variant forms of tunes might illustrate. For instance, the old melody called "Cupid's Garden" is printed by Chappell (*Popular Music of the Olden Time*, II, 728) with two strains. The phrase-design is AB/A′B′, which may further be resolved into abcd / ebcfx: the first strain shows tonic-dominant modulation at the end, and the second is furnished with an extension passage

It may have seemed a piece of gross oversimplification to assert, as I have above, that most of our melodies are made up of two separate phrases that could be labelled A and B; and to discuss our tunes as if they invariably consisted of A- and B-phrases in various alternation-patterns. What of those tunes (it may be asked) which manifestly consist of *four* differing phrases, and thus present themselves in schemes of ABCD? They are certainly noticeable in Anglo-American folk music wherever it is recovered, and they cannot be ignored.[38] Nor do I propose to ignore them; but before dealing with them it was necessary to make the preceding explanations about A-*plus*-B designs, because of the peculiar relations between airs with those designs and the airs with schemes of ABCD. Keeping in view what has been said about the tunes generally, we can make the following observations about these tunes with ABCD phrase-pattern:

I remarked above that internal subdivisions of any phrase in the make-up of a folk melody were to be expected. Now the fact stands out that in the repertories of our folk-singers, a number of the melodies apparently having the independent pattern ABCD are actually found to correspond with one or the other half of longer tunes in the melodic stock—and these longer tunes show phrase-patterns of ABBA, AABA, etc. In other words, the AB of one of these ABCD-tunes is really discernible as equalling the A of a longer air, and the CD is similarly found to correspond with the B of the longer air. This means that, either originally, or through re-creation and varying development, certain tune-phrases have traits that divide them clearly into two subsections which are found everywhere in the variant forms of these phrases. These subsections, also, may on occasion serve as entire phrases themselves. The situation, then, with regard to ABCD-pattern tunes, is often as follows:

Taking the ABBA pattern merely as an example, one of the longer-form airs will show:

1. A　　　　B　　　　B　　　　A

which is found, upon closer examination, to be approximately equivalent to

2. ab　　　　cd　　　　cd　　　　ab

(x). Chappell notes (*ibid.*, p. 727) how singers sometimes "cut" the f-phrase. This version of Chappell's is rare in recorded sets of the tune. A much more widespread version, without either modulation or extension may be diagrammed thus: AA´ / BA, or abac / ebac. It is known in England, Lowland Scotland, Ireland, North America, and even (in one isolated variant) in Flanders—where it was no doubt imported from the British Isles. Forms of the second half only of this more common set are likewise found in tradition. Also, I have recovered, in Pennsylvania and West Virginia, sets that may be rendered in diagrams thus: cfcx and cfcx / eb´cx. Now the question is: Which of these variant forms actually corresponds most to the original? Since we cannot determine this satisfactorily, we cannot actually tell which sets may have been worn first and then rebuilt—or, indeed, whether there has been any wearing down at all in the full-length sets. In the shorter sets (cfcx, etc.) we may indeed plausibly guess at a wearing-down; but we can feel no certainty about the others. When one is confronted with versions varying in this manner, the difficulty in making a decision about their development-relations becomes very real indeed.

[38] It is of course obvious that a number of ballads and songs which we customarily record in the regular, or common, ballad-stanza are set to airs showing the phrase-pattern in question.

This, in turn, we find to correspond with

        3. AB   CD

of some shorter airs, or with

        4.   AB   CD

of others—where the AB-CD of these latter melodies actually corresponds to the cd-ab, or BA, second-half pattern, of the versions of the longer melodies. I freely admit that the foregoing explanation is both generalized and simplified; but it had to be in order to indicate intelligibly a phenomenon that recurs continually in our recorded folk music. To sum up: tune-items with phrase-patterns of ABCD may themselves often be shortened (? worn-down) forms of longer tunes in which is customarily found some alternation-pattern of phrases that could be distinguished by the designating letter A and B (*cf.* the examples set forth in footnote 37).

As a result, we are unable to say definitely that ABCD-patterns are always those of full, independent, properly complete tunes; nor can we declare these patterns to be entirely separate from other A-*plus*-B arrangements found generally in our folk music. It is true that certain melodies consisting of four different phrases may be regarded as retaining their proper, full-length forms.[38a] But such tunes do not by any means all do so. And thus, the mere phrase-pattern of any traditional tune-item cannot in itself teach us anything about the original form, or the proper form, or even the usual form, of the tune of which that item may be a variant. Hence, we have to conclude either that folk melodies in our tradition do not belong to "types" on the basis of their phrase-order patterns only, or else that—even if we arbitrarily classified them thus—such "phrase-pattern" typology cannot serve to identify versions of individual melodies in British-American folk song. As shown above, differences of phrase-order pattern may, and do, exist aplenty among the versions of any individual folk melody, with the result that either the single phrase or the half-tune is the real unit with which we have to work when attempting to identify melodies by means of the highly important features of melodic-interval (melodic-line) and stressed-tone correspondences. Observing the recurrence of those complexes of phrases that stick together as distinct entities in themselves, we arrive at the conclusion repeatedly stated above: that our musical tradition is essentially one of organized, integrated, individual tunes, whose fundamental identities remain perceptible throughout many vicissitudes of oral transmission, re-creation, and reorganization.

Perhaps I have said enough to indicate that while the phenomenon which I call "wearing down" cannot always be satisfactorily detected or determined, the actual presence of tune-versions of varying length and phrase-arrangement

---

[38a]For example, the tune so often found joined with the ballad of "The Golden Glove" as, e.g., in Sharp-Karpeles, *English Folk Songs from the Southern Appalachians*, I, 377 f., and in many other collections. Yet this is one of the tunes uniquely set in Christie's *Traditional Ballad Airs* (II, 114) to a second strain (made up out of material from the first), and thus there appearing in a form double the length of the otherwise universally known version.

in our melodic tradition is a very real fact.[39] Whether a tune was originally in one or another form; or to what extent lengthening or shortening has taken place in transmission; are interesting questions which may or may not become important. But the existence of shorter or longer tune-versions, and the transposition of phrases or entire halves of tunes in tradition, are facts of the first importance to a student either of the music or of the association between the music and the songs.

It occasionally happens that a group of variant texts of a single folk song will appear at first glance to be sung to a number of different melodies. But upon further comparison of all the tunes to those variants, and of other resembling tunes joined to other texts in the tradition, we are sometimes enabled to see that the musical settings to the texts of our song are really diverse forms of a single air—in which variation, transposition of phrases, and shortening-or-lengthening of the entire tune have produced differences that can entirely mislead a hasty or superficial observer. In such cases, it sometimes takes a quite extensive tune-examination of the sort just indicated before we see that the melodies on which we happen to be concentrating are actually all cognates. A discovery similar to that just outlined is one which an investigator of British-American folk song tunes may expect to make repeatedly. Such an experience furnishes one of the most cogent arguments for the study of the music by and for itself, before any large-scale plunge is taken into the exceedingly complicated problems of the history of folk song variants as texttune units. What the organized knowledge of our folk music, when attained, may do to help us with problems of ballad text history is hard to predict. But at least, it should considerably refine our approaches to those problems.

In the preceding paragraphs I have been endeavoring to describe some of the salient variation-phenomena that a student encounters when he pays close attention to our folk music. I must now turn to still other features of oral variation; among them, some which practically force us to theorize about what has happened to our tunes in their passage down the generations. The student often finds himself at close grips with music to which almost anything may conceivably have happened in oral transmission; yet he is deprived of any record of just what actually *has* happened, outside of such information as he may glean from the music itself. And this internal evidence is apt to be profoundly ambiguous just where an investigator wishes it were most explicit.

While the student is trying to envisage clearly all the possibilities lying

---

[39] Phillips Barry once expressed the opinion that "folk melodies are of simple structure, for the most part, with a constant tendency toward greater simplicity." Barry's utterances about folk music are nearly always of an unshakable justice and correctness; yet in this case I wonder if he was not a little hasty? Is it not possible that the relative degree of simplicity or elaboration (both rather uncertain and debatable quantities) in a folk tune may depend to some extent on the type of song to which any version of the tune is set? At any rate it seems plain that recomposition is not always in the direction of greater simplification or abbreviation (cf. note 38). Barry's remark quoted above is in his "Some Aspects of Folk-Song," *JAF*, 25 (1912), 274-283, reprinted in *Folk Music in America*, ed. G. Herzog and H. Halpert (National Service Bureau, Federal Theatre Project, Works Progress Administration, 1939).

behind the record, the realization naturally haunts him that all reconstructions of processes which he may make are conjectural. In the presence of alternate possibilities, there are often no unmistakable indications that will enable him to fix on the correct alternative. This situation yet again forces him to rely on thoroughgoing resemblances between collected tune-items. They in turn, by their continual reappearance, convince him anew of the real existence of separate melodies, widespread in tradition and split up into large families numbering many variant forms. Just as the principal folk tales may be detected through the multitudes of floating traditional stories by the recurrent combinations of their respectively component *motifs*, so certain distinctive folk melodies in this tradition reappear amid the welter of oft-used melodic formulae. This is not remarkable in itself; by analogy with other folk arts, it is to be expected. But what really is remarkable is the overtowering importance of these distinctive tunes in the tradition—their prevailing use wherever the tradition lives.

I stated above that apparent cases of melodic attraction between airs, and instances where an actual mingling of two otherwise usually distinct melodies would seem to have taken place, can often confuse an investigator. It is in precisely these cases, naturally, that one is most troubled by inability to decide between possible alternatives—through lack of clear evidence. These cases merit some effort at brief analysis.

Occasional and passing resemblances between two undoubtedly different airs are to be expected in folk music, of course, and do not cause much trouble. But in cases where a really inextricable fusion of two ordinarily distinct tunes may be seen, we simply cannot discover with any certainty the actual course of events behind the seeming fusion: the possibilities are too many, the indications too few—or entirely wanting. For example, any such case may possibly be the result of what is really the exact opposite of "fusion." It may be a version of a melody out of which, by traditional re-creation, may have developed the two widespread distinct airs whose elements we discern in it. On the other hand, such a tune may represent simple confusion of memory on the part of a singer or singers somewhere along the line of transmission—by means of which two well-known different airs have been mingled unintentionally, and the product of this confusion passed on to other singers. Or, again, the combination of strains or elements from the different airs may have been made in full consciousness, and deliberately, by someone. Or, again, the tune in question may be the product of someone's effort to compose a new melody—in which, however, the would-be composer was overmuch dominated by the memory of a couple of important tunes already current in the tradition, and thus evolved something more imitative than original. In the presence of varying possibilities like these we find ourselves practically helpless.

It must be remarked, however, that what we discern in the versions of distinguishable tunes allows us to envisage one general possibility: namely, that all these fused and indeterminate airs may actually be of later development than the comparatively clear-cut ones. Perhaps in such tunes we witness the beginnings of a newer tune-repertory, which by gradual growth and spread in time—if the tradition were undisturbed—might eventually displace the one out of which it grew. The only basis for a conjecture such as this is the "non-universality" of these mixed melodies. They certainly do not appear to enjoy a currency wherever the English folk songs are sung—as do many other airs whose recurrence we may reasonably expect anywhere in the English folk-song world. Melodies such as these mixed ones occur sporadically. They appear to be made up of the elements of airs known universally, yet they themselves are not so known. They might even be regarded as accidents of tradition, and as transient local phenomena—although any one of them at any time could conceivably become something much more important in the folk song culture.

One hitherto unmentioned aspect of traditional variation bears directly on these "mixed" tunes and upon the problems of melodic attraction in the folk music. That is the fact, clearly apparent to the student, that sometimes a change of mode may greatly increase the overall resemblance of a version of one separate tune to versions of another separate tune. This could easily lead to still more influence of the material of the one tune upon the other, and result in ever-increasing resemblance between some versions of one and of the other. Actually, it is probable that just as folk poems may change theme by theme and slide imperceptibly—and by subtle associations of ideas connected with the themes—into quite different song-families; so also some folk-tune versions, through crisscrossing of modal, formulaic, and general structural resemblances, can come to a point where it is impossible to say to which of two (or even three) large cognate groups they belong. They could be in any; are, in fact, strictly in none. It is also likely that versions of an originally independent tune may gradually become more and more like versions of another (in the way just outlined) so that eventually they are, to all appearances, and in all respects, versions of the tune to which they have little by little been assimilated.

In the British tradition we certainly find some melodies which are quite bewildering because of what look like the results of "multiple attraction" of some of their versions to more than one widespread tune-family. That group of interrelated and interresembling tunes generally sung in old-country English tradition to the ballad "Henry Martin" (Child No. 250) shows extraordinary variety among its members.[40] Now they will appear to be independent tunes; again, they will look like forms of the "Lord Randal" melody, one of the

[40] Reference may be made to S. Baring-Gould, H. F. Sheppard, F. W. Bussell, *Songs of the West*, 2d ed., C. J. Sharp (London, 1905), p. 108; C. J. Sharp, ed., *English Folk Songs* (London: Novello, 1919), I, 1, ff.; this same set also in Sharp's *Folk Songs from Somerset* (2d series; London, 1905), p. 6; *JFSS*, 1, No. 2 (1900), p. 44, No. 4 (1902), p. 162; 4, No. 2 (1910), p. 92, No. 4 (1913), pp. 301-303. The striking variety and different ramifications of these sets, however, come out even more clearly in the numerous versions scattered through C. J. Sharp's MS collection; as also is plainly apparent their interconnection one with another.

commonest of our folk-song airs; still again, they rather seem to resemble another such widespread tune-family, that one which I have arbitrarily christened the "Bailiff's Daughter" air. Some such remarks also apply to the tunes ordinarily sung to the ballad "Young and Growing"[41]—which display at once so much mutual resemblance and so many divergent developments that their actual relations one with another and with any single widespread family of folk tunes seem at present indeterminable.[42] It thus appears that sets of tunes in our tradition may be attracted toward more than one different melody current among folk singers at the same time. If such things actually happened—as seem reflected in the musical record—then the influence of certain melodies which attained universal popularity and continual use all over the British folk-singing world must have been considerable. Such airs would appear to have been prime examples of the folk musical taste and ideals; sources of inspiration and subjects of imitation; regulators of variation; and so, in a sense, shapers of creative melodizing among the singing people. Sooner or later the student of this musical tradition comes to the point of concluding that the power and importance of various universally known individual melodies are hard to exaggerate.

Another feature of oral variation, which is a fruitful source of confusion for uninitiated and experienced students alike, is the phenomenon which I have called "alternating cadential formulae."[43] I have already noticed these manifestations briefly. And I think that, for once, the term just given fits the phenomenon completely. A few words about this aspect of our folk music may be desirable here. It appears to arise through an exchange of formulaic cadential passages all of which may be substituted one for another in many of our tunes. It is, then, just another example of that exchange of musical formulae already discussed. Obviously, it is a melodizing trick that would present no difficulties to a practiced folk singer whose mind was filled with the common tunes of his traditional repertory and with the memories of how he had heard them varied. On the contrary, it is something that would be quite naturally and easily done. I have heard traditional singers substitute one cadential formula for another in the course of their singing one tune to stanza after stanza of a song; and evidently other collectors have heard the like, since such exchanges on the part of one singer of a tune-version also appear in published folk-tune records.[44]

[41] Representative members of this tune-group may be seen in Sharp-Karpeles, *English Folk Songs from the Southern Appalachians*, I, 410; Barry, *British Ballads from Maine*, p. xxx; *Songs of the West*, p. 8; Sharp, *English Folk Songs* (1919), **2**, 20; *JFSS*, **1**, 214; **2**, 44, 46, 95, 96, 206, 274, 275; **5**, 190, 192.

[42] Similarly puzzling are the interrelations of a group of tunes set to English texts of many love songs belonging to the "Turtle Dove-Truelover's Farewell" complex; itself a song-family consisting of texts that are highly complicated in their relations.

[43] Bartók, in *Hungarian Folk Music*, p. 8, notes that Hungarian tunes are "extraordinarily rich in different endings to tune-lines." I am not certain, however, that the phenomenon he refers to is the same as that discussed in the present article.

[44] Perhaps one example may illustrate sufficiently for the moment: the strikingly variant ending to the second line of a Cornish singer's tune to the "Outlandish Knight" ballad (Child No. 4), *JFSS*, 4, Pt. 2 (1910), 116. One of these cadential closes represents an ordinary one for the tune, which is widely known; the other is unusual.

The particular cadence-alterations under discussion at the moment have the effect of ending a phrase of a tune on *different notes* of the scale or mode in which the tune happens to be cast. This fact implies at once that they are not used at the closes of tune-versions—which is the case. Such alterations occur medially: sometimes at the end of the first phrase (mid-point of first strain); also often, at the mid-point of the tune (end of first-strain). At these points, tune-versions that are unmistakably forms of one original melody will vary, turning now up, now down, according to the progression of the inserted cadence-formula.

Thus, there are three places where the melodic line of a tune-version may be confidently expected to vary: at the very beginning (sometimes the variation is considerable, here); at the very end; and at the mid-point cadence, or end of the first half of the set. A tune-version is not necessarily altered beyond recognition by changes at any or all of these points. Indeed, it may be conjectured that if a certain number of these alternating formulae come to be associated in the minds of various singers with the familiar strains of certain tune-versions, that fact itself might work as a conserver of the outlines of a tune. However, the formulae which interchange at these medial tune-cadences are not restricted—as to their occurrence—by rhythmic pattern, by pace or tempo, by strongly marked version-group characteristics, by the immediate function of a tune-version, or by the mode in which a tune-version happens to be sung at any particular time. In other words, we may look for certain variant medial-cadential turns to recur in any sets of any widespread melody, despite the alterations caused by variation of other kinds. Thus, this re-markable manifestation in our folk music actually helps the investigator to detect cognates of a tune as it floats hither and thither on the currents of tradition. On the other hand, it can also—taken with the "falling together" of versions of different folk tunes, due to their being by chance translated into the same mode—bewilder a student, no matter how careful he may be, and divert him from perceiving the main outlines of a given tune. It can disguise from a careless or hasty observer the true affiliations of some melodic item with some widely known family of variants.

However, there will always be some amount of indeterminate material in our tradition, no doubt. We are left in an ignorance of the past of our folk music which prevents us from being able to decide between the alternatives of dispersion *plus* variation; independent invention *plus* assimilative variation; and (deliberate or unconscious) tune-merging *plus* variation, in any attempt to ac-count for the features displayed by some of our airs.

Judging from the testimony of the published musical records, our folk song tunes fall into three main classes, on the basis of the comparative number of their discernible cognate relatives. These classes are: (1) a few tunes which have formed very widely diffused and multiform families—consisting of inex-tricably interrelated sets that dominate the musical scene, and account for the majority of the tunes sung to the songs; (2) A fair number of distinct, independent tunes seemingly less well known, and recorded in fewer variant forms—hence, forming smaller tune-families; and (3) the "indeterminate" melodies just now being discussed.

Melodies of class (2) sometimes have their variants more or less concentrated; or they may show variants widely, but thinly, scattered over the entire area of the tradition. Those of class (3) are varied in their aspects. They are all in a recognizable style, or musical idiom, of the tradition. Sometimes they may partake of the characteristics or elements of various exceedingly well-known airs in the repertory, without yet being clearly members of any of the version-groups of those airs. At other times they are quite nondescript— arrangements of familiar melodic turns or passages—and seem to illustrate perfectly what Professor George Pullen Jackson calls "general melodizing."[45] Furthermore, to judge from published musical evidence, they are mostly not traceable in variant forms from region to region of the English folk-singing area—as are the tune-families of the widely known airs. On the contrary, they occur locally and sporadically—most of them are *hapax legomena*, in fact—so that it is not certain whether they have had any extensive currency, or whether any lengthy history of transmission lies behind them. (I have mentioned above some groups that seem to furnish exceptions to this general principle.) In brief, their occurrence suggests that they are, for the most part, "sports" of tradition—chance, hybrid products of variation—and not integrated, intrenched, widely accepted old melodies, strongly impressed on the popular memory. They seem not to travel about like the great tunes of the tradition; but to be current locally, perhaps temporarily. It may be that they represent the gradually accumulating elements of some exclusively local tune-repertories, or the products of some local worthies in obvious imitation of forms of the really important melodies in the general stock. Indeed, their character itself inevitably suggests that they are usually formed in imitation of (or under the influence of) those already dominant airs in our tradition, and hence cannot be of such age as the latter. If this be actually the case with these non-allocable airs, still another suggestion likewise becomes inevitable: that our folk-song-tune repertory, over its whole area, is not only composed, for the greater part, of diverse forms of a few individual tunes, but that it is essentially *individual tune based*. I mean by this that it gradually grows larger mostly by means of the occasional mergings and slow divergences in transmission of continually varied forms of the dominating, strongly impressed melodies.[46]

---

[45] See Jackson's *White and Negro Spirituals* (New York: J. J. Augustin, cop. 1943), p. 329, note to No. 24; p. 333, note to No. 62, and the airs they refer to; also see page 266 for a brief characterization of this "general melodizing," or "simple repetitive melodizing," as he also calls it.

[46] Or, if it does not grow larger, perhaps, then, it gradually alters in such a way that the repertory itself changes little by little from one stock of tunes(?) The statement that oral re-creation is a cause of gradual growth in our tune-repertory, however, was made by Barry shortly before his lamented death—see *Bulletin of the Folk-Song Society of the Northeast*, No. 12 (1937), p. 11, col. 2—and since there Barry expressed in one sentence the idea that my own studies have, I think, amply evidenced, and are intended to demonstrate, I naturally consider his suggestion the correct one.

I have been trying, at great length, to set forth the most notable features exhibited by our folk music as a whole—especially, however, those aspects that illustrate the nature of the oral variation that our melodies have undergone. Considering those aspects, it seems as though we should fall into a considerable mistake if we tried to account for the rise of any one of the great "tune families" in our tradition merely by cumulative unconscious or involuntary oral variation of an isolated, single, simple melody. We have to recall two basic facts: first, that no traditional melody ever lives or is re-created in a vacuum—it is always liable to influence from other melodies co-existent with it; second, that there is no reason to suppose all variation unconscious—a good part of it may have been not only conscious, but even deliberate, on the part of the traditional artists whose property the music is.

For practically every one of our folk melodies of British extraction, the composer, and the time, place and circumstances of composition are alike unknown and unimportant. It is perfectly plain that the melodies, as we now know them, have been re-created time and again by persons of no mean organizing and artistic talent. It is also plain that—their original forms being unknown or undetectable—we cannot undertake to say how they first came into being. Possibly they were each composed as "new" tunes by some persons at some times in the past. Just as possibly, they arose by endless variation out of some older mass of airs—and once a thoroughly congenial form or outline had been attained, it stayed in popular memory and spread by oral diffusion. Or perhaps some of them arose in the one way, some in the other; we cannot tell. We can be sure of at least two things: that our folk music, as far back as we can trace it, has always been alive and developing; and that certain tunes have managed to retain their identity in the face of oral re-creations that have fundamentally altered the esthetic character of many of their versions.

But from the occurrences and apparent tendencies visible in this music, it would seem not unreasonable to suppose that a big tune-family was built up by a succession—or a combination—of happenings somewhat like the following:

1. A tune, its form once comparatively settled either by original composition or by someone's distinctive revision, would appeal to a number of people, who would learn it and start to spread it abroad orally. During this diffusion it would at once commence to be heard in variant forms; and throughout its subsequent life in tradition, it would never cease to be varied more or less by practically every one of its singers.

2. Because of its wide appeal—and perhaps its adaptability to many different song texts or uses—our hypothetical tune would become exceedingly popular, so that it could be reckoned one of the best-known melodies in the folk repertory.

3. The variant forms of this tune, travelling back and forth, would become known side by side—or in clusters—in many communities. Their similarity one to another would make it easy for singers to merge them involuntarily while

performing; so that variant forms of one tune, found alongside each other in any community, would affect each other mutually, exerting influences one upon another of a most complex and subtle kind. The composite variant forms made by this confluence of more than one already existing variant of the tune might spread anew to other communities, where the process would be likely to be repeated.

4. This merging of parent and derivative variants would tend to fix the basic outlines and important intervals of a tune firmly in the minds of the singing people—so that the pattern and principal formulae of the tune would become a part of the way in which they habitually thought melodically.

5. The reinforcement of the tune's main melodic outline, combined with constant slight variation, would in time cause a number of inextricably inter-related forms to appear—among which a form very close to that of the original melody might or might not survive.

6. Bits of other concurrent melodies might get worked into some of the forms of this group of variants, causing more or less divergence from the common tune outlines, and facilitating the appearance of *versions* of the tune. A change of rhythm, pace or mode (always possible when the outlines of a tune are firmly ingrained in a folk singer's consciousness) would effect the appearance and further development of still other distinctive versions.

7. The variation undergone by these related tunes—traceable both to the influence of other airs and the interchange of elements from their own sets—would make it practically impossible for many singers to hear or think of their forms of the tunes in any single, unvarying way. They would likewise tend to vary their forms by consciously introducing the formulae of other variants which they had heard.[47] And this interchange of variant-material, in turn, would tend to increase the number of usable and interchangeable begin-ning-and-ending formulae which the folk singers would have at their disposal in performing any of their traditionally learned tunes.

8. The formation of distinctive versions of the tune—by means of altera-tions in rhythmic scheme, pace and mode—would not all be natural or uncon-scious; some of it would be intentional. Some folk musicians who thoroughly knew a form or forms of the air would be able to adapt it to another function (marching, dancing, etc.) by deliberately recasting it—in the ways mentioned, or by the elaboration or drastic simplification of its melodic line.

---

[47] Some words of an experienced Irish student and collector may indicate that this postulate is not a mere fancy of my own. In *A Handbook of Irish Music*, p. 190, Fr. Richard Henebry remarks that "it may be useful to explain that whenever a musician heard a note or an ascent passage in a tune that he considered an improvement, he straightway incorporated it in his own version. I particularly remember, in my own case, as a boy, how . . . I used to listen . . . to . . . tramp pipers or fiddlers . . . especially if their style was good . . . in order to assimilate for myself such changes of version or inter-pretation as I considered suitable. And I never knew an Irish musician who did not do the same." Fr. Henebry is here speaking more especially of folk instrumentalists; I, following the internal evidence of our folk song tunes, am assuming that folk vocalists have done the very thing he outlines in the words just quoted.

The capabilities of certain musical instruments might also exert an influence in this process.

9. Because of alterations of mode and interchange of formulaic beginnings and strain-endings, melodies which originally had been quite different from the tune whose development we are following in theory, would be found resembling it much more closely. Some of these melodies, or some forms of them, would become progressively assimilated to forms of our supposed "dominant" tune—until at length they would be as indistinguishable from it, or as inextricable from the mass of its variants, as if they had been forms of the "dominant" tune from the beginning.

10. So deeply impressed would be the outline and basic structure of the tune, throughout its many forms, that we might expect imitations of it to appear. A person of no originality, desirous of composing a new tune (and this sort of person is by no means unknown in folk-singing circles), would be more likely to produce an adaptation of something already familiar to him. And his "new" composition could readily take one of two forms: either what amount (or, in the course of variation, ultimately would amount) to simply another version or variant of our supposed dominant tune; or a hybrid, in which a part of one such dominant tune might be joined to, or mingled with, a part of another air equally widespread in the oral repertory. In this way, the array of versions would be increased by one; or else one of the nonallocable "nondescript" airs of the tradition would be produced.

11. As the derivative forms of the dominant melody continued to be perpetuated by tradition, some would become shortened; others, due to the adaptive faculties of talented folk musicians, might be extended or elaborated, or provided with additional full-length strains or refrain passages. All such alterations would tend (provided they lived and spread) either to establish yet another group of versions in oral currency, or to produce a form so divergent that it could be developed without difficulty into a quite different air.

12. In the course of time one would be able to find among folk singers some individuals who were alive to the likenesses and evident relations between close variants among the forms of this air which they knew; others who were oblivious of such features. And the less obvious versions of the air would be sung without suspicion that they were in any way related. All forms, however, would continue to be re-created by their singers. The derivatives of one traditional melody, cultivated along with others, would thus have multiplied and greatly enriched the communal music tradition.

In accordance with the hypothesis just outlined in the above twelve points —a hypothesis itself depending on observable phenomena in our folk melodies—I can now offer my definition of a "tune family":

A tune family is a group of melodies showing basic interrelation by means of constant melodic correspondence, and presumably owing their mutual likeness to descent from a single air that has assumed multiple forms through processes of variation, imitation, and assimilation.

* * *

The folk music of the British Isles is apt to impress one at first by its really astonishing variety, both of national repertory and of regional style.[48] Of repertories we can distinguish at least five among the land-dwelling population: those of the English, the Lowland Scots, the Welsh, the Irish, and the Highland or Hebridean Scots. To these must be added a sixth distinctive melodic repertory, not peculiar to any nationality: that of the tunes to the shanties, or marine work-songs. Among them all, the most stylistically distinct and melodically self-contained are the tune-treasuries of the shantymen and the Highland Scots.

"Style" in our folk music, or in any music, is terribly hard to characterize. Nevertheless, a few words more may perhaps be set down about the dominant perceivable styles in British traditional tunes. They do not—as has been pointed out at length—correspond necessarily with groups of versions or related airs, nor with any melodic repertories, strictly speaking. They belong to the sort of phenomena which may be often readily perceived, but almost never successfully described; and what one can say about them in words is bound to be exceedingly superficial.

Broadly speaking, and leaving out of account the shantymen's tunes, the folk music of the British Isles, as we have known it, appears in three distinguishable main styles. These we may term the *English*, the *Irish*, and the *Hebridean*; but these terms must be understood as being employed more for convenience than for any scientific reason. The English style, current in English counties and the northeast of Scotland (with local variations of melodic idiom), shows relationship in its mannerisms with Scandinavian traditional music. The two other styles may be roughly included under the term "Gaelic," and are rather closely akin in many fashions of melodizing. The Irish style prevails, naturally, in Ireland, and in the western Scottish Lowlands. The here so-called Hebridean style is that of the Scottish Highlands and the Western Isles. In this music also some observers have (not surprisingly) thought to see Scandinavian influence.[49]

Both English and Irish styles share some qualities to which I have already alluded: their tunes are generally couched in bisymmetric two- or four-line organizations, and have phrase-patterns of AABA, ABBA, ABCD, etc. I hope I have made it plain that the internal structure of these airs is much more varied, complex and subtly organized than any A-*plus*-B scheme of phrase-arrangements could indicate: these schemes are simply indications of fundamental models. The great popularity of the Dorian mode in English music has also been mentioned. In addition, we might say that the English style is characterized by a certain solidity of melodic build—an emphasis throughout

---

[48] This variety is commented on by Werner Danckert, *Das Europäische Volkslied*, (Berlin: Hanhefeld, 1939), pp. 101-104, who considers it the result of much mixture of musical influences from differing cultures.

[49] See, for instance, Marjory Kennedy-Fraser, *Songs of the Hebrides* (London: Boosey & Co.), Vol. II (cop. 1917), p. xiii.

the tune on the strong notes of the mode, like the tonic or dominant tones— and by a preference for the sort of melodic movement which "gets somewhere," which is not held up by hesitating progression or undue overlay of ornamental features. In general, the style is firm and forward-moving, with vigorous rhythm, bold, long-range sweeps, and simple melodism.[49a]

Whereas the English folk poems are nearly all composed in stanzas of four main accents to a line, or in alternations of four accents with three, many Gaelic and Anglo-Irish poems are composed in lines which, from a musical point of view, might be said to contain three, five, or six principal stresses; consequently, we see tunes with five- and six-bar lines in music of the Irish style. Irish singers, as already noticed, seem to show as marked a liking for the Mixolydian mode as English singers do for the Dorian; and the English singer's leaning to relatively straightforward and simple melodic lines is counteracted in Irish tradition by a love of ornament, of multiplying notes, of varying rhythmic patterns by this sort of multiplication. Often, in Irish singing, the skeletal tune is so heavily overlaid with ornamental features that it becomes hard to recognize; yet, too, it is hard to call these features (cadenza-like runs, slides, rapid shakes, grace-notes of various sorts) an "overlay"—they seem to form an integral part of the melody, as well as of the style of performance.[50] This same ornamental tendency, plus the free-time rendition of many song-tunes, and the five- and six-bar line of many others, gives to Irish music in the purest style a quality which Padraic Colum also notes in Irish verse-structure: i.e., the most characteristic Irish song-tunes are "wavering and unemphatic" in their movement.[51] Contributing still further to this impression

[49a] I hope that I have not unduly slighted Welsh folk music in treating its style, by implication as part of the English. What I have just said about the style of the English tunes and versions, however, also applies to the Welsh; and it is a matter of record that, despite the presence of a real national Welsh repertory of traditional airs, some of the very popular Welsh tunes are also common to England and other British nationalities. Furthermore, it looks as though the Welsh harpers have been adopting—and adapting— English tunes for a long while. See the list given by Chappell, *Popular Music of the Olden Time*, I, 64, note *a*—a list by no means exhaustive.

However, Welsh tunes have themselves some distinctive stylistic features—the most prominent among them being tonic-dominant modulation, and a tendency to indulge in melodic sequence; which I take to be elements of instrumental, not vocal, technique in British traditional music. And Welsh tunes have, like the others, travelled about among other British peoples. An instance of how sensitive an earlier collector of folk music could be to national or regional style may be drawn from Simon Fraser's *Airs . . . Peculiar to the Highlands of Scotland*. In commenting upon tune No. 146, p. 69, Fraser says (p. 114) "This air the Editor supposed to be Welsh." He goes on to say that it has not appeared among the Welsh melodies. Fraser was right in the first instance and wrong in the second. The tune is indeed Welsh, being a version of the old harpers' melody "Merch Megan" (Megan's Daughter); and it has certainly appeared more than once in Welsh collections. Versions may be seen, for example, in *British Harmony* (1781)—one of the famous "Blind John" Parry's publications—No. 36, p. 35; and in Edward Jones, *Musical and Poetical Relicks of the Welsh Bards* (London, 1794), p. 149. A version is printed, with commentary, in Alfred Moffatt's *Minstrelsy of Wales*; but I cannot furnish exact reference, since the volume is unavailable to me at the moment.

[50] Examples are the song-airs from Co. Waterford in *JFSS*, 3 (1907-1909), 6-38.

[51] See Padraic Colum, *Anthology of Irish Verse* (New York: Boni & Liveright, 1922), p. 8.

are two other marked features of Irish style. One is a curious tendency to "hold back"—to draw back before starting forward again, as it were; and also to linger on certain notes or tones, by repeating them before going on to another tone, thus almost impeding the onward course of the melody from time to time.[52] The other is a striking tendency to emphasize and dwell on scale-tones that are inconclusive or indecisive—the weak or passing tones, the ones that do not contribute to resolution or finality in the entire phrase or musical utterance, but rather to easy flow and facile continuity.[53] These qualities taken together give the purest Irish airs a peculiarly melodious, graceful softness of flow and outline; a sweetness and smooth ease that seem often on the point of slipping into diffuse weakness.

It is possible that the Hebridean style is the most archaic surviving in British folk music. By contrast with the symmetrical, highly organized tunes of Ireland and England, many of the Highland airs appear almost casually put together. The fundamental phrase-order patterns mentioned as characterising the other two styles are not prominent at all in the Hebridean music. The Hebridean singers have a decided fondness for arranging tune-strains or phrases in groups of three—a habit not characteristic of the other two styles.[54] Also, the Hebridean-style repertory contains numerous airs which it is impossible to bisect. They do not fall into two equal-length halves any more than French folk tunes usually do, and for a similar reason: the lines of the songs in Highland and Hebrid repertories are interspersed with refrains and ejaculations, in such a way that the accompanying music sounds much more improvisational than the tunes of the English and Irish styles. Often it seems as if no clear ending-strain for a Highland tune can be discerned: as if another strain could be added, or one removed, without damaging what organization the entire melody has.

The frequent repetition of short units, or motives, also characterizes the Hebrid melodies. Likewise, the use of "gapped" scales, instead of full, heptatonic diatonic scales is very characteristic of Hebridean singing; and the gaps in these modes are not often filled in or slurred over by the use of passing-tones. The whole tonality of tunes in this style seems vaguer than that of the other styles: shifts from a minor-sounding tune-body to a major close, and *vice versa* are not uncommon. Abrupt switches of register, with wide and

---

[52] Examples are P. W. Joyce, *Old Irish Folk Music and Songs* (London: Longmans, Green & Co., 1909), No. 614, p. 316, "The Cuckoo"; and the second part of "Molly St. George" in Bunting's 1796 collection, ed. D. J. O'Sullivan: *Journal of the Irish Folk Song Society*, Vols. 22-23, 1925-1926 (1927), p. 43.

[53] Compare the air to "A Óganaigh Óig" in D. J. O'Sullivan's edition of the 1796 Bunting collection, *Journal of the Irish Folk Song Society*, Vol. 25, 1928 (1930), p. 12.

[54] A few three-phrase tunes have tuned up in the American repertory of British folk tunes—all of them being shortened from the normal four-phrase form of one of our most widely known airs. These special versions are curiously restricted in their diffusion, being mostly from Kentucky, with occasional scattered examples elsewhere. See, for example, Sharp-Karpeles, *English Folk Songs from the Southern Appalchians*, I, 317-327, to "The Cruel Ship's Carpenter," versions F (Ky.), G (Ky.), N (Ky.), T (Va.).—The three-phrase organization so popular among American Negroes generally affects a set of tunes entirely different from those in our Anglo-American repertory.

frequent melodic leaps (of fifths, sixths and octaves) are quite prominent in this melodic style; yet here may also be perceived sometimes the peculiar "lingering" tendency just described for Irish-style music. In Hebridean tunes the melodic outline is apt to be relatively simple, lacking the florid multiplicity of notes which we often find in Irish music. The graceful and beautiful way in which Highland singers handle slides and short grace-notes has been eloquently remarked by Miss Broadwood.[55] But again, as in Irish tunes, we find, to some extent, the curious prominence given to indecisive tones in the scales; and in melodic idiom generally, the Hebridean style is much closer to the Irish than to the English.

In these three styles we find rendered the national and regional tune-repertories of British folk song singers—except for the sea shanties, which have developed in large measure still another style especially their own. But whatever may be the spread of one of these styles, or the prominence in any region or nation of one of the above-enumerated repertories, not one of these regions has a repertory consisting entirely of airs unknown elsewhere. All share to some extent in melodies known to all the others.

The tune-trading and mutual influence among the national repertories are bewildering—hard to describe, hard oftentimes to determine. It seems that in each of the above mentioned regional (or national) repertories we find certain tunes quite popular and known in many versions, which are peculiar to those parts and are not heard or recorded elsewhere. This, of course, is judging by the published collectanea, with all their acutely realized limitations. Thus, there are some tune-families that would seem peculiar to certain nationalities or regions of the British Isles.

Other tune-families show variant forms in more than one region—or perhaps in all parts. Thus, Highland and Lowland Scotland; England, Wales, Ireland and the Scottish Lowlands; Wales, Ireland, the Hebrides and the western Scottish Lowlands; are seen to be bound up together, musically, in a network of melodies known in common. The music of the Isle of Man has very little peculiar to it, on the whole: outside of a very few airs, like the well-known "Mylecharane"[56] and some *carval* melodies, Manx folk music consists of versions of melodies known to Anglo-Scottish or Irish singers, or to both.

Now many of these tunes, as I said before, are apt to sound English in England, Irish in Ireland, etc. It is therefore often impossible to ascertain in which country the parent tune of a family was composed. When a tune-version travelled from one British region or nation to another, it was naturally re-created in the musical style of the region which adopted it. We can often reasonably infer that a given version of some widespread air is Irish or Scot-

---

[55] In *JFSS*, 4, Pt. 3 (1911), x.

[56] For which see Lucy Broadwood and A. J. Fuller-Maitland, *English County Songs* (London, 1893), p. 36, and *JFSS* 7, Pt. 2 (1924), 124. The tune called "The Sheep under the Snow" (*English County Songs*, pp. 38-39, *JFSS*, 7, pp. 117, 118) would seem, if not an exclusively Manx air, to have taken a very distinctive shape in the Isle. It is not impossible that it is of island origin. See Miss Gilchrist's note, *JFSS, loc. cit.*

tish, for example; but we cannot therefore claim that the air itself was of Irish or Scots origin. The presence of Irish mannerisms in a melody current in midland England, then, indicates only that this version of the melody was presumably evolved in, and brought from Ireland; but it does not allow us to claim that the tune first arose there. Judging from the "traceability" of melodic style in the published records, tune-versions have travelled much and often between the countries of the British Isles. The creeping-in of Scottish- and Irish-style dance music on English country-dance accompaniments is a matter of record.[57] And many folk song tune-versions common in the English countryside are apparently just as well known in Ireland and northeastern Scotland—often quite thoroughly assimilated to the local melodic idiom.

The dominant tune-families of English folk song are about equally wide-spread elsewhere in the British islands, save for the Highlands and Western Isles of Scotland; so much the intensive collecting of the last half-century or so has taught us. Conversely, it looks as though certain dominant Irish tune-families are now also at home in Great Britain. The realization of how un-traceable these melodies actually are has finally halted the rather futile con-troversies over the claims of different lands to various internationally current melodies of merit.

To attempt a summing-up: the tune families dominant among English folk singers are alikewise apparently dominant among the Irish and Lowland Scots. They form what may as well be called the *common* melodic repertory of the British Isles, and we expect to see their versions turning up everywhere and rather constantly in those lands—except in the Highlands and Hebrides, where they have not effected any wholesale penetration, apparently. Nor, on the other hand, does the Highland music seem to have affected the folk song airs of other British regions except (slightly) the Scottish Lowlands. With this exception, the melodic traffic of the various British nationalities and peoples seems to have been extensive. The *common repertory* is everywhere—versions of its tunes even occurring now and then in Highland music and among the airs sung to sea shanties. This *common repertory*, of course, consists of those prevalent tune-families that are the principal concern of the present essay. We must surmise that all the British nationalities have contributed something to this basic melodic fund. And the impressive community of traditional tune-repertory among most of the British peoples cuts right across distinctions of melodic style, as it also blurs the outlines of such exclusively national or regional tune-stocks as exist.

British folk tunes have been flowing across the Atlantic into North America for over three hundred years, presumably. Since members of all British peoples have migrated to this continent, and have undoubtedly brought over goodly shares of their old-world musical inheritance, we should expect to find a remarkable mixture of melodies from all these traditions in the folk song of

[57] The record is not assembled in one place; but the influence of Scots and Gaelic dance music on the tunes to English country dances can be observed by anyone who cares to examine the published collectanea.

this country. Likewise, if the foregoing analysis of the British music is at all correct, we should expect to find that versions of the airs composing the *common* repertory have been imported from all the countries of the British Isles, and have been conserved alongside each other in our own countryside. Moreover, we might assume—in view of the international travels of tunes and tune-versions among the British peoples—that tunes in the melodic style of one country did not necessarily reach this country direct from the land where that style is prevalent. As we have seen, there is reason to suppose that minglings of the national traditions were going on previous to any of the large-scale British migrations to America.

Since we may be sure that British folk music went right on developing during the period of colonization in America, and afterward, we may likewise assume that each group of British immigrants after the first great settlers' waves of the years before 1650 brought over some more newly evolved variant forms of the folk airs to add to the variety of our own tradition here. Also we can see, apparently, that some rather distinctive variant forms of widespread tunes evolved in the tradition of the American countryside.

Hence, the musical influences from the old countries must have come not all at once, but in a series of waves and impacts, each one probably adding some elements to the melodic culture implanted by the English migrations of the seventeenth century. Doubtless the most important of these fresh contributions were made by the Scotch-Irish migrations of the early eighteenth century, and the huge Gaelic Irish influx of the 1840's and 1850's. Folk melodies transplanted to America, meanwhile, have undoubtedly undergone continuous oral variation and development in their new homes, no matter at what period they were introduced.

If the preceding summary embodies an accurate enumeration of the main possibilities, we in America have to cope with a pretty complicated set of conditions in our efforts to discover approximately the true history of our individual folk songs and their music. We seem at present to have four ways of attacking the various problems: 1. by identifying widely current tunes in all their detectable versions; 2. by trying to determine (if possible) the national styles to which tune-versions current in America seem to have the closest affinity; 3. by studying together the texts and tunes of folk song versions in which appear a persistent association of a version of some song with a version of a widespread tune; and 4. by trying to plot the distribution of these close associations of particular text-versions with particular tune-versions, so that their area of currency may be correlated with regions of settlement and routes of settlers' migrations in this country. Obviously, these approaches are all to some extent interdependent.

However, the situation, as a whole, of British music current in America is qualified by several outstanding facts which must be recognized if we want to appreciate properly the relations between old-world and new-world folk song records. These facts may be set forth approximately thus:

1. The Scottish Gaelic tune-repertory of the Highlands and Western Isles

has apparently not survived to any extent among English-language folk singers in America. I do not know what may be preserved among the Gaels of Nova Scotia; but it is obvious that the tune-families of the Highlands have had but little currency or influence over North America as a whole. Tunes in this style are of exceedingly rare occurrence.[58]

2. The same statement may be made about a number of the outstanding tunes peculiar to the Irish repertory. Perhaps their association with songs in Gaelic somehow inhibited their spread outside Ireland. There are indications that some of these distinctively Irish airs have been preserved among members of Irish colonies in our cities; but since no sizable attempt to investigate them has ever been made, nothing more can be said about them at present. However, in our countryside, very few melodies of exclusively Irish style and currency are found. If imported, they have not survived.

3. The *common repertory*—that limited number of internationally known tune-families to whose variants are sung the majority of our folk song texts—is dominant in our countryside, as it is in the British Isles. This is a fact which every successive publication of Anglo-American folk song music simply confirms anew. The different British colonists have apparently succeeded in bringing over (at various times, no doubt) the greater number of the prevailing versions of these tunes, and have preserved them here in forms as clearly recognizable as those we see in old-country collections. It might be plausibly argued, in fact, that here in the folk song of America the common repertory is even more important than it is in its original homelands. On the whole, the traditional divergences of its component tune-versions are less wide than might have been expected, considering the vast reaches of the territory the versions were to cover, and the separation of early pioneering settlements.

4. There appear to be some rather considerable differences in the relative popularity of versions of these common tunes, between the old-country traditions and those of our country. Some of these differences are seemingly due to special relations between folk dance and folk song airs in our countryside: in the way certain dance- or march-versions of common tunes have been converted to the uses of song by American folk artists. This is a matter of such complication that it deserves separate treatment; there is no space for further discussion here.

Another source of difference between British and American repertories, as regards prevalent tunes, is the fact that certain versions that are widely or universally known to our folk singers appear but very little in British collections. For instance, one tune-version which in America is known all over the southern and many midwestern states has been recorded only a few times in Britain—and the recordings are all from the northeast of Scotland. In another instance, a tune-version exceedingly common in our tradition, to both

---

[58] A lone example of a really Scottish-Highland-style tune occurs in the J. S. James edition of the *Original Sacred Harp* (1911; reprinted Atlanta, Georgia, 1929), p. 326, entitled "Weary Pilgrim." The air is there attributed to one L. P. Breedlove, a singing-leader and "composer," one of the revisers of the 1850 *Sacred Harp*.

ballads and lyric songs, has been recorded only once or twice in Lowland Scotland, and two or three times in the Isle of Man. The converse of this proposition is also true: American records fail to show certain versions broadcast in the folk music of Great Britain. In cases like these, one hardly knows how to interpret the available evidence. Perhaps certain little-known versions in the old country have taken on a new lease of life, and experienced an upsurge of popularity over here. On the other hand, they may be much more widely known in British regions than the published material indicates: collectors may simply have passed them by. But if they were actually very well known in Britain, it is hard to see how all collectors except those in one or two districts could possibly have missed them. After all, a purely local version of any well-known air in British-American tradition occurs very rarely indeed.

5. In the course of its further traditional development in this country, the common repertory would appear to have thrown off very widely divergent forms, to have had its component tunes mingled to some extent, and to have produced its crop of composite, indeterminate and nondescript melodies, just as I had presumed that it did in the British Isles. The character and occurrence of these tunes—non-allocable, yet definitely made out of familiar elements—are precisely like the manifestations of the airs of similar character in the old country, as I have described them above. Among the most important examples of this sort of air in the American tradition are the tunes of a number of white folk spirituals.[59] Another group of examples is furnished by many of the tunes developed among the members of the religious sect known as the Shakers.[60]

6. The large mass of folk tunes sung by North American Negroes appears, on the whole, to be an independent creation by that people. The influence of imported (mostly British) folk music is plainly discernible in Negro folk melody, and Negro repertories are shot through with versions of the principal British folk airs and other popular tunes; yet we cannot help recognizing in the music of this people a fund of song tunes generally distinct from that current among the whites.

7. As regards the association of texts of individual folk songs with certain tunes and tune-versions, we observe in the British and Anglo-America records both correspondences and differences which are alike interesting and striking. Many songs have been collected in America joined to the same tunes (in the same variant forms) to which they have been widely sung in British folk singing. On the other hand, we have in our rural traditions some widespread ballads and songs that show persistent musical associations which do not turn

[59] See the camp-meeting spirituals in George Pullen Jackson's *White Spirituals in the Southern Uplands* (Chapel Hill: University of North Carolina Press, 1933); *Spiritual Folk-Songs of Early America* (New York: J. J. Augustin, cop. 1937); *Down East Spirituals and Others* (New York: Augustin, 1943); L. L. McDowell, *Songs of the Old Camp Ground* (Ann Arbor, Mich.: Edwards Bros., Inc., 1937).

[60] See Edward Deming Andrews, "Shaker Songs," *The Musical Quarterly* (New York: G. Schirmer), 23, No. 4 (Oct., 1937), 491-508; same author, *The Gift to be Simple* (New York: J. J. Augustin, cop. 1940).

up in the British Isles at all. It is impossible to guess the age of these tune-text combinations; but some of them are certainly known almost everywhere in our countryside. There are three possible explanations for these phenomena: First, they may reflect the singing of some region not thoroughly explored by British collectors—hence, similar tune-text examples have been overlooked in the old country. Or, second, they may represent the junction of an English song with an air from Germany, or some other non-British homeland. Or, third, they may be the products of American tradition: an association, unmade before, between a British song and tune. What prevents us from making a clear decision one way or the other is the fact that, although different versions of a folk song may be sung to quite different melodies, these melodies are almost always forms of the often used and widely known airs of the *common repertory*. This means that when singers in the past have changed tunes for their songs, they generally shifted from one old stock melody to another—not to some newly introduced air.

8. Among the tunes sung in the eighteenth-century ballad operas, and to the broadside ballad airs of the seventeenth (and perhaps the sixteenth) century—e.g., those tunes which appear in the first (1650) edition of *The Dancing Master* and in other early sources—we find every so often a version of some melody which still has traditional currency among our folk artists. Nevertheless, the fact stands out that most of the known popular broadside ballad tunes of the seventeenth century bear no relation whatever to the melodies of the British *common repertory*. At present we do not know enough to attempt an interpretation of this fact. Are most of the tunes in our common repertory of more recent composition or development than the older dance and broadside airs? Or are they older than the latter, on the whole, and characteristic of a conservative country tradition that resisted the introduction of newer tunes from the town, the center of distribution for broadside verse? Answers to such questions, if they ever are attained, will have to await more exact organization of our knowledge of popular traditional music.

* * *

The foregoing remarks have been assembled in order to provide a background to detailed studies of individual tune-families, which I hope will follow. They have been designed to make as many "blanket" and generalizing statements as possible, and thus to avoid repeated long explanations in those projected studies. Also they have been set down as an attempt to outline—however crudely—a picture of a tradition that is certainly one of the most glorious artistic achievements of the peoples of British descent. The general theory of tune-family growth that I have advanced may or may not be vindicated in the minds of other students by the evidence I hope to bring forward. But whether it be right or wrong, my theory (or any other) can do nothing either to enhance or diminish the nobility of this folk musical tradition.

In closing, one more generalization may be set down. One thing in this essay cannot escape notice: namely, the remoteness of the ideas expressed here from the views of those who insist that all folk tunes must originally have been the compositions of trained musicians, and must at first have been current in cultivated circles before they "sank" to a lower social level and were adopted by the uneducated mass of the people.[61] Naturally, this is no place for a detailed discussion of such a view—which, for that matter, has never figured to any extent in the writings of students of Anglo-American folk music.[62] However, a few statements about the applicability of this theory may not be out of order here.

There exist published British folk tune items which are unmistakably recreated versions of song airs by known musicians of the past. One very typical example is the air in the *Journal of the Folk Song Society*, I, No. 2 (1900), p. 49, to "The Plains of Waterloo." This tune, though simplified and "squared off" to accommodate a characteristic broadside stanza of four lines of even length, is obviously made up out of the first two verse-lines and the last two chorus-lines of "Rule Britannia." However, the air is a *hapax legomenon*: nothing like it has appeared elsewhere in our published folk musical records. And this lone appearance is characteristic of almost all such pieces, which are, moreover, exceedingly rare.

A somewhat different, but equally representative, case is furnished by sets of a tune sung on both sides of the Atlantic to "Sovay, Sovay"—the ballad of the girl who manages to test her truelove's devotion by robbing him in man's disguise.[63] These sets appear to have developed in several different directions and, though apparently interrelated, they differ puzzlingly. However, some of them look as though they might be derived from the melody composed by Robert Jones for "My mistress sings no other song," and found in his *First Book of Airs* (1600).[64] If this be indeed the case, the folk derivatives have

[61] This view, or its practical equivalent, has recently been developed at length for folklore in general by Carlos Vega, *Panorama de la Musica Popular Argentina* (Buenos Aires: Editorial Losada, S.A., cop. 1944), pp. 19-108. Vega's theories are reminiscent of Hans Naumann's concept of *gesunkenes Kulturgut* and of similar notions dating back to Hoffman-Krayer and John Meier (Volkstümlichkeit).

[62] Cf., for folk traditions in general, W. R. Halliday, *Folklore Studies, Ancient and Modern* (London: Methuen & Co., Ltd., 1942), p. 146. Cf. also Rodney Gallop, *Portugal, A Book of Folk-Ways* (Cambridge: at the University Press, 1936), xiv; 198, 199, for pronouncements on folk-music in general, as well as on Portuguese popular airs. Statements such as the last cited show a complete misunderstanding of the so-called "distortion" (i.e., re-creation) of music by folk musicians; of its conventional, traditional, and essentially cultured and *artistic* nature; and above all, of its cumulative potentialities in moulding and forming the traditional music of a group.

[63] Characteristic versions may be seen in C. J. Sharp, *Folk Songs from Somerset*, 2d Series, pp. 10, 11; E. B. Greenleaf and G. Y. Mansfield, *Ballads and Sea Songs of Newfoundland* (Cambridge: Harvard University Press, 1933), pp. 61, 62.

[64] For this tune see the edition of Robert Jones' *First Book of Songes and Ayres*, 1600, by E. H. Fellowes (The English School of Lutenist Song Writers, 2d Series, No. 4; London: Stainer & Bell, Ltd., cop. 1925), pp. 36-39. With the Jones air compare especially the "Sovay" tunes in Greenleaf and Mansfield, *op. cit.*, p. 63; *JFSS*, 3, No. 2 (1907), pp. 127-128 (all three tunes); *JFSS*, 8, No. 4 (1930), p. 225, p. 227, second version; *Oxford History of Music*, Introductory Volume, ed. Percy C. Buck (Oxford University Press, 1929), p. 178.

not only changed in a striking manner, but they also appear to have been very much attracted to forms of the widespread air commonly sung to the ballad of "Young Beichan" (Child No. 53). In other words, we cannot tell whether the "Sovay" tunes are diversely re-created forms of Jones's air, of which some sets are partly assimilated to the common "Young Beichan" tune; or whether the dateless "Beichan" tune has had some of its versions influenced by traditional memories (or renditions) of the Jones air. In the long run, the two possibilities seem to amount to practically the same thing anyway. And the examples just cited illustrate perfectly, in my opinion, the character of the influence that art music has exerted on folk music in our British traditions. Apparently a vigorous folk music tradition can absorb and assimilate outside influences; but these influences do not necessarily arrest the development of the tradition.

I should certainly be the last to deny the influence of art music on our folk tunes. As Marius Barbeau has recently put it, "Folk culture is alive and grasping. It feeds on everything within reach, and often assimilates its material beyond recognition." [65] But I should like to point out that any theory that holds our folk tunes, *as organized, individual pieces of music*, to be merely borrowed court or theater tunes of the past, signally fails to solve one problem or answer one question of importance raised by our recorded melodic versions. Anyone who held such a theory, moreover, would find the burden of proof weighing heavily upon him. The fact is that thus far not a single well-known air of our *common* (i.e. dominating) repertory has ever been traced definitely to any known composition of a trained musical artist. [66]

In such a richly developed and artistically re-created fund of melodies as this tradition possesses, the original authorship of any single tune is—as I said above—not only unknown, but also utterly unimportant. Any folk that can develop the possibilities of a few basic airs as have the peoples of the British Isles can take care of itself in matters of musical culture. It is itself in possession of a musical culture at once cumulative and powerful. It does not have to wait for educated composers to produce simple melodies which it can borrow. It can produce, out of its own funds and resources, its own simple melodies, and can develop them with amazing complexity and variety. [67] And this, I think, is what the untrained and unknown artists among the British folk have done in the past. [68]

[65] *JAF*. 61 (1948). 210.

[66] What may be thought an exception to this rule is furnished by sets of the tune to which is generally sung "General Wolfe," or "The Taking of Quebec." See *JFSS*, 6, No. 1 (1918), 8-10 and accompanying notes; also *JFSS*, 8, No. 4 (1930), 179, 180. This air, however, may be called "thinly scattered" in tradition, and is not related to any of the dominant or widespread tune-families at all. Its versions are few, and its distribution apparently confined to England and Ireland (one recorded version, *v. JFSS*, 6, the notes

cited). What is more significant yet, the recorded versions differ among themselves in a curious way, indicating the progress of folk re-creation of the tune into a shape more congenial to traditional taste than the presumed original, cited *JFSS*, 6, p. 10. On the failure of investigators to find the originals of the great bulk of our folk airs in older art music, see Sabine Baring-Gould, *A Garland of Country-Song* (London, 1895), p. x; R. Vaughan Williams, *National Music* (London: Oxford University Press, 1934), p. 30.

[67] E.g., once more, the melodies of American Shakers and the other white religious groups that produced folk spirituals.

[68] Some words of Bartók are especially to the point here: "Die Dorfkunst kann nur eine spontane Offenbarung sein; sobald sich jemand hineinmischen und sie künstlich lenken will, hat für die Dorfkunst die letzte Stunde geschlagen. Eben deshalb wäre es eine vollkommen fruchtlose Angelegenheit, wie man das neuerdings immer wieder versucht, die Dorfmusik nach dieser oder jener Richtung entwickeln zu wollen, alte Melodien auf dem Dorfe neu zu beleben und ähnliches. Wenn das Volk des Dorfes nicht selbst von sich aus seine Kunst schafft oder sich wählt, ist es auch mit seiner Kunst dahin." *Die Volksmusik der Magyaren und der benachbarten Völker*, Ausdruck: Ungarische Jahrbücher, Bd. XV, Heft. 2, 3; Ungarische-Bibliothek, Reihe I, No. 20 (Berlin: Walter de Gruyter, 1935), p. 19.

HISTORY

CARTOGRAPHY AND ETHNOMUSICOLOGY*
Paul Collaer

Ethnomusicology is concerned primarily with music in the oral tradition and is thus concerned with a direct manifestation of a vital energy which does not come from the written score. Such music is due to intuition and is codified and reasoned out only in more complex phases of its development, as in the high cultures. It is impossible, then, to apply the old history-literary method based on chronology and the interpretation of written documents to the study of such traditional music; rather, the methods of experimental science, above all, those of the biological sciences, apply best to ethnomusicology. The problems which face this young branch of science can be divided into two parts—those of description, and those of comparison.

Where the study is confined to the description of music in a local area, the problem is reduced to using methods of collection and observation which are as objective and exact as possible. Ethnography, sociology, and experimental psychology are useful to the musicologist although his basic question is that of measurement—of vibration frequencies, intervals and durations. And measurement includes as its corollary, notation, for which a system remains to be invented which will faithfully reflect the reality of musical sound. Measurement of instruments, and, when all is said and done, analysis of structure are primary here.

Once the stage of collection and objective presentation of the music has been passed, the question arises of the comprehension of the music, its reason for being and its place in the general history of music, its significance for the general comprehension of the phenomenon of musical creation. The comparative method is here as indispensable as comparative anatomy is for the study of the evolution of animal and vegetable forms. Comparison throws light on the existence of specific types and on the distribution of types common to several countries or peoples; it underlines the importance of melodic structures, scales, rhythms and polyphonic concepts, of musical instruments which are identical or similar found in neighboring or diverse regions; it suggests that certain kinds of music give the impression of existing in symbiotic relationship with other characteristics of culture.

While one can hope to reach some sort of precision and objectivity in the descriptive stage thanks to electrical means of recording and analysis, the comparative stage leads us thus far almost inevitably to the hypothetical. But it is not sufficient to conclude a work simply by presenting a hypothesis;

*Translated by Alan P. Merriam

rather, the idea must be conceived as a working hypothesis to be submitted to the test of comparison with the results obtained in dealing with other cultural characteristics. Only the method of multiple verification can confirm or invalidate the hypothesis advanced, and the greater the number of tests with positive results, the greater the plausibility of the hypothesis. For example, a group X has a musical system in which the intervals are comparable only to those which characterize the music of group Y; on this basis alone it is not possible to assume that X and Y are directly related. But if group X uses specific fishing methods and implements which are identical only to those used by group Y, then we have a positive indication which reinforces the hypothesis of their relationship. Both statistics and cartography can be of great value here.

Statistics, which is indispensable in an area in which values are variable within fixed limits, is still too infrequently employed in ethnomusicology. But we wish to speak here only of cartography.

The importance of cartography for botanical and zoological studies is well known. The areas of distribution (*Verbreitungsareale*) of various animal and vegetable species compared among themselves or with isothermic or geologic maps furnish information which is of considerable importance among the ecological factors on which the existence of these species depends, and such comparison can show as well their zones of origin, relationship with other species, relative degree of antiquity, perhaps even their evolution. The greater the number of agreements among the various maps used, the greater becomes the probability of liaison and interactions among the facts that the maps represent. A plant, for example, cannot live above an altitude of 2,000 meters; is this limit imposed by the minimum winter temperature or by the excessive ultraviolet radiation? When maps showing the geographic distribution of the plant are compared with those tracing minimum temperature curves or representing the composition of solar light for the region under observation, some answers are possible.

The cartographic method can render considerable service to ethnomusicology if it is established in the necessary detail. One frequently sees sketches of such maps, but sketches are not enough, for great detail is vital, and it is only on this condition that cartography can help us go beyond the stage of hypotheses concerning the genesis, transmission and evolution of the first forms of music.

It would be of great interest, for example, to map the anhemitonic pentatonic scale with careful attention to its various modal aspects; at the same time, hemitonic pentatonic scales as well as the prepentatonic (tri, and tetra types) should be mapped. Such work could obviously only follow an exchange of views among the specialists in the genesis of musical scales which would serve to fix the characteristics used—pure pentatonism, "pyen" pentatonism, the coexistence of pentatonism and pre-pentatonism, of pentatonism and heptatonism, etc. Such a map, compared with the areas of distribution of other culture elements (hunting-gathering, pastoralists, agriculturalists, nomadic or sedentary people, etc.) should furnish evidence on which we can base proba-bilities or even certainties rather than mere vague or hypothetical conclusions.

Let us take another example—that of polyphony. Where is it found (and the maps must be on a large enough scale to permit detailed localization)? What is the geographic distribution of each type of polyphony (simple, double, fixed, oscillating bourdon; parallel fourths, fifths, or other intervals; contrary motion; of two, three or more voices, etc.)? Here again, cartography would disclose the most archaic types, those which are universal, those which are due to cultural differences, etc. And it is also possible to see how a detailed map of musical instruments or of specific melodic types, considered always against ethnographic and other maps, could give valuable clues to fix-ing points of origin, as well as to the presence or absence of various outside influences or possibly migrations.

The realization and publication of a work such as that envisaged here cannot be achieved by a single individual or even by a single local or regional organization; if anything good is to come of it, all interested musicologists must agree to the project and give freely of their advice and suggestions. It is in dealing with these various problems that we have proposed the problem of cartography as the principle theme of the Third Colloquium at Wégimont (Liège) of European ethnomusicologists in September 1958. All suggestions received from our extra-European colleagues will not only be received with gratitude but will be conceived as the first step in the labor we propose, as the first gesture in a great collaboration and as the beginning of a common work which we feel to be indispensable to the progress of ethnomusicology.

PLAINS GHOST DANCE AND GREAT BASIN MUSIC
George Herzog

An inquiry into the relation and stability of musical form and function finds in the Ghost Dance songs of the Plains Indians an excellent example for study. In them we have music associated with a movement definitely known to have arisen in a different setting, with the Paiute of the Great Basin. Examination of the musical material brings forth specific answers to some of the basic questions which prompt such an inquiry.

Practically all songs found associated with the Plains Ghost Dance are so closely related to each other that they must be conceived as representing a distinct type, forming an integrated "style" of their own. This style is foreign to the Plains; its patterns are different from those prevalent in Plains music. The style can be traced to the Great Basin: musical evidence reflects the diffusion of the Ghost Dance from that region to and through the Plains. In the Basin the style is not restricted to Ghost Dance songs; it is represented in other song categories so generously that its pattern may be regarded as the strongest and most characteristic element of some Great Basin musical styles. While this pattern penetrated into Plains music as the "Ghost Dance style," it has also found a place in the music of other tribes, unaffected by the Ghost Dance; there naturally it is not associated with the same function.

In this paper the foundation for these statements is offered as briefly and as much freed from technical detail as possible. The presentation of the full evidence with more abundant musical illustration and complete analysis would overstep the limits of this article and must be left to another occasion.

Comparison of all the Plains Ghost Dance melodies available to me (altogether thirty-eight) revealed in most of them a striking similarity amounting to a uniformity of style. The melodic range is usually narrow, essentially a fifth. As a rule there is no accompaniment.[1] Many of the phrases end on the tonic. They fall into sections so symmetrical as to be startling in primitive material. This symmetry is achieved by the most essential feature of the style, a simple structural device: *every* phrase is rendered twice. The emphasis on "every" is important, since doubling one or two phrases is a fairly commonplace feature of many styles, in Indian and other music. Repetition, in one guise or another, is one of the most significant principles of primitive musical form. But this particular repetitive device is quite unusual, and is unique in Plains music. At the same time, just because it is so simple

---

[1] See James Mooney, The Ghost-Dance Religion and the Sioux Outbreak of 1890 (Fourteenth Annual Report, Bureau of American Ethnology, Pt. 2, 1896), p. 921.

and unequivocal, it constitutes a trait which can be traced and treated with ease. Its various forms will be referred to as "paired patterns." Or, since the melody often progresses through phrases of changing melodic content, each rendered twice, the expression "paired progression" will be applied.

Ghost Dance songs are not easy to record. They are either forgotten or are still cherished with especial reverence. Many collectors made no particular effort to get them.[2] The short description above is based chiefly on second hand material. Many of the melodies in the literature were not taken on the phonograph, but merely transcribed by ear. While such material must always be treated with caution, it is reliable enough for present purposes. The salient trait, paired pattern, is so simple that it could not easily be lost through imperfections of notation. However, faulty transcription would be more likely to obscure its presence than to suggest it where it was absent. It was possible to make a check on part of Mooney's melodies, as some of them were recorded on the phonograph.[3] Comparison of No. 1 of the music examples with his Arapaho song No. 67 shows that while the transcriptions in his volume are not in all respects satisfactory, they represent structure with sufficient accuracy. The first version is the transcription made by me of a record in the Bureau of American Ethnology, taken during or perhaps after Mooney's study. The songs in Natalie Curtis' collection,[4] on the other hand, are to be trusted implicitly, so excellent is the workmanship of the volume.

The analysis is condensed below into tabular form. Those traits were selected for the table in which the style contrasts significantly with its setting—Plains music—and which can be treated without cumbersome musical detail. They have been chosen to satisfy not only the requirements of convenience, but also those of fair representation. Such a selection can in no case be avoided in describing a musical style, and the terms in which one style may best be discussed do not necessarily apply to another style. In the present case some features like manner of singing, to which the nature of the material does not give clear clues, have had to be left out of consideration.

The number under "range" gives the interval within which the song is confined, 5 standing for the fifth, etc. The letters under "Structure" stand for phrases or still smaller units, one letter for each. Recurrent letters indicate the recurrence of phrases. If two phrases are almost, but not absolutely, identical they are marked with the same letter but with different index numerals. Purely formal elements of meager melodic or rhythmic content are denoted by x: introductory, connective, or final phrases ("codas"). If the song splits into two sections, a break between the letters indicates the division.

[2] For example, in the collection of phonograph records in the American Museum of Natual History in New York, which contains over four hundred records of Plains music, there seems to be only one Plains Ghost Dance song; No. 8 among the music examples appended to this paper.

[3] See Mooney, p. 655.

[4] The Indian's Book (New York and London, 2nd ed., 1923).

"Phrase" is a unit not easily defined, just as "phrase" or "sentence" are troublesome units in linguistics. The musical phrase does not invariably coincide with a text phrase. Its limits can be established by various means, taking into consideration text, rests, accentuation, divisions of the melodic or rhythmic movement, etc. The musician distinguishes between the longer unit of a phrase and the shorter unit of a motif, but this distinction is not germane to our material. In many Ghost Dance songs the structural element rendered twice may be quite long or quite short; in fact, the unit of structure may best be defined in this style as that element which is rendered twice, irrespective of its length. This in turn strengthens the contention that the essential earmark of the style is the tendency to double. While to most investigators the presence of phrase units in primitive music is no news, some do not mark them in notation, or do not consider their relation to each other in analyzing structure. Consequently much material, especially collections of Plains music, had to be reanalyzed in order to determine the structural types and their distribution.

Under "finals" are indicated the tones which stand at the end of each phrase. Tabulation of such tones as a means of throwing light on the tonal structure of melodies has long been used in the study of European folk song.[5] With certain reservations, it can be used also with primitive songs, in addition to other methods. The tones are indicated by numbers: roman numerals stand for tones below the tonic, arabic numerals for tones above it. The tonic being taken as 1, a second above it is 2, a second below it is VII, etc. The intervals ought to be further specified with sharps and flats, but for the present purposes the procedure may be simplified by dispensing with these signs. Even a much more elaborate table would be a rather rough representation of musical forms. The inadequacies of the present table, the discussion of which would again lead too far afield, do not, however, bolster up the evidence; if anything, they diminish it.

Song	Range	Structure	Finals
Arapaho			
M. p. 990,[6] No. 45	5	aabb	1,1,1,1
C. p. 208[7]	6	aabb	1,1,1,1
M. p. 965	5	aabbcc	1,1,1,1,1,1
M. p. 977	5	aabbcc	1,1,1,1,1,1
M. p. 990, No. 44	5	aabbcc	1,1,1,1,1,1
M. p. 996	5	aabbcc	1,1,1,1,1,1
M. p. 1011	6	aabbcc	1,1,1,1,1,1

[5] See Ilmari Krohn, Welche ist die beste Methode, um Volks- und volksmässige Lieder nach ihrer melodischen (nicht textlichen) Beschaffenheit lexikalisch zu ordnen? (Sammelbände der Internationalen Musikgesellschaft, Vol. 4, No. 4, pp. 643-60, 1903, and Béla Bartók, Hungarian Folk Music (Oxford, 1931), pp. 6-8.

[6] Reference to the page in Mooney on which the song is found.

[7] Page-reference to Curtis' collection.

Song	Range	Structure	Finals
M. p. 1006	6	aabbccdd	5,5,1,1,1,1,1,1
(cf. music example 1)			
M. p. 958	6	aab^{1}b^{1}b^{2}b^{2}b^{3}b^3	VII,VII,1,1,1,1,1,1
F. p. 98–99[8]	5	aabb ccbb	3,3,1,1 3,3,1,1
S.[9]	8	aabbcd	4,4,4,4,2,1
(C. p. 209–10[10]	8	a^{1}a^{1}bcdef ga^{2}cdef	4,4,6,1,3,3,1 4,4,1,3,3,1)
Pawnee			
C. p. 143	8	aabb	1,1,1,1
D. 50[11]	7	aabb	4,4,1,1
D. 52	7	aabb	4,4,1,1
C. p. 140	5	a^{1}a^{2}bb	2,2,1,1
(music example 2)			
D. 55	5	aabbcc	3,3,1,1,1,1
D. 58	5	aabbcc	4,4,1,1,1,1
D. 54	5	aabbcc	3,3,3,3,1,1
C. p. 139	8	aabbcc	1,1,III,III,1,1
D. 51	5	a^{1}a^{2}bbcc	3,3,1,1,1,1
D. 56	6	a^{1}a^{2}bbcc	5,5,1,1,1,1
D. 57[12]	5	a^{1}a^{2}bbcc a^{1}a^{2}ddee	3,3,1,1,1,1 3,3,1,1,1,1
C. p. 141–42	5	a^{1}a^{2}b^{1}b^{1}c^{1}c^1 b^{2}b^{2}c^{2}c^2	4,4,1,1,1,1 1,1,1,1
D. 53[13]	5	a^{1}a^{2}x a^{3}a^{2}x	1,1,1 1,1,1
Caddo			
M. p. 1100	6	aabbcc	2,2,1,1,1,1
M. p. 1096	6	aab^{1}b^{1}b^{2}b^{2}b^{3}b^3	1,1,1,1,1,1,1,1
M. p. 1101–02	6	aabbcc d^{1}d^{2}eee	3,3,1,1,1,1 1,1,1,1,1
Kiowa			
M. p. 1088	5	aabbcc	4,4,1,1,1,1
M. p. 1086	7	aabbc^{1}c^{1}ddc^{2}c^2	3,3,3,3,3,3,1,1,1,1
Comanche			
M. p. 1046	12	(x)xaabbcc	(8,)8,7,7,4,4,1,1
Teton Dakota			
C. p. 67	5	aabb	1,1,1,1
C. p. 66	5	a^{1}a^{2}bbccdd	2,2,1,1,2,2,1,1
(music example 3)			
C. p. 63–65	5	a^{1}a^{2}bccd^{1}d^2	3,4,1,1,1,1,1

---

[8] Alice C. Fletcher, Indian Story and Song from North America (Boston, 1907).

[9] A song in The Southern Workman, Vol. 36, p. 111, reproduced there without any comment, taken down probably from the singing of a Hampton student, by N. Curtis. I am obliged to Dr. A. H. Gayton for this reference.

[10] This is a Crow Dance song; cf. Curtis, p. 201.

[11] References to song numbers in Frances Densmore, Pawnee Music (Bulletin, Bureau of American Ethnology 93, 1929), pp. 78-86.

[12] The song ends, in the last rendition, without the last two (e) phrases.

[13] This melody, together with Nos. 54-56, was sung to dancing incidental in pauses of the hand game.

Song	Range	Structure	Finals
Mo. p. 168–70[14]	5	abccdd	4,1,3,3,1,1
Mo. p. 168–70	7	abcdee	5,3,2,1,1,1
C.[15]	10	$a^1bcc\ a^1bcc\ a^2de\ a^2de$	8,5,4,4 8,5,4,4 8,5,1 8,5,1
Yanktonai Dakota			
H.PR 93[16]	8	abcddee	5,3,1,3,3,1,1
(music example 8)			

The frequent occurrence of paired patterns can be seen at a glance. Simple forms with gradually changing content ("paired progression") are:

aabb	(6 examples)
aabbcc	(11)
aabbccdd	(1)
$aab^1b^1b^2b^2b^3b^3$	(2)

In closely related forms one of the phrases is modified upon its second appearance:

a^1a^2bb	(1)
a^1a^2bbcc	(2)

One song begins with an introductory phrase of slight melodic importance:[17]

(x)xaabbcc	(1)

Once the progression breaks toward its close and reverts to a previous phrase:

$aabbc^1c^1ddc^2c^2$	(1)

In a few cases the song splits into two sections or "verses" which stand in a definite relation to each other. The second section may substitute new phrases for some of the first:

aabb ccbb	(1)
$a^1a^2bbcc\ a^1a^2ddee$	(1)

Or the second section may reproduce the first in a somewhat shortened form, at the same time either modifying phrases or substituting new phrases for old ones:

$a^1a^2b^1b^1cc\ b^2b^2c^2c^2$	(1)
$aabbcc\ d^1d^2eee$	(1)

[14] Warren K. Moorehead, The Sioux Messiah (Archaeologist, Vol. 2, No. 5, pp. 146-49; No. 6:168-70, 1894).

[15] Pp. 141-42 of L. W. Colby, Wanagi olowan kin. The Ghost Songs of the Dakotas (Proceedings and Collections, Nebraska State Historical Society, 2nd ser., Vol. 1, pp. 131-50, 1894-95).

[16] Phonograph record 93 of my collection of Yanktonai Dakota songs in the American Museum of Natural History.

[17] This is the Comanche song, Mooney, p. 1046. On the phonograph record of this song the introduction is repeated in one of the three renditions.

In the great majority of our cases (thirty out of thirty-eight) the paired pattern is clear and practically unbroken. (The third repetition of the last phrase in the Caddo song M. pp. 1101-2 is a rather minor modification.) Of the eight songs that do not conform to the pattern, six have at least a partial doubling of phrases (Pawnee D.53, Arapaho S., Teton C. pp. 63-65, Mo. pp. 168-70, Mo. pp. 168-70, and Yanktonai H. PR 93). Moreover, one of them is a variant of a Teton song which is regular: the text of the Yanktonai song is identical with that of the Teton song C., p. 66, and the melody is similar. (Compare No. 8 of the music examples with No. 3.) The text of Moorehead's first Teton song is almost identical with these two, but the melody is quite different. It is justifiable to assume that the Yanktonai melody is a hybrid form. Of the two remaining examples, the Arapaho song C. pp. 209-10 is not a Ghost Dance song proper but a melody from the "Crow Dance," associated with the Ghost Dance.[18] While its scheme in the table suggests no trace of paired patterning, the structure could be re-analyzed without doing it grave injustice, as $a^1a^1a^2b^1b^2cx \; xa^3 b^1 b^2cx$, which shows a more intimate interrelation between the units. Colby's Teton song, finally, shows little of the tendency for doubling, although at least the two verses are repeated. This exception to the musical pattern may be due to the poetic form: the text represents a dialogue between the "Great Spirit" and the Ghost dancer, alternately singing two phrases each.[19]

Narrow range and the cumulative use of the tonic for phrase-endings (numeral one) are also fairly frequent in the table. There is a relation, although somewhat tenuous, between these two traits; a relation naturally conditioned also by the number of tones within the range. The gradually descending melodies do not have much freedom of movement when con-fined to a narrow space, nor much choice where to repose on the way. But to stop consistently on the same level is not obligatory for them and so the two traits may be considered independent, or only indirectly interrelated.

In a respectable majority of songs (twenty-six) the paired pattern is at the same time "paired progression." The structural principles which in the others supersede or obscure this pattern, or are superimposed upon it, are very strong in the music of the Plains.

Plains songs in general exhibit features different from those of Ghost Dance songs. My analysis of material published so far indicates that the most frequent patterns on the Plains are based on a few simple principles such as:

a) Progression through single phrases, as *ab, abc, abcd,* etc.

b) Modified repetition of a section or verse. The two sections then make up the song, which is usually repeated a number of times. The modification may consist of altering one or two phrases of the first section, $a^1 bc \; a^2 bc$

---

[18] This is a modification of the "Omaha Dance" according to Mooney (pp. 901, 921-22) and not an entirely new growth, which may well expalin the "irregularity" of this song.

[19] See Colby, *op. cit.,* pp. 141-42.

and the like, or of substituting an altogether new phrase: *abc dbc*, etc.

c) Curtailment of a section by leaving out one or two phrases, very often initially: *abc bc*, etc.

d) Reversion to a previous phrase: *aba, abca, abcb*, etc.

e) In a special type the song or its sections are closed by one or two phrases which have occurred already, but which are now rendered an octave below. Common forms could be noted as aba_8, $abca_8$, $aba_8 a_8 b_8$, etc.

It should be kept in mind that in many songs more than one of these principles apply. A structure like $abc\ a_8 b_8$, for instance, at the same time implies "progression," "modified repetition," and "curtailment," in this case at the end. Thus the frequency of these primary types can seldom be precisely determined by simple counting. For present purposes, however, it seemed more fruitful to indicate the general prevalence of these types, rather than to give a more meticulous but overcomplicated count, even though the simpler method understates the case. In the following tabulation of most of the larger collections of Plains music only the simple forms of the types described have been counted and each song is indicated only once, except for the last column. The tabulation ought not to be taken, then, to express much more than the general prevalence of these types on the Plains. Since it is only a general approximation, it would be injudicious to transform these figures into percentages. The heavy proportion of the aba_8 type in Omaha and Pawnee material is significant, however.

	Total	Progressive	Initial curtailment	aba_8, etc.
Mandan and Hidatsa[20]	111	51	15	13
Teton[21]	240	40	62	32
Pawnee[22]	102	12	25	34
Omaha[23]	187	49	30	50

These patterns are not limited to the Plains. Among some tribes of the Northeast, like the Chippewa and the Menominee (whose music must be classed on the whole with Plains music), they are quite as frequent:

Menominee[24]	140	38	8	36

[20] Frances Densmore, Mandan and Hidatsa Music (Bulletin, Bureau of American Ethnology, 80, 1923).

[21] *Idem*, Teton-Sioux Music (Bulletin, Bureau of American Ethnology, 61, 1918).

[22] *Idem,* Pawnee Music, and N. Curtis, *op. cit.*, pp. 117-43. The 94 melodies of the Hako (Twenty-second Annual Report, Bureau of American Ethnology, pt. 2, 1904) are omitted here to avoid heavy weighting by so many songs from a single ritual.

[23] A. C. Fletcher, A Study of Omaha Indian Music (Archaeological and Ethnological Papers of the Peabody Museum, Harvard University, Vol. 1, No. 5, 1893) and A. C. Fletcher and F. LaFlesche, The Omaha Tribe (Twenty-seventh Annual Report, Bureau of American Ethnology, 1911).

[24] F. Densmore, Menominee Music (Bulletin, Bureau of American Ethnology, 102, 1932).

In the music of other regions in North America these patterns also occur, but except for the very simple and fairly general progressive pattern, they are no longer representative. As random examples:

Creek[25]	119	23	3	—
Pueblo[26]	157	13	4	2

The foregoing indicates that the prevailing structural patterns on the Plains are different from that of the Ghost Dance. As for range and phrase-endings, it may be said that the average Plains song has a range of an octave and above, and that the successive finals tend to form a series descending to the tonic, rather than each one striking it.

The question then arises, to what extent are paired patterns found on the Plains at all, outside of Ghost Dance songs proper, and to what extent do they occur in other regions of North America, as far as extant material can show? I have traced these patterns in North American Indian music, analyzing all the larger and many smaller collections of melodies published so far, as well as much unpublished material recorded by myself. The following table gives result for the Plains:

	Total	*Paired*	*Related or modified*	*Doubtful*
Mandan and Hidatsa[27]	111	—	1	3
Teton[28]	240	—	4	3
Pawnee[29]	90	6	4	1
Omaha[30]	187	1	1	1
Osage[31]	283	1	2	1

The six clear Pawnee cases (and one under "related") are hand game melodies, out of eleven such melodies recorded. Most of them were apparently sung to the game itself, while some of the Ghost Dance songs were sung in the intervals of the game for dancing. The paired pattern as such is not common in songs of hiding games on the Plains, except in a delimited

[25] Frank G. Speck, Ceremonial Songs of the Creek and Yuchi Indians (University of Pennsylvania Museum Anthropological Publications, Vol. 1, No. 2, 1911).

[26] Melodies of a collection recorded by me, as yet unpublished.

[27] The melodies are: Densmore Nos. 36; 34, 41, 73.

[28] Densmore Nos. 45, 145, 198, 211; 9, 102, 160. No. 45, interestingly enough, is a song received in a vision which made the visionary proof against arrows and bullets (see Densmore, Teton Sioux Music, pp. 175-76).

[29] F. Densmore, *op. cit.*, and N. Curtis, exclusive of the Ghost Dance songs, Densmore No. 44 is related and 19, 20, 63 may be considered so; No. 69 is a doubtful case. Of ninety-four melodies of the Hako, one has a regular paired pattern (p. 212) and four may be considered related.

[30] Omaha Indian Music, No. 27; The Omaha Tribe, pp. 239, 257.

[31] From the studies of Osage Rituals by F. LaFlesche, in the Thirty-sixth, Thirty-ninth and Fofty-fifth Annual Reports, Bureau of American Ethnology. The respective melodies are in the Thirty-ninth Annual Report, pp. 102; 231, 233; 315.

region in the south.[32] All the hand games known to me from tribes of this region are incorporated in the following table:

Song	Range	Structure	Finals
Pawnee			
D. 39	3	aabb	1,1,1,1
D. 48	8	aabb	5,5,1,1
D. 45	6	a^1a^2bb	1,1,1,1
(music example 4)			
D. 42	4	aabbcc	1,1,1,1,1,1
D. 47	8	aabbcc	V,V,V,V,1,1
D. 40	5	aabbcc bbcc	5,5,1,1,1,1 1,1,1,1
D. 44	6	aabcc	4,4,3,1,1
D. 43	8	abc	2,1,1
D. 46	8	abcd	1,1,V,1
D. 41	7	abcd cdd	5,4,1,2 1,1,1
Arapaho			
C. p. 213-14	6	aabbcc aabb	3,3,1,1,V,V 3,3,1,1
Cheyenne			
C. p. 183	8	aabbcc	4,4,1,1,1,1
C. p. 184	9	aabbaa	1,1,5,5,1,1
C. p. 182	11	aabbc	8,8,4,4,1
C. p. 186[33]	12	aabccx	8,8,4,1,1,1
C. p. 185	8	$a\,{}^{b}_{2}\,bb$	5,1,1,1
C. p. 187	8	aabcdx bbcd	3,3,1,1,1,1 1,1,1,1

In the light of the connection between the dance and the game among the Pawnees, recently illuminated in great detail by Dr. Lesser,[34] the presence of the Ghost Dance pattern in hand game songs of the Pawnee and their neighbors is not surprising. According to him, there are special songs sung before the game proper begins, songs sung in the intervals between the games, and songs sung to the actual playing of the game (Lesser, p. 134). Both old hand game songs and Ghost Dance game songs are used in the modified forms of the hand game (Lesser, pp. 210, 235, 310). Furthermore, "Many of the play songs used at the Ghost Dance hand game ceremonies for the play of the game are songs of a revival nature learned in Ghost Dance visions" (Lesser, p. 321). Dr. Lesser adds, in a letter, "The Pawnee say that the first songs used for Ghost dancing, both in ceremonies

[32] Among the eighteen songs indicated in the previous table (exclusive of the Pawnee), two are hiding game songs; one from the Teton out of nine Teton hand game songs recorded, and one from the Omaha out of four that were recorded.

[33] The phrases marked c are actually a_8 phrases.

[34] Alexander Lesser, The Pawnee Ghost Dance Hand Game (Columbia University Contributions to Anthropology, Vol. 16, 1933). See also Lesser, Cultural Significance of the Ghost Dance (American Anthropologist, Vol. 35, pp. 108-15, 1933).

and in hand games, were borrowed, and that then they made up songs themselves." The material referred to in the table is too slight to warrant tracing these distinctions. It is sufficient to note that at least two thirds of these songs classed in the literature as "hand game songs" are unmistakably in the Ghost Dance pattern. Some of them may be new forms, others remodeled old hand game songs.

An analysis of representative collections from other regions in North America gave the following results:

	Total	Paired	Related or modified	Doubtful
Creek[35]	110	3	4	3
Pueblo	157	4	6	—
Papagǒ[36]	169	5	9	—
Navaho "War Dance"[37]	40	14	4	7
Northern Ute[38]	114	9	6	4
Northern Ute Bear Dance[39]	17	8	3	—

The number of paired forms is negligible (perhaps excepting the Papago) until we come to the Navaho and the Northern Ute. In a great mass of Navaho ritualistic music now being analyzed by me, practically no paired patterns as such have been found so far. However, in dancing songs, mostly exoteric, associated with the Enemy Chant or "War Dance," the pattern is apparently quite common. The Northern Ute data probably have some bearing on this frequency. Of the nine clear cut Ute examples given above, eight belong to the Bear Dance; of the seventeen songs recorded from this dance altogether, only six are clearly not to be referred to this pattern at all. The analysis of the Bear Dance songs follows:

Song	Range	Structure	Finals
D. 2	4	aabb	1,1,1,1
D. 13	8	aabb	1,1,1,1
D. 17	6	aabb	1,1,1,1
D. 1	6	aab^{1}b^2	VII, VII, 1,1
(music example 6)			
D. 6	5	aabb(x)	1,1,1,1
D. 7[40]	6	aab^{1}b^{2}x	1,1,1,1,1

[35] Speck Nos. 16B, 19B, Medicine song 2; 10H, 18B, 18C, 20B; 12A, Medicine song 7, 17A.

[36] F. Densmore, Papago Music (Bulletin, Bureau of American Ethnology, 90, 1929), Nos. 21, 24, 26, 34, 126; 8, 12, 19, 27, 29, 47, 127, 128, 129.

[37] From unpublished material recorded by me.

[38] F. Densmore, Northern Ute Music (Bulletin, Bureau of American Ethnology, 75, 1922).

[39] Densmore, op. cit. pp. 58-72.

[40] The x phrase is a connective, omitted the last time.

Song	*Range*	*Structure*	*Finals*
D. 16[41]	6	$a^1a^2bb\,a^1a^1bb$	1,1,1,1 1,1,1,1
		$a^1a^1bb\,abb$	1,1,1,1 1,1,1
D. 9	8	$aabbc^1c^2$	VI, VI, 1,1,1,1
D. 3	11	$a^1a^2bbc^1c^1c^2dd$	1,1,1,1,1,1,1,1,1
D. 8	8	$aabbc$	1,1,1,1,1
D. 14	9	$(x)aabx$	(9),1,1,1,1
D. 15	8	abb	1,1,1
D. 10	9	xab^1b^2	7,1,1,1
D. 12	9	$abcd^1d^2$	1,VI,V,1,1
D. 5	8	$abc^1\ dc^2$	5,4,1 5,1
D. 11	9	$ab^1c\ b^2b^3d$	1,V,IV 1,1,1
D. 4[42]	9	$abcdcdefghh$	8,1,3,1,3,1,2,1,1,1,1

The comparative frequency of paired patterns in Northern Ute music, in the Bear Dance, supports the information that features of Ute dancing have been incorporated into the Navaho "War Dance."[43] With regard to narrow range and the frequency of phrase-endings on the tonic it should be kept in mind, however, that a scattering of these traits is found in the Northern Ute style as a whole.

Paired patterns are also not exceptional in the music of some of the Yuman tribes:

	Total	*Paired*	*Related or modified*	*Doubtful*
Yuma[44]	82	5	10	6
Southern Diegueño[45]	27	4	–	2
(Mohave[46]	29	–	1	2)
(Cocopa[47]	30	–	–	1)

Among these groups, a number of songs showed a paired pattern in company with the "rise" characteristic for the Yumans (modification or imitation of the fundamental musical phrase on a higher level somewhere in the body of the song[48]); indicating the interpenetration of two distinct syles or at least, stylistic principles.

[41] The paired units are exceedingly small. The melody is repeated, beginning with the ninth unit.

[42] The melody is repeated, beginning with the phrase *c*.

[43] I am indebted to Dr. W. W. Hill for this information.

[44] F. Densmore, Yuman and Yaqui Music (Bulletin, Bureau of American Ethnology, 110, 1932), see especially Nos. 7, 11, 12, 13, and 20.

[45] From my collection, partly published in The Yuman Musical Style (Journal of American Folk-Lore, Vol. 41, pp. 183-232, 1928). See especially Nos. 24, 26, and 33 in that article.

[46] Four melodies in Densmore, *op. cit.*; the rest in my collection, partly published in The Yuman Musical Style.

[47] Densmore, *op. cit.*, pp. 85-98, 168-82, 185-92.

[48] See The Yuman Musical Style, pp. 193, 196.

Published material from other parts of California is at the present time too scanty for our purposes.

Finally, from the Northern Paiute only the few music examples in Steward's study of the Owens Valley Paiute are available at present.[49] The paired pattern is in evidence, but presumably in a larger collection the proportion would be larger. Of eighteen melodies, one is plainly in this style (No. 12); in two others both paired pattern and Yuman "rise" occur (Nos. 4, 13). The rest are about equally divided between Yuman and other forms. In a larger collection of Southern Paiute songs which I had occasion to analyze, of about 200 melodies some seventy have clearly paired patterns (mostly paired progression), partly with slight modifications, besides a number of possible related cases.[50] Aside from an approximately equal number of songs conforming to Yuman types, introduced with mourning songs to the Southern Paiute, about fifty remain that do not have paired patterning in one form or another. As it is planned to publish this material after its study has been completed, the distribution of the different types within the various song categories will not be discussed here. It may be added that comparatively narrow range and clustering of the phrase finals on the tonic are not uncommon in Southern Paiute songs. It is safe to infer that when a sufficiently large Northern Paiute collection is studied, it also will show this preponderance of "Ghost Dance patterns."

Even the relatively small body of material on which this study of Plains Ghost Dance music is based, demonstrates beyond doubt that it has preserved a surprising degree of stylistic unity while spreading on the Plains. In structure, comparatively narrow range, and some other features, the melodies are essentially in the style of the Paiute groups. That these patterns are of old standing in the Basin is suggested also by their presence in Yuman and Nothern Ute music: both of these groups participated little if at all in the Ghost Dance of 1890.

Observations on the text of the songs, the dance movements, and the instrumental accompaniment, if any, are at present insufficient. It is nevertheless clear that the pattern prevalent in Ghost Dance melodies is predominant also in the song text: of 137 texts given without melodies in Mooney's study, 122 have consistently paired text patterns, every line being repeated. This supports musical evidence and, indirectly, strengthens it. But text and melody are not always parallel; there are examples in which the same line is sung to two different musical phrases, and vice versa.

Ghost Dance songs form a style of their own, embedded within the various local styles of the Plains. That is, Plains music did not strongly

---

[49] Julian H. Steward, Ethnography of the Owens Valley Paiute (University of California Publications in American Archaeology and Ethnology, Vol. 33, No. 3, 1933), pp. 279-85.

[50] This collection is at present in manuscript form, containing transcriptions made by J. Sapir of phonograph records taken by Dr. E. Sapir. For the perusal of this manuscript I am indebted to Dr. Sapir; also for the permission to publish a melody from it.

affect the Paiute musical patterns offered to it in the form of Ghost Dance songs. We have, to be sure, pointed to the occasional merging of Plains patterns with Ghost Dance patterns, which at times make it difficult to say whether a Plains melody became remodeled in conformity with paired patterns, or vice versa. That this process did not progress further may be due in part to the exceedingly quick spread of the Ghost Dance movement and to its brief life in many places. Yet where, as in the case of the Pawnee hand game songs, its life was extended, the style continued to cling to its early form. That it was accepted on the Plains without soon suffering modifications may be explained partly by the analogy between the principle of simple progression in Plains music and the principle of paired progression in the Ghost Dance songs. The modifications of the Ghost Dance patterns on the Plains will be better treated when the Southern Paiute material can be presented as a background. More significant perhaps are the effects on the local music of the patterns introduced into the Plains. In a few tribes, including the Pawnee, hand game music became permeated with the new pattern. This bears out Dr. Lesser's suggestion that the Ghost Dance represented a revivifying and reintegrating force in Pawnee life.[51] If the Pawnee revival of the old rituals and societies in the spirit of the Ghost Dance[52] had progressed further than it did, the new style might have penetrated into Pawnee music beyond the hand game songs. Indeed, there is clear evidence in the form of certain hybrid melodies that such a process was already under way. Appropriately enough, these melodies occur in the Bear Dance, itself, according to Lesser, a Ghost Dance revival in recent years.[53] Musical evidence also strengthens the possibility that the Cheyenne as well have incorporated the hand game into their Ghost Dance, and as a result came to have a modified form of the hand game.[54] We know, further, that the Pawnee Ghost Dance is intimately bound up with the Arapaho Ghost Dance, the Pawnee being the receivers. This tallies well with the tables: the salient features of the style are most frequent among the Arapaho examples, with the Pawnee next, and then the Dakota. Taken in the same order, the correlation of the three features selected also becomes less marked.

It has been shown, in the field of European folk music, that single melodies can be diffused with great ease.[55] The music of the Plains Ghost Dance represents a case in which what may be called a tribal or regional style became diffused, as the style of a special ceremonial complex, with

[51] The Pawnee Ghost Dance Hand Game, pp. 106, 116, 117.

[52] Lesser, pp. 106-15.

[53] Lesser, Cultural Significance of the Ghost Dance (American Anthropologist, Vol. 35, pp. 108-15, 1933), pp. 113-14, fn. 6.

[54] Lesser, pp. 322, 323.

[55] W. Tappert, Wandernde Melodien (Berlin, 1890). See also Erich M. von Hornbostel, Notizen über kirgisische Musikinstrumente und Melodien (in R. Karutz, Unter Kirgisen und Turkmenen, Leipzig, 1911), p. 214.

continuous distribution, through processes which we know from historical evidence to have been exclusively those of culture contact. While this illustrates the great persistence with which music can adhere to a ceremonial or other complex, it also indicates that similarities of style between two disconnected regions would not necessarily imply that some elements of the population itself were to be considered related. Nor would they necessarily prove long and very intimate culture contacts.[56]

The Ghost Dance songs may also have a bearing on the question whether, and in how far, formal features of a musical style can be explained or derived from their function in social life. The present finding is obviously negative. Through processes of diffusion a local style has become the style of a ceremonial complex in another region. In a third region, among the Yumans, features of the style are found scattered in various types of songs, apparently not restricted to any song group with a specific function. On the other hand, among the Northern Ute the style is concentrated in songs of the Bear Dance, a ceremonial that even by a generous stretch of imagination has little to do with the Ghost Dance—unless one insisted on the common idea of renewal. A more plausible connection might be seen in the styles of dancing which may prove to be related. Features of the style apparently spread from the Ute to the Navaho, who incorporated it, probably together with features of the Ute dancing, into the curing ritual of the Enemy Chant; mainly into the exoteric parts. These parts of the Enemy Chant form a pool into which individual compositions also may be deposited with considerable freedom, whereas most Navaho music is ritualistic and is not freely augmented, either by composition or importation.

It should not be asserted that such varied functions associated with the same style, or with the same stylistic features, can never have a more profound remodeling effect on the style itself. But the example under discussion suggests that musical form can weather amazingly well the vicissitudes to which it is exposed, although if it comes from a fundamentally different cultural setting, or from a bygone age, it may receive in the new setting a new life and meaning.

---

[56] I have suggested other examples for the diffusion of musical features in Special Song Types in North American Indian Music (Zeitschrift für Vergleichende Musikwissenschaft, Vol. 3, pp. 22-33, music pp. 1-6, 1935).

1. ARAPAHO GHOST DANCE SONG*
(PR Bureau of American Ethnology; cf. Mooney, p. 1006)

2. PAWNEE GHOST DANCE SONG
(N. Curtis, p. 140)

3. TETON GHOST DANCE SONG
(N. Curtis, p. 66)

4. PAWNEE HAND GAME SONG
(F. Densmore, Pawnee Music, No. 45)

*In most music examples taken from the literature I have simplified the signature and the bar lines. The melodies are transposed to the same level in order to facilitate comparison.

5. SOUTHERN PAIUTE ROAN MOURNING SONG
(E. Sapir, PR 16a)

♩=160

6. NORTHERN UTE BEAR DANCE SONG
(F. Desnmore, Northern Ute Music, No. 1)

♩=96

7. NAVAHO "WAR DANCE" SONG
(H. Disk 15 B1)

♩=144

8. YANKTONAI GHOST DANCE SONG
(H. PR 93)

♩=140

A STUDY OF MUSIC DIFFUSION BASED ON THE WANDERING OF THE OPENING PEYOTE SONG

Willard Rhodes

The widespread diffusion of the peyote cult[2] among Indian tribes of the Great Plains between the mid-nineteenth century and the present provides a wealth of musical material that awaits further analysis and interpretation. McAllester has made a significant contribution in the field of ethnomusicology with his scholarly study, *Peyote Music.*[3] Although he has given a clear description of the over-all style of peyote songs with detailed references to the differences he found among the Comanche, Washo, Dakota, Fox, Cheyenne, Pawnee, Kiowa, Shoshone, Ute, Tonkawa, Kickapoo, Arapaho, Huichol and Tarahumare, he calls attention to the complexity of the picture and the need for further investigation. It is the object of this paper to examine several versions of the opening song of the peyote ceremony and to draw whatever conclusions seem justified by the evidence. The validity of such conclusions is necessarily affected by the limited amount of material on which they are based. They are offered, however, with the hope that they will call attention to a significant area of culture that has been imperfectly reported and too little studied, and that other students may be stimulated to investigate further this field.

Though the peyote ceremonial complex is composed of a number of elements essential to the proper celebration of the ritual, it is in the eating of the peyote and singing of the sings that the individual achieves his deepest religious experience. Songs, many of which are received in visions while the singer is under the influence of peyote, constitute the nuclear core of peyotism. They may be regarded as the quintessential expression of the cult. At stated intervals during the all-night meetings the leader sings four songs that are ceremonially determined, the opening song, the midnight water song, the dawn water song, and the closing song. Each of these songs appears as the first of a group of four songs and is sung four times before the leader proceeds to the remaining songs of the group. These are the only songs that are ceremonially fixed, the leader being free to use whatever songs he chooses to complete each group. Throughout the night there is almost continuous singing by the individual members of the cult, each man presenting a group of four songs of his own choosing, each song being sung four times.

In the diffusion of the peyote cult, the four ceremonial songs have passed from tribe to tribe as an integral part of the complex. McAllester concludes "from statements by Peyotists and from the available evidence it has seemed probable that the four special songs in Peyote are essentially the same wherever the cult is practised and that many of the regular songs also have a wide intertribal currency." [4] This finding should not surprise us if we take into account that factor which Linton, for lack of a better term, calls the "inherent communicability" of culture elements. What in man's culture could be more communicable than song? Here is a universal expression of man, an abstract, symbolic art that lives anew with each re-creation in the voice of the singer. Transcending and oft-times avoiding the limitations of language, vocal melody, which by definition includes rhythm as a component part of its substance, crosses tribal barriers with an ease that is not common to many culture elements. All that is needed for the diffusion of song is the contact of a bearer and a receptive receiver in a favourable situation. A receptive receiver would be a person possessed with sufficient aural sensitivity and memory to perceive and retain a melodic pattern, adequate vocal co-ordination to reproduce the melody at will, and an interest strong enough to engage him in the learning process. The average individual in any society would meet these qualifications. Though musical talent within a culture ranges from that of the active singer and maker of songs to that of the passive listener, there are few persons who are completely devoid of musical perception. Anthropologists, while recognising the significance of music in culture, have been prone to exaggerate the specialisation of this activity and material. Conditioned by their own culture in which the prerogative of music making has passed from the folk to the professional, they have come to regard themselves as unmusical, and distrusting their own musical perceptions they have neglected and avoided the ethnological problems posed by music.

The dynamics of diffusion of the peyote have been dealt with in various studies and will not be reviewed here. It may be noted, however, that in the spread of the ceremonial complex the songs figure importantly. In reporting peyotism among the Winnebago, Radin observed that at the time that Rowe introduced the cult "all that took place was the singing of peyote songs. . . . There seems to have been little more (at first) than this singing of songs." [5] It appears that the songs with their direct and immediate appeal through the sensory perception were accepted and sung before the doctrine and teachings of the new cult were understood and assimilated. If this assumption is accepted then it is to be explained in part by the nature of music and man's receptivity to this element of his culture.

Another factor which exercises a strong influence on the diffusion of music is the aesthetic satisfaction which man derives from his activities in this medium of expression. Man is endowed with an aesthetic impulse which impels him to seek satisfaction by moulding the raw materials of his environment into an idealised rhythmic form and order. His creative, re-creative and interpretive efforts are frequently stimulated and seconded by his taste for and interest in novelty. Would it be assuming too much to suggest that the popularity of peyote songs and their ready acceptance among so many tribes may be due in part to the fact that they are distinctly different from traditional tribal music? It is a nice analogy to speak of music as a universal *lingua franca,* but we are obliged to recognise countless dialectic nuances of musical style that differentiate the music of one tribe or culture area from that of another. In the peyote songs the distinct musical style is further emphasised by the vocal technique employed in singing them.

But ènough of generalisations. It is time to examine the opening peyote song which has had an interesting career in its wide and varied wandering. Records of the song as sung by the Lipan and Mescalero Apache who are credited with having passed the peyote on to the Comanche are not available. In their absence we must begin our journey with the Comanche and Kiowa who were responsible for the rapid diffusion of the cult in the plains north of the Rio Grande after 1880. This is the song as sung by George Hunt, Kiowa, recorded at Anadarko, Oklahoma, during the summer of 1941.

EXAMPLE I.   Peyote Opening Song (Kiowa).[6]

A comparative analysis of twelve versions of the song, one Comanche, three Cheyenne, one Kiowa, two Dakota, one Southern Ute, one Winnebago and three Menominee,[7] furnishes an index of the range of variation to be found not only between tribes, but within one tribe, and also in the different performances of the same singer. This observation simply confirms what we have known of the oral tradition of folk music in non-Indian cultures and reminds us that singing is a re-creative activity providing within certain limitations a wide range of variation and expression to the singer. If this observation has significance it lies in the fact that the same general psychological principle operative in the field of secular song is found here in cult music. More surprising, however, is the basic uniformity which these versions present. Unlike the long, poetic chants of the Navajo, Apache and Pueblo tribes, the opening peyote song has no words to give it form and regulate its pattern other than the meaningless vocables, *He-yo-wi-ci-nai-yo.* This sequence of syllables has a rhythm of its own, four short pulsations followed by two long ones. Prefixed by two long pulsations which may be doubled without destroying the distinctive rhythm of *He-yo-wi-ci-nai-yo,*

there emerges a rhythmic motive of six or eight beats, -- ´´´´--, or
---- ´´´´ --. It is this rhythmic nucleus in combination with melodic patterns which reappears in the various versions of the song and assures us that
we are dealing with variations of a prototype. There are many songs which
employ the common peyote syllables, *He-yo-wi-ci-nai-yo*, but I have limited
my study to those songs that offer evidence of musical relationship. The
simplicity of this short rhythmic motive in association with the sequence of
peyote vocables seems to have facilitated the diffusion of the opening song
and contributed to its stability through time and space.

An examination of the tonal aspects of the song reveals a number of
interesting features. In the matter of range, eight songs extend through a
compass of an eleventh, two extend through a compass of a tenth, and two
are confined within the frame of an octave. Only two of the twelve songs
employ a heptatonic scale. These are the Southern Ute song, cast in the
mixolydian mode, which is like our Western European major scale except
for a lowered seventh, and the Cheyenne version reported by Edward S.
Curtis, based on the natural minor scale. The Comanche and Kiowa versions, the two Dakota examples, and one of the three Cheyenne versions
are based on hexatonic scales. All of these follow the pattern of a major
scale without the seventh tone. To this basic scale the Comanche song adds
an extra tone, a minor sixth, used alternately with the major sixth found in
the scale series. One of the Dakota songs introduces a similar variation by
the occasional use of a minor third in place of the major third of the scale
series. Two songs employ pentatonic scales; one Menominee version transcribed by McAllester following a descending tone series, D, B, A, G, F#,
D; the Cheyenne version reported by Natalie Curtis following a descending
tone series, D, C, A, G, E, D. The Winnebago version and two of the
Menominee versions are limited to four-tone scales, but even here there is a
difference in the tonal composition of these scales to be noted. The Winnebago song employs the following tone series, D, A, G, F, D; the two
Menominee songs, both versions by the same singer, are based on the tone
series, D, B, A, F#, D.

A comparison of the melodic contour of the first and second phrases of
the song presents a remarkable uniformity. All of the versions except the
Dakota and the Winnebago begin on the octave above the tonic and after
one or more repetitions of this tone descend to the fifth. The Dakota versions reverse the order, beginning on the fifth above the tonic and without
repetition of the initial tone ascending to the octave above the tonic. The
Winnebago starts on the tonic and after several repetitions of this tone leaps
to the octave above. In all versions except the Winnebago, whose inclusion
in this group of twelve songs is subject to question on the basis of its wide
variation from the norm of the song, the first phrase cadences on the fifth
above the tonic. The Winnebago cadences its first phrase on the tonic. In
all examples except the Winnebago and the Natalie Curtis version of the
Cheyenne song the second phrase or section, discounting repetitions of the

first phrase, opens with an upward movement rising from the fifth or sixth tone above the ground tone to the octave and ends on the tonic. The Edward Curtis version of the Cheyenne song is the only case in which this upward melodic movement starts on the fifth, all other examples except as noted starting on the sixth. The aberrant Winnebago version in its second phrase moves downward from the third above the tonic to the tonic where it comes to a point of repose. The Natalie Curtis version of the Cheyenne song in its second phrase repeats twice in linked succession the pattern of the descending fourth with which the song opens. This cascading, terraced movement, so characteristic of Plains musical style, is more evident here than in other versions. From the evidence presented it is apparent that we have here a melodic-rhythmic configuration with an identifiable individuality and that it has maintained its basic musical structure despite the variations it has undergone in its diffusion. It is re-created with scales of four, five, six and seven tones, varying considerably in their patterns and tonal material, but the song emerges with its personality intact.

In a paper, "Acculturation in North American Indian Music," [8] which I presented at the Twenty-ninth International Congress of Americanists in 1949 I stated, "the highly religious character of the Peyote songs tends to render them inseparable from the whole ceremonial complex in which they function so importantly." At that time, Dr. Omar C. Stewart kindly reminded me of the opening peyote song which has become dissociated from its ritual setting and has had a wide diffusion as a social song. When and how this song broke over into the realm of the secular I am unable to determine, but I present the following facts which I hope will lead to the unearthing of additional information regarding the history of this song and the eventual solution of an intriguing problem.[9]

In 1919 Elizabeth Willis De Huff recorded this song on wax cylinder as sung by two Lujan girls of Taos pueblo. Miss De Huff has kindly supplied me with the following information. "According to their statement (the two Lujan girls), which was corroborated by several other Taos and Navajo pupils at the Santa Fe Indian School, where I collected it, the song originated among the Navajo and was adopted by the Taos Indians to use in their peyote ceremony. At that time, the Government was opposing the use of peyote and I could not find out whether or not the Navajos used the song in a peyote ceremony. That is still a moot question.[10] ... I used it in an Indian play that year and it became popular with all of the Indian pupils and was disseminated when the pupils returned to their homes in Oklahoma, Arizona, New Mexico and among the Utes. It seemed to strike like a spark of dynamite. Homer Grunn used the tune exactly as it was in harmonising it." In 1924 the song appeared in a collection of Indian songs from the Southwest, published by Oliver Ditson Co., Boston, set for solo voice with piano accompaniment arranged by Homer Grunn, who had transcribed the melody from Miss De Huff's recording. It is titled "Navajo Peyote Drinking Song." Sometime later the song was recorded with piano accompaniment and issued commercially under the label, "Peyote Drinking Song, Navaho Indiana" (*sic*), His Master's Voice B2083, Homer Grunn, in Native Dialect, Chief Os-ke-Non-Ton, Canadian Red Indian. Since His Master's Voice is a British company it is doubtful whether this record found wide distribution in the United States and influenced the diffusion of the song. It is not so easy to estimate the extent of the influence of the printed version of the song. Like many professional folk singers of to-day who acquire their repertoire of songs from books, some professional Indian singers, knowing few songs from their own broken cultures have learned their songs from printed scores. These singers unknowingly have been active agents in the diffusion of the printed versions of songs, for other Indians who hear them at fairs, rodeos, pow-wows and ceremonials have learned their songs. War Bow (Harry Nieto) of Zuni recorded this song for me in the summer of 1941. He told me that he had first heard it sung by an Indian "Princess" at the Gallup ceremonial. Since Nieto's performance follows so closely the published version, one is led to believe that the Indian "Princess" either learned the song from the printed score or by oral tradition as disseminated from the Santa Fe Indian School.

EXAMPLE 2. "Peyote Drinking Song, Navaho Indiana" (*sic*)[11]

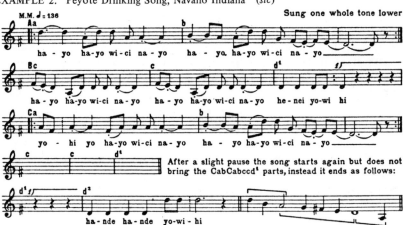

In 1927 George Herzog transcribed by ear a version of a song sung by Mayo Archuleta from San Juan in Saceton, Arizona. It was described as a young men's song, sung for entertainment. Herzog noted, "Mr. Archuleta considered this a San Juan song and didn't think it came from another tribe." During the summer of 1953 David McAllester recorded the song as sung by Walter Taylor, who had heard it sung in 1935 by two Hopis, Robert Lomodofkie from Shungopovi on Second Mesa and Edward Nequatewa, son of Edmund Nequatewa, former caretaker of the Museum of Northern Arizona at Flagstaff. Taylor had heard the song the previous year sung by a Zuni workman on a dig being directed by Frank H. H. Roberts Jr.

EXAMPLE 3.   Song Sung by War Bow (Harry Nieto)[12]

David F. Aberle encountered the song during a dig in the Jemez Mountains in 1938. He writes (I quote his personal communication because it states the problem so succinctly, at the same time contributing further information regarding the linkage of the sacred and secular versions of this song): "We had several Jemez Indian labourers, who taught me a song which they said was an Indian song, and implied it was a Jemez song. The first line of the song was: *Ha-yo-ha-yo itsi-na-yo.* This was definitely a secular song, and at that time I knew nothing about peyote. When I first heard *Ha-yo-wi-ci-na-yo,* I thought I recognised the Jemez song as a debased version of the peyote song. Of course, I heard my first peyote song in 1949, some eleven years after I heard the Jemez song. I once tried singing the Jemez song to a Navajo peyote man, who considered it a familiar secular Indian song. He knew, of course, that it was not Navajo—so, I am baffled. Did I hear a different song in Jemez, or was this a secular interpretation of the peyote song?" I believe that we can safely assure Dr. Aberle that he heard a secular version of the opening peyote song.

Space does not allow a detailed analysis of the several secular versions of this song. In brief, we may note that the De Huff-Grunn version and that of Nieto are almost identical with the majority of examples of the song in its sacred setting. Both versions have a range of an eleventh. The published version employs a hexatonic scale, D, B, A, G, F# E, D; the Nieto version a pentatonic scale, D, B, A, F#, E, D, and the melodic movement of the first two phrases matches the over-all pattern of the cult versions. The Herzog and Taylor versions are very similar. In the latter the range has been contracted to a tenth and the song has been lengthened by an extra repetition of the final phrase.

Several years ago the song appeared on radio and television in a very fancy arrangement as the theme song of the Mohawk Carpet Co., a gentle reminder that acculturation is a two-way process. This is the Mohawk Carpet Co. version of the opening peyote song:

EXAMPLE 4.   Carpets from the Looms of Mohawk[13]

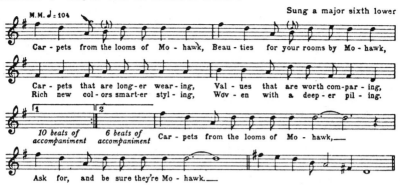

The song has a range of a tenth and employs a pentatonic scale, D, B, A, F#, E, D. Though the melodic movement varies somewhat from that which we have observed in the other examples, the core rhythmic pattern, -- ′ ′ ′ ′ --, repeated four times in the song in the commercial interest of inducing the listener to buy "carpets from the looms of Mohawk," leaves little doubt that this is one more example of the opening peyote song in secular form.

In conclusion we make the following observations:

1. Songs, which constitute the nuclear core of the peyote ceremonial complex, have greatly facilitated the rapid and widespread diffusion of the cult.

2. The ready acceptance and popularity of the songs are in part a result of the nature of music and man's psycho-physical receptivity to it.

3. This psycho-physical receptivity is associated with what for lack of more knowledge, we call an aesthetic impulse and man's curiosity or interest in novelty.

4. The same psychological principles operative in the re-creation of secular music are found also in the singing of peyote songs.

5. Songs from cult music can and do pass over into the field of social music where they live an independent and parallel existence. Songs may also move in the opposite direction, from the secular to the sacred.

6. The complexity of the song is in inverse ratio to its distance from the centre of diffusion. As the song travels there is a trend toward simplification to be noted in a contracted range, limited tonal material, regularity of metre and symmetry of phrases.

7. The opening peyote song has maintained its musical structure and personality intact despite the variations it has undergone in the course of its wandering in time and space.

8. Music, though one of the most intangible, fluid and malleable artistic expressions of man, is one of the most persistent elements in his culture and least subject to change in its basic structure and forms.

9. If the stability of form and resistance to major change observed in the opening peyote song are characteristics of musical diffusion in general,

these facts may be helpful in dating music, establishing time sequences, and postulating movements and contacts of peoples through ethnomusicological studies of their music.

10. The widespread diffusion of this song in its secular form is indicative of a pan-Indian movement in which tribal differences in culture lose their sharp definition and take on a generalised Indianism. This is to be noted in costumes, social music and religion.

11. Though modern Indian music has borrowed little from white culture, the white composer has frequently gone to the Indian for his themes, as observed in the Mohawk Carpet Co. theme song.

Notes and References

[1] This paper is a revision of an earlier paper that was read at the Fifty-second Annual Meeting of the American Anthropological Association in Tucson, Arizona, December 1953.

[2] The peyote cult, also known as the Native American Church, is a syncretic religion in which North American Indians have blended native religious beliefs and practices with the symbolism and teachings of Christianity. The peyote ceremony centres around the eating of the peyote, a small fleshy cactus found in Mexico. This is a source of spiritual power to the participant.

[3] David P. McAllester, *Peyote Music.* Viking Fund Publications No. 13. New York 1949.

[4] J. S. Slotkin, *Menominee Peyotism, a Study of Variation in a Primary Group with a Homogeneous Culture.* With Transcriptions and Analysis of Menominee Peyote Music by David P. McAllester. Transactions of the American Philosophical Society, New Series, Vol. 49, Part 4. Philadelphia, 1952. p. 681.

[5] Paul Radin, *A Sketch of the Peyote Cult of the Winnebago: a Study in Borrowing.* Journal of Religious Psychology, Vol. 7, No. 1, Jan. 1914, p. 7.

[6] Music of the American Indian: Kiowa, recorded and edited by Willard Rhodes, AAFS L35. The Library of Congress, Washington, D.C.

[7] Commanche, McAllester, *op. cit.*, The Songs, No. 2: Cheyenne, McAllester, *op. cit.*, The Songs, No. 58, quoted from Frances Densmore, Cheyenne and Arapaho Music, Southwest Museum Papaers, No. 10. May 1936. The Songs, No. 63, quoted from Natalie Curtis, *The Indian's Book*, New York, 1907. p. 188. Edward S. Curtis, *The North American Indian*, University Press, Cambridge, 1907-30. Vol. 19, pp. 205-6: Kiowa, Music of the American Indian, *op. cit.*: Dakota, Rhodes Collection of Indian Music, Library of Congress, Washington, D.C., 1942, Reel 6, No. 10. 1942 Reel 7, No. 9.: Southern Ute, Rhodes Collection of·Indian Music, Library of Congress, Washington, D.C. 1942 Reel 8, No. 7: Menominee, J. S. Slotkin, *op. cit.* pp. 688-9: Winnebago, manuscript transcription of song sung by Sam Blowsnake furnished by David P. McAllester.

[8] Willard Rhodes, "Acculturation in North American Indian Music." Tax, Acculturation in the Americas, Vol. 2, Proceedings of the 29th International Congress of Americanists. The University of Chicago Press, 1952, pp. 127-132.

[9] There is the possibility that the song was originally a secular song and that it was incorporated into the ceremonialism of the cult by the peyotists.

[10] This statement by Miss De Huff's pupil-informants regarding the Navajo origin of the song fails to stand in the light of more recent research and investigations that have been made by anthropologists. David Aberle, whose intensive study of the peyote cult among the Navajo may be accepted as authoritative, writes, "The Taos would appear to have had peyote at least since 1913, whereas the Ute complex cannot be dated any earlier than 1908 and probably 1914 to 1917 for the Southern Utes. Since the Navajos got it from the Southern Utes and so far as I can tell there were few Navajo

peyotists prior to 1933, and perhaps 1936, I think that the idea of a song spreading to Taos from the Navajos is virtually out of the question. Navajo peyotists themselves regard the Taos as having earlier contact with peyote than they did." (For detailed information consult David F. Aberle and Omer C. Stewart, *Navaho and Ute Peyotism: Chronological and Distributional Study*. University of Colorado Studies, Series in Anthropology, No. 6, 1957.

[11] His Master's Voice B 2083. Transcribed from the record by George Herzog.

[12] Rhodes Collection of Indian Music, Library of Congress, Washington, D.C. LWO 1483.

[13] Carpets from the Looms of Mohawk, produced by Maxon, Inc., New York. 53510.

BAMBOO AND MUSIC:
A NEW APPROACH TO ORGANOLOGY

Theodore C. Grame

Of the many materials from which man, in his ingenuity, has fashioned musical instruments, none is more widely used or of greater significance than bamboo; it plays a large role in the cultures of most of the areas where it grows, for it is used as a food as well as a material for all sorts of construction and artisanship. Moreover, it presents unusual possibilities to the investigator because its physical characteristics are so pronounced and so difficult to alter significantly that its influence on the form and shape of man-made objects is easily traced. Wood, or metal, or clay are easily shaped; they present but little resistance to the craftsman, but bamboo is very nearly immutable. This very quality—its resistance to change—represents both the strength and the weakness of bamboo, for its physical characteristics allow many instruments to be constructed from it with little effort, while for many others it is almost entirely useless. Bamboo is so well adapted to musical purposes that one might almost say that it is only necessary to cut a piece to produce a musical instrument. We might expect, therefore, that the portions of the earth where bamboo grows would possess certain organological features in common with one another; we shall try to show that this, in fact, is the case. Our belief is that many of the peculiarities of the shape of instruments of the present day may be traced to either a material, such as bamboo, a gourd, or horn, or to forgotten technological processes, or symbolic associations. A well-known example, of course, is the horn, which in its name, its shape, and its association with the chase, indicates its relationship with the animal horn from which it stemmed.

Bamboo is a grass, and like most members of its family, it is extremely hard and of exceedingly wide distribution. The areas where it grows include South America and the southern portions of North America, eastern Asia, and Australia and New Zealand. It grows especially abundantly in Malaysia and Indonesia, and is hardy in the northernmost reaches of Japan and to a height of 10,000 feet in the Himalayas. The plant is not to be found in Europe, western Asia, or Siberia, and with the significant exception of Madagascar is not of wide occurrence in Africa or its environs, though it does grow there to a degree, especially in the southern areas. It would be difficult to overestimate the importance of bamboo in these areas; its use as a food, for building, for utensils, as a material for artistic endeavor, and for water pipes, to mention only a few of its practical applications, place it in the very forefront of cultural importance. In China, in fact, bamboo possesses an importance transcending that of the merely physical; it is intimately connected with many of the less tangible aspects of culture: law, measurement, gambling, and music. (Moore, 1960, 96)

The physical characteristics of bamboo are too well-known to be described here, and instruments that are made of, or inspired by, bamboo conform closely to these qualities in that they are usually straight, rather narrow, and cylindrical or semi-cylindrical. Though there are one or two exceptions to the rule that bamboo instruments are straight—notably the Japanese flute, the shaku-hachi (Malm, 1959, 158)—for the most part this rule holds, and it is of some importance, for several other grasses and reeds also possess the qualities of being straight and tubular; they, however, are often easily susceptible to being bent, and this distinction between bamboo, which can only be curved by a skilled and patient craftsman, and other materials, is an important and highly significant one. In the areas that do not have bamboo, notably western Asia, the northerly portions of Africa, and Europe, the chordophones that are typical and seem to be indigenous—the harp, the lyre, and the lute—are based on a curved shape that is un-typical of bamboo, whereas in India, Indonesia and the far East the straight zither holds full sway. It will be objected that the lute and the lyre are not based on a curved shape; in fact, however, it is more than likely that they are. Some of the very early surviving specimens of lutes have curved sticks. One of these is illustrated in several sources (Sachs, 1940, Pl. V, opp., 96), and is from the Egypt of the New Kingdom, while the Sumerian name pantur, meaning bow-small, has been suggested as the parent of the Greek word pandoura, meaning lute. (Farmer, 1957, 245) The lyre, too, in some of its early manifestations seems to preserve a vestige of a curved shape in its arms (Sachs, 1940, Pl. III, opp., 64). However this may be, the zither is certainly not a prominent feature of musical life in the ancient Near East, and, conversely, the lute, lyre, and harp are late accretions to the instrumentarium of the Far East.

The so-called idiochordic priniciple of musical instrument construction is very possibly the one lying behind the decisive difference between Eastern and Western instruments that we have postulated above; in this process a thin strip of fiber is carefully cut out and is lifted from the wall of a tube of cane or bamboo, but is left attached at either end. Once this fiber, or string, is somehow raised by a bridge from the tube, it is able to be either plucked or struck to produce a musical tone, the tube forming a resonator. The idiochordic principle has been developed in two different ways: in areas where the inflexible bamboo grows the strip is supported at each end by a bridge, thus producing an idiochordic zither; in places, on the other hand, where a flexible material such as cane is available the cane is bent so that it becomes bow-like in shape, and the fiber strips are supported by a single bridge in the center of the stock, making a harp-like instrument that is reminiscent of the musical bow. The first idiochordic instrument that we have mentioned, the zither, is commonly met with in many bamboo-growing sections in the East, while the idiochordic harp is known today only in sections of West Africa, notably Dahomey and the Camerouns (Ankerman, 1906, 76). It will be shown that the idiochordic zither is almost certainly responsible for the importance attached to the zither in Far Eastern civilization, but whether a similar statement can be made regarding the influence of the idiochordic harp on the instruments of more westerly areas is much more debatable. Organologists, however, have long been uneasy at the anthropological belief that the musical bow developed from the hunters' implement, though it is undeniable that the hunting bow is frequently used for musical purposes. With similar reason, however, one might find the origin of the drum in the cooking pot, or of the fiddle bow in the bow drill. Further, as Sachs (1940, 56) points out, musical bows are often made of implements that are entirely unsuitable for the chase. It is possible that the similarity of shape between the hunting and musical bows has led to a confusion of function. Further light will be cast on this matter when we know in greater detail the instruments of Africa, and can correlate them with studies in plant geography.

We would be doing less than justice to our subject if we left the subject of Africa without reference to other ways in which bamboo is used musically on that continent and its environs. In Madagascar there exists a highly developed bamboo idiochordic zither, the *valiha,* that includes wire strings in addition to those of bamboo. This instrument was brought to the island by a Malay people, the Hovas, who moved there in the 15th century. This same group was responsible for introducing the bamboo stick-zither with gourd resonator into Africa. (Picken, 1957, 177) There is an additional application of the idiochordic principle to be found in Africa, specifically in West Africa; this is the raft zither, which is made of small pieces of bamboo or cane lashed together in raft shape. A fiber is separated from each piece of cane in the manner usual with idiochordic instruments. The resulting zither may have ten or twelve strings. It would be interesting to delineate precisely the area in which this instrument has been known, for one would like to discover what relation, if any, it bears to the somewhat similarly shaped raft zither of East Africa. One cannot but help, too, from wondering whether this raft zither may form a prototype for the Islamic family of flat zithers that are known as the *qanun* and *santuri.* It is perhaps more than coincidental that both the idiochordic harp and the idiochordic raft zither are found in West Africa.

A list of other instruments that are commonly constructed in part or in their entirely of bamboo would include most of the commonly used ones of East Asia. We should mention particularly the straight trumpets that are found, among other places, in New Guinea, for these may represent prototypes of the straight trumpets of China. The flute too is very often made from bamboo, of course, but it can be made with equal ease of several other types of material and—perhaps largely for this reason—it is of very nearly universal occurrence. Another highly interesting use of bamboo is found in the mouth organ family. The members of this *sheng* family are found in various degrees of sophistication all over the Far East, and were at one time exported to the Near East as well (Farmer, 1957, 444). In these instruments not only are the tubes made of bamboo, but, in the more primitive examples from Borneo and Laos, the reeds as well are fashioned from this material. In China and Japan at the present time the reeds are made of brass, and look much like our harmonica reeds (which were copied from them). One wonders whether this instrument would have developed at all without bamboo, for it is impossible to think of another non-metallic material sufficiently resilient to serve for the manufacture of reeds of this kind. Picken, by the way, has adduced very interesting evidence showing the essential identity of the reeds of the sheng with the jews harp (1957, 185); though this applies only to the reeds as made of bamboo. A final point in connection with the mouth organ is that both in ancient China and in

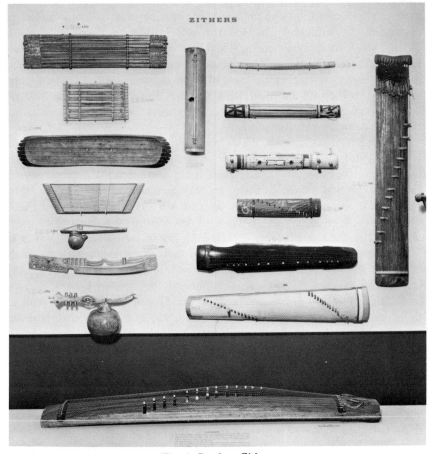

Fig. 1. Bamboo Zithers
Photo courtesy of Museum of Natural History, New York

modern New Guinea, the air chamber is constructed of a gourd; the Indian *vina*, too, is made of bamboo and gourd. This combination of materials has borne unusual fruit in Asia.

In many legends of the Far East bamboo is accorded a most prominent place in the very development of musical instruments and their music. One of the best known stories of this type, first printed by Raffles in his *History of Java* of 1817, has been recently reprinted by Lawrence Picken (1957, 183). "The first music of which they have any idea was produced by the accidental admission of air into a bamboo tube which was left hanging on a tree. The *ankloeng* was the first improvement on this Aeolian music." Another widely printed legend that is of direct concern to us is from the Lake Sentani region of New Guinea (Standard Dictionary, 1949; art: Flute); it concerns the adventures of a man who went out into the forest to pick breadfruit. He climbed a tree and threw the fruit down to his waiting wife, who caught it. At length a large fruit fell onto a dry stalk of bamboo, which was split by the impact. From the fractured bamboo stalk there came a loud snorting and a terrifying buzzing sound. These noises so frightened the wife that she scurried off, leaving her husband alone to watch a large cassowary emerge from the split stalk. The man, after surrounding the cassowary with an enclosure, ran back to the village to spread the good news: at last something had been discovered that would frighten the women! Then all the men went into the forest to cut pieces of bamboo, and after a great deal of experimentation, they managed to fashion their raw material into flutes.

Several inferences can be drawn from these legends, but the most important—and largely overlooked—one concerns the profound significance of bamboo to the music of these areas; it is, as we remarked previously, an essentially musical material. Sachs, in his discussion of the second legend (1940, 45), after pointing out that the cassowary is a rebirth symbol that is the equivalent in Melanesian tradiion of the Phoenix elsewhere goes on to say that the flute in this area is "clearly a charm for rebirth". If this is so, Melanesian symbolism conforms closely to that of the many portions of the world in which the flute is connected with love, courtship, and fertility. One thinks at once of the courting flute of the Apache Indians, and the lore surrounding the divine shepherd of the Hindu, Krishna, who, with his flute, was irresistible to women (*Mythology*, 1959, 380). We shall have further reason to discuss the symbolic significance of the interesting legend from Lake Sentani presently, when we consider the role of bamboo in the music of China.

An additional implication of the legends is found in the fact that in the Javanese legend the "aeolian" music inspires the creation of the idiophonic *ankloeng* while conversely, in New Guinea, the percussive sound of something falling onto bamboo gives man the impetus to develop the flute. No doubt the explanation of these seemingly inconsistent ways of thinking about instruments lies again in the nature of bamboo itself, for a bamboo slit drum is not very different in its construction, appearance, or even playing technique from a bamboo idiochordic zither. Moreover, bamboo flutes and trumpets are very much alike, as are bamboo mouth organ reeds and jews harps. Bamboo imposes its own unity on musical instruments, for the appearance, the technique of manufacture, and the ideas and legends that constitute the lore of instruments are deeply affected by it. It may well have some effect on the timbre of the music as well.

When we examine the role of bamboo in the instrumentarium of China many of the ideas that have been implicit in our earlier discussions become explicit, for many Chinese written records are available to us, and therefore the attitude of the Chinese towards music does not need to be guessed at. China, the influence of which on the technology of the East is analogous to that of Mesopotamia to the West, has long been aware of the profound role that bamboo has played in its culture. Chinese thinking about musical instruments is rather different in many ways, of course, from ours; this is nowhere better indicated than in the Chinese system of classification of instruments, which is based on the material of which they are constructed—or, more accurately, the material of which they were constructed when the system was originally delineated. In this system eight categories are enumerated, with each substance being coordinated with several things: a phenomenon, a musical instrument, a season of the year, and a point of the compass. Thus bamboo, which is one of the eight substances, is coordinated with the direction of East, the season Spring, the phenomenon mountain, and the instrument the pan-pipes. The very idea of a classification system based on material is of interest to us in view of our earlier discussions concerning the difficulty of classifying bamboo instruments by means of our Western system. Beyond that, however, the coordination of bamboo with the season Spring reminds one of the relationship between bamboo and the rebirth symbol, the cassowary, noted in the legend from New Guinea. Bamboo, in fact, is in many parts of the East connected with fertility (*Standard Dictionary*, 1949, art: Bamboo) and this is not surprising, considering its extremely rapid growth and the ease with which it flourishes in difficult locations. Evidence confirming the relationship between bamboo and fertility is found in the following well-known legend written down in the third century B.C. and here taken from Sachs (1943, 114).

"Emperor Huang-Ti, so legend says, one day ordered Ling-Lun to make pitch pipes. Ling-Lun went from the West of the Ta Hia and came to the North of the Yuan Yu mountains. Here he took bamboo from the valley, selected those the internodes of which were thick and even, and cut them between two nodes. Their length was 3 inches 9 lines. He blew them and made their tone the starting note *huang ching* of the scale. He blew them and said 'that's right.' He heard the male and female Phoenix bird and made six notes from the singing of the male Phoenix and six from the female. All were derived from the *huang ching*."

Many Chinese instruments have either an actual or a legendary connection with bamboo, and what is more, in many cases these instruments have a relation to the idea of rebirth or fertility as well. The classical Chinese zither *cheng*, for example, betrays both by its shape and by the inclusion of the radical for "bamboo" in its ideograph that it has its origin in the half tube idiochordic zither (Gulik, 1940, 99). The other traditional zither of China, the *ch'in*, has a nomenclatural peculiarity that is of interest, for its bridge is a Phoenix forehead, while its sides are Phoenix wings. This is true of the mouth organ *sheng*, portions of which are again named after the Phoenix (Gulik, 1940, 100); Sachs notes that it is carried—though no longer played—in Chinese funeral processions and he suggests that this may be connected with its symbolic relation to the Phoenix. In this connection it is of great interest to discover that another bamboo instrument, the jews harp, and one that is very closely related to the *sheng* reeds, is used in courtship among the *Lihuang Mosuo* of Yunnan Province in Southern China (Picken, 1957, 155). When we add that the Chinese straight trumpet too is used in funerals, and that as mentioned above, in the present writer's belief it can be traced to the bamboo straight trumpet as found in New Guinea, we wonder if we have not found indication of an even more general connection than has heretofore been suspected, namely, a widespread, and influential coordination between bamboo, music, and fertility. Certainly a preponderant amount of evidence seems to point that way, for on every level of investigation we have found indication of this connection: in nomenclature, in legend, and in function.

The overall point to be made then, is that studies in the field of organology have paid remarkably little heed to the important effects that the material available for construction has had on the history and development of musical instruments. Under the impact of the growth of technology, more and varied materials have become available to the maker of musical instruments, wherever he may be. (By technology, we do not mean merely recent Western developments, but, rather, all manifestations of a technical nature.) The desire remains, however, to provide some symbolic link, often visual and nonfunctional, with the older materials. Thus plastic flooring is often made to resemble the wood that it has displaced. An instrument then, may well betray by its shape or decoration that its antecedents were constructed of a substance no longer used, one that has nevertheless stamped the later specimen quite indelibly with its own peculiar qualities. Further, we are not confined only to the physical characteristics of an instrument alone, for legend and myth play a large role in the lore of musical instruments; so do the names of instruments, though etymology is especially difficult to apply in a subject that, like music, may well have names that are onomatopoeic. We have here confined ourselves to an investigation of just some of the ways, and some of the places, in which one material has played an important role in the history of music; investigation of the ways in which bamboo has been used in other areas, such as India, will provide more detailed evidence. It seems too, that there are several other materials that, were they to be investigated in this fashion, would elicit results of great interest; among these we might suggest stone, gourd, and horn. In the case of the more malleable materials, such as wood, clay, or metal, we should have to place the weight of our investigation on the technological aspects of the creation of musical instruments. In this case too, the results would be worthy of the effort.

Bibliography

Ankermann, B., 1901, *Die afrikanischen Musikinstrumente.* Berlin.

Farmer, H. G., 1957, "The Music of Islam" in *The New Oxford History of Music* I. New York.

Gulik, R. H. van, 1940, *The Lore of the Chinese Lute.* Tokyo.

Malm, W., 1959, *Japanese Music and Musical Instruments.* Rutland, Vermont.

Moore, A., 1960, *The Grasses.* New York.

Mythology, 1959, *Larousse Encyclopedia of Mythology.* New York.

Picken, L., 1957, "The Music of Far Eastern Asia" in *The New Oxford History of Music* I. New York.

Sachs, C., 1940, *The History of Musical Instruments.* New York.

Sachs, C., 1943, *The Rise of Music in the Ancient World East and West.* New York.

Standard Dictionary, 1949, *The Standard Dictionary of Folklore Mythology and Legend.* New York

HISTORICAL ASPECTS OF ETHNOMUSICOLOGY
Bruno Nettl

Ethnomusicology has traditionally been classified within the systematic branch of musicology rather than the historical, but historical interests and orientations have always played a considerable part in it; indeed, they have at times been the predominant motivating forces in investigation. However, the preference for synchronic and descriptive approaches has evidently caused the historical aspects of ethnomusicology to be left in a methodologically disorganized array. It is the purpose of this paper to work toward a systematization of the various historical aspects; it will utilize approaches followed in the past as well as other theoretical possibilities. Systematizations of this sort have already been attempted in ways which range from early music-historical points of view such as Lach's (1924) through later ones which emerged under the increasing influence of anthropology (Kunst 1955:43-46; Nettl 1955a). The subject matter under consideration has also varied greatly. Beginning with historical speculation in Oriental music (with which we are concerned here only in a secondary sense because of the existence of at least a partially written tradition and a professionalized musical culture) and the role of folk music in the history of European cultivated music, the interests began to follow the trends of anthropological thinking, have occasionally gone their own way, and have sometimes been influenced by other disciplines such as biology and psychology.

In spite of the variety of materials and aims, the historical aspects of ethnomusicology can be grouped into two principal classes, origin and change. Explanation of the origin of various phenomena has been at the root of many developments throughout the field, and has until recently predominated over the study of change. But while the study of origins has in a sense been exhausted or in many cases seems impossible to pursue further, the study of change promises to be of even greater interest when some of the methodological problems have been solved.

The problem of origin can be approached in a number of ways. For example, one may be interested in the manner of origin of a given phenomenon, or in the place of origin. The manner-of-origin approach has been one of the more speculative sides of ethnomusicology, and has provided considerable common ground between that field and general music history. The problem of the origin of music itself falls into this class, although ethnomusicological data can only corroborate or, more frequently, negate. Nevertheless, some theories of the origin of music which indicate the special function of music in primitive culture and its close ties to religion are genuinely based on ethnological information (e.g. Nadel 1930).

The seach for the manner of origin of various generalized musical phenomena is also involved here. For example, the debate on the origin of polyphony carried through the decades (e.g. Adler 1908; Lachmann 1927; Schneider 1934), the arguments for single versus multiple origins of polyphony, the possibility of various types of polyphony developing separately or together, would all be included in this category. Slightly different is the treatment of specialized and localized musical phenomena. The origin of certain types of scales or meters is relevant here, insofar as the approach does not stress the development of one type from another; the latter would properly be included in the "change" category. An example of this category is the investigation of the origin of the unhemitonic pentatonic scale whether it was derived acoustically through the circle of fifths, through the repetition of a two-tone motif at different pitch levels, or through filling gaps in larger intervals. Another such example is the origin of transposition or melodic sequence, which may be interpreted as variety introduced in a repetitive musical structure, or (since it is most frequently downward movement) as repetition modified by the prevailingly descending melodic contour (Kolinski 1957:3), or in still other ways. It would be difficult to exhaust the examples for the manner-of-origin quest in ethnomusicology, for it may be justly said that it has provided the impetus for a large proportion of the research in this field.

The search for the place of origin of musical phenomena, generalized and specialized, has comprised a number of research problems in ethnomusicology.

Thus, the place of origin of medieval European polyphony (summarized by Reese 1940:249-58), of the styles of some Northwest Coast Indians (Barbeau 1934), of certain musical instruments, and even of individual compositions such as the folk songs in European traditions, to cite only a few examples, have provided a variety of studies and theories. The general problem of place of origin has been approached from the nonmusical side as well; musical materials have been used to ascertain the possibility of cultural contact among widely separated peoples, and it is in this area that the historical orientation of ethnomusicology has made its greatest contribution to cultural anthropology.

The problem of change, although often related to and combined with the problem of origin, requires somewhat different approaches. We are interested in the reasons for change (or lack of change), and in its nature, degree, and rate. This applies to various levels of musical organization. We can study the change in individual compositions or in larger bodies of music. We can try to trace the changes indicated by differences among the variants of a single song, and we can try to identify the reasons for them whether they lie within the structure of the piece or in its cultural context. We can try to measure, for comparative purposes, the amount of change that has taken place and try to determine how rapidly it has occurred. Similar matters can be studied, but with greater difficulty, in entire repertories, whether defined geographically or by their cultural milieu. If more than one composition is involved, certain statistical methods may be drawn upon (as in Merriam 1956). Finally, investigations involving change are frequently associated with those concerning the place of origin of a musical phenomenon, for the obvious reason that if a musical item moves from one place to another it is also subject to change, and it would be impossible to evaluate the change without considering the geographic movement.

It is useless to try within a short space to survey all of the studies in ethnomusicology involving historical perspective. However, the approaches of many of these studies are summarized in the following pages, and we shall attempt to give examples of the general conclusions to which they have led and to formulate some of the general tendencies which seem to prevail.

Problems of Origin

The origin of music, as well as of individual musical phenomena, has usually been explained by reference to three possible processes. (The origin theories are summarized in Kunst 1955:46-48 and Nettl 1956:134-36). It may be a coincidence based on the structure of a related phenomenon, it may be motivated by a nonmusical need, or it may be inevitable through some process of evolution in a given direction. Thus, the origin of music in emotional speech (a theory not widely accepted) or in vocal signalling over a long distance (one more widely held) could be based on coincidence. A human need for music, and its resulting invention, are postulated in theories involving rhythmic work and religion as the cradles of music. Music as the human version of mating calls, or as a specialized form which developed from a prelanguage and premusic generalized type of communication (Nettl 1956:136) are examples of the evolutionary views.

Most origin theories involving smaller-scale phenomena are also based on one of these three approaches. For example, most forms of polyphony are attributed to discovery by coincidence or by faulty rendition of monophonic materials. This point of view does not explain why "faulty" rendition (singing of two variants of the same piece simultaneously, overlap in antiphonal singing, or singing the same melody at different pitch levels) should in some cultures lead to the development of polyphonic style, while in others it is simply written off as error. The origin of some instruments is also attributed to coincidence—for example, the origin of the musical bow from the hunting bow.

It is also possible to postulate the development of musical factors in some styles on the basis of esthetic needs. The need for unifying factors in orally transmitted music (explained in Nettl 1957) may bring unity in one element in order to balance the elaboration or heterogeneity in another. It is possible, for example, that a style in which the tonal material is expanded will also introduce melodic sequences in order to offset the diversification. Or a style based largely on repetition of short melodic formulae may introduce and encourage improvisation and variation in order to offset the large degree of unity. This view is supported by the complementary distribution of unifying features in some styles.

The evolutionary view is represented by such hypotheses as that the direction of change remains the same, so pentatonic scales naturally evolve from tetratonic scales if the latter have in turn developed from tritonic scales. The opinion that there are stages through which all (or many) musical cultures pass, discussed below, is also pertinent here.

The problem of single versus multiple origin has occupied ethnomusicologists on many occasions. On the whole, they have adhered to the generally accepted anthropological point of view, using geographic distributions and assuming that the likelihood of multiple origin decreases with the complexity of the phenomenon. They have also used the laws of acoustics (Hornbostel 1910) to explain the presence of the same phenomenon in widely separated areas. The main problem faced here by ethnomusicologists is the measurement of degree of complexity and similarity. This problem is shared with other cultural anthropologists, but is somewhat more specialized here because of the peculiar structure of music. It is possible that musical material, being in its structure relatively independent of other cultural elements and being fairly easy to describe and analyze, is better suited to measuring devices than are many other cultural phenomena (Merriam 1956:465).

Problems of Change

Why, how, and under what conditions does music change? Although these questions have not been answered with scientifically predictable results for any type of music, they have considerable significance even for material outside the scope of ethnomusicology, as have the negative versions of the same questions—the identification of stability and stabilizing factors in music.

It is first necessary to define musical change. In non-Western music, change seems to be a phenomenon substantially different from change in a cultivated, Western tradition. While changes through substitution in a repertory occur in both types of cultures, it is only in those which make use of oral tradition that established compositions are altered. Thus, change in a cultivated musical culture tends to be cumulative, new material simply being added to the old; in an oral tradition it may be change in a real sense, old material being eliminated as the new is introduced.

Changes in a repertory, or beyond the simple alteration of individual compositions, occur in various ways. Individual elements of music may undergo change, while others remain the same. New songs may be introduced into a repertory, causing the older material to change by assimilation; or the new material may gradually change to accommodate the style of the old. Changes in a repertory, if not caused by the substitution of new compositions for older ones, are of course determined by the changes wrought in individual compositions. But when change in a repertory is evident, it is often impossible to determine what has happened to individual compositions. Thus the two levels of change must usually be approached in contrastive ways.

There are many reasons for musical change, and the following discussion is limited to those involved in music in oral tradition. However, the same reasons, and perhaps others, may be relevant to cultivated music. We are not in a position to assert under what conditions, how fast, and how much music changes, and which aspects of it are most subject to change. It is possible to divide the scholarly approaches to change into two main classes: those which make use of strictly musical (or esthetic) criteria, concerned with the characteristics of the musical material itself; and those which make use of nonmusical criteria, such as cultural and racial ones. Of course, these approaches are not mutually exclusive; both must be used, and which is finally preferred depends on the individual case.

The first to be generally accepted were racial criteria; these were partially subscribed to by such men as Carl Stumpf, E. M. von Hornbostel, and Marius Schneider (1946). Today they are not generally credited with great validity, although they have been the subject of technical investigation by Metfessel (1928) and Bose (1952). On the whole, racial approaches tend to concentrate more on musical stability than on change. The musical relationships among members of different races are of course entwined with cultural relationships, and to separate the racial factors is a difficult and sometimes impossible task. Nevertheless, statements have been made (e.g. Schneider 1938:290) that the style of music is determined by the culture, but the manner of performance, vocal techniques, and so forth, are determined by the race, and there have been attempts to associate specific traits with certain racially defined groups. Since members of a race have lived in relatively close cultural contact, the existence of common musical traits hardly proves racial or physically inherited traits. Even when the characteristics of a racial group, such as the African Negroes, are brought from one place to another, such as from Africa to the New World, we have no convincing case for racially inherited musical characteristics. The notion that members of a racial group tend to accept musical materials from physically similar groups more readily than from different ones (Schneider 1946) seems too speculative. Moreover, it is negated by such cases as the distribution of individual compositions through the various physical types of Europe, the influence of Arabic music on the African Negroes, and the relatively similar musical styles of Africa and Europe (viewed on a broad scale) as compared to the musical contrast between the African Negroes and the physically similar Melanesians. The accompaniment of cultural influences by racial ones in many cases obscures the problem even more, and we must conclude that the racial approaches to musical change have not contributed much to this field.

Logically related to the racial approaches are those concerned with movements of populations and contact among peoples. It is probable that most documented cases of changing repertories are due to culture contact. Peoples living side-by-side influence each other, and where there is movement of population groups, the greater number of contacts increases the possibility of musical change. One might conclude from this that a tribe which moves about experiences greater or more rapid musical change than does one which remains among the same set of neighbors. The former tribe might have a high rate of elimination of material; or, holding on to old styles as new ones are introduced, it may increase the total number of styles in its repertory. Thus we conclude that a tribe with many outside contacts may have more variety in its music than one with a stable and limited set of contacts. This approach is illustrated by my study (Nettl 1953) of Shawnee music, in which it is shown that Shawnee contacts with other Indian tribes have resulted in the introduction of new styles; the Shawnee today have music which can be traced back to their contacts with the Northern Algonquians, the Southeastern United States, and the Plains styles. On the other hand, we find that the Pueblos have a rich and complex but rather unified musical style, perhaps because (at least in recent centuries) their contacts with other tribes have been limited. The generally conservative nature of Pueblo culture may also be involved here.

Another problem involving musical change through cultural contact is the direction of influence. This can generally be answered with some degree of certainty: the more complex style tends to influence the simpler one. This does not necessarily mean that the music of the more complex culture is introduced into the simpler one, for occasionally the simpler culture may have the more complex music. A variety of stylistic combinations may also occur, as indicated below in the dicussion of acculturation. In these combinations, however, it seems likely that each culture contributes the elements which it has developed best or to the greatest degree of specialization. For example, the mixture of African and European styles found in Haiti consists of African rhythm, antiphonal singing, and drum accompaniment, but European melodic structure, perhaps because melody is more highly developed in European folk music than in African Negro music.

A musical style may also move from one tribe to another, independently of population movement. It changes the repertories of the tribes through which it passes but it may also undergo change itself, influenced by the tribal styles with which it has made contact. For example, the Peyote style, as defined by McAllester (1949), presumably moved from the Apache and Navaho to the Plains. It retained a feature of Apache music, the use of restricted rhythmic values (only two note-lengths are usually found), but in the Plains it evidently acquired the cascadingly descending, terrace-shaped melodic contour. Possibly the forces described above operated here; the melodic contour of the Plains, a specialized and rather highly developed type, was strong enough to encroach on the Peyote style, but the more generalized rhythmic structure of the Plains was not strong enough to alter

the specialized rhythmic organization derived from the Apache. Thus it may
be justified to assume (although there are as yet few documented examples)
that specialized features in music are less easily changed than generalized
ones, and from this to proceed to the hypothesis that generalized features
are constantly undergoing change in the direction of becoming specialized.
If this were true, a general law of music history could be formulated stating
that generalized features change to specialized ones. On the other hand, this
process would no doubt be modified by many other forces, and the hypothesis may be applicable only in certain cases rather than generally.

Movement of musical material occurs not only in large bodies of music,
but also at the level of the individual composition, where the same forces
seem to operate. In European folk music it is possible to identify tunes
which have moved through large areas. They seem rarely to have influenced
the music of these areas to any great extent, but they themselves have
changed for reasons which are discussed below in another context. It might
be possible to infer that the larger a moving body of music, the greater is
its influence on the repertories through which it passes, and the less it is
subject to change itself.

Another force toward change may be called assimilation, the tendency of
neighboring styles to become similar. While musical material which moves
from one place to another influences the styles in its environment, there is
also a force of attraction among the styles which are in contact. Thus, an
area in which there is little contact among groups is likely to have diverse
style, but one in which the contact is great is likely to have a more unified
style. An obstacle to testing this hypothesis is the lack of measuring devices
for degree of musical similarity. Yet it is possible to compare an area with
much internal communication, such as Europe, with one in which communication is inhibited, such as Oceania, and find the hypothesis substantially
borne out. Of course, the presence of other factors must also be considered
here.

I doubt whether it is possible to make decisions about musical change,
its causes and directions, on the basis of strictly musical information. It is
likely that certain directions of change do predominate and that some can
in some cases, and with the corroboration of other kinds of information,
decide such matters as the relative age of musical styles on the basis of
structural features in the music. In most cases, music seems to move from
simplicity to greater complexity, so it assumed by most scholars that
the simplest styles are the oldest. As indicated above, there may be movement from generalized to specialized features, if it is possible to classify
musical traits in this way. Once a specific direction has been established,
there may be a tendency to continue it. For example, if the tones in a
scale have been increased from three to four, further increases will follow,
or at least a decrease will not ensue. These tendencies are speculative, and
beyond the obvious simple-to-complex movement, they have not been used
in specific investigations.

Other changes due to musical reasons are related to the basic common feature of folk and primitive music, oral tradition. Because there are mnemonic problems in the oral transmission of music, the material must adhere to certain specifications in order to make retention possible (Nettl 1957). The music must be simple, and there must be some unifying device such as repetition in form, a drone or parallelism in polyphony, isorhythmic structure, repetition of a metric unit, a definitely established tonality, melodic sequence or other transposition, or predominance of a single tone. The necessity for these features tends to inhibit change, and to channel it in specific directions. Thus, perhaps a melody with rigidly isometric structure is free to become heterometric after becoming isorhythmic. A melody with a hierarchical arrangement of tones, in which important and secondary ones are easily distinguished, may lose this arrangement after the introduction of sequences, since there is less need for the unifying function of the tonal structure. Again, these forces have not been studied in many examples; they are presented here as a possibility for future research. They can be observed in some European folk tunes which have undergone change while passing from one ethnic group to another, but whether these changes are due strictly to assimilation is an open question.

Measurement of the rate of change in music, and the amount of change in a given instance, awaits the discovery of proper methods. On the basis of impressionistic observation, particularly in the field of cultivated music, we may assume that change takes place irregularly; it is sometimes rapid, sometimes absent. In European music history there seem to be intervals during which musical style changes rapidly, while between them it changes only slightly over long periods of time. Sachs (1947) believes that this is connected with the length of a person's productive life, and in effect blames it on the turn-over of persons in the population. It is often stated that the music of primitive cultures must be somewhat closer to the beginnings of music than is Western cultivated music, and that primitive music must therefore have changed more slowly. It is also possible that the rate of change is proportional to the complexity of the music. This may be caused by the inherent structural traits; for example, where there are more features (i.e. more tones, more voices, more sections) there is more possibility for change. Or it may be caused by the more generally dynamic nature of complex cultures (open to question because of the large number of exceptions). The fundamental values of the culture are also involved.

There is evidence that in at least some cases, music changes less rapidly than do other apsects of culture. Thus, most primitive cultures which have had close contact with the West have taken on more European material culture, economic organization, and religion than European music. Although reconstruction is difficult, there may be similar examples among primitive cultures which lack Western influence. The Apache and Navaho have possibly retained more of the Northern Athabascan musical heritage than of many other aspects of that culture. The Hungarians have retained some of the musical features shared by other Finno-Ugric peoples such as the Cheremis (Kodaly 1956:23-59), but otherwise their culture has become Westernized. The reasons for this slow rate of change probably vary with the example, and comparison of music with other cultural features is methodologically difficult.

There are two ways of studying individual cases of historical change in folk and primitive music. One can try to reconstruct events of the past, or one can observe the changes occurring at the present time. The latter approach has been used in a number of cases involving acculturation (for example, Merriam 1955); the former has been used less often in cases involving individual repertories or styles (Nettl 1953, 1955b), but more often in general questions such as those involving the relative age of musical features. For example, it has been used to reconstruct the history of European folk songs by comparison of variants. There are definite limitations to both approaches. The reconstruction method is limited by inadequate material and by the fact that definite proof is almost impossible to obtain. The study of change in the present limits the amount of time during which change may take place, and involves specialized situations in which the cultures being studied are usually feeling the influence of Western civilization.

The Role of the Individual Composition

The role of the individual composition must be especially considered in historical research in ethnomusicology. It is a problematic role, for there is no clear-cut definition of what constitutes a composition in folk and primitive music, and this very lack accentuates the importance of historical orientation. Should one consider a group of variants with proved relationship a single unit of musical creation? Most scholars would prefer this to a working definition of a single variant or rendition, but they are then faced with proving the relationship. At the other extreme, one could devise melodic types which may or may not have internal genetic relationship, as has been done by Wiora (1953), and call these individual compositions without considering the question of actual genetic relationship. This would have the advantage of grouping similar materials and simplifying the picture. There are other possibilities, all of which show that isolation of the unit of musical creation is much more difficult in folk and primitive than in Western cultivated music.

The problem of measuring degrees of similarity among different musical items in a style is also unsolved. However, it would appear that in some styles, all or most of the pieces are so similar as to be comparable to related variants of single compositions in other styles. For example, most songs of the Plains Indians appear, by virtue of their specialized melodic contour and form and by use of similar scales, as closely related to each other as the variants of a single English folk song found in several English-speaking countries. Thus the criteria used for one culture do not hold for others. Informants' statements may be of help in some cases, and they have on occasion differed considerably from the writer's own calculations.

Another problem is identification or classification of musical items which, although composed at separate times, are based on each other or on a common model. In many cultures, the priority on originality (however one can define this term) is probably not as great as in Western civilization, and there may be cases in which new songs are created simply by copying an already existing song with only slight changes (Nettl 1954a:83-85). For descriptive purposes in all of these situations it is probably advisable to accept the informant's classification, but for comparative work this is usually not feasible.

The very existence of the problem of identifying individual units of composition points up some of the essential differences in historical change between cultivated and traditional material. In some primitive cultures it seems that entire complexes of musical material are built up from a single composition. This process, described by Roberts (1933) and called by her the "pattern phenomenon," may occur, for example, when a ceremony unites a body of music which then tends to become homogeneous by intensifying the specialized tendencies of its style. In some cultures (Nettl 1954a:89), new material is consciously created from the old, either by elaborating songs already in existence or by combining material from several songs to form new units. The extent to which these products are individual compositions may also be questioned. To be sure, a similar problem occasionally appears in cultivated music, as when the ultimate source of a composition is investigated. In traditional music the problem becomes substantially greater in cultures which encourage improvisation and where music may be performed with considerable change in each rendition. One must also consider the problems of defining a composition if each rendition or stanza is different, and of dealing with entirely improvised material. These examples show why the history of individual pieces has rarely been studied, especially in primitive cultures. (An important exception is Willard Rhodes' investigation, published in this volume, of an individual Peyote song.)

Some Methods of Investigating Change

Among the various approaches to historical problems in ethnomusicology and the interpretation of descriptive data in a diachronic manner, three are selected for brief discussion here: evolutionary, geographic, and statistical. We label an approach evolutionary if it recognizes a generally valid series of stages of musical style, into which the data are fitted. The schemes arranging musical material into a time sequence may apply to generalized concepts or to more specific local ones. For example, it is believed by some that each culture goes through a stage of monophonic music, after which polyphony is developed. Cultures which have a great deal of polyphony, such as many in Negro Africa, are thus assumed to be higher in the musico-evolutionary process than those which have very little polyphony, such as the North American Indians. The difficulty with this view is that the results might be reversed if some other elements of music were considered. It could be postulated, for example, that there is an evolutionary process from short, repetitious forms to longer, strophic ones; in this case the Indians would be ahead of the African Negroes, assuming that typical rather than exceptional examples are used. Such a scheme is used by Lach (1929:17) to classify the music of the Finno-Ugric tribes in Russia. He believes that the simple forms of the Mordvin, which are usually repetitious, place that tribe in a lower evolutionary category than the Chuvash, who have many strophic songs with four different phrases per song. The Cheremis, who have many forms which begin in a typically strophic manner and then go on to repeat one phrase several times, are placed in an intermediate category. The same data could be interpreted differently, and without the use of evolutionary schemes. One of the problems faced by the classifier of tribes according to evolutionary principles is the selection of representative material. There would be different results if one used the average or most common, the simplest, or the most complex material within a repertory as a basis for comparison. Furthermore, the assumption that all cultures ultimately pass through the same set of musical stages is invalid unless one makes only the grossest sort of distinctions. Evolutionary schemes must thus be limited, if they are to serve any useful purpose at all, to restricted areas and phenomena, and the existence of other factors must be admitted.

Universally applicable stages for other elements of music have been postulated. They are usually quite logical and would be accepted as valid for most cases even by opponents of evolutionary approaches. For example, the development of scales from two to three and finally four tones probably took place in many cultures, although a development of tetratonic from ditonic without the intermediate tritonic is also possible. Similarly, most strophic styles probably developed from simple repetitive forms, but this does not necessarily indicate the future development of strophic forms in all styles which consist of a simple repetition of single phrases. There has been particular confusion in the case of rhythm. Some students believe that metric chaos, or absence of metric organization, precedes unification into metric patterns. On the other hand, it might be assumed that metric simplicity, repetition of a simple metric unit, precedes heterometric structure which, to the listener, may appear confusing or unorganized. A given piece may be analyzed as metrically unorganized or complex, and many evolutionary statements in ethnomusiology have been made on the basis of such subjective distinctions.

Evolutionary stages have also been hypothesized for the development of repertories. For example, Bartok (1931:12) postulates three stages in the development of folk music. First the repertory is homogeneous; all songs are in the same style. Then special substyles are developed for certain categories of songs, such as Christmas songs, wedding songs, and music for other ceremonies. In the third stage these ceremonies disappear, and with them the correlation between song functions and musical styles. This scheme seems justified for at least some cases, if we take the music of some primitive cultures as an example of the first stage. It is not known whether Bartok also allows for the appearance of intermediate stages caused by the impoverishment of repertories, whether the third stage is even reached in all cases, or whether the disappearing ceremonies and their peculiar styles are not replaced by other similar categories. Answers to these questions would probably qualify the general validity of this scheme.

Other such schemes have been advanced, largely along lines similar to Bartok's. Characteristically, they divide music history into three stages, a fact which in itself renders them suspect. The general validity of evolutionary schemes has never been established because of the many other factors affecting the material. Their greatest value has perhaps been the arrangement and classification of material.

The geographic approaches to historical questions have been more valuable. They have always been accepted for classificatory purposes, and there are few ethnomusicological studies which do not include some statement of geographic reference. There are perhaps two main uses which ethnomusicologists make of geographic concepts: (1) They plot distributions of musical phenomena, entire styles, individual compositions, but most frequently of individual traits abstracted from their styles, which can be present in various stylistic environments. An example of the latter is a scale type found with various kinds of meter or form, so that its distribution is not affected by the other elements in the same composition. (2) They classify the world in terms of musical areas which exhibit some degree of internal unity and contrast with neighboring areas. The results of these plottings and classifications are then used as the basis for conclusions on origin and change in music.

The plotting of distributions of musical traits is fairly clear-cut, but is limited by several factors: the difficulty of obtaining material which is valid for a given point in time for the entire area to be covered; the reliability of samplings represented by a collection; the necessity for positive statements and the fact that one can rarely vouch for the absence of a certain trait simply because it has not yet been observed; and the identification of similar traits when found in different stylistic milieus. However, these limitations do not pose as great a methodological problem as does identification of musical areas.

The concept of a musical area is difficult to handle because it is necessary first to decide how much homogeneity must be assumed. If based on one main trait, it becomes nothing but a plotted distribution of that trait; but if one expects too great a degree of unity, the musical area will shrink to the provenience of a single tribe, and the original purpose will not be served. It is therefore necessary to guard against overly great concentration on a single trait when making such constructions. Furthermore, there is a temptation merely to describe the music of an established culture area instead of basing the musical area exclusively on musical traits. The very fact that it is possible to identify musical areas at all gives us some insight into the nature of musical change. The areas, rather surprisingly, have fairly distinct borders and sometimes well-marked centers. To be sure, the borders show some influence of neighboring areas, but it is nevertheless remarkable that they set off a geographic unit which has common musical traits but which does not coincide with a language area, a culture area, or a natural area. The evidence thus points to some kind of independent development of the musical area.

Although it is subject to many influences, the musical area may in part be determined by an interaction of stylistic traits which appear because they have complementary functions. The presence of one trait may favor the retention of another one. For example, it is possible that the cascading melodies of the Plains Indians, with their wide range and large intervals, inhibit the development of polyphony and favor retention of a monophonic style. The small intervals and ranges of the Caroline Islands may be responsible for the fact that parallelism is the main type of polyphony rather than, say, imitation; with such a melodic structure, imitation would not be perceived as well as with larger intervals. All of this is highly speculative, but the possibility that musical styles develop on the basis of certain musical forces should be considered, and this can best be done through a study of musical areas. Different sizes of areas, and variety in the accompanying degree of homogeneity, have been noted for North American music in several studies (summarized by Nettl 1954:3), for Africa (Merriam 1953), and for the world divided into three huge areas (Nettl 1956:141).

Most historical conclusions drawn from distributional information are based on several hypotheses. One is a generalized form of the so-called age-area concept—the assumption that the more widely distributed a trait is, the greater its probable age. Thus two-tone scales, found in all parts of the world, are assumed to be older than pentatonic scales, which are less widely distributed; rattle types of instruments are oldest because they are found in more places than other types, and so forth. A complementary hypothesis is the theory of marginal survivals, namely, that traits found only at the geographic limits of an area are older than material found only in the center. This theory has dominated discussions of the origin of European polyphony and its relationship to the folk polyphony of the Caucasus, Eastern Europe, and Iceland (Reese 1940:256-258). Similar conclusions have been drawn for European folk music in the United States, which seems to preserve especially old forms. But isolation may not mean retention of old traits, but rather separate development; this fact precludes the possibility of dogmatic statements regarding age-area and marginal survivals. These theories are less often applicable to individual compositions. For example, the presence of a melody throughout Europe does not mean that it is older than a purely local tune.

Related to these hypotheses are those formulated by the Kulturkreis school, as represented in ethnomusicology by Curt Sachs, Walter Graf, and

Werner Danckert, among others. A number of their studies have attempted to reconstruct music history through a study of the distribution of the layers in tribal repertories and in larger areas. This procedure has been subject to many methodological obstacles, but has resulted in some valuable information. Finally, the use of music to establish specific times of contact among cultures has been a contribution to cultural anthropology at large. Common musical traits, particularly if specialized, are usually assumed to be evidence for former contact, if the distribution is not contiguous. The degree of difference among musical styles may indicate the time elapsed since contact. Conversely, if common musical material exists, and the time of contact is known, a minimum age for the material can be established. This is especially applicable to individual compositions, as has been demonstrated by Idelsohn (1921). We may conclude that geographic approaches to historical problems have made greater contributions than have evolutionary points of view.

Statistical approaches have been used only in recent decades, but they seem to be very promising for historical contexts. By statistical we do not mean all approaches which are based on large bodies of music, groups of variants, or other corpora, which attempt to evaluate samplings from a corpus, and which make use of quantitative classification. Statistics in its more technical sense has been used in a recent study by Merriam (1956), which deals with problems not primarily of historical interest. A classical example of a study with historical implications is the description of Suriname music by Kolinski (1936). Here the proportions of African material in music used in the country and in town are compared, and although historical conclusions are not drawn, they are evident. An unpublished study by the present author, comparing variants of British ballads collected in various regions of the Eastern United States, indicates the possibility of using statistics for tracing the history of musical units.

Statistical samplings of the repertories of individual singers and players, and of individual musical elements or traits (considered separately from entire compositions) have yet to be tested. The main problem facing the statistical investigator is again the lack of measuring devices for degrees of similarity, relationship, and importance of musical items, and the necessity of proceeding at present along intuitive lines.

The importance of historical orientations in ethnomusicology can readily be seen. Such orientations can contribute to the knowledge of culture change in general, as well as to a better understanding of the processes of music history.

References Cited

Adler, Guido, 1908, Über Heterophonie. Jahrbuch der Musikbibliothek Peters 15:17-27.
Barbeau, Marius, 1934, Songs of the Northwest. Musical Quarterly 20:107-116.
Bartok, Bela, 1931, Hungarian folk music. London, Oxford University Press.
Bose, Fritz, 1952, Messbare Rassenunterschiede in der Musik. Homo 2:2.1-12.

Hornbostel, E. M. von, 1910, Über einige Panpfeifen aus Nordwest Brasilien. *In* Zwei Jahr unter den Indianern, vol. 2, Theodor Koch-Gruenberg ed. Berlin, Ernst Wasmuth.

Idelsohn, A. Z., 1921, Parallelen zwischen gregorianischen und herbräischorientalischen Gesangsweisen. Zeitschrift für Musikwissenschaft 4:515-524.

Kodaly, Zoltan, 1956, Die ungarische Volksmusik. Budapest, Corvina.

Kolinski, M., 1936, Suriname folk music. *In* Suriname folklore, M. Herskovits ed. New York, American Folklore Society.

Kolinski, M., 1957, Ethnomusicology, its problems and methods. Ethnomusicology 10:1-7.

Kunst, Jaap, 1955, Ethno-musicology. The Hague. Martinus Nijhoff.

Lach, Robert, 1924, Die vergleichende Musikwissenschaft, ihre Methoden und Probleme. Vienna, Academy of Sciences.

Lach, Robert, 1929, Tscheremissische Gesänge. Vienna. Academy of Sciences.

Lachmann, Robert, 1927, Zur aussereuropäischen Mehrstimmigkeit. Kongressbericht der Beethoven-Zentenarfeier. Vienna, Otto Maass.

McAllester, David P., 1949, Peyote music. New York, Viking Fund.

Merriam, Alan 'P., 1953, African music reexamined in the light of new material from the Belgian Congo and Ruanda-Urundi. Zaire 7:245-253.

Merriam, Alan P., 1955, The use of music in the study of a problem of acculturation. American Anthropologist 57:28-34.

Merriam, Alan P., 1956, Statistical classification in anthropology: an application to ethnomusicology. American Anthropologist 58:464-472.

Metfessel, Milton, 1928, Phonophotography in folk music. Chapel Hill, University of North Carolina Press.

Nadel, Siegfried, 1930, The origins of music. Musical Quarterly 16:531-546.

Nettl, Bruno, 1953, The Shawnee musical style. Southwestern Journal of Anthropology 9:160-168.

Nettl, Bruno, 1954a, Notes on musical composition in primitive culture. Anthropological Quarterly 27:81-90.

Nettl, Bruno, 1954b, North American Indian musical styles. Philadelphia, American Folklore Society.

Nettl, Bruno, 1955a, Change in folk and primitive music: a survey of problems and methods. Journal of the American Musicological society 8:101-109.

Nettl, Bruno, 1955b, Musical culture of the Arapaho. Musical Quarterly 41:335-341.

Nettl, Bruno, 1956, Music in primitive culture. Cambridge, Harvard University Press.

Nettl, Bruno, Unifying factors in folk and primitive music. Journal of the American Musicological Society (in press).

Reese, Gustave, 1940, Music in the Middle Ages. New York, W. W. Norton.

Roberts, Helen H., 1933, The pattern phenomenon in primitive music. Zeitschrift für vergleichende Musikwissenschaft 1:49-52.

Sachs, Curt, 1947, The commonwealth of art. New York, W. W. Norton.

Schneider, Marius, 1934, Geschicte der Mehrstimmigkeit vol. 1. Berlin, Julius Bard.

Schneider, Marius, 1938, Die musikalischen Bezeihungen zwischen Urkulturen, Altpflanzern und Hirtenvölkern. Zeitschrift für Ethnologie 70:287-302.

Schneider, Marius, 1946, El origen musical de los animalos-símbolos. Barcelona, Instituto Espanol de Musicología.

Wiora, Walter, 1953, Europäischer Volksdesang. Köln, Arno Volk Verlag.

FUNCTIONALISM

MUSIC IN AUSTRALIAN ABORIGINAL CULTURE— SOME SOCIOLOGICAL AND PSYCHOLOGICAL IMPLICATIONS

Richard A. Waterman

Music in every human culture has many functions of importance both to the society and to the individuals who compose it, and an understanding of these functions in a general way would seem prerequisite to the wise use of music in specific instances as a means of introducing changes in social or individual behavior. This kind of understanding is difficult to achieve if we study only familiar musical scenes.

In our society attention has, for example, been so closely focused on the aesthetic and recreational aspects of music that we have tended to lose sight of most of its other functions in Western Culture. In order to achieve some perspective on the general problem, I shall in this paper desert the Western World completely in order to discuss the musical life of a group of Australian Aborigines camped at or near Yirkalla on the northwestern tip of Arnhem Land, where the western shores of the Gulf of Carpentaria meet the Arafura Sea.

The people of Yirkalla are of the Carpenterian physical type of the Australoid race. They inhabit from time to time, and have traditional property rights in, the territory extending west about 200 miles along the Arafura coast to Milingimbi and south about the same distance to the Rose River. The total population is in the neighborhood of 400. They form in no sense a nation or tribe, but are united after a fashion by the fact that they speak forty-odd mutually intelligible dialects that distinguish them from the Aboriginals to the west and south of their domain.

The arts, in the life of the people of Yirkalla, are unified to an unusual degree, in that the subject matter of all of them—graphic, plastic, folkloric, choreographic, dramatic, and musical—is largely confined to activities of totemic species and totemic ancestors. Within the largest musical category almost every song has a painted iconographic design or hard-wood carving, a story, a dance, and a segment of ritual associated with it. An idea of the preeminence of the songs in everyday life is communicated by the fact that informants identifying food plants and animals for the ethnographer regularly do so by giving first the name of the object, then the name of the "old man," or lineage head, who "sang" it.

Basically, music functions at Yirkalla as an enculturative mechanism, a means of learning Yirkalla culture. Throughout his life, the Aboriginal is surrounded by musical events that instruct him about his natural environment and its utilization by man, that teach him his world-view and shape his system of values, and that reinforce his understanding of Aboriginal concepts of status and of his own role. More specifically, songs function as emblems of membership in his moiety and lineage, as validation of his system of religious belief, and as symbols of status in the age-grading continuum. They serve on some occasions the purpose of releasing tensions, while other types are used for heightening the emotionalism of a ritual climax. They provide a method of controlling, by supernatural means, sequences of natural events otherwise uncontrollable. Further, some types of songs provide an outlet for individual creativity while many may be used simply to conquer personal dysphoria. In every case, the enculturative function of the music in helping to shape the social personality of the Aboriginal in the Yirkalla pattern rather than in some other, is apparent.

That this process is a consistent and continuing one is evidenced by the fact that even the babbling of infants may have musical importance to this society. Cases in which a baby's inept attempts to mimic speech have been interpreted as revelations of secret and sacred song-words are not rare. In fact, this is one of the recognized ways the elders have of "finding" new songs.[1]

There are no lullabies in Yirkalla music. Although an infant may perhaps hear the stylized wailing at his birth, his first musical experience comes somewhat later.

Yirkalla has an institution comparable to that of the baby-sitter in that babies are tended much of the time, after the first few months of life, by little girls. One underlying reason for baby-sitting in our culture, the feeling that infants should be insulated in their own regimented world while adults go about their business, is, however, absent. Even very young babies may be present at any of the social events of camp life. Consequently, the infant comes to a dawning awareness of music by attending minor ceremonies in his mother's arms.

The child's first actual participation in Yirkalla music comes about gradually as a result of his involvement with the little girls' age-group, which functions partly as a baby-tending institution. This group is of some importance in the Yirkalla musical scene. Composed of girls ranging in age from toddlers to ten or twelve-year olds, and occasionally boys up to the age of four or five, it has a certain independence from the rest of the population. While it is essentially a play-group, it conducts foraging expeditions for shell-fish and for wild fruits, holds mock ceremonies in imitation of the elders, and roams around at will. Of importance in the present context,

---

[1] It should be explained that there is no invention or creation of songs at Yirkalla, only discovery. A sacred song based on infantile babbling is considered a song as ancient as any other. The implied idea that all possible songs exist and have only to be found is in complete harmony with Aboriginal attitudes in general toward time and innovation.

however, is the fact that this group forms the most prolific song-creating group in the society.

The songs of the little girls' group are structurally distinct from other Yirkalla songs. Associated with special dance routines, usually mimetic, they are heavily rhythmic and often syncopated. Melodic lines are of two types: the monotone chant, and the tetratonic or pentatonic song. No musical instruments are employed, although a vocal imitation of the Aboriginal drone-tube occurs frequently. Percussion effects are obtained through handclapping and foot stamping; these techniques are employed nowhere else in the entire repertoire of Yirkalla music.

The verses deal with everyday things such as digging roots, gathering firewood, collecting rock-oysters, and seeing animals in the forest. The songs change constantly, and new ones may be added at the rate of one or two a month while others are dropped. Some remain in relatively unchanged form for at least a generation or two according to statements by the few adult women who had not completely forgotten the details of their own earlier participation in this age-class.

One of the main musical preoccupations of the group concerns the teaching of the songs and dances to the babies. From the time they begin to talk, or even before, the little ones are urged to imitate the singing and dancing. The most inept indication of willingness to participate is rewarded with approbation. Thus, the first actual singing of the youngster at Yirkalla takes place in a warmly encouraging atmosphere, and most children become competent in terms of this style by the time they have learned to talk.

As soon as they can walk and run with proficiency—in other words, about as soon as they can get away—the little boys tend to leave to form a group of their own, where the interest in music is entirely displaced by new interests in mock battle and in hunting expeditions for minnows, small birds and animals. The girls stay with the group and graduate to the status of teachers of still younger children. A year or two before first menstruation, however, even the girls leave the group in favor of other pursuits and, to all intents and purposes, leave behind them their musical careers as well, for the only singing permitted a female after this time is the stylized wailing that functions as a ceremonial expression of intense emotion.

Nowadays at Yirkalla, a boy is circumcised at the age of six or seven. The circumcision ceremony has at least two musical aspects that inevitably make a deep impression on the boy. The first is mainly intellectual, and involves the boy's introduction to the *karma* songs of his lineage. These are the sacred songs that are not secret. All his life he has heard these songs, but usually without paying much attention to them. Now he lies motionless in the sand for hours, while a relative paints on his body the complex design of his lineage group, and listens to the sacred songs directed specifically at him. While most of the words are special song-words, or secret words which will not be explained to him until later, he nevertheless receives a concentrated training in recognition of the melody patterns peculiar to his lineage.

When the time comes for the actual circumcision the boy learns another kind of lesson about his music, this time an emotional one. For just prior to, and during the operation, every musical tension-heightening device known to Yirkalla culture is brought into action, and the cumulative effect is considerable.

As the boy is brought by his adult sponsor to the circumcision arena he is surrounded by painted warriors shouting a special kind of song that features unison grunts and shouts produced in a manner that is intended to be terrifying in the extreme to outside enemies, natural and supernatural. It is frequently obvious that this display of fierceness also terrifies the boy himself.

After an interlude of strenuous dancing punctuated with mass shouts and hisses, the warriors close in on the boy and set up a deafening rhythmic pattern of yells and cries. At the same time the women, in a seated group to one side of the arena, begin their wailing cry, gashing their scalps with sharpened sticks and bones manufactured especially for the purpose.

This mass of sound is deliberately worked up to a fortissimo climax that occurs when the boy, held on the prone body of his sponsor, is circumcised and adds his own terrified shrieks to the din. The sponsor then carries the boy aside to treat his wound with heat and astringent leaves, the women continue their wailing for a time, and the men work off their own excitement by means of a few more set-dances. Emotional exhaustion is the lot of almost the entire camp after such a ceremony.

After circumcision the boy is expected to move away from his family to the bachelor's camp. Here he encounters a new musical experience, for the bachelors' group has its own distinctive form of song. This is called the "playing" or "fun" song, and has the function of providing entertainment for the society. The members of the bachelors' group are, in effect, the troubadors and exhibition dancers of the camp. Their songs have no religious or ceremonial connotations at all, and are thus to be distinguished functionally from the rest of the music of the Yirkalla men. In form, too, these "fun" songs differ from the other songs of this culture. With few exceptions, all follow one melodic pattern, and the words, as well, are almost identical through the whole series. What differentiates them from each other is the chanted rhythmic pattern that occurs as a refrain in each song. The songs are about a great many things including shooting stars, high tides, low tides and other natural phenomena, but since the words give no indication of the subject matter, one must almost necessarily be a member of the group in order to learn the rhythmic cues that indicate which song is being sung.

Of musical importance is the fact that in the bachelors' group the boy has his first opportunity to begin to master the wooden trumpet that serves as a ground-bass for these, as well as for the *karma songs*. This drone-pipe is usually the termite-hollowed limb of a eucalyptus tree, about four and a half feet long and tapering in outside diameter from two inches to about three. The smaller end is used as a mouthpiece and the larger is placed in a large shell or, preferably, in a tin can or bucket which serves both as a resonator and as a means of increasing back-pressure on the air column. There is only one main tone, the pedal tone, produced by this instrument, although another tone that sounds a tenth above is used to mark the end of songs. In order to play it properly, the musician must learn not only to produce nine or ten different tone-qualities, which have names, but also to regulate his breathing so that the tone, once started, can be continued indefinitely. This he does by sniffing in air through his nose at points in between the accents of the drone-pipe rhythm pattern, at the same time maintaining enough air pressure in his mouth to keep the instrument buzzing. In spite of constant practice, over long periods, only a small number of men ever approach virtuosity on the drone-pipe. In the bachelors' camp the deep-toned throbbing of the instrument is, however, an almost continuous sound.

Among the functions of the "fun" songs, in addition to providing a mechanism for training instrumentalists, is the socially important one of providing recreation. When camp morale is low, and the ubiquitous undercurrent of blood-feuds begins to come to the surface, the older men often call on the bachelors' group to furnish an evening's entertainment of singing and dancing. There is a great deal of good natured clowning associated with such an event, and good humor is usually at least temporarily restored. Thus, the people of Yirkalla utilize music not only to increase emotional tension, as in the case of circumcision ceremonies, but also to relieve it.

By actual count, over a period of nine and a half months, the songs most often heard at Yirkalla belong to the *karma*, or sacred, but non-secret ceremonial songs. The *karma* songs belong to the lineages, and usually each lineage has one or two lengthy cycles of them, each cycle with a distinctive and recognizable musical pattern that functions as an audible emblem of the lineage.

In overall structural characteristics the totality of *karma* songs has a certain unity, and it is perhaps this fact that permits ready identification of specific song-cycles.[2] The basis of tonality is provided by the drone-pipe, which also provides the more complex rhythm patterns. Pairs of sticks,

---

[2] It should be mentioned, in passing, that Aboriginal informants were unaware of the underlying identity of *karma* songs even after this had been pointed out to them, but were aware of the differences. This is by no means unusual. In the same way, all or almost all Western music is alike, being based on certain basic concepts that include reliance on diatonism, a notion of absolute pitch, and actual or implied harmony and harmonic sequences. Yet one has to realize that most of the world's music does completely without these things before he is in a position to see that symphonies, operas, Dixieland jazz, popular tunes, hillbilly tunes, and so on are simply varieties of the same musical thing, and that in terms of world musical perspective the similarities are much more striking than are the differences to which those reared in the Western tradition pay almost exclusive attention.

usually about ten inches long, are used to mark the rhythm, and for most of the group the beating of these is the extent of their participation. The melodies, sung by one or two men, are extremely small in compass; most utilize no more than two or three pitch-levels. It is the pattern formed by these melodic tones in relation to the pitch of the drone-pipe that makes each *karma* song-cycle distinctive. Thus, if we take the note of the drone-pipe as an octave or two below the first of scale, a *karma* cycle of the *ridajigo*-speaking lineage uses the first, the flatted second, and the flatted third of scale; a cycle of the *komaitt*-speaking lineage uses the natural second and flatted third of a scale, and one of the *magkalili*-speaking lineage the flatted third and the fourth. While other tones, as well as ono-matopoetic sounds, occasionally are employed, the songs of a given *karma* cycle tend to adhere to the basic pattern or "lineage-mode" very con-sistently; this permits them to be identified at a distance even when the words are indistinguishable.[3]

It is to knowledge of these *karma* song-cycles that the youth next pro-gresses. While still in the bachelors' camp he may absorb some of the songs of his lineage, but it is not until he marries and begins to have a family that he embarks on what amounts to a long-term program in musical, adult education. At various stages in his life, on more or less formal occasions, the elders of his group reveal to him and his age-mates installments of the esoteric knowledge that is the mark of the full-fledged Yirkalla man. While this instruction involves legends, paintings, and dances as well as songs, the songs are of primary importance. The young adult learns to sing his own songs, and also becomes familiar with those of other lineages which he may not sing without special permission of the "owners." Thus, his knowledge of *karma* songs is cumulative through the years.

The uses of these songs are many. They figure in all "open" ceremonies, including as we have seen, the important ones for circumcision. They are also used for the frequent small ceremonies dealing with funeral or com-memorative rites, ceremonial cleansing and curing. There are so many pos-sible occasions for minor ceremonies that when, as often happens, a group simply wants to sing these songs a "reason" can always be found. An in-dividual suffering from dysphoria or insomnia may take some comfort from singing to himself, often in the dead of night, the *karma* songs of his lineage.

Beyond the strengthening of kin-group solidarity by providing a musical emblem, the *karma* songs have two other important functions. Since they deal mainly with totemic plants and animals and involve deeds of human

---

[3] The *karma* song-cycle patterns thus follow, in an extremely simplified way, the same system as that used by the classical *ragas* of India, which also depend for certain important aspects of their meaning upon the relationships between a drone and the notes of the song. While the *ragas* have come to have specific emotional, religious and seasonal connotations, the lineage-modes of Aboriginal Australia simply serve as sym-bols of social groups.

and supernatural ancestors, they not only act as text-books in natural history, history, cosmology, and religion, but also serve to reaffirm the individual's kinship with and "ownership" of the various plant and animal totems belonging to his lineage and to stress the antiquity, continuity and permanence of his family line. All of these functions are of inestimable utility in casting the individual's personality in the Yirkalla mold.

At about the same age as the Yirkalla man when he begins to learn the *karma* songs, the Yirkalla woman begins to develop proficiency in the ritual wailing that is the only form of musical expression permitted her. In order to be regarded as a good woman she must be able to perform this song whenever the occasion demands; the ritual wailing thus becomes a status-symbol for Yirkalla womanhood with roughly the same meaning as tidy housewifery is in our own society.[4]

The ritual wail is the stylized expression of intense emotion. It is used on occasions of grief and sorrow, and also when the situation demands an expression of overwhelming joy. Musically it consists of a series of sobbing descending glissandi, often loud and piercing; the words are borrowed from the men's *karma* songs, and the women preferably wail only the words of songs belonging to their own lineages.

While mastery of the ritual wailing technique marks the end of progress in the woman's musical life, the man has more to learn even after he has become fairly familiar with the *karma* songs. Both the remaining categories of Yirkalla songs are learned and sung in special circumstances and auditors are either absent or highly select. The Yirkalla man may, if he be fortunate enough to win the confidence of a practising magician, learn the songs that go with sorcery. These are softly enunciated and repetitive monotone chants, usually sung privately into some substance in order to charge it with magical potency. None of these chants is said to be indigenous in the Yirkalla area; at least a number have been imported and put to use.

As the Yirkalla man grows old, hence, to the Aboriginal mind, sacred, he begins to learn the deeply secret religious songs of his lineage. A full knowledge of these intensely sacred songs, which embody the essential core of Yirkalla religion, is possessed only by the oldest men of each lineage. They are used only for ceremonies regarded as necessary for the maintenance of the world and conducted in the special and remote sacred ground of the old men, from which women and children are rigidly excluded, and to which the younger men are admitted only by invitation.

The words to these songs are essentially those of the *karma* cycles, to which have been added certain awe-inspiring secret expressions that serve to intensify the sacredness. The melodies, however, are entirely different from those of the non-secret songs. They range in compasss from an octave to almost two octaves, and may utilize all the notes of the diatonic scale. Sung without the drone, accompanied only by especially carved and decor-

---

[4] For comparative information on ritual wailing, see K. Berndt, "Grief and the Aborigines" *Oceania* 20 (June, 1950) 306.

ated beating sticks, the effect of the secret songs is one of great solemnity and, at times, intense fervor.

When a man has learned his proper secret sacred songs he has achieved the pinnacle of his musical learning. His knowledge of these songs is a necessary and sufficient indication that he also knows everything else worth knowing, and that he has reached the highest status possible in his society.

This, then, has been a brief outline of the types of music to be found at Yirkalla. A few songs imported from the whites and from other Aboriginal groups, including some Methodist hymns, complete the roster. We have seen how the member of this Aboriginal society is surrounded by music during most of his life, and how this music functions in various ways to educate him in the techniques of existence and to inculcate the skills and values of his society. Since we are in a position to view the Yirkalla society from the outside, we can also see how music in this remote corner of Arnhem Land functions to identify social groups, to delimit statuses and specify roles, to maintain *esprit de corps*, and, in short, to hold the society together and keep it running on its own particular rails.

Note on the pronunciation of Aboriginal words:

/k/ = English k or g
/g/ = English ng (velar n)
/t/ = English t or d
/d/ = single-flap "British" r
/r/ = retroflex "Midwestern American" r
/j/ = voiced alveopalatal groove affricate

* The field research of which this paper is one of the results extended from March 1952 to March 1953, and was supported by a grant under the provisions of the Fulbright Act, supplemented by a grant of the American Philosophical Society.

MUSIC ON IFALUK ATOLL IN THE CAROLINE ISLANDS

Edwin G. Burrows

The music of Ifaluk is exclusively vocal. The people have, to be sure, two sound-making instruments: the conch shell trumpet and a conical roll of coconut leaf with double reed, technically an oboe. But while both of these could be used for making music, and are so used elsewhere, in Ifaluk the conch trumpet is a signalling instrument; the rolled-leaf oboe, a toy. There are neither drums, flutes, nor musical bow. If there is any exception to this general absence of musical instruments, it is either the sticks of the laūra dancers, rhythmically knocked together in a sort of manual of arms; or the sounding of the conch trumpet between lines of an incantation.

The little conical noise-maker with double reed is described, with an accuracy rare outside works of musicology, in the unpublished journal of Donald P. Abbott, marine biologist who worked on Ifaluk from June to November, 1953, with both the first and second parties of the Coral Atoll Project team. During an interval of work on the lagoon, his assistants made some Ifaluk playthings. His journal (for Oct. 23) continues:

> Tachim made a horn. These people have got the principle of the double reed down absolutely pat. You take a green (coconut) leaflet, take out the midrib, and fold the thing double ... making a long, thin (1.5 cm. wide) strip of leaflet, bent double,—crosswise, not longitudinally. This is then wrapped round and round with another leaflet, with a pressure that just barely bends the axis leaflets; these inner ones take on a slight bulge, and leave a space between. When this is done, you take a knife and cut the two ends (near where the winding starts) off cleanly, leaving a thing with the body of a small cornucopia (from the spiralled wrappings, getting bigger as they go away from the mouthpiece), surrounding an axis of two reeds, slightly separated.
>
> Tachim laughed and blew at a great rate, and the thing made enough noise to be heard all the way to Elangelap. Yarof then made an even bigger and louder horn, and Ella's peace was shattered. Wonder whether this is a Micronesian device, this reed horn?

Such an honest question deserves an honest answer; honest, and as nearly adequate as available sources allow.

How widely this noise-maker may be distributed within Micronesia is not certain. Search of the Cross-Cultural Survey files at Yale University reveals only one mention, for Yap (Müller 1917:203, Figs. 299 a-c), where it is clearly the same, or virtually so: "aus grünen Kokosfiedern spiralig aufewickelten, am Mundende flachgedrückten Oboe ..." But Müller's account of Yap is the best of all the early sources, and the fact that we would have missed this toy on Ifaluk but for Abbott's alertness raises the question: how many times has it been missed elsewhere?

However that may be, certain it is that this little oboe is not exclusively Micronesian. André Schaeffner (1936:275-76, Pl. XXIX) speaks of it as "un procédé de facture assez étrangement répandu. Il s'agit d'instruments où se trouve enroulée une lame d'écorce, un copeau de bois ou une bande de feuille." He notes its presence in England (the whithorn of willow bark, formerly blown by the countryfolk about Oxford on Whitsunday), figures one of oak bark from France (Vendée), and cites one of the pandanus leaf from Indonesia (Celebes).

Helen H. Roberts (1925:350-51) reports a "ti leaf whistle" made in this same way. In speaking of geographical distribution of instruments and music like the Hawaiian, she notes the whit-horn of England, a "May-flute" from the lower Rhine, and a *huzule* from Spain (Galicia). Within Polynesia, she finds mention of a similar instrument among the Maori of New Zealand, rolled from a split of *Phormium tenax*, or "New Zealand flax," but this description leaves in doubt the presence of a double reed, and the same is true of a citation from Africa (coastal Nigeria). Miss Roberts' authority, H. Ling Roth, knew of some of the other citations, and called the African ones "similar." Yet Africa is not included in the distribution of this particular device by Schaeffner even though he describes other oboes from Africa. Such an inconspicuous though ingenious device, especially when too perishable to be included in museum collections, can easily escape notice. As to the best name for it, both Hornbostel and Sachs (1914:587-88) and Schaeffner, in his thoughtful amendment to that scheme, call it an oboe.

Let us return to the "exclusively vocal" music of Ifaluk. Most of it is accompanied by dancing, or at least by formal gestures, and songs fall into the same main classes as dances: *arūerū* or lament; *gapengapeng* or invocation; *bwarux* or serenade; *ur*, dance with song to entertain the gods; and *laūra*, stick dance accompanied by a song. Another kind of song—a borderline case—is *bwoongabwoong*, incantation or prayer. In a second border-line case, the *pann* (work-song or chantey), the united pull on a line or heave on a lever produced by responsive declamation at least resembles dance as much as the sounds resemble music. Still a third border-line case, as far as intonation is concerned, is the crooning of texts of any kind of song in a reminiscent way, apart from the dance that accompanies their public performance.

Like dancing, music ranges from something that has barely shape enough to deserve the name, to forms of some interest in themselves, though music never attains a degree of complexity to match the most elaborate dances. To begin with the crooning mentioned above, this has both rhythm and recognizable pitch (mainly a monotone), and as a rule, the long syllables of the text are accented at fairly regular intervals while syllables of less importance are worked in on short notes, like grace-notes. The effect can be indicated fairly accurately in our musical notation. Songs crooned in this way are usually either *bwarux* or *arüerü*.

Arüerü, when performed "in earnest"—that is, in wailing or keening over a person recently dead or moribund—are quite different from reminiscent crooning. Attempts at description written in a note-book just after hearing performances of this kind follow:

About September, 1947.

> The dying man lay covered with a new loin cloth, decorated with flowers, with two (white) plumes rising above his head-dress. Mourners (his mother and a sister) sat on both sides, facing him. Now and then men joined in the wailing. As they wailed (or sang?), they would extend the right arm and hand, palm down, and wave, swaying the torso from side to side, over or toward the recumbent form. At the end of phrases, most of them would bend forward, bowing their heads. Some would beat their breasts. The mother seemed to scratch her face a few times.
>
> The wailing, while not regular, followed a general pattern. Starting on a high note (how high varies from a shrill shriek to a medium tone), the voice descends in a whine, *portamento*, to a low pitch, repeated with slow, equal time value. Then up a minor third for one tone, down again for one or more. This rise and fall of a minor third sometimes repeated.
>
> Sometimes all sang in unison. Again one group sang low, another higher. Several times, when I tested the interval between them, it was a perfect fourth, or nearly enough to sound so to me. The interval from the first high note to the low monotone varied, but was often an octave or very near it. The last tone often broke into a shuddering sob. At the end of some phrases, a short wail, one or a few notes.
>
> Later—wailing much quieter, intervals diminished. The first descending glide now rather definitely a fifth rather than an octave. What was a rise of a minor third at first, had become definitely a major second. The short wails variable.
>
> *Next morning.* Man dead. Chanting much faster.

WAILING OVER MORIBUND MAN; 1947

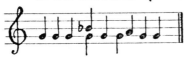

IN THE MORNING (AFTER THE DEATH)

Fig. 1

Similar notes after a later death:

> In the wailing for a dead woman, October 10, 1947, the intervals were smaller than in the earlier wailing for a man. This whole mourning for the woman seemed rather perfunctory, not nearly so intense as that for the man. This recalls the question raised by Helen Roberts, as to the expansive effect of emotion on melodic intervals.

On a third occasion (January 15, 1948):

> She died late in the afternoon. The first wailing was a short burst; a few howls, then some words on a monotone. It did not settle down to the regular pattern until evening, when all the relatives and friends were sitting about.
>
> Each line of the song—they are known songs, not improvisations, for all the people sang the same words—was sung mainly on a monotone, with the occasional rise of a minor third noted earlier. Sometimes the rise amounted to a major third. Between each two lines was a long cry, without definite pitch. There was great variation in these. Some could be called shouts, others howls, still others shrieks. Then the voice would drag down, *portamento*, to the pitch on which the lines were being intoned. There was some singing in parallel parts. Noted major third and fourth.

On another occasion, when men in a canoe-house were rehearsing a lament in anticipation of the impending death of the chief Paliuilimar, a different kind of part-singing was heard in which the upper part continued in a monotone while the lower part moved up and down.

Striking resemblance to this Ifaluk wailing elsewhere has been noted by von Hornbostel (1922:371) among the Kubu who are (or were) nomads inhabiting the jungles inland from Palenbang in Sumatra. The utterance of interest here is not a lament, but a *Zuruf im Walde*, call in the jungle:

Fig. 2

The *gapengəpeng* or simply *gapeng* is a hymn of invocation to the god

Tilitr. The ceremony begins with the assembling of worshippers about a
sanded ring, bedecked with upright rods representing the most important
sky-dwelling gods. Those immediately around this altar hold in their hands
long fringes made of half leaves of coconut, with the midribs trimmed and
about six inches of leaflet left on. These are held so that the fringes just
clear the ground and swing back and forth as the people chant the first
part of the long hymn of invocation. The singing, as heard in 1947-48, was
to an extremely simple, rather uniform melody, that moved up and down
about a semitone, oscillating around a principal pitch or tonic.

GAPENGƏPENG (INVOCATION TO TILITR)   1947-48

Fig. 3

The same strain could often be heard in the evening from native houses
whose inhabitants had kindled a fire or lit a kerosene lantern, and were
holding a "prayer meeting."

One night of unusual excitement, when evil spirits were reputed to be
abroad, was recorded in the Journal irregularly kept by the author:

September 22—

   I noticed unusual noises—singing (not so rare, yet not a matter of
course), and the blowing of a police whistle—or, more likely, a boat-
swain's whistle.

   We scouted out. There was singing in both directions. One proved
to be in the house of our neighbor just beyond the canoe-house. They
sing a good deal there; but this was different. The tune was that of
the invocation to the god.

   In the other direction, we traced the singing (and whistle) to the
platform of the house where the man died a while back. A circle of
young men was sitting there, and Arogeligar, with the whistle, was
sort of egging them on. He seemed pretty drunk. They too were singing the invocation to the god, with a lot of spirit, in all sorts of
pitches simultaneously—forming successive major thirds, fourths, major
seconds, and I don't know what-all. Talimeira, our boy, explained that
the god had come upon Arogeligar and might come upon all of them.
Mats were dragged out for us, and leis put on our heads.

   Then Arogeligar announced, through Talimeira, that they were going to call on Paliuilimar and Totogoetin (our Tom). We went with
them, the boys singing out lustily along the road as the spirit moved
them. Paliuilimar gave a pandanus-wrapped roll of tobacco to the god.
Then on to Tom's. After a bit more singing there, Arogeligar said

(through Tom) that we two had better go home now. They were about to go around and exorcise the devil that had been the occasion of the god's coming. We came back, reluctantly, because it was an exciting show. Though some of the enjoyment of the boys was like Hallowe'en, there was real tension; and the fervor of the singing made the air tingle. There seemed to be really both fright and faith in them.

In the public ceremony, after the first invocation with waving of coconut fringes, a drink is prepared and, by calling down the blessing of the gods, empowered to keep off disease. The invocation for this purpose is not part of the long hymn of invocation. I was never given the text of this part, though I asked the chiefs for it. The music begins as follows:

Ngai i-i-i tanga i   mwa·re mwa·re mwa·re   ma--E mwaratri E mwaratri!

(opening nonsense syllables) flowers flowers flowers O – – – garlands – One later line ends in "mai" (breadfruit); another in "pulax" (swamp taro).

Fig. 4

During one of the performances of this chanted prayer, the young men seated about the cauldron of medicine sang a passage in three parts which maintained the usual parallel movement although the polyphonic intervals were smaller than usual, including seconds and thirds and possibly a diminished fifth triad.

The *laūra*, or stick dance, is performed by all the men of a particular district. Each of the four districts has one or more versions of this dance, as of the *ur(u)*. The men form in two lines carrying sticks about a yard long. Those in one line face right, those in the other left, thus changing the lines into columns, and they then tap sticks together in an elaborate fixed pattern. In the one performance witnessed in 1948, the *laūra* was performed to a tune melodically the same as the *gapeng* in that year, but at a much faster tempo,—more than twice as fast.

LAŪRA STICK DANCE 1948 (tune virtually same as *gapeng*, but taken faster)

Fig. 5

Fig. 6

The *bwarux*, or serenade, has a melodic pattern of its own.

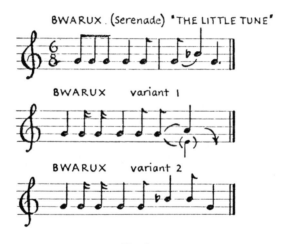

Fig. 7

Fully as distinctive of *bwarux* as "the little tune" is the manner of singing. When the pitch rises, at the point written as the beginning of the
second measure, the voice is carried up in a slur or *portamento*, maintaining
a "chest tone," so that some versions sound as much like shouting as singing. The final descent in pitch is similar, sometimes a downward *portamento*
without definite pitch. The whole gives a rather boisterous effect for love-
making. (See Variant I.)

Don Abbott, whose experience in Ifaluk overlaps my own, recognized
"the little tune" when special circumstances enabled him to hear the singing
and dancing of *bwarux* late in 1953. Use of this "little tune" is recent, to
judge from Herzog's transcription of records taken on Ifaluk during the German expedition and marked *"laure"* (Herzog: 1936). These resemble rather
the intonation of the present *ur(u)*, and so, indeed, did the singing of
bwarux heard one night in 1947. The experience is recorded in a Journal
entry for the next day:

October 4—At night we heard singing. Reconnoitered, and it was in the house next door. At first I didn't think it was the invocation hymn, but it turned out to be, with the intervals widened so that it suggested our major mode, rather than the minor it usually does . . .

We called in at the house next door. It was women and girls singing. One woman's voice had an ecstatic quaver in it, very pronounced. Somebody set out a candle in our honor. Then we could see that the excited woman was a young thing whose face looked as though she might have been drunk, but I couldn't be sure. She was throwing herself into the song, slapping her thighs, swinging and swaying, part of the time making dance gestures with her hands (that reminded me of those made over the dying man during the wailing). The young widow of the household sat beside her and joined in, but without any such wildness. In intervals between singing, the woman would laugh in a giggly, out-of-control way. All very graceful.

The journal identifies the song as *gapeng*, but—trusting from memory—I think that *bwarux* were sung later on because of the frequent repetition of the word *taremwanni* (young man) in the words, of which otherwise I could understand very little. This later singing was not intoned to the main theme of the *gapeng*, nor to the usual little *bwarux* tune. It was rather—trusting to memory again, for the journal fails to mention this point—chanting, mostly on a monotone, but with an occasional note a major second higher, as in much of the singing that accompanies the *ur(u)* dance.

Some of Herzog's notations from Sarfert's records, identified as *bwarux*, are also in this two-tone or *do-re* pattern. This raises two questions: first, is the more frequently heard *bwarux* recent—since 1909? Second, does a woman singing *bwarux* to her lover—the true performance—follow the "little tune" heard in public, or does she use the more general two-tone chanting pattern shown in Herzog's transcription?

Somewhat different was the following, heard during a *taurang* rite, which celebrates a girl's first menstruation.

FRAGMENT OF SONG ACCOMPANYING *TAURANG* TRANSITION RITE

E ma -   ROO-U! (No more!, deprecating rain)

Fig. 8

Maroligar, when asked about it during the first performance seen, said—with appropriate embarrassment and lowering of voice—"All same *bwarux*." The melodic formula, however, is not the same.

Still another definite pattern or formula characterizes the singing of the *ur(u)*-dance with song to entertain the gods. Like the dance, this musical formula is the most elaborate of all. The first, very slow movement of the dance is performed to a theme of rather more melodic interest than any other of the standard formulas which was recognizably the same through all district versions of the dance, though the words to which it was sung were quite distinct in each version.

Fig. 9

The only variation noted in the tune of the slow movement of the *ur(u)* was in one of the versions of the dance called "Peiran;" specifically, that ascribed to the Falahrik district, the northernmost district of the more northerly of the two inhabited islands on the atoll. The difference is thus described in field notes written during a period of nightly rehearsals for these dances.

> The slow theme in the Falahrik *Peiran* is based on the same melodic curve as in the Rauau *Ungarik* and *Ulimatol.* But the embroidery, instead of consisting of oscillation on an augmented second between the second and third notes, is a descending bit that comes in between the repetitions of the theme. Only the leader sang variations (c and d) as far as I heard; but the others put a good deal of emphasis on the low note below the tonic.

Incantations, which are private property and are kept secret, are whispered rather than sung, and are uttered only in undertones so that the uninitiated may not understand. Consequently, though I witnessed the utterance of several incantations, it was always too far away to hear how the words were intoned; at the same time texts of a number of them were obtained from informants who gave them as a rather special personal favor.

Summary

Looking back over this rather sketchy account of Ifaluk music, it seems permissible to venture a few generalizations, especially by comparison with George Herzog's more general account (1936) based upon records made by the Hamburg South Seas expedition which include nine taken by Fritz Sarfert on Ifaluk in 1909. In the first place, most of Herzog's generalizations are confirmed, so far as Ifaluk is concerned. The music of the Carolines, he says is "extremely primitive," and this characteristic is especially pronounced "on the islands farthest west," which include Ifaluk. Again, in the style of the western and central Carolines, the intonation is frequently uncertain (*schwankend*), but the rhythm pronounced and strict (*straff*, p. 265).

Short, introductory passages half sung, half declaimed, also noted as characteristic of the west with special mention of Merir and Sorol, are less distinct on Ifaluk, though the opening wail of a lament (and the wails between lines of the text) could be so characterized. There are said to be frequently performed *glissando* (p. 264): presumably what I have called *portamento*.

Further points noted in Herzog's specific comment on the Ifaluk records are not so clear in my material. To begin with, the first two selections are marked *dagar*, a term quite unlike any I heard on Ifaluk. The mention of shouts at the end suggests *ur(u)* dance songs, in which each "movement" or "canto" ends with a shouted passage, but concluding shouts were also heard in the records marked *waluch (bwarux)* and *laule (laūra)*.

The part-singing in Sarfert's records is characterized by narrow minor thirds below the main melody which could well happen on some particular occasion; as Sarfert only stayed on Ifaluk for 10 days, his records were presumably all collected at one time. But this would not be characteristic of the part-singing as a whole, judging from my experience. Rather, the part-singing during two periods on the atoll, one of nearly seven months, the other of three, should be described as parallel movement or *organum* in a variety of intervals, with fourths most common. Bits of pedal-point or *bordun* were also noted in the performance of several kinds of song.

The most conspicuous showing of this account—that little melodic formulas characterize most of the main kinds of song, or perhaps more precisely, most of the main occasions for singing—does not appear in Herzog's material. Such formulas have been recorded in this article in wailing for the dead; in the singing of *bwarux* in public; in the *gapengəpeng*, and in the reminiscent crooning by men of the texts of any song, mainly *arūerū* or *bwarux*. There is a little too much variety in them for the word "tune" or "melody" to cover the case; yet, that would be nearer than "style" which is far too ambitious for such little uniformities.

These formulas suggest, rather, rudiments of the *ragini* of India although the extreme simplicity of the Ifaluk patterns makes comparison with that elaborate development seem presumptuous. In the case of the "main theme" of the *gapeng* (Fig. 3) and the slow opening "movement" of the *ur(u)* (Fig. 9), the similarity is so close that all versions might well be called one melody. There is not much more variation in the "little tune" of the *bwarux*. (Fig. 7).

The fact that the records transcribed and analyzed by Herzog give no suggestion of such little formulas raises the question of whether they have developed since 1909, the year of Sarfert's visit? If so, this is a striking development within so short a time (38 years), in an art so meager in total content.

Absence of the characteristic formulae from Sarfert's records may be due to another factor—the occasion on which the song is performed. The "little tune" for *bwarux* was heard only in exceptional public, choral performances: at an *ur(u)* dance; when the men were rounding up a school of bonita in the lagoon; when a woman sang a farewell to one of the men aboard a departing canoe evidently acknowledging her love to him; and when a troupe sang *bwarux* for the visiting chiefs from Woleai.

That such changes should occur within 50 years is no surprise. Changes have been noted in the foregoing pages in the five years between 1947-48 and 1953; in the *gapeng*; in the *laūra*; in wailing for the dead, heard only during the earlier visit; and in women's *ur(u)* heard only during the later one. Changeability must be noted as another prominent characteristic of local musical style.

References Cited

Herzog, George, 1936, Die musik der Karolinen-inseln aus dem phonogramm-archiv, Berlin, *in* Aneliese Eilers. Westkarolinen, *in* G. Thilenius (Ed). Ergebnisse der Südsee-Expedition 1908-1910, Pt. 2B, v. 9, pp. 263-351.

Hornbostel, Erich M. von, 1922, Uber die musik der Kubu. Sammelbände für vergleichende musikwissenschaft 1:361-77.

Hornbostel, Erich M. von, and Curt Sachs, 1914, Systematik der musikinstrumente. Zeitschrift für ethnologie 46:553-90.

Müller, Wilhelm, 1917, Yap, *in* G. Thilenius (Ed). Ergebnisse der Südsee-Expedition 1908-1910. Pt. 2B, v. 2, pt. 1.

Roberts, Helen H., 1926, Ancient Hawaiian music. Honolulu: Bernice P. Bishop Museum Bulletin 29.

Schaeffner, André, 1936, Origine des instruments de musique. Paris.

HANUNÓO MUSIC FROM THE PHILIPPINES
Harold C. Conklin and Jose Maceda

CULTURAL BACKGROUND

Harold C. Conklin

The Hanunóo

One hundred miles south of Manila and at the northern end of the Sulu Sea lies Mindoro, the seventh largest island in the Philippines. On the fertile coastal plains of this island live Tagalog and Bisayan farmers (Christian Filipinos) while in the rugged and largely unknown interior live at least eight different groups of pagan mountaineers known collectively as *Mangyan*.

These forest-dwelling non-Christian groups live in sparsely settled communities, speak mutually unintelligible languages, have little direct contact with each other or with the coastal Christians, and are largely self-sufficient. They are peaceful folk devoting much of their time to hunting, gathering, and shifting cultivation.

The most populous of these relatively unassimilated pagan groups are the *Hanunóo* (numbering approximately 6,000) who inhabit the jungle and grass-covered hills of southeastern Mindoro, inland from the Christian towns of Mansalay and Bulalacao. The mountainous terrain in the remote area around Mt. Yāgaw is traversed only by narrow and often dangerously steep foot trails. Nevertheless, it is a pleasant and productive home to the happy folk who live there. By careful field rotation and considerable agricultural skill, the assiduous Hanunóo farmers cultivate a surpising number of food and other economic plants in their hillside swiddens ("kaingins," or fired clearings). The Hanunóo also garden, gather wild and protected forest foods, hunt, fish, trap; and raise chickens, pigs and humped cattle (zebu). But swidden activities predominate. Beyond their immediate needs, the Hanunóo usually manage to produce enough surplus crops to purchase, by trade with marginal Christians, the few luxuries and some necessities—such as Italian "seed" beads (for ornament, offerings, and local currency), scrap iron, and needles—which must come from the outside.

Most Hanunóo settlements are on promontories centrally located in relation to the swiddens cultivated by their inhabitants. An average settlement consists of about six dwelling houses, each occupied by a single family.

Such houses are sturdy, four-cornered structures raised several feet from the ground on wooden posts, hip-roofed usually with cogon grass thatch, often floored and walled with whole sections of bamboo which have been cracked and beaten flat like boards, and provided with verandas of the same material.

Making a Gitgit

Most Hanunóo are monogamous and the primary economic group is the nuclear family occupying a single dwelling. A man's residence usually shifts to his wife's settlement after marriage, but in most aspects Hanunóo society is structured in a completely bilateral fashion, and is very loosely stratified. Except for the eldest close kinsmen in any given local group, there are no recognized leaders even of a jural sort, and political integration is very weak. There are no chiefs, no headmen, no servants; and there is no warfare.

Most economic activities are participated in by both sexes and by all age groups except infants. Iron working and cloth weaving are exceptions. Men forge and repair blades for knives, axes, bolos, spears, etc. using a piston bellows type of Malayan forge. Women plant, pick, gin, spin, dye (with swidden-grown indigo), and weave cotton cloth for blankets and garments. In general, most wood carving, bamboo work, heavy construction, and lashing are done by men; most baskets are woven by women. None of these activities is restricted to specialists. All women spin and weave, all men have had some experience in metal working. And even the most expert smiths do not spend more than a small fraction of their time at the forge. Swidden cultivation and ancillary food-getting activities are the primary concern of all able-bodied Hanunóo.

Some degree of social distinction may be gained by an individual who becomes a fast loom-weaver, a skilled blacksmith, or an expert basket maker—but it is very slight. Perhaps the most respected members of Hanunóo society are the mediums, some of whom are able to compel their benign spirit familiars to combat and drive off the perpetual enemies of the Hanunóo, the invisible but superhuman *labang*. Even such mediums are indistinguishable from the average Hanunóo farmer except while practicing their supernatural rites in the event of illness, crop failure, or the like.

Hanunóo men present a striking appearance, with their long, white homespun loincloths, and tight-fitting shirts, bead pendant earrings, red headcloths, neck beads and arm bands. The women wear cotton skirts and blouses, waist and breast bands of woven rattan and fern stems, beaded neck pieces and bandeaux. Men and women keep their hair long, wear finger rings, tapered rattan pocket belts which hold charms, mirrors, knives, and beads. Both sexes also file their incisors flat and chew shavings from the aerial roots of certain plants, which coat the teeth with a shiny black substance. Their lips are vermillion most of the time from the constant chewing of the betel masticatory (areca nut, betel pepper leaf, slaked lime, and tobacco leaf).

As indicated above, Hanunóo ritual practices are often predicated by a fear of evil spirits (*labang*) who must be propitiated or repulsed through the services of mediums. The most important single class of spirits, however, is that of the ghosts of recently deceased relatives. Disrespect for them may be repaid with sickness and misfortune. Thus, the bones of a dead kinsman are appropriately exhumed in the next dry season following initial burial, carefully cleaned, housed, fed, danced with, and comforted in other ways during a two- or three-day socio-religious feast known as a *panlūdan*. With elaborate offerings, the bone bundle is finally set in a local cave.

Such a feast for the dead may be attended by hundreds of kinsmen and is always the most important social event of the year for the settlement in which it is held. Months of preparation are required. Special dance pavil-

Playing a Nose Flute (Lantuy)

ions, bone houses, and offering structures are built; and individuals concentrate on preparing special clothing, fragrant and colorful personal ornaments, new musical instruments, etc. During the feast, everyone seems to enjoy himself in a typically extroverted manner, courting, singing, gossiping, exchanging gifts, dancing, learning songs, playing noise-producing instruments of all sorts, storytelling, and consuming huge quantities of rice and other foods. The behavior of the ebullient crowd on these occasions reflects many of the strongest values in Hanunóo culture. For a Hanunóo, being an attractive, unmarried but eligible youth is the acme of social existence. At a *panlūdan* everyone appears to act as if he or she were a young dandy or a marriageable maiden irrespective of actual age group or status affiliations. Grandparents and preadolescents join the 16-year-olds in bedecking themselves with perfumes, ornamental leaves, beaded fillets, and tasselled ear pendants. Eyebrows are trimmed or shaved, teeth are restained, and instruments used primarily for serenading are carried by old men and youngsters alike. A small boy may compete with his elder brother and granduncle in a dancing contest, and a middle-aged woman may outsing a young bachelor at his own game—repartee in chanted, metaphoric verse.

At a *panlūdan* the continuous playing of dozens of hair-strung guitars and diminutive three-stringed fiddles, sword-bean-pod rattles, bamboo flutes, and jew's-harps provides an unceasing medley of instrumental *kalīpay* ('multi-sonous merrymaking') as an appropriate setting for the courting and sere-nading carried on by young lovers. One's popularity in such amorous pur-suits depends to a considerable degree on one's repertoire of *'ambāhan* or *'urūkay* songs. The wording of these chants is most important. Thus, an en-terprising youth takes advantage of large gatherings to increase his stock of love songs by trading lyrics with friends and kinsmen from other areas. The words, syllable by syllable, are carefully inscribed on the smooth outer sur-face of bamboo lime tubes and other betel chewing paraphernalia, to be memorized later. Such secular and—to the Hanunóo—highly practical use of writing is undoubtedly an important factor in explaining their surprisingly high rate of literacy (60-75 per cent in a number of areas) in their 48-character Indic-derived script, despite the total lack of formal instruction! Adolescents learn the syllabary on their own initiative by observation, in-quiry, and imitation.

As a result of their relative isolation and strong cultural conservatism, the Hanunóo still exist in a world quite removed from other parts of the Philip-pines. Social and political changes among the Christian Filipinos have vir-tually no direct effect on Hanunóo daily life, although some syncretism of Hanunóo and lowland culture is taking place gradually. There are, however, numerous indications that the Hanunóo retain much of what may be con-sidered pre-Spanish Bisayan (or central Philippine) culture.

Hanunóo Music

A wide variety of vocal and instrumental forms of Hanunóo sound pro-duction can be described within the framework of five broad cultural con-texts: courting, merrymaking, relaxing, working, and communicating with spirits.

(1) *Courting.* Serenading, essential in all Hanunóo courting, requires the memorization of chanted verses and the use of several musical instruments. The verses are of only two forms: *'ambāhan* or *'urūkay*. There are four main courting instruments: *gitgit* (3-stringed fiddle) and *kudyapi'* (6-stringed guitar) usually played only by men; *lantuy* (bamboo flute) usually played by women; and *kinaban* (bamboo jew's-harp) played by men or women. Such verses and instruments are used in other contexts, but their primary use is in such circumstances as the *panlayīsan* (courting sequence) where a young man exchanges *'ambāhan* (playing his *gitgit* between verses) with a girl he is visiting.

He may speak to her in *pahāgut*, i.e. using a form of voice disguise achieved by inhaling while talking. This method of concealing one's identity is much used at night among unmarried folk, especially before gaining entry into a girl's house, or when within hearing distance of her elders.

All forms of Hanunóo poetry are frequently chanted. Verses known as *'ambāhan* (or *'umbāhan*) are distinguished by having seven-syllable lines and a predominantly Hanunóo vocabulary,. Those called *'urūkay* have eight-syllable lines and a predominantly non-Hanunóo vocabulary. These latter forms, which seem to have been introduced from islands in and bordering the northern part of the Sulu Sea (cf. Kuyunon *'erékay*) during the past few centuries, have retained the vocabulary (including many Spanish loan words) of that area. Hesitation vocables and "nonsense" lines are known in both forms but they are relatively rare. Most verses are meaningful and abound in metaphor. Some *'urūkay* and *'ambāhan* have only three lines, others have more than 30. There is also considerable variation in chanting style from individual to individual. The Hanunóo classify their *'ambāhan* by vocabulary (some contain many words from other Mindoro languages, such as Budíd), length (long or short), content and intent (according to wording), and actual use (serenading, jesting, as a lullaby, etc.). There is a similar, but less extensive, categorization for *'urūkay*.

The lover's song notated in example II:13 is typical of the longer *'ambāhan*. Because of the stylistic "creaking" or "stretching" of the last syllable (an emphatic device frequent also in Hanunóo conversation) some of the lines seem to have an extra syllable. Occasionally the first line of a verse will be longer or shorter than those that follow.

An example of a short form of the *'ambāhan* is the following, sung as a lullaby (*'iyāya*):

> *dānga maglumi-maglumi'*
> *kita madnugan kuti'*
> *kuti' gin sa siyangi'*
> *mag'ingaw magyangyangi'*
> *kita 'ud may 'ibāwai'*
> *kanta bangkaw nabāri'*
> *kanta 'utak nalumbi'*

Free translation:

> Don't cry any more
> Or we'll be heard by the wild cat,
> The wild cat from Siyangi;
> Who will let out a terrifying cry.
> And we can't do anything about it
> Because our hunting spear is broken
> And our bolo is bent in two.

The themes of the verses of *urūkay* love chants are often subtle and completely metaphoric in expression. Some, however, are more direct, as in the mild request for betel ingredients implicit in the following:

> *sanda būnga sanda būyu'*
> *sa 'āpug 'anang lisfīnu'*
> *'anang palad sa tabāku'*
> *bisan man dili 'umagtu'*
> *sa panlulūba kaw sirtu'*

> Areca nut and betel leaf
> With burnt lime are essential
> As is also some tobacco;
> Even if you remain at home,
> Your last desire is satisfied..

The diminutive 3-stringed rebab-like *gitgit* is played with a tiny bamboo bow strung with human hair. (Twisted human hairs serve as strings for both *gitgit* and *kudyapi'*, though nylon cordage and steel wire are occasionally obtained by trade for these purposes.) Bow resin is provided by pitch-candle droppings stuck on the sides of the *gitgit* body. Hanunóo *gitgit* players usually make their own instruments. Light, resonant woods are preferred, and considerable skill goes into the cutting, shaping, boring, gluing, pegging, stringing and decorating of a 2-piece wooden *gitgit* body. A man may own three or four of these fiddles which are rarely more than a foot and a half in length. If right-handed, a player puts the base of the instrument against his right thigh and pivots the entire *gitgit*—instead of moving his bow hand—to shift from one string to another. The *gitgit* is played while walking, standing, or sitting. There are several tunings and six or more methods of playing the *gitgit* (i.e., tunes). The *gitgit* may be played alone, with a flute, with many other instruments, or in accompanying an *'ambāhan* chanter.

The 6-stringed *kudyapi'* (or *gitara*) is to *'urūkay* chanting what the *gitgit* is to *'ambāhan*. Men who know more *'urūkay* than *'ambāhan* also tend to be more skilled in making and playing the *kudyapi'*, though many individuals do both well. Hanunóo guitars range from 15" to 30" in length and are usually made by the players themselves from only two pieces of wood, selected on the basis of weight, color, tree size (for large guitars), and tone (loudness and "brilliance"). *Kudyapi'* types differ most in overall length, then in shape and construction of the guitar box (e.g., some are of materials like coconut shell). *'Urūkay* verses are often inscribed on the back. The strings are strummed (*kaskas*), or plucked individually (*timpara*) with the tips of the fingers, and occasionally the guitar box is thumped with the palm of the hand. The strings are tuned in one of three ways, and a large number of *kaskas* techniques and *timpara* melodies are known. The *kudyapi'* is not usually played in duet fashion with other single instruments. Several guitarists, however, will sometimes tune their *kudyapi'* together and strum

Young Man Playing Bamboo Jew's Harp (Kinaban)

them in unison. Small guitars are particularly popular with adolescent boys who like to play them rapidly and incessantly when courting or at *panlūdan* feasts where crowded conditions make larger instruments cumbersome. The smaller *kudyapi'* are played while walking, standing, or sitting in cross-legged fashion.

The 5-stopped bamboo *lantuy* is usually played as a mouth-blown transverse flute, and when so used it is often referred to by the loan word, *palawta*. When used as a nose flute, the closed-node end of the bamboo tube is placed so that it blocks the passage of air coming from one nostril. Fingering techniques remain the same, but the tones produced are considerably softer than when the flute is played orally. The *lantuy* is primarily a woman's instrument and is usually made by the flutist herself. Three or more are made at a time from a single length of thin-walled *bagākay* bamboo (*Schyzostachyum* sp.). Stop positions are marked off according to traditional finger-width measurements and the holes are burned with a hot metal point. Final testing may require shortening or notching of the open end of the tube with a knife to produce a loud, clear tone. Duds are thrown away, though a flutist may always have 5 or 6 good flutes on hand. Finished transverse flutes average 12"-16" in length and are 1/2"-5/8" in diameter. Because *bagākay* bamboo stems are only 1/16" thick, *lantuy* are easily broken. Therefore, when a flutist is especially fond of a particular *lantuy* she will take every precaution to protect it. She will place it high in the roof thatch or in a basket of cotton when not in use, and will not allow others to practice on it. Several girls may play their *lantuy* together. The *lantuy* is often played with *gitgit* accompaniment. The most frequent context for the latter is during serenading activities.

The Hanunóo occasionally make a 3-stopped endblown flute known as *bangsi'* or *pawīli'*. Its dimensions are similar to those of the *lantuy*, but it is more often made and used by men, and for purely recreational purposes.

Bamboo jew's-harps are widely used by both sexes—and often in courting contexts such as described above. These *kinaban* (known as *subing*, if the tongue is weighted with a spot of beeswax for greater vibration) are usually cut by men from the hard outer layer of the stems of the thick-walled bamboos *kiling* or *kawāyan*. The latter (*Bambusa spinosa*) is preferred because it "sounds louder." *Kinaban* dimensions range from 4-1/2" to 9" in length, and from 3/8" to 1/2" in width. The base which is held firmly in one hand may be of varying dimensions; the thin, narrow, stepped tongue is almost always cut to about 2-1/2" in length.

Making such an instrument is a delicate task and the ratio of rejects to usable *kinaban* is high. Because of their fragile nature *kinaban* are kept in long bamboo lime containers. A jew's-harpist usually twangs his *kinaban* unaccompanied by song or other instruments, but several players may huddle together and follow the same rhythmic pattern. Dissonant jew's-harps are not played together in this fashion.

(2) *Merrymaking.* In the Hanunóo sense, *kalīpay*, or merrymaking, is roughly equivalent to jubilant and multisonous sound production. Musical and other sound instruments are essential; singing, which is usually done in a very soft—even hushed—manner, is not. All such instruments are known as *kalīpay*-producers (*pangālipay*, which is the closest Hanunóo equivalent for 'musical instrument').

In the *panlūdan*-feast type of merrymaking as many as ten different kinds of instruments may be played simultaneously. In addition to guitars, fiddles, flutes, and jew's-harps already discussed, bamboo buzzers and zithers, whistles, bean-pod rattles, and bronze gongs are played. Hanunóo stamp dancing may also add to the din as on Side I, Band 10. Some form of *kalīpay* is essential at all Hanunóo feasts and gatherings. Even during the

Playing the Transverse Flute Known as Lantuy or Palawta

rites of exhumation preceding secondary burial, attendant musicians play miscellaneous *pangalípay* to please the spirits of the deceased.

For maximum group enjoyment the Hanunóo rate the loudest of instruments, bronze gongs, first. Two of these shallow-bodied *águng* (ca. 2" deep and 12" across) are held vertically a few inches above the dance floor and less than six inches apart. One of the gong holders, taking a round wooden stick in his free hand, beats out the main rhythm on the bosses. A faster but coordinated rhythm is usually tapped out simultaneously on the rims of both gongs with light flat sticks held by two other players. These gongs are not made by the Hanunóo but are heirlooms probably obtained originally from Moro traders who brought them from Borneo or Mindanao. In the whole Yāgaw area in 1953 only one good set was available for festive occasions.

Hanunóo stamp dancing is done only to the fast beat of gongs, or to the loud strumming of large guitars. Most dancers are men or boys; the best gong-players are women. There are three or four principal gong rhythms and with each there are associated dance steps. The latter are always vigorously executed by individual performers who dance in place. The upper part of their bodies remain relaxed and slightly bent forward. All energies are spent in keeping up with the gongs by the forceful, rapid, and rhythmical pounding of their feet on the resilient bamboo-board floor. The feet are always brought down flat producing the loudest noise possible. Such dancing often takes the form of an endurance test or contest between dancers, or between the dancer(s) and the gongers, to see which participant can hold out the longest (usually not more than five minutes). Dancing and gong playing are expressions of jubilance and are the essence of group *kalípay*.

For festive occasions, Hanunóo children often make simple bamboo whistles (*tanghup* and *pītu*); and idiochords. The latter are of two types: zithers (*kudlung* or *tabungbung*) and buzzers (*batiwtiw*). Zithers are made from a single closed internode of smooth bamboo (*kiling, Bambusa vulgaris*) split from one end and kept open about an eighth of an inch with a bamboo sliver. The two (sometimes four) self "strings" are cut from the exterior surface of the bamboo and kept raised by small bits of bamboo at each end. When such a string breaks it is quickly replaced by cutting a new one from the bamboo surface next to it. One string is played at a time with a small bamboo plectrum held in the hand. Many children may play their zithers at the same time or together with other instruments. The *betiwtiw* is similar in size and construction to the *kudlung* except that it is closed by a natural node only at one end and has only one self-string which is raised in the middle by a notched stick set at right angles to the axis of the instrument. The characteristic buzzing of the *batiwtiw* is produced when this stick is set in vibration by a bamboo plectrum.

At *panlūdan* festivities young women use the large dried pods of the sword bean (*būray-dīpay, Canavalia gladiata*)—cultivated for no other purpose—as rattles. The large lima-like beans serve as pellets; the hard outer pod casing forms a natural receptacle. Girls tap these 10"-12" long *būray-dīpay* in the palm of their free hand. Rhythms similar to those played on the bamboo idiochords are common. They are very fragile and even though they are used only on important *kalípay*-producing occasions they seldom last for more than a year. Some girls decorate their *būray-dīpay* with wrappings of colored cotton yarn.

(3) *Relaxing.* Whenever there is a lull in the agricultural work of the day, while waiting for food to cook, after meals, and in the evenings, there is hardly a moment in any settlement when one does not hear a *lantuy, gitgit, kinaban,* or *kudyapi'*. Such leisure is also the time for practicing and learning new and old *'ambāhan,* or for copying *'urūkay* verses from weevil-ridden sections of bamboo onto freshly cut internodes or lime tubes, and for making and repairing instruments.

Youth Dressed for Courting with Three-Stringed Gitgit

(4) *Working*. Daily food getting and other essential economic activities involve foot travel to and from swiddens, forests, streams, and neighboring settlements. Except during the rice and maize growing season when destructive environmental spirits might be attracted to the maturing crops— certain instruments are played while hiking. Young men often practice on their *gitgit* fiddles and women hikers of all ages carry sticks known as *kalū- tang.* One of the *kalūtang* sticks is held firmly and is struck against the other which is held loosely. By rotating one or both sticks two or three tones are produced. The sticks vary greatly in size and the sides of some of them are cut flat to increase the tonal quality or provide the tonal interval desired. The sticks are cut green from second-growth forest trees like *bayug* (*Ptersospermum* spp.) and *danglug* (*Grewia* spp.), peeled, tested, and then

kept or rejected. Usually they are not decorated or given special care. When starting out on a trail together, several *kalūtang* players select their stick pairs so that the different tones produced will not "fight each other."

During all seasons, Hanunóo men, women, and children enjoy calling back and forth along the trail by means of short melodic phrases known as *'ūwi*. This is almost always done when leaving or approaching a settlement. By adolescence, a Hanunóo child develops his or her own distinctive *'ūwi* which serves also as a form of identification. Many musical forms such as certain *'ambāhan* chant melodies are thought by the Hanunóo to have come from these individualistic *'ūwi*.

When clearing forest swiddens, carrying heavy loads, and in doing other forms of hard physical labor, the Hanunóo believe that by repeating short but piercing yells known as *pagrit* the task involved becomes less burdensome and one becomes reinvigorated. Such *pagrit* are also used as warning cries, as in the equivalent to our "Timber-r-r!"

Many daily activities such as the pounding, winnowing, and separation of rice before cooking involve rhythmic patterns.

For signaling purposes, as in summoning relatives from distant settlements, a heavy, handled, bamboo slit gong (*barimbaw*) is used by some Hanunóo (though not in Yāgaw today) in much the same way that pagans in the northern part of Mindoro bang with pestles on the giant buttresses of large primary forest trees. Light signal "bugles" or *budyung* are made from bamboo internodes about the size of those used for zithers. These are used normally only in case of emergency.

Spherical brass cascabels (*gurunggurung*) of probable Chinese origin are worn around the waist by women or are tied in shoulder-slung betel baskets worn by either sex. They are rare today but are much desired because of the tinkling sound they produce.

(5) *Communicating with spirits.* Hanunóo mediums known as *pandaniwan* call upon their supernatural familiars at night and in total darkness. Communication between medium and spirit familiars is effected by means of prolonged humming, and chanting (*ngāyung*) and intermittant hissing (*pamyus*). Parts of this monotonous sequence contain audibly distinct vocables many of which are easily understood Hanunóo words, but most of the medium's *ngāyung* "conversation" is hummed in a way that is incomprehensible to the listener. On rare occasions, when the powers of a single medium's spirit helpers are insufficient to combat the evil *labang* in the vicinity, several mediums may combine their efforts. During such ritual activities certain mediums (not in Yāgaw, however) are said to twang a musical bow resting on a bamboo resonator. This instrument, called *bayi batingan*, is unknown in other contexts.

Summary. Yāgaw Hanunóo musical forms are not the product of a few specialists but are widely known, appreciated, and participated in by most of the population. Every youth is able to make, tune, and play at least one of the courting instruments and sing some of the traditional verses. With the exception of *ngāyung*, all musical forms are primarily secular. The strongest positive values associated with music and sound production are those of courting, multisonous merrymaking, and festive rejoicing.

Hanunóo instrumental music is both more complex and more clearly distinguished than are its vocal forms. In the latter, emphasis is placed on words and meanings, on rhyming and metaphor, rather than on melody or other musical qualities. *'Ambāhan* and *'urūkay* are formally defined in terms of poetry, not music. On the other hand, instrumental forms exhibit great independent significance in Hanunóo culture. *Kalīpay*, in its most emphatic expression, requires the use of many instruments—and even of dancing—but not of vocal music. Courting without the use of musical instruments is impossible.

The fourteen musical and sound instruments used by the Yāgaw Hanunóo include 5 idiophones, 4 chordophones, and 5 aerophones; there are no membranophones:

idiophones	chordophones	aerophones
*kinaban	*gitgit	*lantuy
*kalūtang	*kudyapi'	bangsi'
*'āgung	kudlung	tanghup
būray-dīpay	batiwtiw	pītu
gurunggurung		budyang

The six main (i.e., most commonly-used) Hanunóo instruments are starred above. They include two hair-strung chordophones (*gitgit* and *kudyapi'*) used mostly by men; two idiophones (*kinaban* and *'āgung*) used by both sexes and a flute (*lantuy*) and musical sticks (*kalūtang*) used primarily by women.

References

Conklin, Harold C., 1949, Preliminary Report on Field Work on the Islands of Mindoro and Palawan, Philippines (American Anthropologist, n.s., vol. 51, no. 2, pp. 268-273, Menasha).

Conklin, Harold C., 1949b, Bamboo Literacy on Mindoro (Pacific Discovery, vol. 2, no. 4, pp. 4-11, California Academy of Sciences, San Francisco).

Conklin, Harold C., 1953, Hanunóo-English Vocabulary (University of California Publications in Linguistics, vol. 9, Berkeley and Los Angeles).

Conklin, Harold C., 1954, An Ethnoecological Approach to Shifting Agriculture (Transactions of the New York Academy of Sciences, Ser. II, vol. 17, No. 2, pp. 133-142, New York).

Estel, Leo A., 1952, Racial Types on Mindoro (University of Manila Journal of East Asiatic Studies, vol. 1, no. 4, pp. 21-29, Manila).

Gardner, Fletcher, 1943, Philippine Indic Studies (Witte Memorial Museum, San Antonio).

Gardner, Fletcher and Ildefonso Maliwanag, 1939, Indic writings of the Mindoro-Palawan Axis (vols. 1 and 2; Witte Memorial Museum, San Antonio).

Heine-Geldern, Robert, 1933, Trommelsprachen ohne Trommeln (Anthropos, vol. 28, pp. 485-487, St. Gabriel-Mödling bei Wien).

Meyer, Adolf Bernhard and A. Schadenberg, 1895, Die Mangianenschrift von Mindoro (Speciell bearbeitet von W. Foy; R. Friedländer and Sohn, Berlin).

Miller, Merton L., 1912, The Mangyans of Mindoro (Philippine Journal of Science, vol. 7, no. 2, sec. D, pp. 135-156, Bureau of Printing, Manila).

Romuáldez, Norberto, 1935, Filipino Musical Instruments and Airs of Long Ago (Encyclopedia of the Philippines, vol. 4, pp. 86-128, Manila).

Schebesta, Paul, 1947, Menchen ohne Geschichte (Verlag der Missionsdruckerei, St. Gabriel, Mödling bei Wien).

Schneider, Marius, 1951, Musica filipina (Anuario Musical *del* Instituto Español de Musicología del Consejo Superior de Investigaciones Cientificas, vol. 6, pp. 91-(105), Barcelona).

The Music

by José Maceda

General Remarks

The variety of instruments and the different applications of music to daily living among the Hanunóo are matched by imaginative ways of making this music sound simple, yet alive and colorful.

1. Vocal examples are made up mostly of syllabic recitations akin to Gregorian psalm singing.

2. The phrase lines of instruments and the tones that make up the chants involve diatonic and pentatonic constructions as well as hexachords, tetrachords, and three-note structures. Rhythm is both free and unmeasured. A characteristic use of triplets does not divide the groups into notes of equal values. Free rhythm does not have a steady beat or pulse.

3. Simple triadic harmony is used in playing plucked instruments; and seconds, thirds, and fourths are sounded by tone-producing sticks. A sort of counterpoint without theory but with some cohesion in the juxtaposition of parts exists in the flute and fiddle combinations and the flute duet.

4. The use of the zither with the whistle, and ensemble-playing of several instruments present unorthodox forms of musical merrymaking. Chants follow the verse forms of the text, while instrumental selections do not have a definite beginning and ending.

5. There is a clear idea of relative pitch, but no measurement of a fixed referring tone.

Notes on the Musical Forms

MIXED INSTRUMENTAL MERRYMAKING (KALĪPAY). General merrymaking involves the combined use of all Hanunóo instruments, partly represented here by gongs (*'ăgung*), guitars (*kudyapi'*), and the 3-stringed fiddles (*gitgit*). For notes on these instruments, see I: 2, 6, 7, 8, 9, and II: 6, 11, and 12.

CHANTS ('URŪKAY), USED IN COURTING. Most Hanunóo chants (see also example I: 4 and 11 and example II: 13) are recited parlando style, somewhat in the manner of Jewish psalmodies, but each is different from the other and shows the variety of musical expressions that can be obtained from a specific singing style. The mood or quality of voice, a syllabic enunciation, the presence of a reciting tone, organization of phrases, and a rhythmical freedom, are some of the aspects that explain this vocal tradition, and from which certain ideas may be formed for comparison with similar music of other cultures based on a written tradition.

F is the tonal center of the scale used in these *'urūkay* (I, 2, example C). The notes used around it stress even more the pull of that center. The notes above it form diatonic and triadic progressions as well as tones of the pentatonic scale. Diatonicism includes the use of the tetrachord and whole steps up to the third interval (I, 2, example a). A seven-tone scale does not include all the notes, but there is a leaning toward such a structure in the superimposition of one tetrachord over another, B flat to F and F to C.

On his guitar the singer plays in simple rhythm a tonic and dominant triadic harmony which shows a basic relation to the tonal center, but which does not have a detailed rapport with the singing voice (I, 2, example b). Most of the playing comes between verses or towards the end of lines.

The six strings are tuned after the *'inustāba* arrangement found also on example I: 7. There is a difference in harmony and rhythm when playing a solo and when accompanying a chant. A distinction is also made between major and minor chords played with the same tuning. For further details, see example I: 6 and 7.

FLUTE (LANTUY) SOLO, BY A YOUNG GIRL. Pivot notes of this selection are G and C, and the direction of flow alternates between these two poles. C serves as tonal center (I: 3, example b).

The tones of the Hanunóo flutes (see also example II: 1 and 2) all have a diatonic sequence with the same step relation between them (cf. I: 3, example a; II: 1, example a; II:2, example a). No other flute scale is known. Slight variations in pitch are due to inaccuracy of measuring distances between holes. Some notes within the fast groups sound less clear because the fingers involved tend to be raised almost simultaneously rather than to be articulated individually.

The range of these instruments is clearly doubled by free and uncontrolled use of harmonics that portray the coloristic effects of two flutes with different timbres (flute duet, example II: 2). Long-held high-pitched notes and a quick,

free rhythm of tones in between give an ethereal and improvisatory character to
Hanunóo flute music.

LULLABY ('IYĀYA). Certain qualities of the singing voice mark lullaby
style. A sort of yawn (I: 4, example b), the dragging, sleepy quality of the voice,
and an exhalation of the breath at certain spots (I: 4, example c), all contribute
to the feeling of drowsiness. Phrases that are complementary to each other
are separated by rests or long-held notes. The different note values present
more variations in rhythm than are found in the other chants. The
presence of the note F in the ensuing scale (I: 4, example d) accounts for
diatonic passages in an otherwise pentatonic structure of the whole chant.

BOY'S GUITAR (KUDYAPI'): KASKAS AND TIMPARA. Explanation of
the tuning (I: 6, example a-f): The tones of the strings are notated in I: 6,
example c. The strings are tuned in pairs, showing that an organized idea of
relative pitch has been related to the positions of these strings on the guitar
box (I: 6, example a) and their arrangement in the peg box (I: 6, example
b). Thus, the manual side of tuning is made easy even at night.

Strings 2 and 6 (I: 6, example d) are tuned first; then strings 1 and 5
(I: 6, example e) shown in a position opposite to that of the previous pair
(I: 6, examples a-b). Their tones are a third, fourth, and fifth apart from
the B flat and C of strings 2 and 6. Strings 3 and 4 are the innermost pair
whose pegs are at the top, and are tuned an octave higher than F of string
5. This type of tuning is called kinursāda'; there are other kinds of string
arrangements with their own distinct melodies and ways of playing.

Explanation of the music (I: 6, examples g-i): Chordal (kaskas) and
monodic (timpara) sections alternate. The former are played with simple
stops to produce harmonies with a tonal center which is the F triad, and a
dominant chord which is in the second degree of the scale. This shows that
adaptation of European harmony does not copy the I, V relationship found
among the neighboring lowland and coastal folksongs (I: 6, example g).

The monodic part (I: 6, example h) with pizzicato effect, contrasts with
the broad strummings of the preceding section. Much use is made of the
open strings resulting in a pentatonic melody which becomes the prevailing
construction. In the scale formed (I: 6, example i), the note A occurs providing a half-step progression which shows a momentary merging of diatonic
and pentatonic elements. Notice the absence of the note E which would
have provided a full diatonic scale not altogether foreign to this culture. In
such monodic sections, there is no pulse or regular beat.

GUITAR (KUDYAPI'): KASKAS. The 'inustaba tuning completes the
Chinese five-tone scale (I: 7, example a). The two middle strings are a
whole tone lower than the kinursāda' of example 6. As noted above kaskas
consists of harmonic or chordal strumming. The constant tuning even in the
midst of a piece demonstrates how the keen ear can detect well the strings
that go out of pitch. A simple harmony with tonic, supertonic, and sub-
mediant relations has a lilt that is due partly to the stresses made by the
downward pluck of the hand.

GONG-BEATING AND TAPPING: BINALINSAY. An accelerando tempo neither diminishes the clarity of the rhythm nor reaches a speed that becomes unplayable. When struck on their bosses the two gongs produce sounds with scattered overtones; hence, the notes are rather unfocused. In the following example (I: 8), the note F is about a quarter tone higher and E is about a quarter tone lower than notated. A similar rhythm with added sixteenth notes is played on each rim sounding an octave higher. There are different kinds of rhythms each with specific names.

GONG-BEATING AND TAPPING: DINULUT. The rhythm on the bosses is slower in example 9 than in example 8. The beats and arrangements of eighth and sixteenth notes also differ. Per group of five notes, there are three E's in this example, and three F's in the preceding one. The rhythm used in rim tapping follows the main one on the bosses.

STAMP DANCING (TARUK). The dancer's feet resound on the bamboo floor following the rhythm of the gongs (cf. I: 8 and I: 10). Other instruments, including guitars and fiddles, provide additional accompaniment.

RITUAL CHANTING (NGĀYUNG) OF MEDIUMS (to rid the settlement of malign forest spirits). The low, slow and moaning quality of the voice gives an atmosphere of mystery and prayer to this chant. The principal voice has an entirely pentatonic construction (I: 11, example b), while the

Transcribing 'Urukay Verse to New Bamboo Internode

other voice forms a separate scale (I: 11, example c), a hexachord with an added minor third. (For more remarks regarding scales, see example I: 2). Intervals of seconds, thirds, fourths, fifths, and octaves are formed with the other voice (I: 11, example a).

FLUTE (LANTUY) SOLO BY A YOUNG GIRL (II: 1, example b). The tonal center is F. The line of fast notes is longer here than on I: 3. There are more notes per group involving different kinds of turns that tend always to go back to the center.

FLUTE (LANTUY) DUET BY A GIRL AND HER MOTHER. Dissonance produced by this chance counterpoint of two flutes is explained by a clash in their scales. One instrument has a tonal center of C (similar to the flute on I: 3); the other has a tonal center of A (II: 2, examples a-b). The long and short notes of both instruments sound sometimes together, and at other times one after the other. This happens at random, but occasionally one pauses and waits for the other (II: 2, example c).

MUSICAL STICKS (KALUTANG). (Example II: 3). These pairs of sticks play a simple harmony of unisons, seconds, thirds, and fourths that can be found in a combination of four notes belonging to the pentatonic scale (II: 3). Two contrasting features may be noted: variation and repetition. A consecutive grouping of two or more phrases shows an irregularity and variety of patterns which are possible with the long-short-short-long rhythm. Repetition of such a rhythm is a form in itself, and has an insistent and somewhat hypnotic effect.

BAMBOO JEW'S-HARP (KINABAN): 3 SELECTIONS, EXAMPLE II: 4. The different tongue positions vary the pitch and qualities of sound produced with the mouth cavity acting as a resonant chamber. The retards of the beat between eighth notes are deviations from a steady pulse common among most players. The thumb that plucks the harp away from the body takes that much more time to come back and repluck in the same direction. Some discernible rhythms are shown.

TRAIL CALLS ('ŪWI). Some of the identifiable tones are notated (II: 5, examples a-f). Except for the fifth example (II: 5, example c). all have three-tone constructions showing a good variety of rhythm and melodic outline within the limits of a few notes. When joined together they make up a Chinese scale. The note E in II: 5, example c shows again how half and whole steps complete a tetrachord, half of the seven-tone scale.

COURTING SEQUENCE (PANLAYĪSAN): COURTING SONGS ('AMBĀHAN), FIDDLE ACCOMPANIMENT (GITGIT), AND DISGUISED TALK (PAHĀGUT). The 'ambahan chants are based on only three tones forming incomplete tetrachords similar to the chants on II: 13. In playing the gitgit the pentatonic scale is used. The note E, marked x in II: 6, provides the only foreign element, and is used like a leading tone, showing again the merging of pentatonic and diatonic examples. The gitgit is played mostly between verses. There are three ranges of voices; the man has the bass part, the gitgit the other extremity, and the woman the middle range.

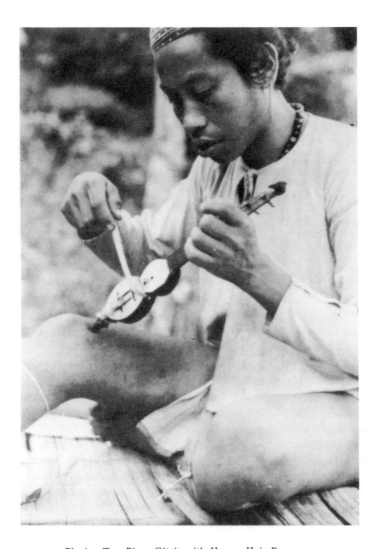

Playing Two-Piece Gitgit with Human-Hair Bow

In spite of inexact tuning, the relation bewteen the tones of each range is evident. The note F is the central point to which all the voices refer. At the end of certain lines a sliding voice may be noted.

BAMBOO ZITHERS, BUZZERS AND WHISTLES. With slight variations the rhythms used are shown in II: 8-10. The third rhythm illustrates one similar to the rhythms heard on I: 7 (guitar) and II: 4 (jew's-harp).

FLUTE AND FIDDLE DUET, EXAMPLE II: 11. The flute tune is similar to that of I: 3, and the fiddle melody to that of II: 6. The difference in rhythm between the two melodies presents ideas in counterpoint. One has a steady pulse, slow, and in triple time, (II: 11, example c), while the other is improvisatory with fast notes in between long-held tones (II: 11,

Beating the Dance Gongs

example a). Since their pitches are related to each other, the dissonances are not as stark as in the flute duet (II: 2); Both employ a diatonic construction with different ranges. In the flute it is a sixth, expanded an octave higher by overblowing (II: 11, example b), while in the fiddle it is an octave (II: 11, example d). In both cases, the seventh degree is omitted. In the fiddle melody, characteristic phrases are made up of whole steps and a major third, avoiding the half-step between E and F, and describing much of the pentatonic scale. In the flute tune, the presence of a half-step discloses a diatonic progression within the space of four, five, and six consecutive whole and half steps, without completing the expanse of two tetrachords.

FIDDLE (GITGIT): SINIDSĪRUY. A more extended melody based on the diatonic scale, Aeolian mode (II: 12, example c), appears clear and full in this piece with a central note, degrees of tension and distension, and a contour, showing a possible relationship to the musical constructions known to Christian groups on Mindoro. The uncertainty of pitch and unsteadiness of tempo are parts of the process of adapting this musical construction to local tastes. The *sinidsīruy* is the name of this particular kind of melody played on a specified tuning of strings (II: 12, example b). There are other kinds of tunings with other melodies.

AN ʻAMBĀHAN CHANT, SUNG BY A LOVER, EXAMPLE II: 13. This recitation is the simplest of the chants recorded (I: 2, 4, 11). Only three notes are used in which E flat serves as tonal center within an interval of a fourth. The suggestion of a complete tetrachord adds up to the variety of interval combinations formed by all these chants. The prolongation of the tone at the end of verse lines emphasizes the assonance of *ʼambāhan* chants.

Young Girl Playing Musical Sticks (Kalūtang)

Miscellaneous Hanunóo Instruments

The lowering of the voice at the end of the last word signifies the end of
the piece. There are variations of the text either when said or sung, but
singing encourages more improvising both in the text and music.

> My loved one, Ma'ayan
> Don't feel so low
> Our elders will help us
> And we will exchange gifts
> To strengthen the bond;
> If things work out
> If all goes well
> We will meet again.

MUSICAL EXAMPLES

The Kudyapi'

Numbers correspond to numbers of strings

diatonic   pentatonic

Scale of example b

I: 8

a. rhythm played on bosses of both gongs

b. rhythm of one player on one rim

c. rhythm of second player on other rim

I, 9   I, 10

R = right foot, L = left foot

I: 11 a

b   c

II: 1 a   b

Notes marked x are about a quarter tone
lower than notated.

scale formed

II: 6 Man's part: Woman's part:

Violin:

Tuning of 3 strings

II: 8-10 a b c d

↓ = down pluck of the hand

II: 11 a Flute part:

b Scale: c Gitgit part:

d Scale: e Tuning of strings

II: 12 a

b c

Tuning of strings   Scale formed

II; 13

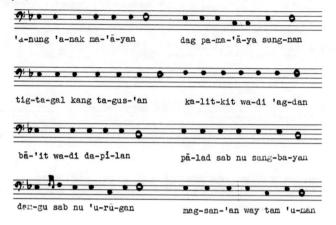

'a-nung 'a-nak ma-'a-yan   dag pa-ma-'a-ya sung-nan

tig-ta-gal kang ta-gus-'an   ka-lit-kit wa-di 'ag-dan

ba-'it wa-di da-pi-lan   pa-lad sab nu sang-ba-yan

dem-gu sab nu 'u-ru-gan   mag-san-'an way tam 'u-man

INDIAN MUSIC IN THE SOUTHWEST

David P. McAllester

Among the Indian tribes of North and South America a number of vital musical traditions exist today. From the point of view of the arts, humanities and social sciences this music is important because of its own intrinsic beauty and also because it embodies many of the unique artistic, religious and philosophic values of the cultures in which it is found.

In a discussion of the music of the Apache, Navaho and Pueblo peoples of the Southwest, some generalizations can be made that will apply to most North American Indian music as well. A striking feature is that it is almost entirely vocal. Except for a few flutes, and whistles, the musical instruments are largely for the purpose of accompanying the voice and consist of a wide variety of drums, rasps and rattles. Only a few instances have been noted of Indian groups using some form of part-singing; unison is almost the universal rule. In the rare instances when men and women sing together it is usually in parallel octaves.

The songs are characteristically performed in a vigorous, emphatic manner. Though pitches range from a deep bass to a piercing falsetto, the overall impression is of a high, tense quality in which emphases are sometimes marked with sharp yells. Occasional bird or animal calls may be introduced as part of the song. Fine voices do not go unnoticed, but there is little effort to cultivate a "pleasing" voice for its own sake. People come to hear famous songs rather than famous singers. A good memory is more important than a pleasing voice even though different areas have distinct vocal techniques which most singers follow.

The melody most frequently starts high and, in the course of the song, moves down over an octave or more until it comes to rest on a bass note which we call the tonic in our tradition. Often a song contains a number of such figures with the later beginnings lower than the earlier ones and all coming to rest on the base note. The result is a "collapsing" melodic line in which the tonic is given a very great solidity and all movement seems drawn to it as though to a magnet.

The meter tends to be regular throughout, most often in duple time. However it has the flexibility to be expected in melodic (as contrasted with harmonic) music; measures or phrases of uneven length frequently occur to accommodate differences of text in succeeding verses, or for other reasons.

The texts very often contain long sections of vocables or nonsense syllables such as *he-ne-ne-ya* or *heyo-heyo-ho-ho-wa*, which may outweigh the meaningful words in the song by as much as three or four to one. Often

215

entire songs may consist of vocables only, yet they are fixed for a particular song and the types of vocables used vary consistently from tribe to tribe. Though there are song series with meaningful texts of epic dimensions and high literary quality, the short rhapsodic text surrounded by vocables is prevalent enough to be called the usual mode. This Apache song is a good example:

> Heyoneya, heyoneya,
> ' A way no yo 'awe heyo, ne yanga
> ' A way he yo 'awehe ya neya
> Heyoneya, heyoneya,
> The girls of Deshiko go downstream two by two,
> Heyoneya, heynoeya, etc.

American Indian singing is group singing for the most part. There are leaders who introduce songs, singing the first few notes solo, or who by themselves carry one part of an antiphonal piece, but even the ceremonial practitioner who is master of a large complex chant is usually the center of a chorus made up of anyone who wants to hum along with him or knows even a few phrases of the work in hand. Though there are certain songs, such as lullabies or corn-grinding songs, that are specifically for women, one is struck by the absence of women's voices in North American Indian music as a whole.

Most of the music is religious. This is a corollary of the integrated quality of American Indian life in which art, theater, medicine, and religion are not separated into different categories but overlap each other to such an extent that there are often no separate terms for them in the native languages. Religion pervades the daily life with an immediate practical force rare in our own culture. It has little theology, not being concerned with questions of belief, but functions largely to maintain the order of the universe and to get necessary things done. Women have a clearly delineated role and generally this does not include leadership in ritual. Many Indian cultures are matrilineal; women may own most of the property and the home and give their family name to their children, but ceremony tends to be in the hands of the men.

Music of the Pueblos

The tightly organized theocratic towns known collectively as the "Pueblos" (Spanish: "towns") of Arizona and New Mexico had their beginnings in wandering bands of people living in brush shelters or simple pithouses and gathering wild foods in the desert. By about 200 A.D. they had obtained corn from peoples to the south, and were creating farm communities and making pottery. By 900 A.D. the pattern of Pueblo culture was clearly set and adobe villages were established near good farm land in peaceful regions or in fortified caves, as at Mesa Verde, when the people were under attack. For various reasons, which certainly included a long drought, the inhabitants of the agricultural towns moved south to the Rio Grande where their descendants live today, and, further west, established the desert Pueblos of Acoma, Zuni and the Hopi. Though there are some twenty towns and four quite separate languages among them, there is a striking similarity of culture.

Corn Dance by Theodore Suina   Collection: Denver Art Museum

The calendrical round of ceremonies is oriented toward bringing rain and ensuring good crops. The most common family organization is matrilineal—a man is at home in his mother's house. His important role is as a farmer and a keeper of ceremonies: his membership in religious societies is the dominant aspect of his life. In his hands is the curing of the sick and the turning of the seasons.

Song and dance are an inseparable part of the religious ritual. There is much emphasis on preparation and training in the underground chambers (kivas) where the religious societies meet. As a result the ceremonies are highly polished performances: the deep pulsing choruses, chanting the long periods of sacred formulae, sing as one man. The costumes are beautifully refurbished for every ceremony and the dancers move with clarity and precision. The cooperation and organization evident in the music and other aspects of ritual are reflected in many phases of Pueblo life.

As might be expected, of the sophisticated town dwellers of the Southwest, Pueblo music has great variety. The music of the great rituals is performed in the plazas before audiences of all ages. The singers, costumed, painted and often masked, represent deities related to rain, crops and the changing seasons. They dance as they sing. The movement is in contained, formal figures, highly repetitive, and the songs too are repetitive and chant-like. Part of the dance is often mimetic gesture, emphasizing and clarifying the lesson to be imparted. Corn, Butterfly, Kachina, Snake and Buffalo Dances invoke the help of deities, celebrate the beauty of clouds and rain and of creatures associated with rain, and instruct the people concerning these sources of life and happiness. Here is an example from Acoma:

> There in the west is the home of the raingods,
> There in the west is their water pool,
> In the middle of the water pool is the spruce tree
>   that they use as a ladder,
> Up from the water the raingods draw the crops
>   which give us life,
> East from there, on the place where we dance,
>   they lay the crops,
> Then up from that place the people receive crops and life.*

Other dances have a secular as well as a sacred context. Comanche, Forty-nine, and Squaw Dances are examples which not only bring rain but are also considered to be recreational or social dances. The accompanying songs are likely to have texts entirely of vocables or largely of vocables with brief jocular phrases added such as:

> Weya he yaheye yaheye yaheyo ha he yo,
> Weya he yaheye yaheye yaheyo ha he yo,
> Weya he yaheye yaheye yaheyo haheyoho ya weya heyo weya.
> Oh yes I love you Sweetheart,
> I don't care if you marry sixteen times,
> I'll get you yet oweya yaya.
> Weya hayo weya hayo hayo.

There are also many kinds of songs not necessarily associated with dances. The corn grinding songs mentioned above are examples. There are animal or bird songs with stories, and game songs that accompany various forms of gambling. Lullabies are widely known in the Pueblos and may describe creatures such as owls and deer by their appearance and actions, or compare the baby to a beetle, puppy or rabbit.

Pueblo culture has been unusually resistant to influences from outside.

Music of Acoma, Isleta, Cochiti and Zuni Pueblos, by Frances Densmore, Smithsonian Institution, Bureau of American Ethnology, Bulletin 165, Washington, 1957, p. 46.

The native religion and many other traditions have been jealously preserved by a strong priesthood even in towns that have been nominally Roman Catholic since the Spanish Conquest four hundred years ago. In the face of such conservatism it comes as a surprise to find the Pueblos quite distinctly cosmopolitan in some aspects of their musical life.

Though the Pueblos are reticent about the more deeply sacred music, they are often willing to record the public recreational songs, and they borrow very readily from the music of other cultures at this level. Navaho "Yeibichai" songs and dances are used at the end of the great midwinter Shalako festival at Zuni: corngrinding songs are freely traded from Pueblo to Pueblo and also borrowed from the Navahos. Many "Comanche Dance" songs are Plains Indian melodies made over in a Pueblo mold. "Forty-nine' songs are picked up from recordings or are learned at Indian shows or Indian schools where members of different tribes come together.

A certain high point in cosmopolitanism is shown at Zuni where a song recording a conversation between a Navaho man and a Hopi girl is entirely in those two languages and where at least one veteran of overseas action can sing "Auld Lang Syne," in Korean. An imitation Indian song has been recorded at Zuni in which an intelligent Indian woman follows exactly the style demanded by non-Indian Americans when they want to hear "Indian" music.

The composition of new songs is a constant process in Pueblo music. Songs are created for the sacred ceremonies as well as for social dances by singers noted for their invention. There are learned, rehearsed and used for a season or two after which they may be replaced by still newer songs. Some of these compositions become so well-liked that they may be used longer than usual. Some sacred songs have passed into the popular repertory for this reason after their ritual service was accomplished.

The Apaches and Navahos

The Apaches and Navahos are closely related Athabascan speaking migrants who began filtering into the Southwest in small groups around the turn of the first millenium A.D. Armed with powerful sinew-backed bows, they lived as hunters and marauders organized in self-sufficient bands under strong leadership. It seems likely that it was these invaders who forced the Pueblo Indians to retreat into their fortified villages and cliff dwellings in the 12th and 13th centuries. It also seems clear that it was the Pueblo revolt against Spanish dominion in 1680 that led to the differentiation of Navaho from Apache culture. For many years whole villages of Pueblo peoples, fearing reprisals by the Spanish, hid away in the back country in close contact with the Athabascan hunters and taught them gardening, sheepherding and weaving. The two groups intermarried and began to spread over the countryside in agricultural family settlements. To the east and west of this zone of mixed culture the other Athabascans continued in their small tightly organized hunting and raiding bands and became the Eastern and Western Apaches. Meanwhile, in northwestern New Mexico, the hunters-turned-farmers prospered greatly, spread westward into Arizona and became the Navahos, the largest tribe in the United States. Today their population is approaching 100,000, while the nine divisions of the Eastern and Western Apaches together total hardly a tenth of that number.

Music of the Apaches

"Apache" the world over is a synonym for daring and relentless warfare. Sometimes a mere handful of these warriors was enough to engage the full operations of the U.S. Army for months on end: for decades their economic base consisted of booty from raids and tribute from terrified Mexican towns. Today cattle ranching on beautiful upland range in the mountains of Arizona and New Mexico, and tribal income from timber and mineral resources, provide for several of the bands, notably the White Mountain and San Carlos of the Western Apache and the Mescalero and Jicarilla of the Eastern group. Though there is variety in detail in the cultures of the various bands, certain features distinguish them all as part of a single tradition.

Much interest in Apache life is focused on the puberty ceremony for young girls. This is a time of celebration and blessing for the whole community. The girl dances for hours and observes ritual tabus that indicate the sacred forces now inherent in her body: for example she must drink through a tube because the touch of her lips would have a powerful effect on all water and make it unsafe for others to drink. Gifts and food are exchanged, symbolic of the wealth and happiness implied by the fertility celebrated in the ceremony. The girl runs in the four directions as an earnest of her future energy and physical well-being, and a beautiful woman molds her body to ensure symmetry and perfection.

Other rituals are similarly centered on the individual, particularly in case of sickness which is considered a disruption of harmony between man and the forces of nature. Deities such as White Shell Woman, Monster Slayer, Child of the Water, White God, Black God, Snake and Mountain Gods, are invoked in night-long chants to aid the sick person. Some of these beings are depicted in colored sands in dry-paintings laid out on the floor in the ceremonial shelter. The design serves as an altar and is dismantled immediately after it has been used. Small dry-paintings are sometimes made with pollen on buckskin and the power of the beings represented is transferred to the sick person by application.

Beneficent Mountain Gods are represented by kilted dancers in black masks crowned with carved and painted wooden slats. By their presence at puberty rites or curing ceremonials these deities bring sacred power and help to the people. Their spectacular dance, commonly called Crown Dance or Devil Dance, with its dramatic angular movement and the comical, befuddled clown, is much admired in the Southwest: some outstanding dance

Apache Crown Dance by Allan Houser   Collection: Denver Art Museum

teams give public performances at "pow-wows" and Indian shows.

Apache music sounds very different from the measured choruses of the Pueblos. A tense, strongly nasal voice production is used and there is a technique, uniquely Apache, of suddenly releasing this tension and almost "swallowing" the voice. Songs begin high, often very high in a powerful falsetto, and descend to the tonic where several phrases may be repeated on that one tone alone. The songs begin with a chorus, very often built solely on the open triad (do-mi-sol-do), and usually with a vocable text. Then comes the meaningful text, usually chanted on one or two tones with the jerky, swallowing technique mentioned above. Songs often contain two balancing verses with the chorus at the beginning and end and also between the verses. The first verse usually refers to male deities and attributes and the second verse to female. The balance between male and female appears in many aspects of the ritual and mythology.

The individualism of Apache culture is apparent in their music. Though nearly all formal singing is choral, personal variations are pronounced; it is a group of individuals singing rather than a choir in which all voices are merged in one effect.

Besides strictly ritual music the Apaches have social dance songs, often associated with ceremonies; moccasin game songs; songs of famous warriors; and social songs that may accompany the convivial drinking of tulpai, a native beverage made from fermented corn. In all these songs the vocal technique and formal structure is very much the same as in the ceremonial music described above.

The Lipan, Carrizo and Mescalero Apaches are early links in the movement of the Peyote religion from Mexico to the Plains tribes of the United States. This pan-tribal sect which has long been organized as the Native American Church has a considerable body of sacred music. The Eastern Apaches, who have practiced the religion since well before white contact, may have contributed much to its style as it is sung today from Mexico to Canada and all through the Western and Middle-western states. Long introductory and codential phrases on the tonic, the prevailingly downward melodic movement, a prevalence of the open triad, the consistent use of a separate note for every syllable of text and the restriction of the time values of these notes to only two, a long and a short, are all features of Apache music and are characteristic of Peyote style. The water drum used to accompany Peyote music may also be a development from the Apache water drum described below.

The Apache fiddle, almost the only stringed instrument of native make found anywhere among North American Indians, is small, rarely more than two feet long, made on a hollowed out mescal stalk. It has a bow, strung with resined horsehair, and one or two horsehair or gut strings which emit a faint squeaky sound when bowed. Brief melodies based on favorite tulpai songs constitute the repertory. It is a chamber instrument, played at home to oneself or a small group.

The Apaches also make a whistle flute of river cane with three stops which usually produce notes approximating do-mi-fa-sol of the European scale. Brief melodies on these notes are repeated over and over with a breathy quavering technique. Flutes and flute-playing are associated with love and love magic. The characteristic Apache drum is a water drum made on a large iron pot. The buckskin drumhead is stretched over the opening and bound in place with buckskin thongs or narrow strips of inner tubing. The rasp, a notched stick held on a gourd or basket resonator and rubbed with a bone or another stick, is used in some rituals. For example, a rasp made of manzanita wood was used in a curing ceremony involving the sacred power of mountains and bears since bears like to eat manzanita berries.

Music of the Navahos

In many ways, Navaho culture seems to be an elaboration on the basic Southern Athabascan pattern still shown by their cousins the Apaches. Their greatest fame, of course, rests in their fine tapestry-weave rugs and their silvercraft. These arts, learned from the Pueblos and the Mexicans, respectively, epitomize the Navaho flair for developing ideas and techniques and making them into something Navaho. The same thing has happened with their ritual. Quite possibly it was their long contact with the Pueblo refugees and the relative leisure of agricultural life that helped to create a loosening of tradition and a willingness to invent new forms. Whatever the causes, they now possess an integrated series of some thirty or forty ceremonials ranging up to nine nights in length and endowed with a tremendous richness of symbolic detail.

As with the Apaches, the purpose is to restore and maintain harmony with the forces of nature and is focused on an individual in need of this effect. The major chants have as many as two or three dozen dry-paintings associated with them. The sick person, the "one sung over," and his family choose from among these possibilities for the particular performance in mind, according to their budget and their specific needs. The larger dry-paintings may be ten or twelve feet square and in their creation may require several hours of intensive work by the ceremonial practitioner and a half dozen assistants.

Quite typically the ritual program consists of several days of exorcism during which all danger and evil are banished from the individual and from his family and all others who are present. Then follows a period of invocation of blessing and help is sought from the deities appropriate to the illness of the "one sung over." In essence the performance is the retelling or re-enactment of parts in the creation myth. For example, where someone is suffering from shock or apprehension after having been bitten or frightened by a snake, the Shootingway may be performed. The episode of a hero living with the Snake People and obtaining their power is re-enacted in the songs, in the scenes depicted in the dry-paintings and in the formal ritual procedure of the singer. In the ceremony, the one sung over is the protagonist in a drama which vividly portrays his attainment of kinship with, and power over snakes:

> He is gliding along, head lifted, he is gliding along, head lifted,
> He is gliding along, head lifted, he is gliding along, head lifted,
>
> Now Holy Young Man is gliding like a snake, head lifted,
> Now the Great Dark Snake is gliding along, head lifted,
> He is traveling in the dust, head lifted,
> He is traveling in the dew, head lifted,
> He is full of menace, gliding along, head lifted,
> He trembles at the danger, gliding along, head lifted,
> Life forever, harmony everywhere, he is gliding along, head lifted.
>
> She is gliding along, head lifted, etc.
> (second verse is the same except that it refers to
> Holy Young Woman and the Great White Snake.)

The two most common Navaho ceremonials, on which are concentrated much of the interest and zest in the daily life of the culture, are Enemyway and Blessingway. The former is a war ceremonial to protect Navahos from the ghosts of alien peoples. Its private ritual contains formidable ghost-killing magic and its public aspect includes the Navahos' only social dancing and a tremendous body of popular songs.

Blessingway is the best loved of the ceremonies and involves only the invocation of good. Its songs are "songs of good hope." It is frequently performed for a pregnant woman shortly before the child is expected, or for someone about to undertake a long journey. It is the shortest and simplest of the ceremonies and the most sacred. It is described by the Navahos as the "root" or the "backbone" of their religion. Parts or all of it are incorporated into most of the larger ceremonies. The purificatory bathing and drying of the protagonist is the climax of this rite and is a re-enactment of the bathing and drying of Changing Woman, the principal Navaho deity. The cornmeal powder with which she was dried, mixed with the loose skin from her body, is the substance from which man was created.

A great variety of shorter or longer, or combined forms of the chants may be performed, again according to the particular needs of the individual for whose sake all this complex of ritual, dance, drama and music is set in motion.

The music is much like that of the Apache ceremonials: chorus-verse-chorus, with the greater melodic movement on the choruses and a considerable use of the open triad. Even the sacred texts have the same or very similar phrases that constantly reappear in both cultures. Navaho vocal style is also nasal and individualistic but less markedly so than that of the Apaches. In the verses of the former the melody is less restricted in range and smoother in delivery than in the latter. But in music, as in other things, the Navahos show their interest in new forms. In the popular public music of the Enemyway, for instance (the "Squaw Dance" songs), there are several different kinds of songs such as Circle Dance, Skip Dance, and Sway songs, which do not follow the pattern described above but are highly melodic throughout and in which the texts are largely vocables with only a few meaningful phrases. Some Skip Dance songs are being composed today using material borrowed from Rock'n'Roll and other popular music that is heard on the radio and then made over according to Navaho patterns of music.

The dance songs of the Nightway are another case in point. Masked dancers, impersonating male and female gods (Yeibichai), perform with a clown much like the one that accompanies the Apache Mountain Gods, and sing striking songs which start with the cry of the gods and then soar into falsetto cadences very unlike the chant style.

Along with the Navahos' freedom in the elaboration of ritual and the invention of new forms in religion, art and music, there is a sense of secrecy of esoteric ritual and knowledge which is more reminiscent of the Pueblos than of the Apaches. Apache women sometimes join the sacred chanting and are likely to link arms and dance forward and back in graceful lines wherever there is music: Navaho women seem more excluded from religious participation, rarely sing at all, and dance only in "Squaw Dances." Indeed, even at Squaw Dances there are nights when only a few girls come

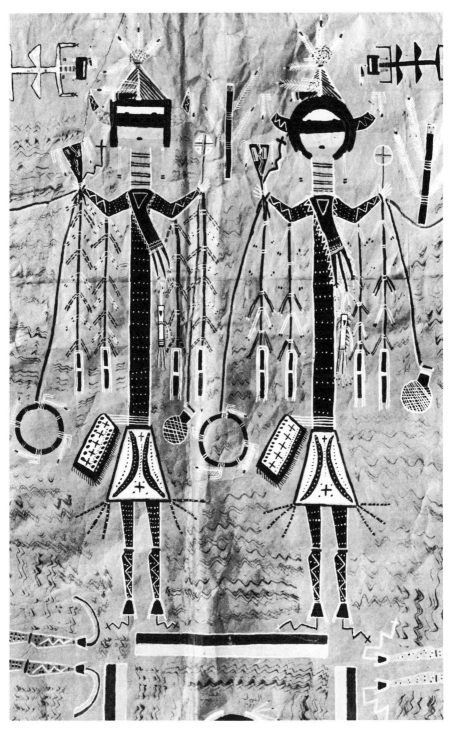

Detail from reproduction of Shootingway Sandpainting showing Sky Woman and Man holding hide rattles in right hand and wearing otterskin collars with reed whistles attached.

Collection: The Taylor Museum.

out to dance, and that only briefly, or when no dancing occurs at all. Convivial drinking is part of the ritual at Apache ceremonies; liquor is illegal at Navaho ceremonies, at least nominally. Parts of Navaho rituals are private; strangers, especially non-Navahos, are not welcome. Even as regards other Navahos, there is a belief that it is unsafe for those not initiated in certain kinds of ritual to be present. Some forms of Navaho music, such as flute playing and corn-grinding songs, have become virtually extinct, very likely because of increasing restrictions surrounding their performance.

Navaho musical instruments consist of a small water drum made of a tall gray pot often only five or six inches in diameter at the opening, the bull-roarer, ritual whistles some of which are played with the distal end in a cup of water to give a burbling sound in imitation of songbirds, rawhide and gourd rattles and a basket turned over and thumped with a drumstick made of yucca leaves. All of these are specific to certain ceremonies and are never used out of their religious context.

In the last twenty years many hundreds of Navahos have joined the Native American Church. They seem to have taken the peyote songs and instruments from their neighbors the Utes, or from Plains sources, with little or no modification. Some students of Navaho culture have predicted that in time the Navahos will turn the peyote ritual into another Navaho chant. It remains to be seen whether their genius for absorption can prevail over the fixed forms of this strongly identified sect.

SONG STRUCTURE AND SOCIAL STRUCTURE

Alan Lomax

Music-making is one of the most strictly patterned forms of human behavior. Its modes of communication are so limited that even a casual listener can distinguish quickly the best performers and identify the pieces in an idiom of whose technique and content he knows nothing. For many centuries and in many cultures, musical adepts have had at their disposal elaborate systems of notation and theory. The musicologists of our time have inherited this treasure of knowledge and have refined greatly their analytic tools. Thousands of volumes of accurately notated music exist, alongside of carefully wrought critical studies. Yet, it seem, none of us is much closer to understanding what music is and what it says than are the singers of primitive cultures. As one of America's leading musicologists remarked to me a year ago, "No one knows anything about melody." If melody, a possession of all human beings everywhere and at every stage of development, is a mystery, what of rhythm, harmony, and the superstructures erected with these three magic tools?

The suggestion of this paper is that ethnomusicology should turn aside, for a time, from the study of music in purely musical terms to a study of music in context, as a form of human behavior. In the first stages of such a study it is not necessary that all that is known and notatable about music be accounted for. It would be a positive step forward to delineate the varying shapes of musical behavior and to begin to frame this behavior in its precise cultural setting. It should then be possible to discern the bonds between musical patterns and the socio-psychological traits available to other humanistic disciplines.

As a working hypothesis, I propose the common-sense notion that music somehow expresses emotion; therefore, when a distinctive and consistent musical style lives in a culture or runs through several cultures, one can posit the existence of a distinctive set of emotional needs or drives that are somehow satisfied or evoked by this music. If such a musical style occurs with only a limited pattern of variation in the similar cultural setting and over a long period of time, one may assume that a stable expressive and emotional pattern has existed in group A in area B through time T. Thus we might look forward to a scientific musicology that could speak with some precision about formative emotional attitudes pervading cultures and operating through history. In this first stage of investigation we need not be concerned about the way that musical symbolism works, but only with a method that would locate sets of musical phenomena cross-culturally.

Until recently, the musical habits of mankind were not well enough known to make such a cross-cultural study possible. In the past twenty years, however, excellent field recordings from a wide sample of primitive and folk cultures have been published. We need no longer depend upon notations of music from exotic sources. Unlike the musicologists of the past, we need no longer evaluate the varied music of the peoples of the world from a perspective of the fine-art music of Western Europe, for we now have adequate comparative data and can examine them at leisure on their own terms.

In the summer of 1961 a Rockefeller grant enabled me, with my musicologist assistant, Victor Grauer, to assemble and to review approximately 400 sets of recordings and tapes from about 250 culture areas. Each selection was played over ultra-high-fidelity equipment through a pair of matched speakers, one for each listener, and was rated in a comparable manner. In this preliminary survey we could not, of course, completely control the size or the authenticity of the sample from all areas. Normally each culture was represented by from six to twenty selections on an LP recording, edited by the field recordist. We believe that, on the whole, these editor-collectors, most of whom were anthropologists or ethnomusicologists, chose representative materials for these LPs. Elsewhere I had to trust my own judgment, gained in a lifetime of field work and editing field tapes. In any case, our analytic technique—which was designed to look at gross traits rather than the detail of music—obviates this difficulty to a considerable extent. The method shows up stylistic pattern so quickly and in such bold relief that, even when a very large sample was available, we found it unnecessary to analyze more than two or three pieces; additional data usually confirmed the first observations.

Furthermore, we found that our descriptive method took care of the normally troublesome distinctions between the more or less "authentic" or "genuine" songs in the sample. As long as the material was recorded on the spot from native informants, even strongly acculturated music from an area conformed in most respects to the profiles established for conservative and traditional songs. For example, we found that "folk," banjo-accompanied, American mountain ballads differed in only two or three particulars from contemporary hillbilly songs; both could be classified legitimately as adhering to the same performance style, at least in terms of our level of analysis. Many similar experiences made us confident that, even when the sample of data from an area is small and acculturated, our method always tells us something important about the structure of the musical performance in that culture.

Cantometrics

This method is called *cantometrics*. Cantometrics is a system for rating a song performance in a series of qualitative judgments; one day it may be a way of using song as an indicator of social and psychological pattern in a culture. Cantometrics takes into account the phenomena described by European music notation—melody, rhythm, harmony, interval size, etc.—but it looks beyond these European basics at many other factors present in and (as far as we could tell by intensive listening) generic to the song style of other areas. These factors include the size and social structure of the music-making group; the location and role of leadership in the music-making group; the type and the degree of integration in the music-making group; the type and the degree of melodic, rhythmic, and vocal embellishment in a sung performance; and the qualities of the singing voice normally effected by the chosen singers in a culture. Since these features of a performance are judged by our system in a summary fashion, we also looked at the purely musical traits at a similar level. For example, rhythm was rated, not in terms of the precise meter that occurred in a selection, but in terms of levels of increasing complexity—from the simple one-beat rhythm, often found among Amerindians, to the free, almost meterless rhythms common to much Oriental singing. In addition, however, we looked at the type of rhythmic organization of both the singing and instrumental groups, here again rating the sample in terms of increasing levels of integration, from simple unison to complex counterpoint. Thus our rating system, for rhythm, quickly summarizes in four judgments much of the information that would be obtainable from painstaking notation and analysis of hundreds of examples by normal methods of music notation.

Cantometrics does not depend, except at one or two levels, upon formal musical analysis, but is limited, I believe, to those features of a sung performance which are available and important to a "normal listener" anywhere. Using the cantometrics system, a trained observer can make the same series of defined observations about any song that he hears, whether recorded or "live." These judgments are recorded in a series of 37 rating scales on a standard data sheet. Each one of these parameters or lines contains from three to thirteen points, each point being the locus of a proximate judgment in relation to the other points on the same line. The number of levels was limited to 37 by the size of the coding sheet, and the number of points on any line was limited by the thirteen punches available in a column on an IBM card. No more points were included on any line than we felt could be handled by an attentive listener.

These 37 lines, with 219 points, are set forth in a symbolic map on the right side of the coding sheet. The symbols, which are abbreviations for the distinctions made in each line, greatly facilitate learning and using the system. The listener records his judgments on the symbolic map and then transfers them to a number map on the left, which also serves as an IBM data sheet. Here the numbers are arranged and spaced so that they match the corresponding lines of symbols. With some practice, cantometrics enables a listener to describe a recorded song from anywhere in the world in a matter of minutes. The results of this notation may be compared and then averaged with material from the same culture, until, within a short working period, a master profile in numerical or linear form is ready for cross-cultural comparison.

The Coding Sheet

The cantometric coding book now ready for publication runs to more than

Figure 1: Sample Cantometric Coding Sheet

CODE SHEET - The Musical Situation - Source: **MEAD - SCHWARTZ TAPE 3 NO. 2**
Group or Song: **LAMENT** · Language: **MANUS** Location: **MANUS, NEW**
male singer - Joseph Mataway **GUINEA**

Line				
1) Vocal Gp.	[2] 3 4 5 6 7 8 9 10 11 12 13	∅ (L/N NA) -L L/N N/L L/N N/L L÷N N÷N L(N N(L N(N W
2) Orch. Relationship	[1] 2 3 5 6 8 9 12 13	∅ /o /0 0/ 0 //o //0 (o (0
3) Orch. Gp.	[1] 2 3 4 5 6 7 8 9 10 11 12 13	∅ (L/N Na) -L L/N N/L L/N N//L L÷N N÷N L(N N(L N(N
4) Vocal Org.	▬[4] 7 10 13	∅ (M) U H P
5) Tonal Blend-V	[1] 4 7 10 13	(∅) b b̲ B B̲
6) Rhy. Blend - V	[1] 4 7 10 13	(∅) r r̲ R R̲
7) Orch. Org.	[1] 4 7 10 13	(∅) M U H P
8) Tonal Blend-O	[1] 4 7 10 13	(∅) b b̲ B B̲
9) Rhy. Blend - O	[1] 4 7 10 13	(∅) r r̲ R R̲
10) Words to Non.	[1] 4 7 10 13	(WO) wo wo-no wo-NO NO
11) Overall Rhy - V	▬▬▬[11] 13	∅ R1 R- R-v R★ R★v (R1) Rpa
12) Grp. Rhy.-V	[1] 3 5 7 9 11 13	(∅) Ru RH RA Rp Rpm Rc
13) Overall Rhy-O	[1] 3 5 6 8 9 11 13	(∅) R1 R- R-v R★ R★v R1 Rpa
14) Grp. Rhy.-O	[1] 3 5 7 9 11 13	(∅) Ru Rh Ra Rp Rpm Rc
15) Mel. Shape	▬[4] ▬[9] 13	(A) T (U) D
16) Mel. Form	▬▬[10] 11 12 13	t+St★V St★v St★ StV Stv StL★V L★vL (LV) Lv L C
17) Phrase Length	[1] 4 7 10 13	(P) P P p- p
18) No. of Phrases	▬▬▬[13]	8+ 5/7 4/A 4/S 3/A 3/S 2/A (1/2S)
19) Pos. of Final	[1] 4 9 11 13	(f) f̲ F F̲ F̲
20) Range	▬▬[7] 10 13	1-2 3-5 (5-8) 10+ 16+
21) Int. Width	▬▬[7] 10 13	∅ w (w̲) W W̲
22) Pol. Type	[1] 3 6 8 10 13	(∅) DR Ic Pc H C
23) Embell.	▬▬[10] 13	E̲ E e̲ (e) é
24) Tempo	▬▬[9] 11 13	t-- t- t t̲ (T) T̲ T-
25) Volume	▬[4] 7 10 13	PP (P) N f ff
26) Rubato-V	▬[5] 9 13	))) ( ))) ∅
27) Rubato-O	▬▬▬[13]	)))))) (∅)
28) Gliss	▬▬[9] 13	(((((((∅)
29) Melisma	▬▬[13]	M m (∅)
30) Tremulo	▬[7] 13	TR (tr) ∅
31) Glottal Sh.	▬▬[13]	GL gl (∅)
32) Register	▬[7] 10 13	V-Hi Hi (Mid.) Low V-Low
33) Vo. Width	▬▬[8] 10 13	V-NA NA Sp (Wi) V-Wi Yodel
34) Nasality	▬[4] 7 10 13	V-NAS (GT.) Intermit. Slight None
35) Raspiness	▬[4] 7 10 13	Ext (GT.) Intermit. Slight None
36) Accent	▬▬[10] 13	V.Force Fo Normal (Relaxed) V-Re
37) Conson.	▬[4] 7 10 13	V-Prec. (Pre) No. Slur. V-Slur

50 pages and thus can be only summarized here. Therefore, in what follows, each rating scale, which is fully defined in the coding book, is explained in the briefest terms. An exception is Line 1, with which this article is particularly concerned. Unless otherwise stated, Point 1 in each line stands for the nonoccurrence of a trait, and the line itself, reading from left to right, is a scale from nonoccurrence to maximal occurrence of a trait. Figure 1 reproduces a sample cantometric coding sheet, coded for a lament recorded by Margaret Mead and Theodore Schwartz in Manus, New Guinea. A line-by-line explanation of the coding system follows.

(1) *Organization of the Vocal Group,* rated in terms of increasing group dominance and integration. This line asks the question: Is the performance a solo by a leader (L) with a passive audience (N) and the resultant situation that of the leader completely dominating the group (L over N), or is the group (N) in some way active in relation to the leader (L)? Point 2 indicates complete leader dominance (e.g., Orient, Western Europe). Points 3 and 4 represent other solo singing situations (e.g., Southern Spain). Points 5 and 6 denote simple unison singing in which leader and group sing the same material in the same way and in concert (e.g., Amerindian and many other primitive peoples). In 5 (L/N), the leader is dominant more than 50 per cent of the time, whereas the reverse relationship prevails in 6 (N/L). Point 7 represents the situation in which both L and N are active in singing the same melodic material, but one part slightly trails the other and often adds small melodic or rhythmic variations (e.g., Oriental choruses, Watusi). Point 8 (L+N) is noted when L sings a phrase and then N separately repeats it. Point 9 (N+N) is indicated when N sings a phrase and another part of the chorus (N) repeats it. Points 10, 11, and 12 denote what we term interlocked relationships, i.e., when a part of a singing group overlaps another or performs a supportive function for the other (e.g., Negro Africa). L(N, in 10, indicates an interlocked relationship between L and N in which L is dominant; N(L, in 11, indicates a similar relationship with N dominant; N(N, in 12 denotes a similar relationship between two groups. Point 13 (W) indicates complete interlocking (e.g., Pygmy hocketing style, European contrapuntal choir).

(2) *Relation of Orchestra to Singers.* Point 1 denotes absence of orchestra or accompaniment. Point 2 indicates a simple accompanying relation by one to three instruments; Point 3, the same with a larger orchestra; Point 4, the same with a dominant big orchestra. Point 5 indicates a big orchestra alone. Points 8 and 9 denote the trailing relationship with a small and a big orchestra; Points 12 and 13, the interlocked relationship with a small and a large orchestra.

(3) *Organization of the Orchestra,* rated in terms of increasing group dominance from left to right, as in Line 1.

(4) *Type of Vocal Organization.* Point 1: no singer. Point 2: monophony. Point 3: unison singing. Point 4: heterophony. Point 5: polyphony, i.e., any consistent use of part singing, no matter how simple.

(5) *Tonal Blend: Voices.* This line rates voice blending in the chorus from none to homogeneous to well integrated.

(6) *Rhythmic Blend: Voice.* This line rates the rhythmic integration of the chorus in five degrees, from poorly to well integrated.

(7) *Type of Orchestral Organization.* Rated as in Line 4.

(8) *Tonal Blend: Orchestra.* Rated as in Line 5.

(9) *Rhythmic Blend: Orchestra.* Rated as in Line 6.

(10) *Words to Nonsense.* This line rates the relative importance of meaningful words as against nonsense syllables (including vocal segregates) in a sung text. Point 1: words important and dominant. Point 2: words less important. Point 3: words with some nonsense. Point 4: nonsense more important than words. Point 5: nonsense only.

(11) *Over-all Rhythm of the Vocal Part,* rated in increasing degrees of metrical complexity. Point 3: one-beat rhythm. Point 5 and 6: simple meters such as 2/4 or 3/4. Points 8 and 9: complex meters such as 7/8. Point 11: irregular meter. Point 13: no consistent meter.

(12) *Linking Rhythm of the Vocal Group,* rated in terms of increasingly complex

integration. Point 3: unison. Point 5: heterophony. Point 7: accompanying rhythm. Point 9: polyrhythm. Point 11: polymeter. Point 13: rhythmic counterpoint.

(13) *Over-all Rhythm of the Orchestra.* Rated as in Line 11.

(14) *Linking Rhythm of the Orchestra.* Rated as in Line 12.

(15) *Melodic Shape.* Point 1: arched. Point 2: terraced. Point 3: undulating. Point 4: descending.

(16) *Melodic Form,* rated from through-composed (1), through five increasingly simple types of strophe (2 to 6) and five increasingly simple types of litany (7 to 12), to Point 13, which represents the special type of litany typical of much Pygmy singing.

(17) *Phrase Length.* The length of the basic musical ideas which make up a melody is rated in five points, from extremely long to extremely short phrases. Complex strophes are generally composed of long phrases, litanies of short phrases.

(18) *Number of Phrases in a Melody,* rated from left to right in eight degrees, from eight or more phrases to one or two in each melodic section.

(19) *Position of the Final,* rated in five degrees from left to right, from the final on the lowest note to the final on the highest note of the scale used in a given tune.

(20) *Over-all Range,* rated in five degrees, from a second to two octaves or more.

(21) *Average Width of Intervals,* rated in five degrees, from dominance of narrow intervals (microtones) to dominance of wide intervals (fourths and fifths).

(22) *Type of Polyphony,* rated in six degrees of increasing complexity from none to counterpoint.

(23) *Embellishment.* The degree of melodic ornamentation is rated in five degrees from left to right, from highly ornamented to virtual absence of ornament.

(24) *Tempo,* rated in six degrees, from very slow to very fast. Point 9, the center point (walking pace), has about sixteen beats per minute. Point 13 was not used.

(25) *Volume of Singing,* rated in five degrees, from very soft to very loud.

(26) *Rubato: Voice.* The degree of rubato (rhythmic freedom) which affects the over-all vocal rhythm (Line 11) is rated in four degrees from left to right, from very great to none.

(27) *Rubato: Orchestra.* Rated as in Line 26.

(28) *Glissando* (voice gliding between notes), rated in four degrees from left to right, from maximum to none.

(29) *Melisma* (two or more notes per syllable), rated in three degrees, from great to none.

(30) *Tremulo* (voice quavering), rated in three degrees, from great to none.

(31) *Glottal Shake.* Rated as in Line 30.

(32) *Register(s)* most commonly used, rated in five levels, from very high to very low.

(33) *Vocal Width* normally used by the singer, rated in five degrees, from very narrow and squeezed to very open and relaxed (the yodel).

(34) *Nasality.* The amount of nasalization characteristic of a singer is rated in five degrees, from very great to none.

(35) *Raspiness* (any type of harsh, throaty voice quality), rated in five degrees, from very great to none.

(36) *Accent.* The forcefulness of the singing attack is rated in five degrees, from very forceful to very relaxed.

(37) *Consonant Enunciation.* The precision of enunciation of sung consonants is rated in five degrees, from very precise to very slurred.

This coding system has its crudities and its areas of vagueness. Even so, I have been able to teach it to other students of folk music and have discovered to my delight that they concurred in most of the judgments Victor Grauer and I had arrived at separately. I do not know whether cantometrics will survive the examination of my colleagues for a short or a long time, but I can commend it in several respects. It produces consistent profiles when applied to the music of large culture areas that both anthropology and musicology tell us share a common cultural history. These profiles enable us to recognize and describe song performance structures for the Amerindians of North America, for Negro Africa, for Western European folk song, for the folk song of Eastern and Central

Europe, for Mediterranean and Middle Eastern folk song, for the music of the high culture of the Orient, for Polynesia, and for perhaps a dozen other musical culture areas. These structures shape the music of very large areas and may be presumed to have had such formative influence for centuries, perhaps for millennia. Regional and tribal variations of appropriate dimensions are also exhibited by the coding sheets, and it seems likely that cantometrics can point up important differences as well as links between contiguous cultures. This paper, however, will concern itself only with contrasts between the profiles of large areas.

A final word of explanation is perhaps necessary for the way in which these large-area profiles were prepared. Normally the songs coded from any one area conformed to one, or at most three, profiles. Generally one of these was far more common than the rest. We presumed that this was the favorite mode of song performance in this area, and we brought all these matching profiles together into sets. Then we reviewed each number column and chose the most frequent number in each parameter. This list of numbers was then arranged on a master sheet, and a new profile was established, which became the master profile for the area. Random tests of this master profile indicated that it took care of the majority of song performances from its area. Deviations in subordinate profiles usually concerned minor matters which did not affect the over-all impression of stylistic unity.

Musical Acculturation

The usefulness of cantometrics is, perhaps, most quickly apparent in relation to the troubling problems of musical acculturation. The American folklore school, led by George Pullen Jackson (1943), studied the available musical scores and concluded that most so-called Negro melodies were variants of old European tunes. Africanists, such as Melville Herskovits (1941), pointed to the survival of African musical habits and institutions in the New World. A comparison of the cantometric profiles of song performance from Negro Africa and from a wide sampling of Afro-American groups provides the answer to this apparent paradox (see Figure 2).

In most respects the African and Afro-American performance profiles are identical and form a unique pair in our world sample. The social organization of the musical group, the degree of integration of the musical group, the layout of the rhythm, the levels of embellishment, and the voice quality sets conform to the same ratings in both Negro Africa and Negro communities in the New World. These paired profiles differ from each other principally at the level where Jackson discovered Western European influence, i.e., in Lines 16 and 17, which deal with melodic form and phrase length. The African profile codes 10 (simply litany) on Line 16 and 10 (short phrases) on Line 17. The Afro-American profile codes 2 to 12 on Line 16, which means that American Negroes sing every type of strophe as well as every type of litany; it also codes 7 and 10 (phrases of medium length as well as short phrases) on Line 17.

Figure 2: African and Afro-American Profiles
(Left and Right, Respectively)

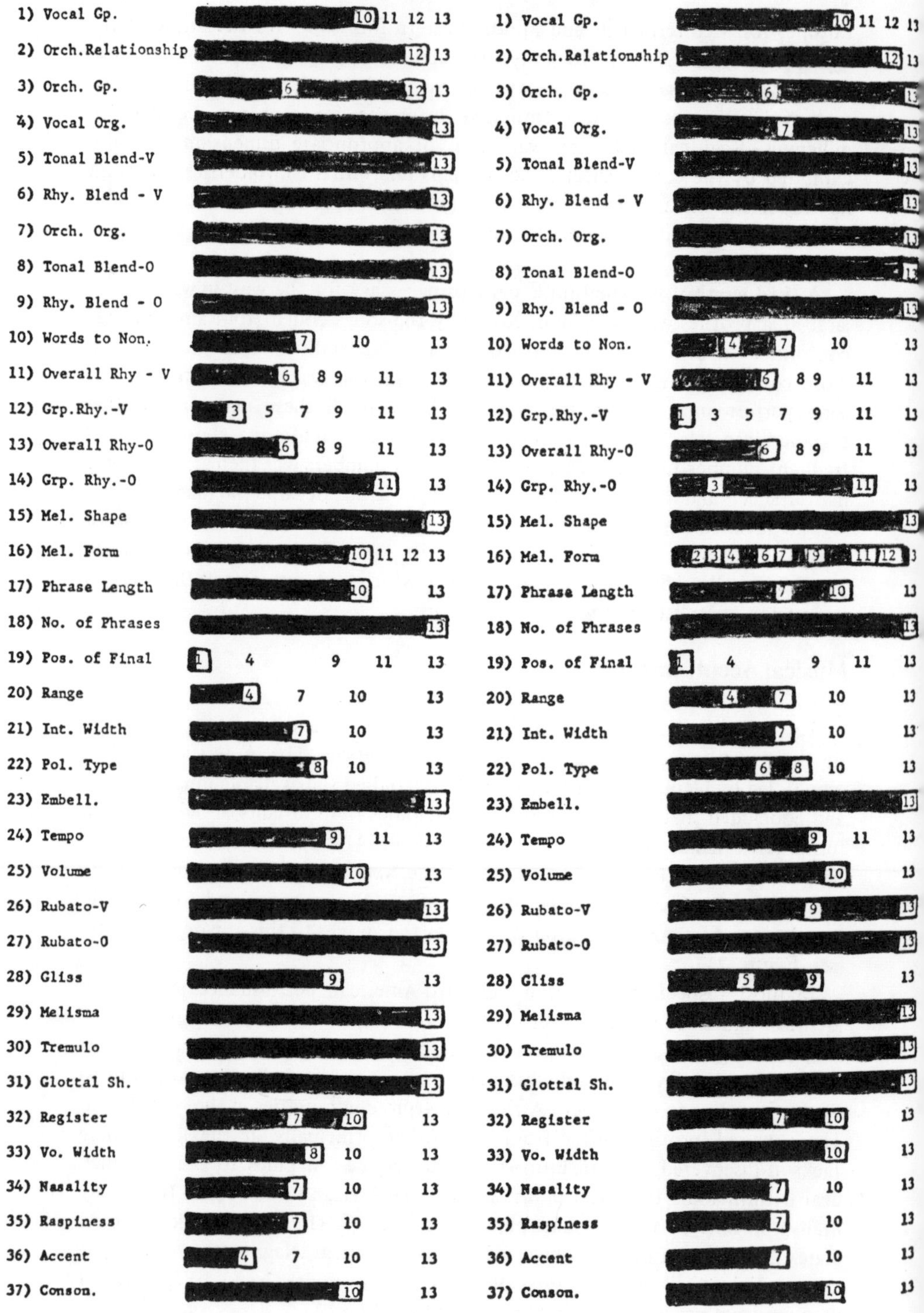

#	Measure	African (scale points)	Afro-American (scale points)
1)	Vocal Gp.	10 11 12 13	10 11 12 13
2)	Orch.Relationship	12 13	12 13
3)	Orch. Gp.	6 12 13	6 13
4)	Vocal Org.	13	7 13
5)	Tonal Blend-V	13	13
6)	Rhy. Blend - V	13	13
7)	Orch. Org.	13	13
8)	Tonal Blend-0	13	13
9)	Rhy. Blend - 0	13	13
10)	Words to Non.	7 10 13	4 7 10 13
11)	Overall Rhy - V	6 8 9 11 13	6 8 9 11 13
12)	Grp.Rhy.-V	3 5 7 9 11 13	1 3 5 7 9 11 13
13)	Overall Rhy-0	6 8 9 11 13	6 8 9 11 13
14)	Grp. Rhy.-0	11 13	3 11 13
15)	Mel. Shape	13	13
16)	Mel. Form	10 11 12 13	2 3 4 6 7 9 11 12 13
17)	Phrase Length	10 13	7 10 13
18)	No. of Phrases	13	13
19)	Pos. of Final	1 4 9 11 13	1 4 9 11 13
20)	Range	4 7 10 13	4 7 10 13
21)	Int. Width	7 10 13	7 10 13
22)	Pol. Type	8 10 13	6 8 10 13
23)	Embell.	13	13
24)	Tempo	9 11 13	9 11 13
25)	Volume	10 13	10 13
26)	Rubato-V	13	9 13
27)	Rubato-0	13	13
28)	Gliss	9 13	5 9 13
29)	Melisma	13	13
30)	Tremulo	13	13
31)	Glottal Sh.	13	13
32)	Register	7 10 13	7 10 13
33)	Vo. Width	8 10 13	10 13
34)	Nasality	7 10 13	7 10 13
35)	Raspiness	7 10 13	7 10 13
36)	Accent	4 7 10 13	7 10 13
37)	Conson.	10 13	10 13

The cause for this shift of emphasis in the Afro-American profile seems clear. Perhaps the most prominent and powerful trait of Western European folk song is its attachment to the strophic melodic form, composed of phrases of medium length. It has exploited this trait pair (2 to 6 plus 7) to develop a body of melodies unmatched in the world for number and variety. It appears, then, that Negro singers, coming to the New World, were impressed by the European strophic form and added it to their musical resources, meanwhile keeping their own system more or less intact in other respects. As melody makers, they retained their interest in the litany, short-phrase form but learned how to use and to create melodies in the potent European style.

For another example of musical acculturation, we may look at modern Polynesian song. One of the most notable traits of old Polynesian music is the choral performance in perfect tonal and rhythmic unison of long and complex texts, where every syllable is clearly enunciated. In some areas, a rudimentary form of polyphony occurs: one of the voice parts rises in pitch and maintains this level while the chorus continues to sing at the original pitch, thus creating a simple drone harmony.

Shortly after contact with European explorers and missionaries, this older style was submerged by an acculturated choral style, which most Polynesians mastered. They astonished, delighted, and sometimes horrified European observers by choral performances in perfectly blended and often extremely banal Western European harmony. Indeed, a casually organized group of Polynesians could soon sing in the European harmonized style more skillfully than most Westerners. Recordings of these performances became popular hits in Europe and America, and today this Euro-Polynesian style is spreading into Indonesia, South Asia, and even aboriginal Australia.

The cantometric coding system provides a basis for understanding this historical development. In both Western Europe and Polynesia, text is of paramount importance. European singers, however, perform mostly in solo. Choral singing is rare in this area, and, when it occurs, it is badly integrated unison. In order to organize a polyphonic chorus, Western Europeans must be drilled to pronounce, attack, and accent each syllable together and in one manner. This ability to chant in perfect unison, which is a precondition for effective Western European harmonic singing, is a normal Polynesian culture trait. Ancient Polynesia had, as noted above, a leaning toward choral singing indicated by the presence of drone harmony, but it did not have a sophisticated harmonic system. Such a system was provided by the missionaries, eager for Polynesians to sing Christian hymns. European block harmony, when well executed, increases the tonal blend of a chorus to its maximum. Polynesians, concerned about voice blending, quickly adopted Western harmony as a part of their musical system and thus achieved maximal voice blending. In many other respects, however, the profiles of modern Polynesian song continue to conform to standards of the music of old Polynesia.

The stability of the profiles produced by the cantometric coding system is confirmed by a further discovery. I have said earlier that most folk and primitive cultures seem to erect their song structures on one or two or, at most, three models. Whatever the function of a song in a culture, it conforms to one of these models. Thus we have moved on beyond the crude analogies which functional-ism has so far provided ethnomusicology—work songs, funeral laments, ballads, game songs, religious songs, love songs, and the like. On the whole, style, as a category, is superordinate over function, in song performance as in other patterns of culture. Therefore, the cantometric diagrams of song style, which represent the song-producing models in a culture, may stand for formative and emotional patterns that underlie whole sets of human institutions.

This extremely general statement must be qualified in one respect, but one that will be of special interest to ethnologists. Whenever a special profile is attached to a body of song with a special function, this exceptional phenomenon can often be explained by the survival, the adoption, or the recrudescence of an entire style in a culture for historical reasons. The Euro-Polynesian and Afro-American acculturated song styles are both pertinent instances of this process, but perhaps another, more general, example should be set forth.

In an earlier paper (Lomax 1960), it was suggested that an older choralizing, well-integrated singing style has survived in mountain areas, on islands, and, in general, on the fringes of Western Europe, largely submerged by the more modern and familiar solo-balled style of folk song. Cantometric study has strongly confirmed and sharpened this hypothesis. We have found that, in those areas where people sing naturally in well blended choruses and sometimes in harmony, melodies tend to be in litany form, metrical pattern is more complex, melodic embellishment is less important, and voices are lower pitched, wider, more relaxed, less nasal, and raspy. In other words, the stylistic profile characteristic of this "Old European" area strongly resembles the model of simpler African song styles.

There are also choral-litany song types embedded in the repertoire of modern Western European folk song, notably the sea chanties of Britain, various types of work songs, children's game songs, and certain survivals of pagan ceremonial such as the Christmas and May carols of England. All of these song types integrate, strengthen, and direct group activity in various ways. With the exception of the children's games, however, all these functional song types seem to be survivals that are passing out along with the activities and the forms of social organization that supported them. In our society only the children know how to organize and dramatize their feelings in the ancient, collective fashion. That the need for such song types still exists among adult Westerners is evidenced by the recent popularity of highly charged, choral-litany song patterns, rooted in erotic dance forms and created by Afro-Americans. This summary exposition indicates how stylistic models maintain and renew themselves, by working hand-in-hand with history, to weaken or support functionally based song types.

Enough has been said to indicate the general nature and usefulness of the cantometric system. It looks at a level of musical activity which is highly patterned, resistant to change, and superordinate over function. The remainder of the paper will relate certain levels of song performance structure to social structure.

Pygmy-Bushman versus Western European Song Style

One of the universals of song performance seldom remarked upon by musicologists is the working organization of the musical group. There is a difference in kind between the main performance structure of Western European folk song, where a lone voice dominates a group of passive listeners (L over N), and the situation in which every member of a group participates, not only in the rhythm and the counterpoint of a performance, but in recreating the melody, as in the Pygmy hocketing style (W). Figure 3 compares the master profiles of Pygmy-Bushman music and Western European folk song—and exhibits their contrasts. A comparison of the structure of interpersonal relationships and of role-taking in the two societies shows the same order of contrast, strongly hinting that musical structure mirrors social structure or that, perhaps, both structures are a reflection of deeper patterning motives of which we are only dimly aware.

The general shape of Pygmy music must first be summarized. Colin Turnbull, who has done field work among the forest-dwelling Pygmies, discovered that they had concealed the very existence of their musical system from surrounding tribes for centuries. He told me that solo song does not exist among the Pygmies except in the form of lullabies; that their choral songs may be begun by anyone, no matter what his talent; that leadership, during the course of a song performance, shifts from an accomplished to a less accomplished singer with no lessening of support from the whole group; and that the chief delight of the singers is to listen to the effect of group-produced counterpoint as it echoes through the dark cathedral of the jungle. This situation we code 13 (W) on Line 1 and 13 also on Lines 4, 5, 6, 16, 17, 18, and 22. At the bottom of the code, where we deal with register, timbre, and other voice qualities, it turns out that the Pygmy voice is generally low, lacking in nasality and rasp, relaxed, and slurred—13 in Lines 32, 33, 34, 35 and 37. This group sings with yodeling tone which, in the estimation of laryngologists, is produced by the voice in its most relaxed state. When a singer yodels, all of the vocal dimensions, from the chords through the resonating chambers, are at their widest and largest. This extraordinary degree of vocal relaxation, which occurs rarely in the world as an over-all vocal style, seems to be a psycho-physiological set, which symbolizes openness, nonrepressiveness, and an unconstricted approach to the communication of emotion.

Our coding studies show that a high degree of choral integration is always linked with a relaxed and open manner of vocalizing. This connection is strikingly dramatized by the Pygmy-Bushman style. These stone-age hunters normally express themselves in a complex, perfectly blended, contrapuntal singing at a level of integration that a Western choir can achieve only after extensive rehearsal. Indeed, the Pygmy-Bushman profile represents the most

Figure 3: Pygmy-Bushman and Western European Folk Song Profiles
(Left and Right, Respectively)

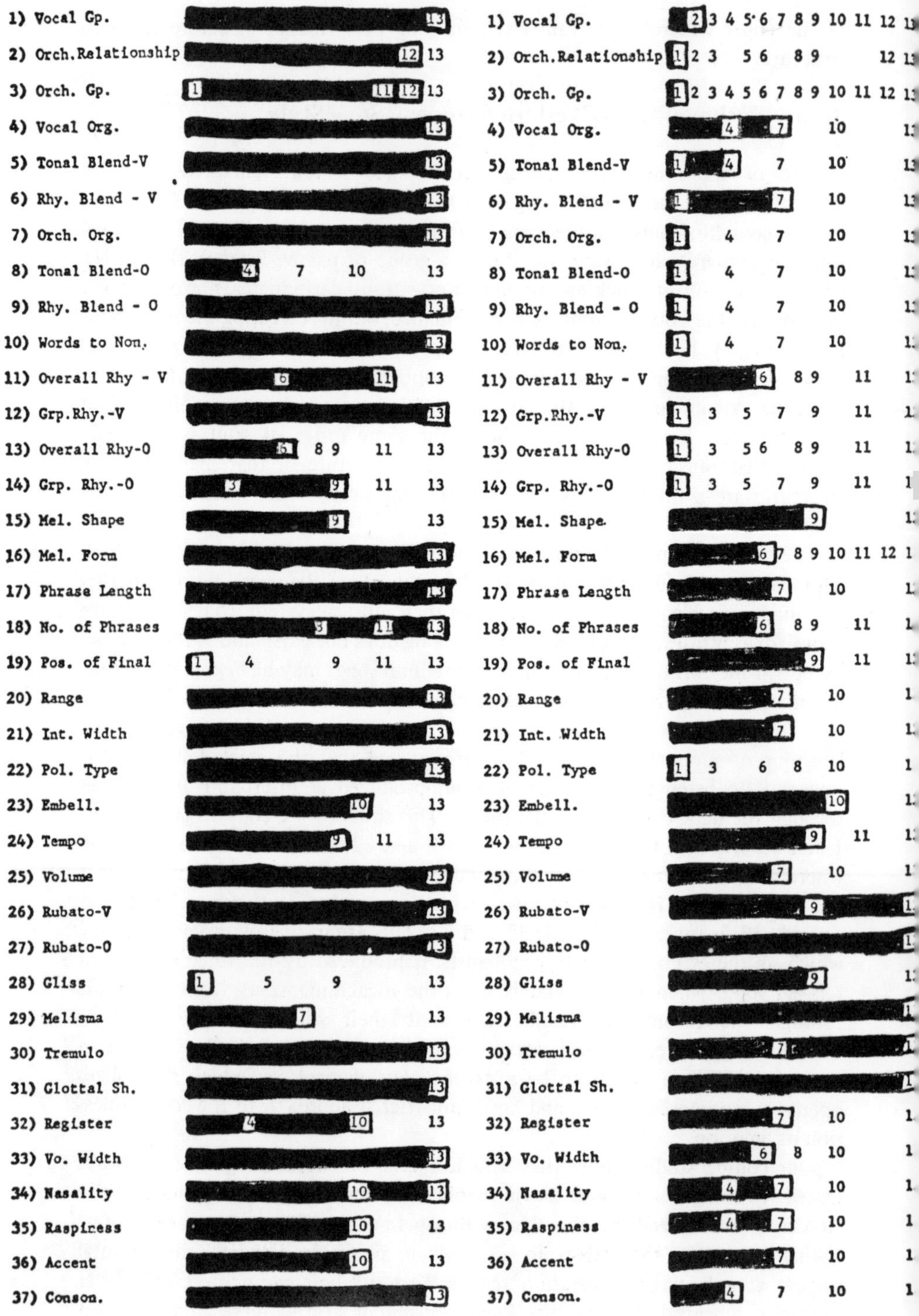

Left (Pygmy-Bushman):

1) Vocal Gp. — 13
2) Orch. Relationship — 12 13
3) Orch. Gp. — 1 ... 11 12 13
4) Vocal Org. — 13
5) Tonal Blend-V — 13
6) Rhy. Blend - V — 13
7) Orch. Org. — 13
8) Tonal Blend-O — 4 7 10 13
9) Rhy. Blend - O — 13
10) Words to Non. — 13
11) Overall Rhy - V — 6 11 13
12) Grp. Rhy.-V — 13
13) Overall Rhy-O — 8 9 11 13
14) Grp. Rhy.-O — 3 9 11 13
15) Mel. Shape — 9 13
16) Mel. Form — 13
17) Phrase Length — 13
18) No. of Phrases — 3 11 13
19) Pos. of Final — 1 4 9 11 13
20) Range — 13
21) Int. Width — 13
22) Pol. Type — 13
23) Embell. — 10 13
24) Tempo — 9 11 13
25) Volume — 13
26) Rubato-V — 13
27) Rubato-O — 13
28) Gliss — 1 5 9 13
29) Melisma — 7 13
30) Tremulo — 13
31) Glottal Sh. — 13
32) Register — 4 10 13
33) Vo. Width — 13
34) Nasality — 10 13
35) Raspiness — 10 13
36) Accent — 10 13
37) Conson. — 13

Right (Western European):

1) Vocal Gp. — 2 3 4 5 6 7 8 9 10 11 12 13
2) Orch. Relationship — 1 2 3 5 6 8 9 12 13
3) Orch. Gp. — 1 2 3 4 5 6 7 8 9 10 11 12 13
4) Vocal Org. — 4 7 10 13
5) Tonal Blend-V — 1 4 7 10 13
6) Rhy. Blend - V — 1 7 10 13
7) Orch. Org. — 1 4 7 10 13
8) Tonal Blend-O — 1 4 7 10 13
9) Rhy. Blend - O — 1 4 7 10 13
10) Words to Non. — 1 4 7 10 13
11) Overall Rhy - V — 6 8 9 11 13
12) Grp. Rhy.-V — 1 3 5 7 9 11 13
13) Overall Rhy-O — 1 3 5 6 8 9 11 13
14) Grp. Rhy.-O — 1 3 5 7 9 11 13
15) Mel. Shape — 9 13
16) Mel. Form — 6 7 8 9 10 11 12 13
17) Phrase Length — 7 10 13
18) No. of Phrases — 6 8 9 11 13
19) Pos. of Final — 9 11 13
20) Range — 7 10 13
21) Int. Width — 7 10 13
22) Pol. Type — 1 3 6 8 10 13
23) Embell. — 10 13
24) Tempo — 9 11 13
25) Volume — 7 10 13
26) Rubato-V — 9 13
27) Rubato-O — 13
28) Gliss — 9 13
29) Melisma — 13
30) Tremulo — 7 13
31) Glottal Sh. — 13
32) Register — 7 10 13
33) Vo. Width — 6 8 10 13
34) Nasality — 4 7 10 13
35) Raspiness — 4 7 10 13
36) Accent — 7 10 13
37) Conson. — 4 7 10 13

extreme case of total focus on choral integration in our world sample, and in this sense it is unique among folk cultures.

The vocal empathy of the Pygmies seems to be matched by the cooperative style of their culture. All that Turnbull has told us about the Pygmies in his remarkable book and his many papers (Turnbull 1957, 1959, 1960a, 1960b, 1961) confirms this point. Normally the group never goes hungry. Their environment furnishes them what they need for food and shelter. The men hunt in groups, and the women gather in groups. A precise system of dividing food assures every individual of his exact share. There are no specific penalties for even the greatest crimes, such as incest, murder, or theft, nor do judges or law enforcement exist. The community expresses its vociferous dislike of the criminal, and he may be belabored and driven out of the group for a time, but soon he will be pitied and welcomed back among his people.

A Pygmy baby lives, literally, on his mother's body, his head positioned so that he can always take her breast, her voice constantly soothing him with a liquid-voiced lullaby. Children grow up in their own play community relatively unhampered by their parents. When a girl begins to menstruate, the whole tribe joins in rejoicing that a new potential mother is among them. Her joyful maturation ceremony concludes with marriage. Pygmy men do not impose on their sons a painful puberty ceremony; in Pygmy terms, a boy becomes a man simply when he kills his first game. The Mbuti sometimes permit the Negro tribesmen with whom they live in symbiosis to put Pygmy adolescents through a rite of passage, but this is only one of the many ways in which the Pygmies tactfully pretend to conform to the desires of their Negro neighbors in order to live at peace with them and to conceal the existence of their own forest culture. When the Negroes have gone back to their village, the Pygmy children are given the bull-roarer and the fetishes to play with, and the little hunters laugh together over the childish superstitions of their black masters. During the initiation ceremonies there is ritual whipping of the boys by the Negroes, but when this takes on a sadistic character the Pygmy fathers intervene.

The forest Pygmies do not share the magical beliefs of their Negro neighbors; indeed, the Pygmies look down on the Negroes because of their superstitious fears and their focus on evil. They have no myths and little formalized religious belief. Their only religious ceremonies occur in times of crisis, when they sing to wake the beneficent forest and to remind it to give them its usual protection. When the tribe gathers after the hunt, joy-filled dances and songs knit the group into a cohesive and fully expressive whole. In our code the Pygmy musical form emerges as a static expression of community joy sung in liquid, open-throated style.

I have dwelt upon this extreme, rare, and somehow utopian situation because it runs counter to most of the music we know and thus illuminates the rest of human musical activity in an extraordinary way. It points to the close bonds between forms of social and musical integration. The choruses of these hunting-gathering peoples sit in a circle, bodies touching, changing leaders, strongly group-dependent. Even their melodies are shared pleasures, just as are all tasks, all property, and all social responsibilities. The only parallel in our coding system is found at the peak of Western European contrapuntal writing, where again all the separate interests of a variegated musical community are subordinated to a desire to sing together with a united voice about universal human values.

Thus far we have assumed an identity between Bushman and Pygmy musical styles, and, indeed, this is what our profiles indicate. Perhaps no two peoples, so far separated in space (3,000 miles), living in such different environments (desert and jungle), and belonging to different racial and linguistic groups, share so many stylistic traits. Even after pointing out numerous musical idiosyncrasies, this cross-cultural mystery sill disturbs the two researchers who have most closely examined it, Yvette Grimaud and Gilbert Rouget. Rouget (1956) speculates upon the possible influence of a common cultural heritage of similar environmental adaptation, then leaves the problem. It seems to me that he has neglected one important piece of evidence.

Solo songs are common among the Bushmen and rare, except in lullaby form, among the Pygmies. Otherwise, as far as cantometric analysis is concerned, the styles are, indeed, identical. Bushman males sing plaintive solo songs to the accompaniment of the mouth bow, which, like our blues, dwell upon loneliness and isolation. This sense of personal deprivation grows out of a special Bushman situation that does not exist among the Pygmies. Their harsh desert existence, beset by thirst and hunger, results in a scarcity of women. Thus, in order to have a mate, Bushman men often betroth themselves to infant girls. The result is long years of waiting for marriage and consummation, then a union with a capricious little girl who may be anxious to postpone the duties of a mother and a wife. Meantime the Bushman men, battling for their group's existence in a barren waste, suffer the deprivations common to lonely males everywhere, and they voice this emotion in their solo plaints (Marshall 1959).

In all other important respects Pygmy and Bushman social and musical structures are extremely close. Both groups share; both are acephalous. Their hocketing, polyphonic, polyrhythmic, maximally blended style seems to mirror this sytem of closely integrated relationships. The Bushman solo "blues," the only major deviation from this pattern, thus suggests the influence of environment on an otherwise consistent social and musical structure. It does not matter whether this Bushman solo song style has been borrowed from a neighboring group. A musical structure stands for a social adjustment, for the fulfillment of a commonly felt emotional need, whether borrowed or not. There is no better proof of this hypothesis than this one divergence of Pygmy and Bushman musical structures.

For further evidence of the link between song structure and social structure we may look at the other extreme of the coding system—a leader dominating a passive audience (L over N)—the principal pattern of Western Europe folk song (see Figure 3, right). This profile shows only slight variation for most folk songs from Norway, Holland, the British Isles (apart from old Celtic areas of Wales, Cornwall, and the Hebrides), Western France, Central Spain, and colonial United

States. Text is dominant and rhythm simple for three or four phrase strophes set in diatonic intervals, with an octave range and some degree of embellishment. Voices are from middle range to falsetto, with strong characterizers both of throat and nose and a clear enunciating pattern. The connection between voice type and the degree of integration in group song is reflected in unison singing with poor tonal blend and poor to moderate rhythmic coordination. We may think of the singing of a Rotarian meeting, a football crowd, a regiment on the march in World War II, or a pub group in Britain. Each of these situations is a gathering of extremely individualized specialists, each singing in his own normal tone of voice and uncompromisingly independent of others at the level of vocal empathy.

The familiar pattern in British and Kentucky ballad singing is for the singer to sit quietly with his hands passive in his lap as he sings; his eyes are closed, or he gazes unseeingly over the heads of his listeners. He tells his stories in simple strophes that permit a concentrated narrative pace and demand the full attention of his audience. Thus, during his song, the listeners must remain silent and physically passive. Any movement on their part would interfere with the story. Any distraction would break the ballad singer's spell. When the first singer has finished a number of such songs, another may take his place, and the same pattern is repeated.

The leading singer commands and dominates his listeners during his performance. His association with his audience, is, in sociological terms, one of exclusive authority, a principal model for conduct in Western European culture (see Parsons 1949: 43, 140-147, 178-179, 286-295). When a doctor or a lawyer takes over a case, his authority is absolute for the duration of the relationship. The same unspoken pact joins boss and worker, priest and penitent, officer and soldier, parent and child. Dominance-subordination, with a deep sense of moral obligation, is the fundamental form of role-taking in the Protestant West. Our cooperative enterprises are organized in terms of an assemblage of experts, each one temporarily subordinating his separate, specialized, and exclusive function to an agreed-upon goal. Workers on belt lines cooperate in this way to produce automobiles for Ford or bombers for Lockheed, just as instrumentalists combine to make the big symphonic sounds. Ultimately, this leader-follower pattern is rooted in the past, e.g., in the European concept of lifelong fealty to the king or the lord. Ignatius Loyola inculcated the same principle in his teaching of the Jesuits: "In the hands of my superior, I must be a soft wax, a thing . . . a corpse which has neither intelligence nor will."

This degree of compliance is precisely what the contemporary symphonic conductor demands and gets from his orchestra—and from his audience as well. In its role relationship the symphonic audience, quietly listening to a work of one of the masters spun out under the baton of the conductor (whose back is to his admirers), differs from the ballad audience only in its size. Even the most group-oriented and fully integrated Western music is produced by a collectivity, organized in a manner fundamentally different from that of the acephalous

Pygmy chorus, where all parts are equal, where subordination does not exist, as it scarcely exists in the society itself.

A western table of organization or a belt line or a symphony depends upon a series of clear and explicit commands, arranged in a clear pattern agreed upon in advance. Our Western European folk songs are arranged in the same fashion—a series of compact, clearly outlined strophes and stanzas, each of which bids the listener to view such-and-such an aspect of a sung tale in such-and-such an explicit fashion. While this series of explicit and well constructed packages of fantasy or fact are being delivered to the listeners, the leader-singer must not be interrupted. If he is, he will very likely refuse to sing any further. "If you know so much, sing it yourself," he will tell his rude listeners, much as a doctor might tell an anxious patient, "If you don't like my medical procedure, get another man."

According to Turnbull, a long Pygmy performance may, as a maximum, contain only enough text to make a normal four-line stanza. The rest of the phonating consists of hooted vocables or variations on one phrase of text. Tiring of this material, another singer is free to introduce another bit of text, which in its turn is torn apart into syllables and played with for a while in somewhat the manner of a child or a musing adult in our culture. Here language loses its cutting edge and becomes a toy in a delightful game with sounds. This contrast is noted in Line 10 of Figure 3, which deals with the relative importance of text as against nonsense syllables. Western Europe codes 1; Pygmies and Bushmen, 13.

The Bardic Style of the Orient

Having now described two styles which lie at the extremes of the cantometric system—one solo-unaccompanied and the other contrapuntal-hocketing—let us now consider three master codes that lie between these extremes and that show again how musical structures rise out of, or reveal, the general shape of their social contexts. First, there is the area which, for want of a better term, I call "bardic." Here solo performance is again dominant, but various levels of accompaniment support and reinforce the authority of the soloist-leader. Linking together several large subareas, this bardic style shapes most of the music of southern Europe and Moslem Africa, of the Near and Middle East, of the Far East, and indeed of most of Asia aside from certain tribal cultures.

A searching portrait of the societies which gave rise to the bardic tradition can be found in the analysis of the system of Oriental despotism by Karl Wittfogel (1957). Wittfogel argues that, wherever an agricultural system depends upon the construction and maintenance of a complex of great canals and dams, a despotic control of labor, land, political structure, justice, religion, and family life arises. All the great hydraulic empires—of Peru, of Mexico, of China, of Indonesia, of India, of Mesopotamia, of Egypt, of the Moslem world—conformed to the same over-all pattern. The center owned and controlled every person and all the means of production and power. Complete and blind obedience was the rule. The way to approach the throne was on the knees or the belly. Deviation was immediately and ruthlessly handled by capital punishment, imprisonment, confiscation, or torture. The ancient rulers of Mesopotamia asserted that they received their power from the god Enlil, who symbolized power and force. The ministry of justice in ancient China was known as the Ministry of Punishment. The Egyptian peasant who failed to deliver his quota of grain was beaten and thrown into a ditch. A court favorite could be executed or deprived of his perquisites at the whim of the emperor.

Wittfogel points out that this system results in a state of total loneliness for the top as well as the bottom of the society. The peasant or small official knows that no one will dare protect him if he disobeys; the king or the pharoah knows as well that he can trust no one with his confidence or, for that matter, with his life—neither his closest adviser nor the members of his family, and especially not his son and heir.

Depersonalized conformity to authoritarian tradition is the norm for such a society. Everywhere in the hydraulic world song styles shows an analogous set of traits. The singer learns to use his voice in a formalized way and then masters a complex set of rules for starting and improvising a theme, and he displays his talent by showing how far he can develop this theme without breaking the rules that apply. The growth of modal systems, with the elaborate set of beliefs and customs surrounding them, reminds one strongly of a society in which social stratification strictly limits the development and growth of each individual from birth to death. Above all there is one voice, expressive of doom and pain and anger, which speaks the varied moods of the center of power. It is a testimony to the noble spirit of the poets and musicians of the past that within this structure they created universes of plastic and plangent beauty.

The Oriental bard is a highly idiosyncratic solo singer, a master of subtly designed verse and of complex, shifting, and sometimes meterless rhythm. He performs highly complex strophes composed of many long phrases, with maximal ornamentation, vocal rubato, melisma, and tremulo, in a voice that is usually high or falsetto, narrow and squeezed—with maximal nasality, raspy, and often characterized by forcefully precise articulation. In places where a primitive type of feudalism still prevails, as in Mauretania and Afghanistan, bards are generally attached to a big or powerful chief and their duty is to celebrate the magnificence of their lords before their world. The bardic voice quality is generally tense, high, thin, feminine, and placatory. Sometimes it is harsh, guttural, and forceful, symbolizing ruthless power and unchecked anger. Its marked nasality, tremulo, and throbbing glottal shake and its quivering melodic ornaments speak of tears, of fear, of trembling submission. These vocal mannerisms are the norm among Eastern mystics, muzzein, and cantors—the bards of God—as well as among the epic singers and the composers of praise songs for the king.

King David, like the great singers of early high culture, probably sang in the bardic manner. This inference is strong, since the style still survives in the whole Orient today, reaching its apogee in the court music of Japan, Java, India, and Ethiopia. A profusion of musical flowers, representing a sort of conspicuous

Figure 4: The Oriental Bardic Profile: Near and Far East
(Left and Right, Respectively)

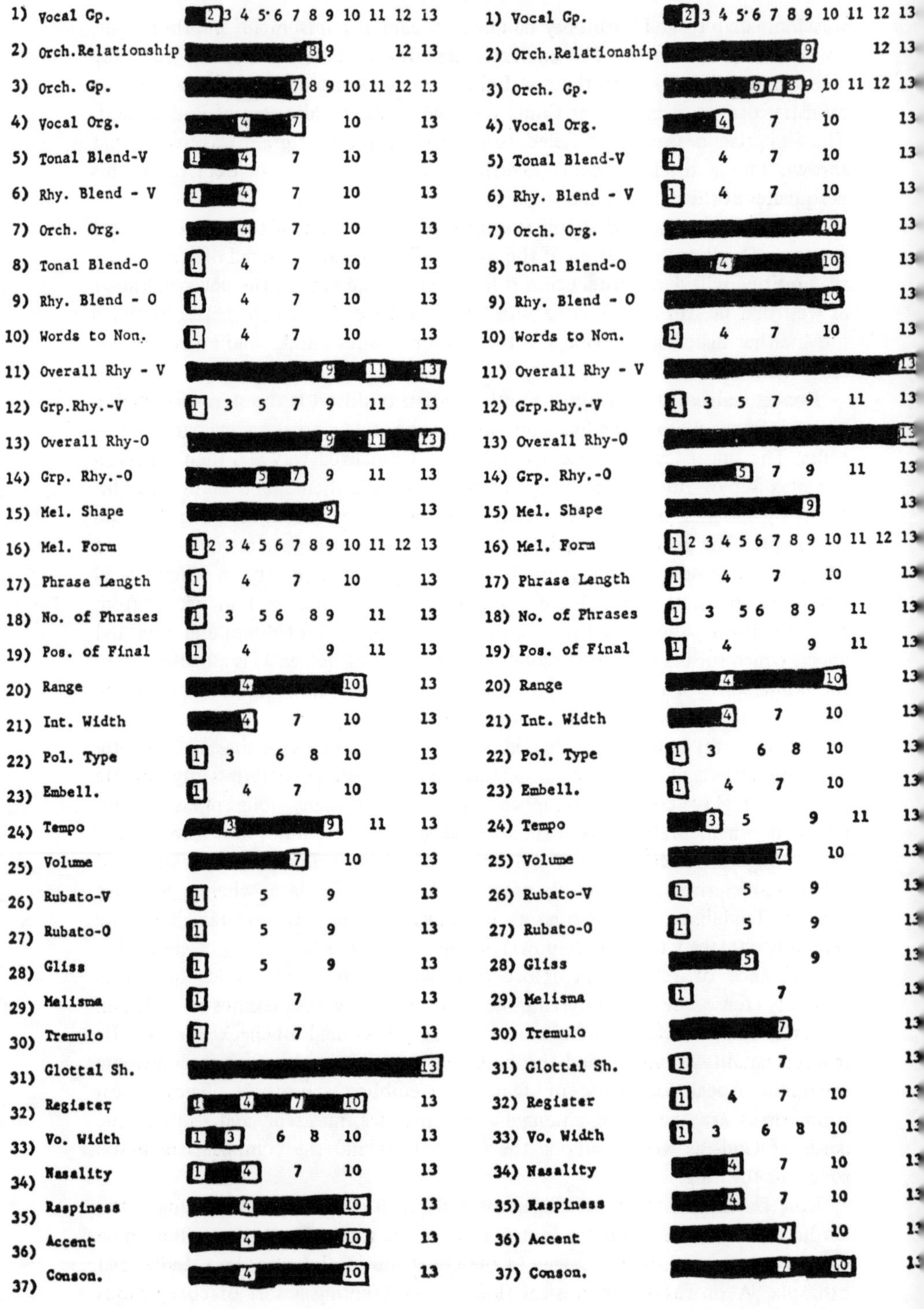

Near East (Left)

#	Parameter	Scale values
1)	Vocal Gp.	2 3 4 5 6 7 8 9 10 11 12 13
2)	Orch.Relationship	8 9 12 13
3)	Orch. Gp.	7 8 9 10 11 12 13
4)	Vocal Org.	4 7 10 13
5)	Tonal Blend-V	1 4 7 10 13
6)	Rhy. Blend - V	1 4 7 10 13
7)	Orch. Org.	4 7 10 13
8)	Tonal Blend-O	1 4 7 10 13
9)	Rhy. Blend - O	1 4 7 10 13
10)	Words to Non.	1 4 7 10 13
11)	Overall Rhy - V	9 11 13
12)	Grp.Rhy.-V	1 3 5 7 9 11 13
13)	Overall Rhy-O	9 11 13
14)	Grp. Rhy.-O	5 7 9 11 13
15)	Mel. Shape	9 13
16)	Mel. Form	1 2 3 4 5 6 7 8 9 10 11 12 13
17)	Phrase Length	1 4 7 10 13
18)	No. of Phrases	1 3 5 6 8 9 11 13
19)	Pos. of Final	1 4 9 11 13
20)	Range	4 10 13
21)	Int. Width	4 7 10 13
22)	Pol. Type	1 3 6 8 10 13
23)	Embell.	1 4 7 10 13
24)	Tempo	3 9 11 13
25)	Volume	7 10 13
26)	Rubato-V	1 5 9 13
27)	Rubato-O	1 5 9 13
28)	Gliss	1 5 9 13
29)	Melisma	1 7 13
30)	Tremulo	1 7 13
31)	Glottal Sh.	13
32)	Register	1 4 7 10 13
33)	Vo. Width	1 3 6 8 10 13
34)	Nasality	1 4 7 10 13
35)	Raspiness	4 10 13
36)	Accent	4 10 13
37)	Conson.	4 10 13

Far East (Right)

#	Parameter	Scale values
1)	Vocal Gp.	2 3 4 5 6 7 8 9 10 11 12 13
2)	Orch.Relationship	9 12 13
3)	Orch. Gp.	6 7 8 9 10 11 12 13
4)	Vocal Org.	4 7 10 13
5)	Tonal Blend-V	1 4 7 10 13
6)	Rhy. Blend - V	1 4 7 10 13
7)	Orch. Org.	10 13
8)	Tonal Blend-O	4 10 13
9)	Rhy. Blend - O	10 13
10)	Words to Non.	1 4 7 10 13
11)	Overall Rhy - V	13
12)	Grp.Rhy.-V	1 3 5 7 9 11 13
13)	Overall Rhy-O	13
14)	Grp. Rhy.-O	5 7 9 11 13
15)	Mel. Shape	9 13
16)	Mel. Form	1 2 3 4 5 6 7 8 9 10 11 12 13
17)	Phrase Length	1 4 7 10 13
18)	No. of Phrases	1 3 5 6 8 9 11 13
19)	Pos. of Final	1 4 9 11 13
20)	Range	4 10 13
21)	Int. Width	4 7 10 13
22)	Pol. Type	1 3 6 8 10 13
23)	Embell.	1 4 7 10 13
24)	Tempo	3 5 9 11 13
25)	Volume	7 10 13
26)	Rubato-V	1 5 9 13
27)	Rubato-O	1 5 9 13
28)	Gliss	5 9 13
29)	Melisma	1 7 13
30)	Tremulo	7 13
31)	Glottal Sh.	1 7 13
32)	Register	1 4 7 10 13
33)	Vo. Width	1 3 6 8 10 13
34)	Nasality	4 7 10 13
35)	Raspiness	4 7 10 13
36)	Accent	7 10 13
37)	Conson.	7 10 13

consumption of music, is everywhere pleasing to the ears of kings, and thus to the almighty, whatever his name or names. In the same way, the lover in the bardic area abases himself before his mistress, showering her with flowery compliments, telling her with trembling voice and lavishly ornamented melody that he is utterly her slave.

Thus the Oriental bard was a specialist and virtuoso of a high order. He was the product of long and rigorous training. He conformed to rigid and explicitly stated esthetic theories. In fact, it was in the bardic world that the fine arts of music and poetry arose, alongside of highly developed metrical and melodic systems. Here, too, instruments were refined and developed and complex orchestras established.

In his paeans of praise of the king or of God, the bard spoke for or about the all-powerful center, and it was important that these praise songs be as grand and impressive as possible. He extended this manner to all his productions. Normally he sang at length—in long phrases, long and complex strophes, often in through-composed style, characteristically in song or verse forms that lasted for hours and ran to thousands of lines. He also used his voice in a depersonalized manner, appropriate to the voice of the king, of the god, or of one of his ministers or supplicants. Generally the bard was unsupported by other voices; in an absolutely despotic situation, only one voice should be heard—the voice of the despot or his surrogate.

Thus group singing in the bardic area is at a minimum. Normally, when it occurs, it is unison with poor rhythmic or tonal blend, or it is heterophonic. One thinks here of the choirs of Ethiopia or Korea or the heterophonic style of the Watusi or the enforced unison of the royal choirs of Dahomey. Yet the bard, like the king, needs support. He finds it in an elaborate accompanying style. The court orchestras of the Orient are generally large and play together heterophonically, that is, each instrument speaks the same melody but in its own variant, with many voices independently following the same line. Always, however, a high-pitched nasalized singer or an instrument with a similar timbre leads and dominates the orchestra.

An Amerindian Pattern

When Europeans first encountered Amerindian tribes, they could not understand how Indian society worked at all, for there were apparently no permanent authoritarian leaders. Walter Miller (1957) shows that American Indians and feudal Europeans followed two completely opposed concepts of authority. Europeans swore allegiance for life and carried out the commands of the representative of their king. Indians took orders from no one and bore allegiance to no one except on a temporary basis of personal choice. An Indian war party might be organized by a war chief if he were persuasive enough, but the braves who set out with him would desert if the enterprise encountered difficulties. A sizeable percentage of such enterprises ended in failure, and the participants straggled back to the village with no loss of face.

Figure 5: Profile of North American Indian Song

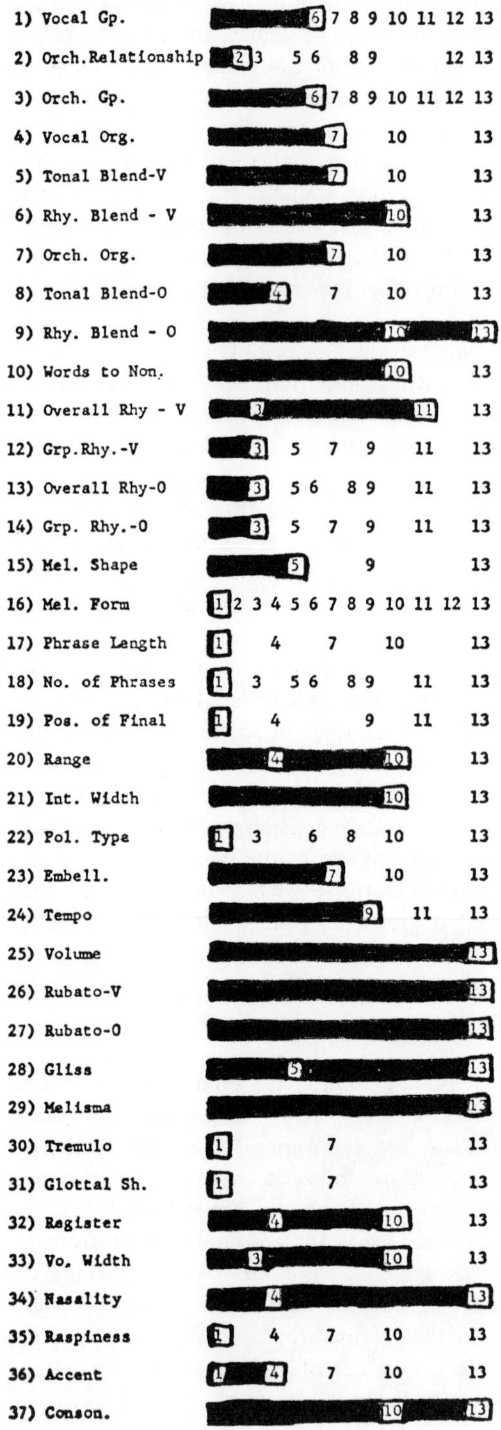

#	Feature	Values
1)	Vocal Gp.	6 7 8 9 10 11 12 13
2)	Orch. Relationship	2 3 5 6 8 9 12 13
3)	Orch. Gp.	6 7 8 9 10 11 12 13
4)	Vocal Org.	7 10 13
5)	Tonal Blend-V	7 10 13
6)	Rhy. Blend - V	10 13
7)	Orch. Org.	7 10 13
8)	Tonal Blend-O	4 7 10 13
9)	Rhy. Blend - O	10 13
10)	Words to Non.	10 13
11)	Overall Rhy - V	3 11 13
12)	Grp. Rhy.-V	3 5 7 9 11 13
13)	Overall Rhy-O	3 5 6 8 9 11 13
14)	Grp. Rhy.-O	3 5 7 9 11 13
15)	Mel. Shape	5 9 13
16)	Mel. Form	1 2 3 4 5 6 7 8 9 10 11 12 13
17)	Phrase Length	1 4 7 10 13
18)	No. of Phrases	1 3 5 6 8 9 11 13
19)	Pos. of Final	1 4 9 11 13
20)	Range	4 10 13
21)	Int. Width	10 13
22)	Pol. Type	1 3 6 8 10 13
23)	Embell.	7 10 13
24)	Tempo	9 11 13
25)	Volume	13
26)	Rubato-V	13
27)	Rubato-O	13
28)	Gliss	5 13
29)	Melisma	13
30)	Tremulo	1 7 13
31)	Glottal Sh.	1 7 13
32)	Register	4 10 13
33)	Vo. Width	3 10 13
34)	Nasality	4 13
35)	Raspiness	1 4 7 10 13
36)	Accent	1 4 7 10 13
37)	Conson.	10 13

Among the Fox Indians, whom Miller particularly studied, each person had his own supernatural protector, whom he venerated when fortune smiled upon him but reviled in periods of bad luck. The permanent village chiefs had no direct authority; indeed, they were not much more than permanent presiding officers at a village council of equals. Individuals were trained from childhood to venture self-reliantly into the wilderness. Collective activity was at a minimum, and, when it occurred, it was unforced, each individual participating, not upon command, but because he knew from tradition what he should do and how and when he should do it. Just as the individual Indian might ask for and obtain power directly from a supernatural source, so he might acquire a medicine song from the spirit world that would give him the power to heal or to lead a war party.

The shape of the American Indian musical group conforms to the pattern of role-taking briefly sketched above. The solo singer uses a chesty voice, wide rather than narrow, yet with strong characterizers of nasal resonance and throaty burr and with forceful accent—a voice which is expressive of a full-blown and unrepressed masculinity or, perhaps better, of a strong bodily orientation. The major manner of Indian song performance, however, is that which we code as N/L—group superordinate over leader. The leader initiates the song but then is submerged in a chorus performing the same musical material in unison. This chorus links their bassy, resonant voices with moderate tonal blending (varying to well-integrated blend among the Iroquois and some Pueblo groups), but in precise rhythmic concert. Individual voices in these choruses can still be heard, and the effect is of a loosely knit but well coordinated group of individuals cooperating in relation to a common goal. Here, as with the Pygmies and in contrast with the West and the Orient, the importance of text is often minimized. Indian songs normally consist of a few phrases padded out by repetitions and vocal segregates, to form long strophes of complex structure, which the whole group knows how to perform.

Many Indian melodies may be described as through-composed, that is, basically open-ended, leaving the decision for extension and termination to a collective impulse. The strongest element in this situation is a dominant, one-beat rhythm that unites the group in a simple, highly physical reenactment of their adventures on the hunt, on the war path, and in the supernatural world. Hardly anywhere in this system, except at this nonstratified rhythmic level, is the individual asked to conform either vocally or musically. The very style of conformity in group performances exhibits the principle of individualism.

The profile of Amerindian song remains remarkably constant throughout most of North America and many parts of South America. This consistency of style explains why Amerindian music has been so remarkably resistant to change and how it is possible for Indians to swap songs, as they frequently do, across linguistic and cultural barriers. Indeed, the solidity of this framework confirms a common-sense impression that there is an Amerindian music, distinct from other world musical systems and congruent with an over-all Amerindian culture pattern.

The Negro African Pattern

We have designated the working structure of West African song style as L/N. African music might be called interlocked antiphony. A leader initiates and a group responds, litany phrase by litany phrase, but the group does more than respond and overlap with the leader's part, and the leader usually does more than overlap with the chorus. Very frequently both L and N support and comment on the other part with murmurs, bits of chords, or snatches of musical laughter and with a complex pattern of counterrhythms from hands, feet, and orchestra, not to mention kinesic comment from the dancers. In the solo line, itself, a playful lead voice shifts from open, ringing tones to strong nasalization to powerful rasp, from falsetto coo to bass grunt. Indeed, without such exhibitions of vocal display, an African song leader is soon replaced by another.

Yet, despite the shifting vocal timbre of the African singer, the choruses blend their voices in striking tonal effects. Visible speech analysis shows how this is possible. Although rasp and nasalization are present in the harmonic pattern of the solo voice, they are controlled and precisely placed instead of being pervasive characteristics, as is the case with the vocal characterizers that Western European bardic and Amerindian voices handle. Also, the harmonics are well and widely distributed—signs of the well-tuned voice.

A leader and a chorus part are normally implied in Negro African song, whether or not the performance is solo, for both elements are essential to African song structure. The song leader never performs for long without complex counterbalancing comment by the instrumental or vocal chorus. Furthermore, our research indicates that the length of the leader's part varies roughly with the importance of tribal chiefs over against the tribal council. In more or less acephalous African tribes, song leaders usually perform against a constant background of choral singing. Where chieftainship is paramount, vocal solos are longer and more prominent.

This hypothesis is strengthened by our coding of the ceremonial music of the Kingdom of Dahomey and the court songs of the Watusi of Ruanda-Urundi. In Dahomey, long solos are again important; no polyphony is permitted and highly embellished chromatic passages, rare in Negro Africa but common in Oriental song, become prominent. Among the royal Watusi, highly embellished hetero-phonic singing, meterless rhythm, long bardic performances, and other traits link Watusi style with that of the hydraulic empires. It would be improper not to observe that, in both these cases, song functions as a support to a powerful ruling hierarchy rather than playing the role normal in most simpler African societies. Along the southern border of the Sahara, among peoples strongly influenced by the culture of Islam and in many tribes where powerful kingship systems dominate large nations, solo bardic singing of the type described previously is common. It is my conviction, however, based on examination of a number of cases, that bardic singing of a strongly Oriental type is not of significant importance except in those African societies where institutional patterns akin to despotic Oriental societies shape the whole social system.

This brief sketch of African song performance structure, as exhibited in the cantometric profile in Figure 2, matches in a remarkable way the gross structure of most African Negro societies (see Murdock 1959). An African normally belongs to several interlocked groups—to a tribe, then perhaps to a series of segmentary patrilineal kin groups, to one or more cult groups, to a work organization, to an age group, to a political faction, and so on. Each of these groups may have a different head, and in each of them an individual may achieve a varying degree of prominence in accordance with his talents and his status. Although the society is stratified, it is quite possible for a witty man with a highly developed sense of political maneuver to rise to the top of one or several of the organizations of which he is a member. If he is an hysteric, he may become a religious leader and prophet. This provides an exact analogy to the emergence of a talented individual in the African musical group. African music is full of spaces. The loose structure of this musical situation gives the individual dancer, drummer, or singer the leeway to exhibit his personality in a moment of virtuosic display. He will then be replaced, but later on he may preempt longer and more elaborate solo passages, thus establishing himself as a recognized and talented musical leader.

Since music is keyed to group integration in a wide variety of African activities, a strong musical personality may be or become a religious or political leader. Yet the very structure of African melodies stands in the way of the L over N dominance pattern, for African melody is litany and responsorial, made up of more or less equal contributions from solo and chorus, with the chorus part dominant more often than not. Thus, in Negro Africa, musical performance structure and social structure mirror one another, reinforce one another, and establish the special quality of both African music and African society—whether in Africa or in African enclaves in the New World.

The strong rhythmic bias of African music also represents this many-goaled, many-headed, group-oriented culture. African rhythm is usually anchored in a strongly accented two or four beat rhythm, but around and through this positive, thrusting, rhythmic unity plays a variety of contrasting counterrhythms on numbers of instruments that give voice to the diverse groups and personalities bound together in tribal unity. At any moment, one of these tangential rhythms can seize the imagination of the group and become dominant, just as in a West African cult ceremony an individual may be mounted by his cult deity and rise from obscurity to total group dominance for a period.

Nor does the Negro group discourage women from taking leading roles in singing, as do many primitive peoples. Here Negro society reflects the comparative importance and independence of women, recognized in other spheres by their ownership of land, their control of marketing activities, and their part in religious ritual.

Perhaps, too, the prominence of polygyny in Negro Africa (cf. Murdock 1959) finds its expression in African musical structure. African education and custom place great emphasis on sexual matters—on fertility, on potency, and on erotic skill. This focus of interest supports the system of polygynous marriage, where a man must be able to satisfy several wives and a woman must compete for the favor of her husband with a number of co-wives. African dance prepares and trains both sexes for strenuous love-making, and the swinging, off-beat, rhythmically climactic rhythms of Africa motivate and support this frankly erotic dance style. Yet not all African dancing is a dramatization of courtship and love-making, just as not all group rhythmic activity in Africa is dancing in the strict sense. Collective rhythmic activity runs like a bright thread through the web of African life and is, indeed, one of its organizing principles. Work is done, journeys are made, law cases are argued, myths and legends are told, social comment is made, religious rites are conducted to rhythms which can be danced and sung by leader and chorus in accordance with the main structures of African music. The result is that the whole of African culture is infused with the pleasurably erotic, community-based pattern of African song and dance style. The attractiveness of African music for all the world today may, indeed, lie in the fact that it is so practical, that it operates successfully in more of life's activities than any other musical system.

It is my hope that the preceding thumb-nail sketches have indicated the usefulness of the cantometric approach for both ethnomusicology and anthropology. Several viable concepts seem to be indicated by the research at this stage. First, that, as long as music is considered cross-culturally as a whole and in behavioral terms, it is possible to locate structure comparable to known culture patterns. Second, that these esthetic structures remain relatively stable through time and space. Third, that these stable structures correspond to and represent patterns of interpersonal relationship which are fundamental in the various forms of social organization. Fourth, that analysis of cantometric structures may provide a precise and illuminating way of looking at the cultural process itself. Fifth, that, since the cantometric coding system deals with expressive material which all societies provide spontaneously and unself-consciously, it may become a tool for characterizing and, in some sense, measuring group emotional patterns. Finally, the way may be open for us to make the all-important distinction, first discussed by Sapir (1922)—the intangible yet grave distinction that all human beings respond to—between spurious and genuine culture.

I should like to add one word about the troubling problem of esthetic level. The structures that appear in our coding system are basic to the acceptance of a musical performance in a cultural setting. Without the proper structure, a song is felt to be foreign, or unsuitable, or simply of no interest. The more closely a song conforms to the norm indicated by a given profile, the more acceptable and familiar it seems to be in its cultural setting, yet the beauty of a bit of music depends upon the way the performer and/or composer handle another and narrower level of patterns, which cantometrics is not equipped to examine.

This essay provides evidence that the principal messages of music concern a fairly limited and crude set of patterns; otherwise, they would not be so easily available to such a system. The art of music, however, lies in its capacity to repeat these main messages again and again in slightly disguised and subtly different ways. Here, at the level of musical conversation, we enter a limitless realm of nuance, where reinforcement never brings surfeit or fatigue, where the ear delights in playing with a scale of tiny differences, and the restatement of the familiar is not a command but an invitation to return home.

Note

1. The substance of this paper was read at the annual meeting of the Society of Ethnomusicology in Philadelphia, November 15, 1961. The research was sponsored by Columbia University and supported by the Rockefeller Foundation. Many of the ideas developed in the paper grew out of informal discussions with Professor Conrad Arensberg, under whose general direction the research was carried out.

Bibliography

Bargara, D.A. 1960. Psychiatric Aspects of Speech and Hearing. Springfield.
Herskovits, M.J. 1941. The Myth of the Negro Past, New York.
Jackson, G.P. 1943. White and Negro Spirituals. New York.
Lomax, A. 1959. Musical Style and Social Context. American Anthropologist 61:927-954.
Marshall, E. 1959. The Harmless People. New York.
Miller, W.B. 1955. Two Concepts of Authority. American Anthropologist 57:271-289.
Moses, P.J. 1954. The Voice of Neurosis. San Francisco.
Murdock, G.P. 1959. Africa: Its Peoples and Their Culture History. New York.
Parsons, T. 1949. Essays in Sociological Theory. Glencoe.
Rouget, G. 1956(?). Music of the Bushmen Compared to That of the Babinga Pygmies. Paris and Cambridge.
Sapir, E. 1922. Culture, Genuine and Spurious. American Journal of Sociology 29:410-430.
Turnbull, C.M. 1957. Initiation Among the Bambuti Pygmies of the Central Ituri. Journal of the Royal Anthropological Institute 87:191-216.
Turnbull, C.M. 1959. Legends of the Bambuti. Journal of the Royal Anthropological Institute 89:45-60.
Turnbull, C.M. 1960a. Field Work Among the Bambuti Pygmies. Man 60:36-40.
Turnbull, C.M. 1960b. Some Recent Developments in the Sociology of the Bambuti Pygmies. Transactions of the New York Academy of Sciences, ser. 2,22:267-274.
Turnbull, C.M. 1961. The Forest People. New York.
Wittfogel, K.A. 1957. Oriental Despotism. New Haven.

Record Bibliography

For an extensive list of selected records, see Lomax (1959). A wide range of material is available on Folkways Records and, in a more condensed form, on Columbia Records. A few representative long-playing records are cited below for each master profile.
Africa and American Negro
French Africa. Columbia Records KL 205.
British East Africa. Columbia Records SL 213.
Bulu Songs from the Cameroons. Folkways Records P 451.
The Topoke People of the Congo. Folkways Records FE 4503.
The Big Drum Dance of Carriacou. Folkways Records P 1011.
Folk Music of Jamaica. Folkways Records P 410.
Cult Music of Cuba. Folkways Records P 453.
Venezuela. Columbia Records KL 212.
Afro-Bahian Music from Brazil. Library of Congress Record 13.
The Roots of the Blues. Atlantic Records 1348.
Negro Prison Songs. Tradition Records 1020.
Afro-American Blues and Game Songs. Library of Congress Record 4.
Ray Charles at Newport. Atlantic Records 1289.

Pygmy and Bushman
   The Pygmies of the Ituri Forest. Folkways Records FE 4457.
   Music of the Bushman and Pygmy. Peabody Museum and Musée de l'Homme LD-9.
Western European Folk Song
   France. Columbia Records KL 207.
   England. Columbia Records KL 206.
   Ireland. Columbia Records KL 204.
   Scotland. Columbia Records KL 209.
   Folk Music of Norway. Folkway Records FM 4008.
   Anglo-American Ballads. Library of Congress Record 1.
   Wolf River Songs. Folkway Records FM 4005.
   Pete Steele. Folkways Records FS 3828.
Bardic
   Wolof Music of Senegal. Folkways Records 4462.
   Musique Maure. Musée de l'Homme Records.
   Folk Music of Ethiopia. Folkways Records FE 4405.
   Cante Flamenco. Westminster Records WAP 301.
   Modern Greek Heroic Oral Poetry. Folkways Records 4468.
   Arabic and Druse Music. Folkways Records P 480.
   Music of the Russian Middle East. Folkways Records P 416.
   Folk Music of the Mediterranean. Folkways Records P 501.
   Folk Music of India. Folkways Records FE 4422.
   Music of Indonesia. Folkways Records P 406.
   Japan, the Ryukyus, Korea. Columbia Records KL 214.
American Indian
   Eskimos of Hudson Bay. Folkways Records P 444.
   Canada. Columbia Records KL 211.
   Songs from the Iroquois Longhouse, Library of Congress Record 6.
   Music of the Sioux and Navajo. Folkways Records FE 4401.
   Music of the Indians of the Southwest. Folkways Records FE 4420.

THE BOUNDARIES OF SPEECH AND SONG

George List

A primary element in scientific investigation is the categorization or classification of the phenomena studied. We are concerned here with the development of a method of classification by which distinctions can be made between two forms of human sound communication, speech and song. This method should also make feasible the proper classification of any existing intermediate forms and should indicate their relations to each other and to speech and song as such.

There are several thousand languages in the world and it can be assumed that there exist at least an equal number of fairly well differentiated cultures. No one scholar shall ever be competent to develop a valid classification system of the type envisaged on the basis of his own work only. Nor has the problem to be discussed here been much investigated in the past. All that can be done at this time, then, is to survey a few of the problems involved in carrying out such a project and to outline a tentative system of classification which may possibly be useful as a springboard for further development in this direction.

There exist other types of human sound communication besides speech and song. Among these are various signalling devices as, for example, drum, horn, and xylophone speech, and whistled speech. In addition to these forms there is instrumental music, hummed melodies, and imitations of animal cries. The post-prandial courtesy belch of the Orient is also a form of human sound communication, although it may defy classification.

Speech and song display certain characteristics which, taken as a group, set them apart from the other forms listed. Both speech and song are 1) vocally produced, 2) linguistically meaningful, and 3) melodic. None of the other forms of human sound communication that have been mentioned share all three of these traits. The first two characteristics of speech and song, vocal production and linguistic meaningfulness, could undoubtedly be utilized in developing a classification system. However, the problems involved are so complex that these traits have at this time been omitted from consideration. We shall therefore, in general, base our classification system upon the third characteristic only, that of being melodic. Nevertheless, some discussion of the second trait or characteristic, meaningfulness, is necessary in order to define our terms.

When we state that speech and song are linguistically meaningful, we are referring to meaningfulness in the dictionary sense. Not all vocables utilized in these two communication forms are meaningful. Meaningless syllables, for example, are almost invariably present in the songs of the American Indians but are rarely found in their speech. Should we accept meaningfulness in the dictionary sense as an invariable characteristic of speech and song, we must of necessity omit from consideration any form which does not include some meaningful utterances. Thus the "chin music" of the English folk, the vocal production of instrumental dance melodies utilizing meaningless vocables only, must be excluded. So must certain vocal forms found in tribal societies be excluded, forms which are composed entirely of meaningless syllables.

We must also come to a decision concerning certain borderline cases. Many ritual chants are performed in a language intelligible to the celebrant but not always to the listener. Among these are chants in Latin performed in the Roman Catholic liturgy and chants in Sanscrit which form part of the Buddhist ritual. The Australian and North American aborigines commonly borrow songs from other tribes whose languages they do not understand. These songs often remain in the repertory of the tribe that borrowed them and are performed relatively unchanged. Since these forms are meaningful to the celebrants of the chant or to the performers in the culture to which the songs are indigenous, it would seem that they should be included within the compass of speech and song.

The melody of speech is produced either by the intonations or inflections common to the particular language, by the tonal structure if the language possesses phonemic tones, and by a combination of the two phenomena when both are present. The tones are meaningful at the phonemic level, that is, in the dictionary sense. Intonation is meaningful but at a level less susceptible to exact analysis than phonemes or tones.

Certain elements, such as pitch, duration, and stress, can be isolated and analyzed in the study of melody. Pitch may be relatively stable, remaining at a reasonably constant rate of vibration or cycles per second, or relatively unstable, wavering or gliding upwards or downwards. The range of a melody can be assessed whether the pitch is stable or unstable. On the other hand, scalar structure can only be determined when the pitches are reasonably stable.

Comparision of pitch ranges does not seem to be useful as a means of classification. As the writer pointed out in an article concerning Thai speech and song (List 1961), the range of speech may easily exceed that of song. On the other hand, the comparison of scalar structure can be a useful tool, but only when considerable pitch stability exists.

On first thought it would seem that duration, the comparative length or shortness of sustained pitch, would be a useful criterion to incorporate in our system. It is probably a common conception, in our own culture at least, that song exhibits pitches of greater duration than speech. This assumption is not necessarily valid. Length of vowels is of course a phonemic characteristic of a number of languages. Songs in these languages may or may not assign greater duration to these vowels than speech. In other languages, as those of the Australian aborigines, there is apparently greater sustenation of pitch in speech than in song. In length these sustained pitches are comparable to those found in song in our culture. In contrast, communication forms referred to as song among the Australian aborigines are characterized by use of the relatively short vocables common to their language.[2]

Figure 1 is a transcription of a short section of *wangka*, speech or talking, by an informant of the Nyangumata tribe of the Western Australian desert. The informant relates the incidents of a journey which he had recently made. The horizontal lines above the text indicate the use of sustained pitches. The sustention of pitch has the same function here as a superlative suffix in European languages. It conveys the fact that the journey to the East was of considerable length.

tʸuŋkaŋaku   nʸuŋuŋuku kaŋinʸaku   kakaratʸiriku ↑ yu ↑ wuraṇaṇala   //

for-in-earth for-in-this for-driving for-east   yes   I-told-him

yu ↑ palatʸalu //   palaŋa maṇaṇa mutuka   #   kakara mititʸiṇiyiṇi::

yes   then   there I-took motorcar   east   we-went

kanʸaṇa mutuka pala ŋatʸulu::   wika maṇayiṇi patitʸiri #

I-drove motorcar that   I   firewood we-got midway

palaŋulu kakara mititʸiṇiyiṇi:: // ŋapi   // miŋkul #

then   east   we-went   what's-its-name   Minguel

miŋkulŋulu palaŋa tuṇaptʸarinyiṇi //

from-Minguel there   I-turned-off

Fig. 1. *Nyangumata*, Speech

Nor is stress an invariable characteristic of the two means of human sound communcation under consideration. Very little if any stress or accent, for example, is found in the vocal part of the lament for the dead of the Tibetan lamas. Stress can be phonemic or non-phonemic, that is, it may or may not have an effect upon word meaning.

In English stress affects word meaning, in other languages it may not. Accented syllables can be heard in Japanese speech. However, the accent heard is a function of intonation and can be placed on any syllable of a word without affecting word meaning.

Certain further definitions are necessary before we can develop our classification system. Speech is defined here as casual utterance, as in conversation. Other types of speech, those found in more socially structured situations such as dramatic representations, the delivery of sermons, or the telling of jokes and tales, will be classified as "heightened speech," a form somewhat intermediate to speech and song. Song, itself, will be defined in the light of our own concepts of this means of communication, as a form exhibiting relatively stable pitches, possessing a scalar structure at least as elaborate as the heptatonic, and showing little, if any, influence melodically of speech intonation.

It is quite possible that investigators who are members of a culture differing considerably from our own might assign forms with characteristics very much unlike those selected here as the two ends of the continuum. Certain cultures make a distinction between what is referred to as speech or talking and what is referred to as song or singing. Other cultures do not necessarily make this distinction. Other cultures distinguish forms other than speech or song which to us may seem to be intermediate forms. The nomenclature applied to these intermediate forms will vary considerably from culture to culture as will the social function of the form.

The Hopi Indians of northwestern Arizona distinguish between speech, *laváyi*, song, *táwi*, and announcing, *túngava*. What they refer to as an "announcement" may be described as a type of chant utilizing two unstable pitches approximately a fourth apart, the upper pitch seeming the most used. This chant form exhibits many vocal glides as well as sharpening of the upper of the two chant tones. Each section or paragraph is concluded by a fairly long and slow descending glide which serves consciously as a punctuation device.

Fig. 2. *Hopi*, Announcement of a Rabbit Hunt

The forms referred to by the Hopis as *táwi*, song, cover a very wide range indeed. Some are basically monotonic chant occasionally enlivened with auxiliary tones. Should only one auxiliary tone be utilized, it is usually a fourth above the principal tone. Figure 3 is a transcription of a didactic section from a long Kachina song in which the chiefs are reminded of their responsibilities.

Fig. 3. *Hopi*, Owák Kachina Song

Other Hopi songs exhibit fairly well defined and more developed scalar structures. Figure 4 is a transcription of a section of a social dance song.

Fig. 4. *Hopi*, Buffalo Dance Song

To the writer's knowledge, the Hopis make no distinction between these widely divergent forms of vocal communication. They apparently possess no term to describe what we might refer to in our culture as "chant." From the point of view of the Western musicologist, Figures 2, 3, and 4 represent quite divergent forms.

In the language of the Maoris of New Zealand, a Polynesian people, there are three terms referring to the types of sound communication under consideration here, *koorero*, speech, *karakia*, ritual chant, and *waiata*, song.[3] There is, in addition, a fourth form, *haka*. The term *haka* refers to the dance which this communication form accompanies.

We should describe both *karakia* and *waiata* as generally monotonic chants which display a few auxiliary tones and, in particular, descending vocal glides.

These glides are terminals of phrases as in the Hopi announcements. Figure 5 is a transcription of a section of a *karakia,* in this case a ritual chant designed to drive away unwanted flocks of birds. Figure 6 is a transcription of a section of a *waiata*, a warning song by a sentinel guarding the village.

Fig. 5. *Maori,* Ritual Chant

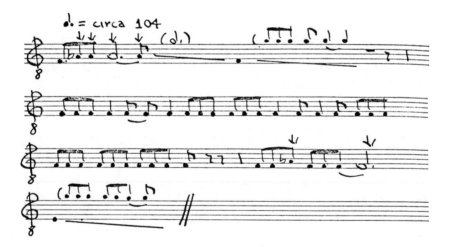

Fig. 6. *Maori,* Sentinel Song

Haka, on the other hand, is quite a divergent form. In it speech intonation seems to have been amplified and developed into a free form. Figure 7 is a transcription of a spectograph made of a section of a recording of a *haka,* a narrative celebrating the exploits of a famous chief. In the transcription only the fundamentals are given, the overtones have been elided. Each horizontal line to the left of the graph represents 50 cps. Each vertical line above the graph represents the elapse of four-tenths of a second.

It is apparent that other considerations than melodic type are usually operative in distinguishing one communication form from another. Distinctions

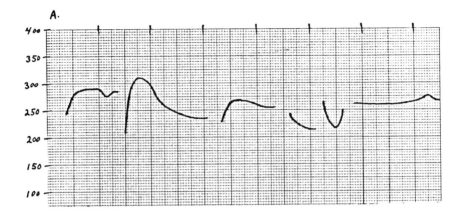

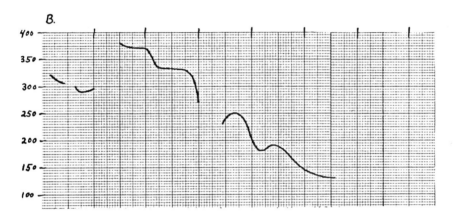

Fig. 7. *Maori*, Haka

made according to function rather than melodic type are also common in our society. "Auctioneering," the form of communication used by the auctioneer, is not usually considered "song" or even "chant." Nevertheless, "auctioneering" often takes the form of a monotonic chant in which the monotone and the few auxiliary tones used are quite stable. On occasion, types of melodic cadences are also used.[4]

When speech is heightened in a socially structured situation, such as a dramatic production or in the telling of a tale, two opposite tendencies appear. The first is the negation or the levelling out of intonation into a plateau approaching a monotone. The second is the amplification or exaggeration of intonation, especially of the downward inflection that serves in most languages as a phrase, sentence, or paragraph final. Figure 8 is a transcription of a spectograph of one sentence, "I have worked a great deal of magic for you in my time, your Majesty," spoken by the King's magician in a recorded play by James Thurber, *Many Moons*. The contour of this sentence is a clear example of the operation of these two divergent tendencies. The range of the transcription is approximately 60 to 120 cps. The first phrase or plateau section hovers between 110 and 115 cps. The dips to 80 cps in this phrase represent the onset of consonants and are therefore more an acoustic than an intonational pheno-menon. To the ear this section of the transcription has very much the character of a monotone. The last part of the transcription, representing the salutation, "your Majesty," is a lengthy downward glide covering approximately 45 cps. In this low cps band this downward inflection represents approximately the interval of a perfect fifth.

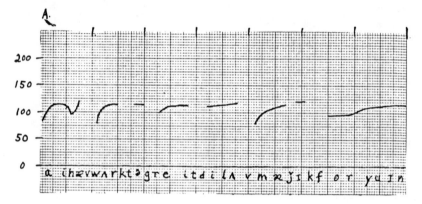

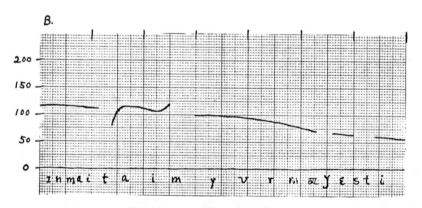

Fig. 8. Line from Play, *Many Moons*

The classification system which we shall now develop is based to a great extent upon these two divergent modifications of speech intonation. The chart or graph, Figure 9, is analogous to a hemispheric map of the world. At the north pole is placed casual speech. Song, as previously defined, is found at the south pole. The forms found north of the equator are those which seem to have more characteristics of speech than song. The forms south of the equator exhibit to a greater extent the traits associated with song.

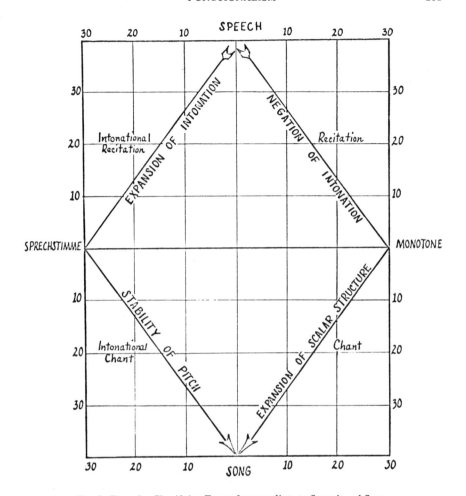

Fig. 9. Chart for Classifying Forms Intermediate to Speech and Song

Movement to the east represents the diminution or negation of the influence of speech intonation. Movement to the west represents either the expansion of intonational contours or of scalar structures. Modification is continuous along the diagonals and each area marked extends its influence with decreasing magnetism in the three possible directions. Thus, the use of lines of latitude and longitude permits the placement of forms at midpoints both horizontally and vertically.

Since the example of heightened speech given in Figure 9 shows both negation of intonation, the first phrase or plateau section, and expansion of intonation, the long and deep terminal glide, this form will be placed on the diagram at latitude 30° north on the central axis.

At latitude 20° north, midway on the diagonal moving to the southeast, we shall place forms such as the counting out or jumping rope rhymes of American children. These forms, while basically speech, make limited use of intonation.

What intonation is present, usually short terminal glides, revolves around a central speech monotone which is ornamented with one or two auxiliary tones. The form is described here as "recitation." Figure 10 is a transcription of the first section of a jumping rope rhyme as recited by an eight-year-old American child. The recitation of poetry by small children in our culture is comparable form.

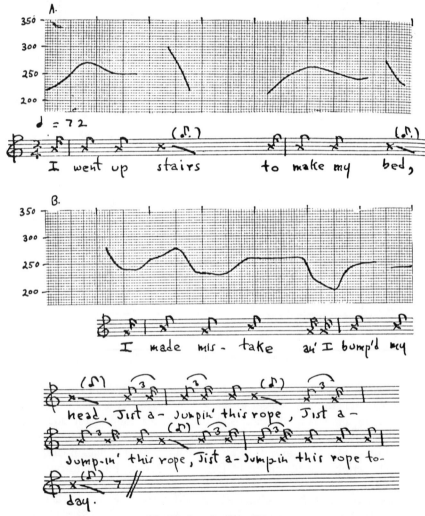

Fig. 10. Jumping Rope Rhyme

When the line representing the continuous negation of speech intonation reaches the equator, the area of the complete monotone is reached. Certain Buddhist chants in Thailand exhibit pure monotone.

Fig. 11. *Thai*, Buddhist Chant

The midway point between the north pole and the equator on the diagram moving to the southwest has been assigned to forms displaying amplification of speech intonation. This type has been designated "intonational recitation." This communication form is found, for example, in the singing of the women of Palau, one of the Caroline Islands in Micronesia. In group singing the leader customarily recites a short text which several women then repeat in an improvisatory type of part singing. The "lining out" by the leader is what is termed here "intonational recitation."

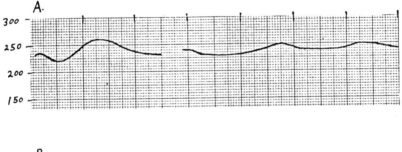

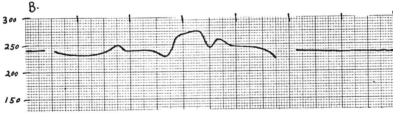

Fig. 12. *Palau*, Intonational Recitation

At the point where the westwards moving diagonal meets the equator is found not merely the greatest amplification of intonation contours but their development into a free melodic form. This area has been labelled *sprechstimme*. The term refers to the type of elevated or heightened speech characteristic of the melodrama and is best known by its application by Arnold Schoenberg to the type of vocal communication displayed in his *Pierrot Lunaire*. The Maori *haka* (Figure 7) is an example of *sprechstimme*.

It will be noted that the range of the Palauan "intonational recitation" is approximately 220 cps to 275 cps, or approximately a major third. In contrast the Maori *haka* has a range of 130 to 380 cps, approximately an octave plus a perfect fifth. The latter therefore has an ambitus more than four times larger than the former.

The forms found to the southwest of monotone along the diagonal leading to SONG all display reasonably stable pitches. The influence of the monotone pervades until the halfway mark, to the area marked "chant." Along the diagonal to this point will be placed monotonic chants displaying an increasing number of auxiliary tones. Figure 13, a transcription of excerpts from a recording of a tobacco auction in North Carolina, is an example of a fully developed form of "chant." Four auxiliary tones are utilized.

Fig. 13. Tobacco "Auctioneering"

From this point south to SONG will be placed forms increasingly independent of monotonic influence and exhibiting increasing complexity of scalar structure, ditonic songs of the Vedda, tritonic taunts of American children, tetratonic Bulgarian folk songs, etc.

Along the diagonal moving southeast from the equator to latitude 20° south will be placed chant-like forms exhibiting contours related to speech intonation. They will be placed here in descending order of intonational complexity and increasing order of pitch stability. The Hopi "announcement" (Figure 2) is an example of "intonational chant."

Further south on this diagonal will be placed song-like forms which exhibit instability of pitch or some aspects of speech intonation. Since the songs of the

Australian aborigines simultaneously exhibit a reasonably clear scalar structure such as the pentatonic and considerable instability of pitch and use of glides, they find their place here at latitude 30° south. The following American Negro song (Figure 14) will be placed at the same latitude on the central axis.

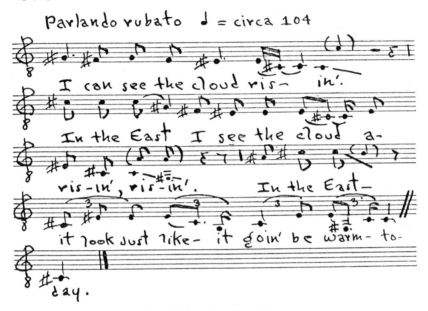

Fig. 14. American Negro Song

Of the two Hopi songs discussed above, the Kachina song (Figure 3), a monotone embellished with one auxiliary, would be placed on the east diagonal a few degrees south of "monotone." The second (Figure 4), which possesses a pentatonic scale and exhibits few vocal glides, would be placed on this diagonal at latitude 30° south. The Maori chant (Figure 5) and song (Figure 6), both exhibiting monotone, a limited number of auxiliaries, and a highly developed use of terminal intonation, would be placed on the central axis, a few degrees south of the equator.

Unfortunately, this chart is not too well adapted to the classification of forms found in cultures whose languages are tonal. The classification of forms in tonal languages presents innumerable difficulties. Tone becomes a third variable to be controlled, making necessary the construction of a three-dimensional diagram. In organizing such a classification system, it is also necessary to take into consideration many complex and little investigated relations existing between tone, intonation, and musical melody. Tones may be fairly stable, as register tones, or unstable, as contours. In Chinese, a tone which coincides with an ascending movement of intonation is further amplified. The reverse occurs when a tone coincides with a descending intonation (Chen 1956:53). Mandarin Chinese has segmented tones and certain elisions of segments are conventional (Chen 1956:53). In Thai one tone may be substituted for another under specific circumstances (List 1961:19-20). In Ashanti heightened speech, tone groups may be reversed.[5] There is some evidence that there exist in Ewe elaborate conventions regulating the modification of speech tones in song (see Schneider 1961).

The present chart is only useful in the placement of forms which follow the tones with great regularity. Chinese singsong (Chao 1956:53-54) or the type of recitation utilized by small children in Thai schools follows the tones with great fidelity and is devoid of intonation (List 1961:17-19). This form may be placed on the chart in the same position as "monotone." Chinese opera recitative follows the dialect used rather closely (Chao 1956:57), but exhibits a tremendous expansion of speech intonation. This form may be placed in the

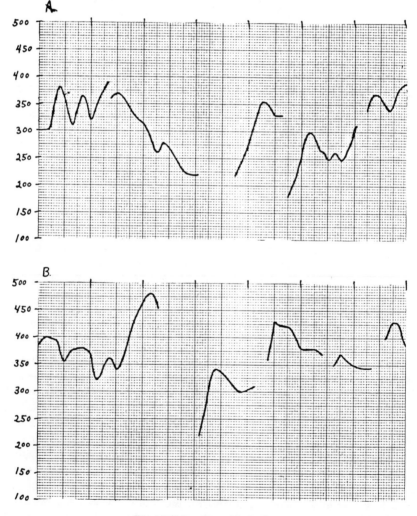

Fig. 15.*China*, Opera Recitative

same position as *sprechstimme*. The excerpt transcribed exhibits a range of from 180 to 480 cps or an ambitus a little larger than a major ninth. This style of *sprechstimme* thus has a slightly smaller ambitus than that of the *haka*, but it shows a more rapid oscillation between peaks and valleys.

The classification system presented here does not of course permit the placement of forms with a fine degree of accuracy. Much more data is needed concerning the intonational contours utilized in each language under consideration before a more exact classification is possible. The further utilization of acoustic devices such as the spectograph or melograph would be very useful as a check upon the ear. When a large number of representative forms from a number of diverse cultures have been plotted upon the chart, they will probably form clusters and these clusters can then be utilized as types.

Or, as our knowledge increases, the utilization of other criteria than the melodic may be added and this system discarded in favor of one that will be both more accurate and more complex.

References Cited

Chao, Yuen Ren
     1956 "Tones, intonation, singsong, chanting, recitative, and atonal composition in Chinese" *in* For Roman Jakobson (The Hague: Mouton), p. 53.
List, George
     1961 "Speech melody and song melody in Central Thailand," ETHNOMUSICOLOGY 5(1):24-26.
Schneider, Marius
     1961 "Tone and tune in West African music," ETHNOMUSICOLOGY 5(3):204-15.

Notes

[1] This article is a revised version of a paper read at the Sixth Annual Meeting of the Society for Ethnomusicology held jointly with the American Anthropological Association in Philadelphia, Nov. 17-18, 1961. The original paper was illustrated with recordings.

[2] For recordings of the *yinma* or song of the Nyangumata tribe of Western Australia, see those made by Geoffrey O'Grady in 1953, Indiana University Archives of Folk and Primitive Music, Tape Library No. 1759.

[3] The writer is indebted to Dr. Bruce Biggs of the University of Auckland, New Zealand, for information concerning the Maori language.

[4] For examples of "auctioneering," see recordings made during a furniture warehouse sale in Bloomington, Indiana, by Wyatt Insko, Indiana University Archives of Folk and Primitive Music, Tape Library Nos. 985-986.

[5] The writer is indebted to Mr. J.H. Kwabena Nketia of the University of Ghana for information concerning the tones of Ashanti.

Acknowledgements

The writer wishes to acknowledge with thanks the assistance of Mr. Geoffrey O'Grady, who provided the transcription and translation of Nyangumata speech (Figure 1), and of Mrs. Judith McCulloh, who undertook the arduous task of transcribing the spectographs (Figures 7, 8, 10, 12, and 15). The writer is also indebted to Professor Fred Householder, Chairman of the Indiana University Linguistics Program, for preparation of the spectographs and for advising Mrs. McCulloh in their transcription.

Figures

Key to Signs Used in the Transcriptions in Musical Notation

Instability or indefiniteness of pitch is indicated by the use of an 'x' rather than a note heard.

Vocal glides are indicated by diagonal lines. Short glides take their time value from the previous note. The length of long glides is indicated in parentheses above the glide. Should more than one syllable be utilized in the glide, the rhythmic pattern is indicated above in parentheses. Note heads without stems indicate the pitch at which glides begin.

Half bars indicate the ends of phrases rather than measures. Where half bars are used accidentals apply for the entire stave. Slanted double bars in initial position indicate that material occurring before this point has been omitted, in medial position that a section has been elided, in final position that the vocal communication continues past this point.

Meter markings in parentheses indicate that the melody follows this meter in general but not consistently.

An upwards pointing arrow above a note indicates that the pitch is approximately a quarter step sharp, a downwards pointing arrow indicates the pitch is approximately a quarter step flat. An arrow curved to the right followed by a dotted line and "simile" indicates that the melody continues at a level approximately a quarter tone sharp.

Dots beneath or above a note head indicate breath accents.

Sources of the Figures

1. Nyangumata, *Wangka*. Recorded by Geoffrey O'Grady in Western Australia in 1953. Indiana University Archives of Folk and Primitive Music, Tape Library No. 1766.4.

2. Hopi, Announcement. Recorded under the supervision of J. Walter Fewkes at the Grand Canyon, Arizona, in 1926. Gennett Records, 10-inch, 78 RPM, 5759 B.

3. Hopi, Kachina Song. Recorded by George List at Polacca, Arizona, August 8, 1960.

4. Hopi, Buffalo Dance Song. Recorded by George List at Polacca, Arizona, August 8, 1960.

5. Maori, *Karakia*. Recorded by Bruce Biggs in New Zealand IU AFPM, Tape Library No. 1557.6.

6. Maori, *Waiata*. Recorded by the New Zealand Broadcasting Service in cooperation with the Maori Affairs Department, Government of New Zealand. Folkways Records, LP Album FE 4433, Side 2, Band 4.

7 Maori, *Haka*. Folkways Records, LP Album FE 4433, Side 1, Band 5.

8. *Many Moons*. Columbia Records, 10-inch, 78 RPM, MJV 46-1.

9. Chart drawn by Sheridan Schroeter.

10. Jumping Rope Rhyme. Recorded by George List at Bloomington, Indiana, August 27, 1955.

11. Thai, Buddhist Chant. Recorded by Howard K. Kaufman at Bangkok, Thailand, June 1954. IU AFPM, Tape Library No. 801.4.

12. Palau, Recitation. Recorded by Cecilia Hendricks in the Caroline Islands in 1950. IU AFPM, Tape Library No. 324.2.

13. Tobacco "Auctioneering." Recorded by Barbara Currin Smetzer in North Carolina. IU AFPM, Folklore Tape Library No. 112, Item 1.

14. American Negro Song. Recorded by Richard A. Dorson, February 7, 1953.

15. China, Opera Recitative. Recorded in China. Folkways Records, LP Album No. FW 8882, Side 1.

UNIVERSALISM AND RELATIVISM IN THE STUDY OF ETHNIC MUSIC

Leonard B. Meyer

It is remarkable with what persistent and single-minded intent human beings strive for inner security and psychic certainty. We cling tenaciously to familiar ways and accepted explanations, blandly disregarding or rationalizing away incongruities and inconsistencies, if only we may be permitted the tranquillity of a system and certainty of a set of principles. Only a few can tolerate ambiguity and its attendant tensions.

Perhaps it is this need for the reliability of order and regularity that compels the mind to obey the principles of pattern perception formulated by the Gestalt psychologists: the psychological organization will always be as good as prevailing conditions allow; a motion once begun will tend to continue in the simplest possible way; changes in memory traces will tend to improve shape; and so forth. In the realms of philosophy, science, and mathematics a similar need leads us to accept as "best" or "true" those explanations which are the simplest and most economical—as, for instance, in the principle of Occam's Razor.[1]

(Observe, incidentally, that in subsuming the theories of Gestalt Psychology and the principle of Occam's Razor under a single general concept, I am obeying the very tendencies which I am discussing.)

Not only does a principle of parsimony govern our perception of music, through the unconscious operation of principles such as those of simplicity and good shape, but it also influences the explanations we give of the nature of music, the development of musical styles, and the relations of music to the culture in which it arises. In short, it shapes both musical experience itself and our thinking about musical experience. And it seems possible that the operation of this principle is responsible for the strong tendency toward simplistic monism which has marked our thinking in the area of Ethnic Music.

I.

Fifty years ago music was generally considered to be a universal language. Obvious differences between music of different cultures were explained away as being apparent rather than real. Beneath the profusion of seemingly disparate styles, it was argued, lay fundamental absolute principles which governed the structure and development of all music everywhere. It was only necessary to discover these basic underlying laws. But when these laws were not discovered, this form of monism was largely discredited and went out of fashion.

Then the warm winds of academic opinion began to blow in the opposite direction—toward an equally monistic relativism which sought to study each culture and each music "in its own terms" and which looked with suspicion upon any search for universal principles. Although scholars of this persuasion gathered much valuable data, for various reasons—perhaps above all precisely because it avoided cross-cultural questions such as those concerned with characteristics common to cultures that are unrelated ethnologically and geographically—relativism failed to produce fruitful hypotheses which might have led to new types of data and provided new insights into the nature of man, culture, and their interrelationships. As a consequence, this form of monism has come to seem less and less satisfactory.

There is, however, no transcendent logic compelling us to choose between these antithetical positions. Instead we can merely ask which features of music, if any, tend to be common to different cultures and which vary from culture to culture. The study and analysis of this material would presumably indicate which aspects of music are universal and which are culturally determined. Hypotheses might then be formulated to account for the findings and, of course, to explain the exceptions.

Unfortunately the matter is not so simply solved. Appearances are often deceptive. For instance, two cultures may appear to employ the same scale structure, but this structure might be interpreted differently by the members of each culture. Conversely, the music of two cultures may employ very different materials, but the underlying mechanism governing the organization of these materials might be the same for both. The possibility of such discrepancy calls attention to the importance of methodology and definition.

Strange though it may seem, such common terms as melody, mode, rhythm, form, and the like have been used in two different, though related, senses; and considerable confusion has resulted from the failure to keep these different uses separate and distinct.

Such terms have been used in a purely descriptive way to refer to sound stimuli and the objective relationships among them. Thus the tonal materials of a musical style can be analyzed, the relative frequency with which particular tones or intervals appear can be calculated, patterns of melodic repetition can be studied, minutiae of performance can be scrutinized and so on. A *descriptive* method such as this treats music like a physical phenomenon—as something to be observed, measured, classified, and compared.

However, the interpretation of such objective data is not without difficulties. For interpretation and explanation involve the use of general laws or hypotheses which serve to order and make understandable the diversity and disparity of observed particulars. In physics the laws explaining, say, the behavior of masses are, like the empirical data itself, essentially descriptive. Thus the law of gravity is a formula which stipulates a constant relationship among mass, distance, and force of attraction. It does not posit causes, it describes.

Because of the number of variables and the complexity of their interaction, the data assembled by descriptive ethnomusicology yields relatively few observable regularities. Furthermore, music is so patently a human product that, even when they can be found, purely descriptive laws do not seem really satisfying. For we still want to trace these observed regularities to their human source and to correlate them with the more general laws governing all human behavior. Thus the initial descriptive data of music must ultimately be explained in terms of the mental behavior, needs, habits, and culture out of which it arises.

It is when such explanation begins that the meanings of terms become changed. They are no longer purely descriptive. Rather they refer to psychological experiences. A mode is no longer a constant set of individual tones. It is a set of subjectively felt tendencies among the tones. The scope of ethnomusicology has changed too. It now requires not only knowledge of the stimulus, but also knowledge of the responding individual—whether composer, performer, or listener—for whom the stimulus has significance; and such knowledge includes an understanding of mental behavior as it operates within the context of culturally acquired habits and dispositions.

Without belittling the importance and the many contributions of descriptive ethnomusicology, the nature and limits of the information it can yield need to be understood. For it has at times employed concepts and reached conclusions which were unwarranted because they rested upon unrecognized or untested assumptions of a pyschological sort. For instance, descriptive data of a statistical nature has occasionally been made the basis for inferences about tonality. But tonality is a psychological phenomenon—a subjective sense of the tendency relationships among tones. And though I am inclined to believe that some sort of correlation exists between statistical frequency and felt tonal tendency, such a subjective response cannot validly be inferred from or correlated with descriptive data unless the relationship betwen them can be empirically demonstrated and theoretically explained.

In short, a purely descriptive method provides data rather than explanations (theory). In itself such data tells us little about music as a form of human activity—about its significance for the peoples who make and enjoy it. And when significance is, so to speak, thrust upon it, descriptive data is apt to be misleading because objective similarities do not necessarily give rise to correspondingly similar psychological responses and because, conversely, objective differences may be products of essentially similar psychological mechanisms.

This calls attention to a point of some moment. What we should ask about, when considering the problem of universals, is not whether the data itself is common to different cultures—any more than we decide whether there are scientific laws on the basis of particular physical events. What we should ask is whether, beneath the profusion of diverse and divergent particulars, there are any universal principles functioning. Stated thus it becomes apparent that the descriptive method is less than satisfactory for dealing with the problem of universalism vs. relativism precisely because it ignores those psychological concepts which might provide common principles for interpreting and explaining the enormous variety of musical means found in different cultures.

II.

Understanding of the process of musical communication too has been muddled by the tendency of critics, theorists, and aestheticians to treat alternative modes of signification as mutually exclusive. Indeed, the monistic approach to the question of universalism vs. relativism is in part a product of this prior monism which sought to exclude as spurious or fortuitous all but one type of musical meaning. But communication is thus limited. At least two basic modes of signification—the connotative and the kinetic or syntactic—can be distinguished.[2]

By connotations are meant associations—whether consciously intellectualized or unconsciously felt—made between the musical organization and some aspect of extra-musical experience, be it an idea, an object, a quality, or an activity. For our purposes the term will also include what has been called the "mood response" to music. As differentiated from the purely subjective, intrapersonal associations evoked by image processes, those involved in connotation are more or less standardized, having the same significance for, and producing the same attitudes in, all members of the cultural group. When a particular musical idea or pattern is used to refer to a *specific* concept, object or event—for instance, Wagner's Leitmotifs or the cannon in the 1812 *Overture*—it may be said to have denotative significance, though such denotation does not preclude the possibility of concurrent connotation.

It should be noted that few connotations are simple. What is communicated is a group of interrelated associations—a connotative complex.[3] For instance, night, winter, cold, death, solemnity, and sadness, constituting a kind of interwoven, inclusive musical metaphor, might be simultaneously signified by a single musical event.

Though any particular connotation is generally the product of both, two mechanisms of association can be distinguished: association by contiguity and association by similarity.

In the case of contiguity, some aspect of the musical organization—an instrumental timbre, a mode, a melody, etc.—becomes linked by dint of repetition with a concept, quality, activity, or mood. The organ is, for instance, associated for western listeners with religious concepts and attitudes; in Arabian music the strings of the lute were associated with actions of the soul, times of day, seasons of the year, and so on; the various Hindu ragas are associated with ethical concepts, moods, hours of the day, and seasons of the year.

Such associations by contiguity are culture-bound. A particular raga will not, for example, evoke the appropriate associations in a western listener unless he has learned its "meaning." The sound of an organ will not arouse religious associations in the members of a primitive tribe which has not been visited by missionaries—if such a tribe exists. Because contiguity creates associations which are contingent rather than necessary, they are subject to change and modification. Old associations die out and new ones arise.

However important associations formed by contiguity may be, their role in connotative signification is a relatively minor one. Most connotations arise as the result of similarities which exist between our experience of music, on the one hand, and our experience of concepts, objects, activities, qualities, and states of mind found in the extramusical world, on the other. Generally associations formed by contiguity modify and delimit those formed by similarity.

As Hornbostel has observed, perceptual experience is one.[4] Both music and life are experienced as dynamic processes—as motions differentiated both in shape and in quality. Such motions may be fast or slow, continuous or disjointed, precise or ambiguous, calm or violent, and so forth. Even experiences without literal, phenomenal motion are somehow associated with activity. Sunlight, the pyramids, a smoothly polished stone, a jagged line—each, depending partly upon our attitude toward it, is felt to exhibit some characteristic quality of motion and of sound.

The problem is not, as some have argued, whether music evokes connotations. An overwhelming amount of evidence proves that it does. Nor from the standpoint of ethnomusicology is the problem that of the propriety and aesthetic validity of connotative significance. The question is whether the processes of association are the same in different cultures; whether similar musical processes and structures give rise to similar or analogous connotations in different cultures. A modest sampling of the evidence indicates these processes are cross-cultural. The problem is an important one, of interest not only for ethnomusicology, but for aesthetics and psychology as well. It deserves thorough and carefully documented investigation.

One final point. It must be remembered that the musical characterization of an activity or concept depends upon the attitude of the culture toward the concept as well as upon the psychological mechanisms of association. Ostensibly similar concepts may be characterized differently in different cultures, or even within a single culture, not because the process of association is inconstant, but because the concept is viewed in different ways. In our own culture, for example, Death is generally considered to be solemn, fearful, and mysterious; but it has also been regarded as an expected friend or as the sardonic mocker of human pretensions. Obviously each of these views would give rise to a different musical characterization.

The kinetic-syntactic mode of signification refers to those essentially intra-musical experiences in which tonal stimuli have meaning because they are understood as the products of earlier musical events and point with varying degrees of probability to future events, creating a sense of movement toward and away from purely musical goals. Words such as tension, expectation, surprise, and delay are verbal descriptions of this mode of musical experience.

Note that, far from being antithetical, the connotative and kinetic modes of signification complement and qualify each other. Just as the behavior of an individual—his language, manners, decisions, and the like—play a part in shaping our opinion of his character, so the kinetic "behavior" of a piece of music (whether continuous or disjointed, expected or surprising) colors our feeling of its connotative significance. The converse of this also holds: connotations influence our expectations as to the way in which a piece will probably procede syntactically.

As was the case with connotation, two aspects of the process of kinetic communication can be distinguished: the grammatical and the psychological. In the grammatical are included the tonal materials of a musical style (its vocabulary) and the rules governing the ways in which these materials may be combined (its grammar). The grammatical aspect of music varies from culture to culture and from style to style within a culture. What remains constant are not scales, modes, harmonic progressions or formal procedures, but the psychology of human mental processes—the way in which the mind, operating within the context of a culturally established grammar, selects and organizes and evaluates the musical materials presented to it. For instance, the desire of the human mind for completeness and stability is a psychological constant. Consequently when a structural gap, such as a skip of an octave is perceived, the mind expects it to be completed, to be filled in. But the particular way in which it will be filled depends upon the tonal materials available and the rules governing their combination, that is, upon the grammar of the style. This will generally vary from style to style.

These observations too need empirical, cross-cultural confirmation. Such confirmation is difficult because, as Nettl points out, native informants find it difficult to verbalize about tonal organization, form, and the like.[5] But direct interrogation is not the only way to get evidence, nor the only way to discover what the norms and the permissible deviants of a style are and what rules and probabilities govern their use. Rather the enthnomusicologist, like the linguist, must learn to use the materials he wishes to study; he must learn to perform the music himself. For instance, by performing a group of carefully designed musical variants for an informant and asking questions such as: "is this a possible beginning phrase?" "which of these ways is better?" "can one do this?"—he can gradually discover the grammar and syntax of the style. Such a procedure supplemented by a statistical, descriptive study of the repertory of the culture should provide a reasonably detailed and accurate account of the kinetic features of the style being studied. It would also enable cross-cultural investigation to be more rigorous, more precise, and more revealing.

III.

Because the limitations imposed by an exclusively descriptive methodology have all but precluded an adequate analysis of signification, the problem of musical value, when it has been considered at all, has generally taken the form of an inventory of the uses made of music in a particular culture. Thus it has been observed that music is employed, and presumably valued, for its therapeutic properties, its magical powers, as an adjunct of ritual, and as a kind of recreation. Such observations, important though they may be, are relevant to the study of *cultural* choices and values rather than to the study of musical values.

Treated thus, the problem of musical value is not logically different from that of the value of basket-weaving or of puberty rites. What is needed in addition to this data is an account of what constitutes excellence in the music of a particular culture—an account, that is, of the musical decisions made by musicians and audiences.

Although an adequate discussion of musical value is beyond the scope both of this author and of this essay, the problems involved are so intimately related to those of signification, that some tentative remarks may perhaps not be out of place.

It is possible, I think, to make a plausible distinction between cultural values and individual values. The former, which are analogous to the culturally dependent processes involved in association by contiguity and in the grammatical structure of style, determine the uses made of music in the culture, the emphasis placed upon connotative vs. syntactical signification, and the degree of conformity demanded (or deviation permitted) by the culture. Individual values, which are analogous to the mechanism of association by similarity and the laws of pattern perception, arise out of the psychological organization and needs of the individual. The satisfaction of these needs is controlled by, and takes place within, the context of culturally established modes of behavior.

Of special relevance to the understanding of individual values is the psychological need for novelty—or, as some have put it, for information.[6] Its importance as a basic human drive is implicit in recent studies of creativity, developmental psychology, and stimulus privation.[7] It seems possible that the need for information is in part responsible for the tendency of composers and performers to deviate from established stylistic norms. Or, to put the matter in a different way: exact repetition is dull, clichés are boring, and familiar tasks tedious—without value—because they yield very little information.

If the distinction between cultural values and individual values has merit and if the need for novelty can be shown to be a basic principle of individual value—as the need for good shape is the basis for the laws of pattern perception—then the study of musical value need not be confined to cataloguing cultural usage.

What follow from this are not infallible answers, but rather a myriad of intriguing questions. If novelty is a basic human need, why do some cultures place severe restrictions upon it? Can one discover any pattern between the type or the degree of restriction and other features of the culture? Is such restraint a function of cultural level? For instance, does the need for novelty act as a correlate of value only when music becomes differentiated from other aspects of culture as a special, *aesthetic* object? In what ways do the norms of a culture channel and govern the permissible modes of deviation?

These questions—and one can think of many more—might well lead to a more fruitful and enlightened analysis of the nature of value in western music as well as non-western music and at the same time help to clarify the correlative problem of universality vs. relativity of values.

Notes

[1] The search for mental security is not a product of psychological inertia or mental sloth. We are obviously willing to expend much effort and energy in order to simplify shapes and rationalize explanations. Rather the need for psychic certainty would seem to arise out of man's awareness of time and his consequent need to predict—to know the future.

[2] These two types of signification are discussed at some length in my book Emotion and Meaning in Music (University of Chicago Press, 1956). However, in that book the term "embodied meaning," was used to designate what is here called "kinetic-syntactic signification."

[3] See Meyer, op. cit., pp. 264-266.

[4] E. von Hornbostel, "The Unity of the Senses," Psyche, VII, 1927, 83-89; also see K. Koffka, Principles of Gestalt Psychology (New York: Harcourt Brace & Co., 1935), p. 303.

[5] Bruno Nettl, Music in Primitive Culture (Cambridge: Harvard University Press, 1956), p. 59.

[6] See Leonard B. Meyer, "Some Remarks on Value and Greatness in Music," Journal of Aesthetics, XVII, 1959, 486-500.

[7] See, for instance, Frank Barron, "The Psychology of Imagination," Scientific American, 199 No. 3, Sept., 1958, 151-166; J.W. Getzels and P.W. Jackson, "The Highly Intelligent and Highly Creative Adolescent: A Summary of Recent Research Findings," The Third Research Conference, 1959, on the Identification of Creative Scientific Talent, ed. Calvin W. Taylor (Salt Lake City: University of Utah Press, to be published in 1960); Woodburn Heron, "The Pathology of Boredom," Scientific American, Vol. 196 No. 7, Jan., 1957, 52-56; John Rader Platt, "The Fifth Need of Man," Horizon, Vol. I No. 6, July, 1959, 106-111; Morris I. Stein, "Creativity and Culture," Journal of Psychology, 36, 1953, 311-322; William R. Thompson and Ronald Melzack, "Early Environment," Scientific American, Vol. 194 No. 7, Jan., 1956, 38-42.

THE ORIGINS OF MUSIC

S. F. Nadel

I.

From of old, learned minds have grappled with the problem of the origins of art, of music. Every thorough-going discussion regarding the nature of art and the true inwardness of human civilization, as well as every historical survey of art-evolution, must, in point of fact, be somewhere confronted by the ultimate question: What was the original source of art, and how did music come into being? Mythical folk-lore deals with this problem, the philosophy of the ancients sought to solve it, the ecclesiastical philosophers of the Middle Ages explained it after their own fashion. The problem has never quite disappeared from the sphere of scientific speculation, and it has been attacked with renewed zeal of late and in our own day.

Now, it can readily be seen that a definitive, wholly unimpeachable solution will probably never be arrived at. The ultimate sources of our art will always be deduced only by some hypothesis, some colorable theory. The possiblity will ever lurk in the background, that new discoveries of prehistoric research, or additional data concerning the artistic usages among present-day primitive peoples, may distinctly modify our conclusion. It is, however, absolutely essential for the probability of our hypothesis that it should be in conformity with our understanding of the nature of art, and with that line of artistic evolution which we can follow, as it were, through the visible sector of the developments in art and culture.

In this inquiry into the origins of art, music occupies a place peculiar to itself. In an investigation of the beginnings of art it is a self-evident assumption that we should be able to describe, in general terms, the real nature of art; we must be able to say positively whether any given case bears the criterion of what we call art. But here again there is no easily and positively defined limit; and especially in the domain of early and primitive art, which we view, so to speak, in a state of flux, it will be very difficult to draw the line, say, between the shaping of some utensil for practical use, and its artistic adornment; between the accidental and the intentional ornamentation of some woven fabric; or where art commences in some epic, or in the presentation of some legendary or religious theme. Music, however, exhibits in its very material an exact demarcation between that which is "art" and that which serves other, non-artistic purposes. The material of plastic art is, on primitive levels, the same as that employed in everyday, practical pursuits—stone, bronze, wood, woven work. The material of poetry is words, which also find employment in speech, in the intercourse of ordinary life.

277

But the tones are not met with, in this form, in the field of practical human activities; the production of tones in song reaches out beyond the "natural" employment of the vocal organ; instruments must be "invented." Even before the element of artistic purport enters into action, the precise dividing-line in music is already sharply marked. We can say that the material of music is artificial, a superaddition to natural expression through sound, and so not found in this latter.

Let us inquire, first: What are the most obvious differences between the material of the tones and the affiliated "natural" material, that of spoken sounds? Consider only such forms as we can define as the most primitive, relatively undeveloped forms of music: those forms of unison song that we find in the music of primitive races and likewise on certain low levels in the evolution of our occidental music, for example, in what we are wont to conceive as the earliest form of ancient Greek music, or in the music of the early Middle Ages. Here, too, a specific difference is quite plain. Speech employs fluctuating pitches; when we speak, the pitch shifts up and down without fixed points, without a determinate formation; whereas in music this shifting of the tones, superadded to the words and sense of speech, acquires a meaning all its own. The pitches of the tones are fixed, held fast on determinate points. The up-and-down fluctuation of speech resolves itself into definite patterns, which are, for music, the first manifestations of real importance; tone-progressions, intervals, are engendered, motives and themes are formed. This fixation of the pitches or, rather, this engendering of fixed intervals, this production of definite motives with the voice, is also, considered as pure technique, by no means a "natural" gift materializing without effort.

We can already see that this primordial "unnaturalness" of the material of music lays a formidable obstacle in the path of every theory concerning the origin of music. For "natural deduction, logical explanation," are the foundations of every scientific theory, and the sole safeguard of so hazardous an hypothesis as any explanation of the origin of music. In fact, the overcoming of the "unnaturalness" of the tone-material occupies the centre of attention in almost all theories regarding the origin of music. It has been attempted to discover some natural cause of the engendering of the "non-natural" tone-material. It is clear, that the theoretical foundation of this cause must be of the broadest; a foundation that can be fitted in some manner into the general scheme of human existence; otherwise it were impossible fully to explain the wide dissemination and commanding position of music in the world of men.

II.

The celebrated Berlin philosopher Karl Stumpf has characterized the principal groups of preceding theories by the ingenious and apposite titles: "In the beginning was love; In the beginning was the word; In the beginning was the deed." What he meant by this was simply a broad general characterization of the principles whereby the ultimate origins of music can be logically and naturally demonstrated. Employing other words to define these principles, we find that the above three groups represent the three great systems of Biology, Psychology, and Sociology; we find the origins of music embedded in the spheres of (1) the sexual instincts in man and animal, (2) the human will to expression and communication, (3) human activity.

(1) "In the beginning was love." In this conception the theory was brought forward for the first time by Charles Darwin,[1] and thus the origin of music, as well as of art in general, finds its place in Darwin's system of "The Origin of Species." The dominating principle in Darwin's theory of selection, the law of natural selection, is also a deciding factor in the generation of what we have termed the "non-natural" realm of tones.—In one sphere of Nature we find music prefigured—in the song of birds. Now, the song of birds is held to play a special rôle in the mechanism of Nature. It is a well-known fact that handsome men are generally preferred to ugly men by the fair sex. In the animal kingdom, too, the male must strive to please; almost everywhere we find the male handsomer, more brilliant in color, and—fonder of singing. Above all during the season of love-making, the time of sexual excitement, the males deploy all their arts; as they flaunt their gay plumage, so they glory in song. With seductive calls, with the highest tones and trills of their voices (the so-called falsetto tones), they woo their mates with passionate song. And man, like them, is supposed to become an artist, a singer, under the stress of sexual excitation. In his case, too, this special, quasi artistic branch of the law of natural selection supposedly applies.

In so far as Darwin's theory refers to the animal kingdom, it seems eminently consistent and logical. But when it is stretched to include mankind, its weak points are apparent. First of all, the birds, which alone among animals emulate musicians, are biologically quite remote from the line of evolution that leads up to Man. Whereas the animals of high and highest rank among the mammals, which we may consider as steps in the transitional progress towards Man, do not sing; their desireful cries and howls hardly merit the honor of inclusion in the ancestry of human music. Furthermore, the birds also sing outside of the mating-season. And so what we had assumed to be one important characteristic of music proves untenable, namely, that music presents an unusual mode of vocal expression at variance with the normal mode. To be sure, it has often been attempted to prove that the mating-songs of birds also differ, in an objectively unequivocal fashion, from the "ordinary" bird-songs, i.e., with respect to the employment of special tone-material. This would be a reason for conceding that birds have a music of their own. But when we seek to apply this reasoning to human music, we must inquire what analogy thereto can be found in human songs of the primitive level; for on that level one should be able to identify traces of the incipient evolution. But, on examining the songs of the primitives to that end, we find a large majority to be of an entirely different nature; mythical, religious and warlike songs occupy the foreground; love-songs are much rarer, or of later origin. In the few love-songs of the primitive that are known to us, however, there is no trace of causation by love-yearning, by wooing or by flirting. A love-song of the Papuas—which is, besides, accompanied by the most unequivocally erotic text conceivable—may serve, with its expressive and monotonous melodic line, as a specimen:

(2) "Music derived its origin from speech." Not from ordinary speech, but from the speech, the intonation, of excitement. It may readily be observed how the pitch of the speaking voice rises, the more excitedly we speak. In a state of extreme excitement, of intense emotion, we employ high tones far exceeding the pitch of our normal, natural speaking voice. Moreover, it seems that in the tone of intensified speech, in speech sustained by any psychic exaltation whatsoever, the intonation characteristic of normal speech intensifies itself in a certain measure; it seems to be more strongly marked, to stabilize itself, to become more interval-like. Speech seems to take on definite melodic form, and in this form presents itself as the first grade of music. For example, when we enunciate the question "Kommst du?" (are you coming?), it presents a tone-line of a certain pitch; on repeating this question a few times *crescendo*, the tone-progression becomes more and more strongly marked, and seems finally to take on the features peculiar to a musical motive. Thus music arises, according to this theory—which was developed by Herbert Spencer[2]—from emotional speech, from speech that expresses strong psychic emotions. We instantly perceive that the dissimilarity in the placing of the musical tone-material from that of the ordinary tone-material of speech is here very clearly demonstrated. The connection between beginnings of music and psychic emotion is also obvious. From this perception, above all, follow the important theories of the origin of music from speech, the theories of Rousseau, Herder, and Richard Wagner.

Conclusive as the theories concerning the rise of music out of speech may appear in this particular regard, they nevertheless do not bear closer scrutiny. For (a) it is precisely what is characteristic in the expressiveness of the melody of speech that stands in opposition to the nature of musical tone-speech. In speech a gliding flow of tones, their pitch fluctuating rapidly and spontaneously up and down, must combine with the words in order to show whether we are sad, merry, excited, low-spirited, curious, or imperious; whereas, in song, the fluctuating tones must be fixed, stabilized, and limited to definite pitches and intervals. Even in the "Sprechgesang" (recitative) of primitive music one definite pitch, a sort of prototype of the tonic, persists, or some definite interval appears to be chosen as a melodic center. Speech, however, must be ready, as the concept of its expressive power plainly implies, to press the entire available range of tones into its service.—(b) Further, the culminating point of excited speech is the shriek. Now, if this theory were consistent, would not the nature of music be most clearly derivable from that point, from the emotional outcry? But from the shriek no way leads—even in a purely physiological sense—to tone and song.—(c)

The intonation, the melody, of speech differs greatly according to the individual and, above all, the nationality. The Scandinavian languages employ quite other inflections of intonation than the German; their normal delivery sounds to us like an eternal interrogation.

Would not the necessary logical consequence be, that we could not understand their music? Again, we find dialects of certain languages, and even the mode of speech in certain places, more "singing" than in other regions where the same language is spoken; would not that influence the "musicality" of the given region, or even of the particular place?[3]

(3) Abandoning the above collective theory, let us go over to the last group, which seeks the origin of music in human activities. Here we have to take into account two theories, the one by Karl Bücher, the other by Karl Stumpf. The well-known view advanced by the economist Bücher in his book on "Arbeit und Rhythmus" (Work and Rhythm) may be stated as follows: In concerted rhythmical labor there arise spontaneously certain rhythmical bursts of sound that apparently tend to facilitate the task; they develop into the characteristic work-calls, as they may be heard wherever concerted labor is going on. Now, according to Bücher, these calls lead to the formation of intervals and motives, developing into characteristic work-songs [such as the seamen's chanties], which we are to accept as the earliest, original musical creations of man.—However, when we scrutinize the primitive songs, we find, first of all, no specially prominent, sharp clear rhythm whatever. On the contrary, one chief characteristic of primitive music is its uneven, often highly capricious or very complicated rhythm, which hardly any kind of work could follow smoothly. Besides this, these work-songs by no means stand in the forefront of primitive music. And the work-songs with which we are familiar—rowing-songs, harvest-songs, and the like—did not properly take their rise in the work itself, but were rather devised as an after-thought, as compositions written *on* labor. Very often, too, they express an entirely different meaning; they have a *cabalistic* signification. A typical instance is found in the rowing-songs of the natives of the Solomon Islands.[4] While they are rowing [paddling?] hard, the natives are silent; during intervals of less strenuous labor, however, they sing, though not to make their rowing easier, but rather (so they say) to "to unburden their souls." Again, the South American Indians sing pertinent songs while rubbing the manioc roots, not for the purpose of facilitating the work, but for their magical influence in making it prosper. The aborigines of New Guinea, when out to capture the dugong, sing a special song, not while the hunt is in progress, but after the animal is securely caught in their nets; before dragging the prey into the boat they strike up this song, which also surely possesses magical significance.

Karl Stumpf likewise seeks the origin of music in a detail of the practical activity of primitive man.[5] When one wishes to send out a call over a considerable distance, the voice is raised spontaneously; one can make himself heard more easily when the pitch of the tone is sustained and the intonation of the words stabilized. Hence (so he holds) a musical tone and a musical motive are engendered, and in this acoustic sign-language he finds the origin of song.

This view of Stumpf's finds no support in primitive music. We have no knowledge of any such vocal sign-language. On the contrary, we do know a very exact and widely disseminated drum-signal speech of barbarians who form their signals solely by the rhythm and the number of the beats, the element of pitch being wholly disregarded. And then, considered by itself, a vocal sign-language would entail a far too complicated and inexact system of signals. The words would become inaudible at a great distance; tones carry further than vowels and consonants, than words. On the primitive level of musical development, however, we can hardly expect to meet with a fixed coordination of definite significations, with definite tones or motives. The drum-signals are countable, exact, cannot be falsified. A complete contrast is found in the idiosyncrasy of the primitive singer, as everywhere observed, who alters and unconsciously varies every melody or motive when singing it repeatedly.

III.

Precisely the last two hypotheses have brought into strong relief one attribute common to all the foregoing theories. These theories sought, first of all, to bring to light the earliest discoverable traces of man's acquaintance with tone-production. They claim that tone, as such, first entered human sense-perception through the channel of instinctive sexual selection, or the emotional outcry, or the work-call or vocal signal. The further evolution of the tones into what we may rate as music would then come about somehow by itself; chance, curiosity, experimentation, imitation, etc., would supervene, broaden the understanding for tone-production, promote the invention of instruments, or add to the tone-material already known.

But does not such a conception shift the basic position of the question? Does it give us, even if proved correct, a satisfactory explanation? Tones are always and everywhere presented to observant human perception; the birds sing, a taut bowstring gives out a tone, a hollow tree trunk resounds. Chance, curiosity and experimentation may well have opened possibilities of tone-production to man. This idea was not foreign to the thought of the ancients. The Greeks have a myth about the invention of the lyre; how the god Hermes happened to strike with his foot against an empty turtle-shell, out of which the sun had burned all the flesh; only a couple of sinews still were stretched inside, and so the shell, when struck, gave out such a sweet tone that the god created an instrument after the same pattern. And the Hindoos regard their god Shiva as the master both of the hunter's bow and of the bow used as a musical instrument.

This being established, however, we have arrived only at the beginning of the real problem: How did men come to employ *intentionally* this chance discovery of a previously unknown possibility in new and unaccustomed ways of tone-production? to appropriate it purposefully as the material for a consistent artistic system of expression—the tone-material of music? It is clear that not each and every impression that enters into human consciousness can engender art. The elements of music evidently bore within themselves characteristics that marked them as predetermined for art. But wherein lay this predetermination for art? According to the myths and legends of folk-lore, music was a gift of the gods to man. The philosopher Heraclides tells us that Amphion, who received his artistry from his divine father Zeus, was the inventor of music. To the Egyptians their god Thot was the giver of music. The Chinese musical system was the gift of the magic bird Fung-Hoang. The earliest songs of the Hindoos, the sacred Ragas, were magical songs sung by the gods. What more does all this mean, than that all peoples distinctly felt that music does not issue from the necessities of everyday life; that music signifies something *withdrawn from* the conditions of ordinary existence, something at variance with the natural order of things.

In primitive music the close relation between art and the non-natural, the non-realistic, is yet more distinctly marked. In the religion of the primitives music and the dance are numbered among the gifts bestowed on man by God. As an Australian tribe has it, the first man taught those created later all ceremonies, the dances, and music. The Good Spirit of another tribe taught the medicine-men the proper songs.

We have already remarked that religious and ritualistic songs occupy the foreground with almost all primitive peoples. Everywhere we find music conjoined with regular solemn, magic ceremonies. All important occurrences in the life of the tribe are solemnized with certain sacred rites in which music and dancing play a chief part. At the ceremony of circumcision, or when the youth of either sex become adult, at seedtime and harvest of the principal foodstuffs or in the seasons set apart for "taboo," on all such occasions certain ritually prescribed songs are sung. Even the place where the singing and dancing at these festivities are carried on is selected by special ritualistic regulations. For example, the Uitotos in Colombia sing and dance on the graves of the departed in order to renew the power of their totem;[6] in Assam, the burial-place of the hereditary priest serves as dancing-ground.[7] Magic songs, spirit-songs, songs of exorcism, are everywhere disseminated. In South America and Australia, Sumatra and New Guinea, the medicine-man heals the sick with his music. For example, the medicine-man of a South American tribe of Indians exorcises the malady with the following song.[8]

The belief in the healing power of music reaches upward into the higher civilizations of the Egyptians, Greeks, and Hindoos. Moreover, a ritual and religious significance is attributed to the various elements of the music itself. Certain instruments are "taboo" with the primitives; they are kept in specified places, and are to be seen only on certain festival occasions. Other instruments must always be concealed from the eyes of the women. Various instruments, again, are marked by branded or carved pictures of gods or sacred animals, sacred symbols, and the like, as genuine ritualistic implements. Both the Egyptians and Greeks incorporate the laws governing musical tones, the tonalities, the number of the harpstrings, etc., in their cosmogonical and theological systems. Thurnwald tells of a very interesting custom among the inhabitants of the Solomon Islands;[9] in this particular case the tuning of the national instrument, the Pan's-pipes, is combined with a highly characteristic ritualistic ceremony:

> When a specially important Unu (rite of initiation into the League of the Vendetta) is about to be held, the men of the chieftain who proposes to ally himself with the principal chief proceed to the latter's habitation; . . . each takes along two or three Pan's-pipes, that have already had a preliminary tuning at home; on the way, too, a halt is made at every place of assembly to try the instruments. On nearing the dwelling of the principal chief, a sham battle sets in at the entrance to the clearing, during which the men of the principal chief attempt to wrest the Pan's-pipes from the visitors. After this the instruments are exactly tuned to the standard model kept by the principal chief, to the accompaniment of a ceremonial dance. (Every principal chief possesses such a standard model, it being a symbol of his dignity.) This ceremony of tuning continues for two or three days.

As we see, a very close relation subsists between the incipient art and the speculative sphere of the supernatural, the out-of-the-ordinary. But do not we, too, recognize that the laws of our highly developed art are laws lying beyond the ordered spheres of conception of our daily life? The evolution of the material of every art plainly goes its own way, a way not dictated by nature. The verse and rime of language, the bounds wherein a painter frames his picture, the steps and figures of the dance—all these signify what might be termed an abnormalizing of the normal, a formal recognition of a realm of law remote from "natural" life, they signify a transformation, an artistic refining of the "natural," and therewith its translation to the sphere of art. As we clearly perceive, the "non-natural" in the material of music does not imply an hiatus in the evolution of music out of any given natural law of existence that requires bridging over. It meets us at every point explicitly and sensibly as an essential characteristic of music.

At one point in the theories of Spencer, Rousseau and Wagner, mentioned in the foregoing, we find a significant suggestion: What Spencer calls the "musical" melody of speech, that sustained and intensified by strong emotion, is to be imagined as transferred in due course to instruments as melodies in pure tones, speech-melody thus becoming a genuine, typical "absolute" music.—For us the essential point resides in the *transference* to some other material of expression. For all art is the "carrying-over" of some form of experience into an artistic—i.e., artificial, out-of-the-ordinary—form of expression, which in itself does not arise out of any necessity of practical experience. Whatever we experience we can—voluntarily or involuntarily—distinctly set forth through means of expression arising from the necessities of practical experience, through speech, gestures, or signs. And all this we can reenact designedly, quite apart from any practical necessity, on the higher level of the artistic form of expression, in poetry, song, dance and imagery.

From this it follows that the question we raised above, "Wherein did the predetermination of the tones for art lie?" answers itself. We now perceive that the elements of music, as representing a non-natural, out-of-the-ordinary sound-language, appear for that reason adapted to become the elements of an artistic language of expression. In the fact that they obey *other* laws of generation and exposition than do the elements of normal expression by sound, lies—if we may use the term—the *dignitas*, the high distinction, of the tones in becoming the material of an art. Here the circle closes; logic in the generation of art demands, so to speak, this first illogical step in the generation of the material of art.

IV.

It is our belief that we have shown here the origin of the *meaning* of music, of music as an art. We may, indeed, be able to determine the very point where the tones themselves must come into being, where music is superadded to speech.

The musical usages of the primitives, the conception of music among many higher civilizations, clearly point, as noted above, to the origination of music for ritualistic customs. The medicine-men of the primitives wear special ritualistic costumes, masks, all manner of significant ornamentation, when performing their ceremonies. The priests of all religions must don special robes and sacred emblems when about to appear before their god. Robes, gestures, all the proceedings, are sharply contrasted with the uses of everyday life by means of special regulations and lifted into a higher, sacred sphere. Should not the spoken words, the speaking voice, likewise assume a special vesture, as it were, an out-of-the-ordinary tone to parallel the loftier rites, and so translate speech into song?

The status of song among primitive peoples is, in fact, intimately related to the ritualistic custom of the masked dances. Among almost all primitive tribes the dancers and singers wear distinctive ritual masks, while performing their ceremonial songs and dances. The legends of such tribes apprise us that these masks are the faces of demons, which the medicine-men of remote antiquity tore from the demons in battle. And now when men put on these masks, they become the equals of the gods or demons; they *are themselves* the demons, and wield their powers. This belief of the primitives, which we call canimism, the notion that we obtain power over anyone when we get possession of a part of his substance, evidently implicates music among other things. The out-of-the-ordinary, supernatural tone-speech of song is held to be the language of the gods and demons. And in order to invoke them, to rise to an quality with their supernatural powers, one must be master of their supernatural, superhuman language. Song is one of the most important functions and acquirements of the medicine-men. The primitives fancy that the medicine-man holds forth in the language of the demons when weaving his magic spells around them. The animal totems of the North American Indians always accompany their rites with singing; it us supposed that they lent this speech to men for invoking the good spirits. The inhabitants of the Solomon Islands declare that they learned their songs from spirits. Similarly, among many tribes the songs and masks are regarded as most valuable booty which, captured from the conquered enemy, may be used by the victors to enhance their own powers.

We find special evidence in support of the opinion that music was a product of man's purpose to create for his own use a "peculiar" magic language of invocation and exorcism. The essential feature in the spoken magical incantations and formulas in invocation resides, in great part, in the combination of *unmeaning* words. Furthermore, words from foreign languages are often used with no idea of their real import. A mysterious spell is always cast by these unintelligible words; thus there arises a distinct, non-natural cabalistic language. With the addition of music their magical influence is necessarily intensified. And it is a fact that the songs of the primitives preferably employ such meaningless texts. They continually dwell on the idea that it is not the part of song-speech to be understood. The songs of incantation, for the taboo, etc., are, in particular, made up of such unmeaning words, quite unintelligible to the singer himself.

To be sure, another, highly significant factor plays a part here—the strong, thrilling emotional effect of music on the human spirit, which in all ages has provoked comparison with the state of *ecstasy* (the Greeks knew and feared the "ethos ekstatikon" of music), and the state of intoxication. The musical usages of the primitives, as well as those of many highly developed Oriental civilizations, and even our own "romantic" conception of music, recognize only this state of ecstasy and strongest psychic emotion in the enjoyment of music. Bear in mind how intimately this state of entrancement has been connected, in every period, with the mystic and religious experiences of mankind. In this state we again see the principle of the supernatural, the out-of-the-ordinary, illustrated. This emotional effect of music should, therefore, have still more firmly knit the bond between religious cult and music, and have made the "music as intoxicant" a collaborator in the creation of the "music as art."

History also furnishes proofs of this process of development; we possess Babylonian tablets of incantation prescribing the songs and accompanying music for the magic rites. The prophets of the Jews sang their predictions, or were transported by music into the prophetic state; in the Bible it is said of the prophet Elisha, when he was to prophesy before King Joram: "But now bring me a minstrel. And it came to pass, when the minstrel played that the hand of the Lord came upon him." The Pythia prophesied in verses accompanied by music. For the Romans the term "vates" signified both seer and singer. Even in the Christianity of the Middle Ages the "moralitas artis musicae," the peculiar ethical virtue supposed to reside in music, promises those true believers who appear singing before their God a more binding claim on everlasting bliss.

V.

Art does not remain forever bounded by the cult. Out of these earliest manifestations it grows into a new, independent estate; it makes unto itself new laws for its own life. Similarly, too, must grow, in a plain and unbroken line out of the law that determine the first beginnings of art, the principles which apply to the entirety of evolutionary art, to art as we apprehend it today.

Our view of the origin of music can be, like any hypothesis of the kind, only a conjecture. But as a basis for this conjecture we have at the start established the necessity that it should accord with our understanding of the nature of art and of the evolution of art. And perhaps we may venture to consider, as a support of the probability of our hypothesis, that it finds in its explanation of the origin of music a key to the entire complex of the manifestations of music. In the earliest form of music that we recognize as such, as an out-of-the-ordinary, supernatural language, are already clearly incorporated the two great principles of art that are recognized, by philosophers and adepts in the study of art, as the essence of art, as the essence of music, and that embrace all the manifold forms of art and artistic evolution—the formative principle and the objective principle.

The Formative Principle.—Art is the transformation, translation, organization of whatever we wish to express into an artificial, artistic material, according to laws which do not arise out of the practical necessities of the will to expression. Primitive man, when for the first time thanking his god, invoking his familiar spirit, or intensifying any word or sentence to an exorcism, by consciously working up some familiar natural possibility of expression into a new and artificial form, has thereby reached the highest intensification within the sphere of his cult, and at the same time created *art* in the cult.

The Objective Principle.—In this new, set form of experience, the experience detaches itself from its erstwhile subject; the subjective psychic content is transformed, by its presentation in a material foreign to and exalted above reality, into a form that is more objective and more independent of the subject. That which was but now a fleeting experience of my innermost self, something I may have uttered by chance in evanescent tones born of momentary impulse, is straightway condensed, as it were, moulded according to objective rules, made into a new, independent entity obeying its own laws; it becomes a work of art. Thus do verse and rime fashion some utterance into poetry; the frame of the picture isolates some typical section from the infinity of things; the involuntary gesture becomes a mimic figure.

What is mentioned here are principles that regulate and shape the material of presentation only in a primitive and outward manner. But the whole evolution of art is, viewed from this standpoint, nothing else than a perfecting and organizing—voluntary or involuntary—of these principles of transmutation.

The first steps in this comprehensive evolutionary process of music can be distinctly noted in many details of primitive musical usages. One such significant and marked step in musical evolution may be seen in the transition from song to pure instrumental music among the primitives. The consciousness of a primitive form of objectivation and organization is well developed in many half-civilized peoples; it is a widely disseminated habit in the singing of these races to execute their songs in unnatural falsetto tones; "With the natural voice," so they say, "everyone speaks; that is not art." Another case in point is the objectivation of the musical speech of expression by the steadily advancing fixation of the tones, their connection and disposition in ordered sequences and systems, the rules for the leading of tones, etc.—Indeed, in certain details the tone-production of the primitives still reverts to the earliest beginnings of music, to the boundary between art and all that is not art; we can very clearly perceive the intrusion of natural, raw, still quite unorganized realism into the artistically ordered form. Certain phases of experiences have not yet been brought, so to speak, under ordered control, set apart from every-day reality. And so they now and again break in upon the pure "sphere of art," as when, in a warsong of the Papuans, shrill shrieks interrupt the melody with which the singers triumphantly proclaim the number of enemies slain:

Here we may also mention the report, assuredly based on fact, of a missionary; how, when tribesmen were once performing a war-dance in the presence of some white men, these dancing and singing warriors seemed gradually to forget that they were merely imitating a fight in dance and song; of a sudden they started a real butchery, of which nearly all those present were the victims. The realism of the action shattered the artistic sphere; the reality was too strong for the formative and purely imitative capacity of art.

We are well aware that all these are incipient, primitive forms of a still external and unstable organization and objectivation in the art-work; but they plainly point to the path that the long-continuing evolution of art must pursue. This evolution takes its rise in the early form-phrases that we have recognized as a mere transference, a "carrying-over," and leads further into the most *intimate* transformation, the realization of the *true inwardness* of the artistic material. Not before attaining to a complete realization of the will to expression and the organization of expression can those laws of subjective artistic balance that we designate as beauty and esthetic propriety become effective.

Goethe remarks somewhere: "Art is long in forming, before it is beautiful." And again: "Art, as it manifests itself in the greatest artist, creates a form of such living potency that it dignifies and transfigures *any subject-matter.*" The evolution of art does not pursue a plain, unswerving course, whose beginning, end, and intermediate stations can be exactly charted. What we can clearly make out in the line of evolution are only landmarks, certain ideal extremes of the evolutionary process. Such landmarks are found in the above citations from Goethe, and between these bounds flows the entire vast flood of art-evolution, whose earliest phases we have attempted to depict: the first steps in the creative synthesis of the will to expression and the organization of expression, of material and form, of experience and art.

(Translated by Theodore Baker.)

Notes

[1] Darwin, "The Expression of the Emotions in Men and Animals."

[2] Spencer, "Psychology, Sociology."

[3] Rousseau actually arrives at this ultimate conclusion (in his "Essai sur l'origine des langues"). He thus denies the possibility of a national French music and admits, for his own period, only the Italian language as a possible generator of an art of music.

[4] Richard Thurnwald and E. von Hornbostel, "Die Musik auf den Salomoneninseln."

[5] Karl Stumpf, "Die Anfänge der Musik."

[6] K. Th. Preuss, "Archäologische und ethnologische Forschungen in Kolumbien."

[7] From I.H. Hutton, "The Angami Nagas."

[8] From Koch-Grünberg and Hornbostel, "Vom Rorofma zum Orinoco."

[9] Thurnwald and E. von Hornbostel, "Die Musik auf den Salomoneninseln."

REGIONAL
STUDIES

INDIA'S MUSIC
Robert E. Brown

I. Introduction

Music seems to have been held in high esteem by the Hindus from earliest times. It has remained such a powerful cultural force that it was able to withstand successfully even the heavy onslaught of Islamic puritanism during the Mughul period. This epoch, in fact, became one of important musical developments. Given the Hindu propensity to absorb and accommodate many varieties of cultural divergence, it is not surprising that India has been one of the two major wellsprings of musical influence in Asia, the other main center being China. The mainstream of India's art music tradition, broad and deep, has been fed by countless smaller streams through centuries of evolution. Even today many musical systems exist side by side in India, especially on the folk and tribal level. The musical richness of the subcontinent is now making itself felt more and more strongly in the West as modern media of rapid communication break down the barriers of time and distance that isolated Indian music in the past.

To survey this vast and varied tradition it will be helpful to group India's music into familiar categories: folk, tribal, popular, religious, classical, ancient, modern. It is well to remember, however, that in India, more than in the West, these categories often tend to blur into one another, and such categorization over-simplifies a situation that is in reality anything but simple. All Indian musical traditions are essentially oral traditions. Until much more than the smattering of folk music now available has been recorded or described, for instance, we cannot speak with much authority on that particular subject. In the case of the ancient music, there are enormous difficulties in working with the lengthy technical descriptions of a music that has disappeared as sound. Even with the classical music of present day North and South India, much that is important lies in the minds and fingers of individual musicians who carry the tradition. As in the West, theory often exists as a subject related to, but distinct from, music as sound. However, as elsewhere the theoretical system can have a fascinating life and development of its own. It is more difficult to discuss Indian than European music as theory and history, since in the West a particular kind of documentation has been possible because of the relatively highly refined system of musical notation. However, many contemporary western composers feel that our notation has closed off important avenues for expression. The Indian musican approaches his art 'through his ears,' commits astonishing amounts of musical information to memory, and has the opportunity for a full expression of self by improvising within a rich and varied musical tradition.

Artistic experience is generally equated with religious experience in India, and music has been described as one of the quickest paths toward the realization of divinity:

> We adore that Supreme Being of the form of sound [Nāda-Brahman] which is the one bliss without a second, and the light of consciousness in all beings that has manifested itself in the form of the universe. By the adoration of sound [nāda] are also adored Gods Brahmā [the Creator], Vishnu [the Preserver], and Maheśvara [Shiva, the Destroyer], for they are the embodiments of sound.[1]

The Vedas allude to a number of musical instruments, mainly drums, stringed instruments (probably harps), and flutes. Musicians are listed among the victims in the human sacrifice ritual (puruṣamedha). Indians have always looked upon the chanting of the Vedas, especially the Sāma Veda, as the source of their classical music tradition. The names of famous legendary musician-sages—Nārada, Bharata, Tumburu—have come down from the ancient past, and a special class of demigods, the gandharvas, provided the celestial music of Indra's heaven. Myths about music are numerous and emphasize the importance of accurate performance as well as the proper mental attitude, one of humility and reverence.

A theory of aesthetics based on eight (later nine) emotional states, the rasa, united music with the arts of dance, dramatics and poetry, and was already elaborately systematized by the beginning of the Christian era. Certain musical modes, rhythms, and instruments properly used could help to develop specific emotional states in a theatrical production when combined with the corresponding verse forms, gestures, movement, etc., and instructions for their employment are compiled in the Nāṭyaśāstra, ascribed to Bharata. Later, the burgeoning of the Rādhā-Kṛṣṇa cult and the bhakti movement had important influences on musical development, as did the mingling of Islamic and Hindu cultural patterns in the Mughul period.

One of the great difficulties for the outsider attempting to penetrate musical thought is its enormous technical vocabulary, principally Sanskrit, without which it is impossible to discuss theoretical concepts. Most of the terms suffer distortion in translating, and there are unique areas of melodic and rhythmic theory that have no parallel in the West. As the various categories of Indian music are now taken up in order, the most essential terms will be introduced and briefly explained.

---

[1] From the 13th century musical treatise, the *Saṅgītaratnākara* of Śārṅgadeva, cited in Wm. Theodore DeBary (ed.), *Sources of Indian Tradition*, New York: Columbia U. Press, 1958, p. 275.

II.   Vedic Music

A glance at the Vedic chant, perhaps the oldest continuous musical tradition in the world, may illumine some basic concepts and premises of music in India.

In general, the recitation of the oldest of the Vedas, the Ṛg Veda, is a kind of heightened speech on a principal reciting tone embellished by a tone above and a tone below to help emphasize the grammatical accents (udātta, anudātta, svarita). There are seven principal poetic meters, and although vowels are either short or long and this length is essential to the meaning, Vedic prosody is based on the number of syllables (either long or short) in a line, as opposed to the later Classical Sanskrit prosody, in which elaborate metrical schemes are based on repetitive patterns of long and short syllables. Sensitivity to the durational aspect of syllables in language, rather than dynamic stress, is directly linked to the concept of rhythm in terms of durational units in music.

Among those responsible for the oral transmission of the Vedic corpus, there has been a constant attempt to prevent any possible change in the text, or in the manner of reciting it. Among devices used were bodily gesture (head movement, finger counting), one of the oldest systems of musical notation (derived from the syllabic writing system), and a type of mathematical permutation of the order of syllables in the text without regard to rational meaning, called vṛtta. All of these can be related to later, specifically musical, practices. In spite of such safeguards, several styles of recitation (Kauthumī, Raṇāyanī, Jaiminī, etc.) developed. Nevertheless, the differences in Vedic chant styles are relatively small when one considers the antiquity of the tradition.

The Sāma Veda is the most developed musically, and may be thought of as a melodically heightened version of the Ṛg Veda. Meaningless syllables called stobhas were inserted profusely and aided melodic development in a range extended to six tones. The style of singing the Sāma Veda is more melismatic than the straight-forward chanting of the Ṛg Veda that has predominantly one vocal tone for one syllable of the text.

Until recently it was extremely difficult to study or record Vedic music, for it was closely guarded by the carriers of the tradition. Detailed studies of the musical aspects remain to be made, but certain general concepts are clear: an agogic (length rather than dynamic stress) principle in the textual rhythm, strict attention to clear and accurate intonation of musical tone, a modal and basically diatonic concept of melody, bodily gesture combined with tone production, and the mathematical process of permutation applied to a series of basic elements (in this case the syllables of the text).

Recording: A Musical Anthology of the Orient. India I (Vedic Recitation and Chant). Barenreiter BM 30 L 2006.

III.   Ancient Classical Music

A flourishing tradition of court music is represented plastically in early Buddhist sculpture, beginning with the 2nd century B.C. stone carvings on the gateways of the stupa at Sāñchī. The same music is alluded to descriptively in such literary monuments as the Śilappadigāram, a Tamil work of the 2nd century, and in the somewhat later poems and dramas of Kālidāsa. The theory of this music has come down to us, albeit in a partially corrupted textual version, in the most famous of theoretical treatises, the Nātyaśāstra, ascribed to the sage Bharata. This impressive manual on theater in all aspects devotes some six of its thirty-six chapters to music. The present English translation[2] leaves much to be desired, although it must be admitted that the descriptive details of the original text are often ambiguous or unclear. The main features of the ancient music are readily apparent, even in translation, and provide a recognizable foundation for development of the rāga and tāla systems of contemporary India.

Music in India is divided into two aspects: gīta ('song') and vādya ('instrument'), although the technique of melodic instruments is never far from the vocal idiom. The earliest general term for 'music' (gāndharva), gave place to the term now in use, sāngīta ('all the songs'). Although the word tāla (literally 'base') is used in the Nātyaśāstra to refer to the rhythmic side of music, the word rāga ('that which pleases') is used for the melodic side only from about the 5th century A.D., when it appears in Matañga's Brhaddeśi.

Instruments are grouped in four categories: tata (strings), avanaddha (drums), ghana (solid, or ideophones), and suśira (winds), a rational classification for instruments arrived at by European curators and musicologists only in the late 19th century. The usual orchestra accompanying the dance in early sculpture consists of one or more arched harps, a flute, one or more drums, sometimes a long-necked lute, and often a group of three or four singers, one of whom keeps the time measure with small hand cymbals. From text and sculpture we can ascertain the stopping of harp strings with the fingers to produce more than one tone per string, the production of ornaments and use of half-open holes on the flute, and the command of several drums by one player, undoubtedly to produce different tones from each of the (generally four) drumheads. All of these refinements have something to say about the sophistication of the music, just as the number of varied gestures and poses in the sculpture make silent comment on the subtlety of the dance.

Several important melodic concepts pertaining to Indian music are described in the Nātyaśāstra. Division of the octave into twenty-two fixed microtonal intervals called śrutis is worked out mathematically and also demonstrated practically with two harps, differently tuned. Only a certain number of śrutis, generally 5, 6, or 7, would be used at one time. These

[2] Nātyaśāstra, transl. by Manmohan Ghosh, Calcutta: the Asiatic Society, Vol. 1, 1951; Vol. 2, 1961.

are arranged in ascending scalar progression. Each scale step is called a svara, and there is a maximum number of seven: ṣaḍja, ṛṣabha, gāndhāra, madhyama, pañcama, dhaivata, and niṣāda. Abbreviations of the first syllable of each of these scalar degrees (sa, ri, ga, ma, pa, dha, ni) have been used as a solfege in India since at least two thousand years ago, and are still prominently used, for instance, in South Indian vocal improvisation. Once the pitch of the key note (sa) has been established, the fifth (pa), if it is present, is always an interval of a perfect fifth above sa. However, the other svaras may each be one of several different possible pitches, but they must always appear in the same sequence Ri, for instance, is always above sa and below ga, although the exact interval relationship of the three tones can vary from one mode to the next.

In the early music there were two basic source scales called grāmas. Sachs[3] speculates that the sa-grāma and ma-grāma stood in the same relationship to one another as our medieval authentic and plagal modes, that is, that they represented related tonal groupings, one in medium, the other in a lower range of the voice. Earlier there had been a third grāma, the ga-grāma, described as having 'retreated to Indra's heaven.' Indian pundits are still debating the exact nature of the grāmas, but it is at least clear that they were a certain basic selection of seven tones from the twenty-two śrutis (fixed microtonal intervals). By treating each of these seven tones in turn as a new tonal center (sa), seven mūrchanās, or modal inversions having different interval structure, could be worked out. This too, bears an astonishing resemblance to western medieval theory as applied to the Gregorian chant. The mūrchanās were called pūrṇa (full) if all seven tones were used, ṣāḍava if six tones were used, and auḍava if they were pentatonic. Within each of the mūrchanās were a number of possible jātis, or melody-types, that seem to resemble the later rāgas. These were classified as either śuddhā ('pure') or vikṛtā ('modified'). For each there were certain predominant tones (amśa), permissible notes for beginning phrases (graha) and ending them (nyāsa), etc. The different jātis were associated with certain sentiments (rasas) and their effective use in a dramatic production was specified. Different types of embellishment (varṇa and alaṃkāra) gave them color and grace, and they were employed with poetic text in dramatic songs of complex form called dhruvās.

Especially interesting for the western student is the systematic theory of rhythm that later came to be called the tāla daśa prāṇas ('ten life-breaths of rhythm'), for this aspect of music has been strangely neglected in European theory.

Several different methods for working out a basic unit for the measurement of time are described. One of the more poetic involved taking a stack of one hundred lotus petals, through which one was to plunge a needle.

<hr/>

[3] Curt Sachs, *The Rise of Music in the Ancient World*, New York: W. W. Norton, 1943, p. 168.

The time taken to pass through one petal was called a kṣana ('instant'), a unit of time too small for human perception and discernible only by the gods. After several stages of doubling, it was elongated to a basic, musically useful, time unit, the mātrā. Another way of determining the approximate length of the mātrā was to recite the first syllables of five important groups in the Sanskrit syllabary, kacatatapa, at a normal rate of speed.

From the mātrā were derived three metrical units, the laghu (one mātrā), guru (two mātrās), and pluta (three mātrās). These three angas ('limbs') could be combined in different ways to form an āvarta, or metrical cycle of the tāla. For example, one such tāla in the ancient Mārga Tāla system was called Caccatputaḥ, and had the aṅga structure: guru-guru-laghu-pluta (2-2-1-3). This eight-beat metrical cycle was repeated over and over as the musical measure of a particular composition.

Various hand gestures, called kriva, were used by singers to 'keep the tāla' in visual form. The krivas were divided into two types: saśabda ('with sound'), for instance a handclap, and nihśabda ('soundless'), such as the stylized wave of the hand in different directions or finger counting. For some kinds of music, small hand cymbals outlined the tāla structure. Still today, one will find South Indian singers 'keeping the tāla' with handclaps, waves, and finger counting. The nāgasvaram, or reed pipe, player is accompanied by the tavil drum and the tālam, small bronze hand cymbals to indicate the aṅga structure.

The setting of a melody in a tāla is treated under the prāṇa heading of mārga ('way, path'), and the subdivision of the mātrā under the heading, kala. Main phrases of the melody might begin on the first beat of the tāla cycle, or just before or just after it. The various possibilities were systematized under the heading graha. Exploitation of the rhythmic tension that can exist when the beginning of the melodic phrase and the beginning of the tāla cycle do not coincide is an important technique in contemporary composition and improvisation in South Indian classical music.

Five basic lengths of rhythmic units, the jātis, were found useful. Listed in the order of importance, they are caturaśra (4), tiśra (3), miśra (7), khaṇḍa (5), and saṅkārṇa (9). Tempo is analyzed under the heading of laya. The three basic tempi were vilambita laya (slow), madhya laya (medium), and druta laya (fast).

Two prāṇas of special interest are yati and prastāra. Yati is a concept of rhythmic design based on geometrical shape. This idea might be applied to various aspects of rhythm, such as the sequence of tempi, arrangement of aṅgas within the āvarta, rhythmical phrase patterns of drumming, etc. The six possibilities are sama yati, in which all components are of equal size: śrotovaha ('river'), going from smaller to larger; gopuccha ('cow's tail'), going from larger to smaller; ḍamaru ('hourglass drum'), larger to smaller to larger; mṛdaṅga yati ('barrel drum'), smaller to larger to smaller; and viṣṣma yati ('unequal'), for designs not covered in the other categories. Prastāra concerns applications of the mathematical process of permutation to deter-

4. Relief from Bhārhut stupa (early 1st cent. B.C.). Note musical instruments. (copy from Benjamin Rowland, *The Art and Architecture of India*, Baltimore: Penguin Books, 1953, Plate 17).

mine, for example, all of the possible combinations of aṅgas that could be used in creating a tāla of a given number of mātras. The roots of the prastāra concept can be traced to the vṛtta rearrangements of syllables in the memorization of Vedic texts. The principle appears today in such practices as svara prastāra, improvisation of ever-changing combinations of notes (svaras), as well as the permutation and combination of small phrase patterns to create constantly new rhythmic phrases in drumming improvisation.

It is significant that the elaborate theory of ancient Indian music is most fully expounded in a manual (śāstra) on the drama (nāṭya), for the arts were intermingled and fully integrated within the rounded and unified cultural pattern of that time. Sculptured poses of Bhārhut, Sāñcī, and Amarāvatī come to life in the famous description of the heroine Mādavi's debut as a dancer in the 2nd century Tamil epic *Śilappadikāram*. Here we catch glimpses of the musical life of an ancient city Madurai, seat of the Pāṇḍyan dynasty. Although the terminology is mainly Tamil, it is evident even in a brief excerpt that theory and technique were systematically imparted in the careful training of dancers and musicians.

The talaikkōl, or the staff, was the central shaft of a splendid white umbrella captured in the battle-field from monarchs of great repute. It was covered over by purest jāmbunāda gold, its joints bedecked with nine gems. This staff represented Jayanta, Indra's son, and as such was worshipped in the palace of the protecting king of the white umbrella (the Cōḷa).

On the day on which this staff was to be used by the dancing-girl, she had to bathe it with holy waters, brought in a golden pitcher, and afterwards to garland it. Then it was handed over with a blessing to the State elephant, already adorned with a plate of gold and other ornaments on its forehead. To the accompaniment of the drum proclaiming victory, and other musical instruments, the king and his five groups of advisers were to circumambulate the chariot and the elephant and give the talaikkōl to the musician-poet on the top of the chariot. Then they went round the town in a procession, and entering the theatre they placed the talaikkōl in its appointed position.

After this the instrument-players occupied their allotted seats. The dancing-girl (Mādavi) placed her right foot forward, and stepping in, stayed by the side of the pillar on the right, according to the ancient custom. Likewise her older assistants who followed the old custom gathered themselves by the side of the pillar on the left. The two kinds of prayer (vāram) were sung in turn so that virtue might increase and vice might disappear. At the close of the prayer all the musical instruments held by the respective players were sounded. The lute was in tune with the flute, and the mṛdangam with the lute. The resounding note was in tune with the mṛdangam, and the āmantirikai with the sound of the pot. Each was in perfect harmony with the other. Two beats made one maṇḍilam, and eleven such maṇḍilams were executed in conformity with the established theatrical practice. When this musical act, called antarakkottu, was over, the auspicious pālaippan was sung without the slightest violence to its rigid measure.

The four parts of the auspicious song were suitably introduced. Beginning with three maṇḍilams (or ottus) it ended with one ottu (ēkatāḷam); with this captivating maṇḍilam the dēśi dance came to an end.

Mādavi also danced the vaḍuku dance. Then it appeared as if the five-beat-mode of each of the two styles of dancing, dēśi and vaḍuku, was concentrated in one style—so captivating was her dance. In her quick movement she looked like a golden creeper animated with life. Because her dance was perfect and scientifically correct, the king, who protected the world, in due recognition, presented her with a green leaf-garland and one thousand and eight kaḷañjus of gold, which was the customary present given to dancers who held the talikkōl and exhibited their talents for the first time.

Fawn-eyed Mādavi handed over a garland to a hunchbacked woman, and asked her to stand out in the street where the rich citizens of the city passed to and fro, as if she was offering it for sale, and to announce that 'this garland is worth the sum of 1008 kaḷañjus of very excellent gold. He who buys this garland becomes the husband of our creeperlike lady.' The garland representing the large lotus-eyed Mādavi was purchased by Kōvalan, and, accompanied by the hunchback, he entered Mādavi's bridal chamber, and as he embraced her he was captivated so much by her charms that he forgot himself and did not like to part from her. In sooth, he forgot his own unsullied home and wife.[4]

[4] Aḍiyārkkunallār, *The Śilappadikaram*, transl. by V. R. Ramachandra Dikshitar, Madras: Oxford University Press, 1939, pp. 102-105.

5. Relief from Pawaya (1st cent. A.D.). Note musical instruments. (copy from Curt Sachs, *The Rise of Music in the Ancient World*, New York: W.W. Norton, 1940, facing page 192.)

IV. North Indian Classical Music

The great musical treatise of the medieval period, the Saṅgītaratnākara of Śarṅgadeva, is known to have been written between 1210 and 1247, in the central Indian city of Devagiri (modern Daulatābād). It sums up the Nāṭya-śāstra, as well as a number of less important intervening works, and develops in great detail the theory of the rāga and tāla systems of that age. These were the ancestors of present day North Indian, or Hindustani, music, which was nurtured and flourished in the cosmopolitan atmosphere of the Mughul courts.

Unlike the Nāṭyaśāstra, the Saṅgītaratnākara is devoted entirely to music, although there is a chapter on the dance. Because all later works refer to it, it may be considered the keystone work of Indian musical theory. The outlines of melodic analysis given in the Nāṭyaśāstra are expanded in detail, as is the rhythmic theory. Expansion of the musical practice itself is indicated by the much larger number of modes, now called rāgas, which Śarṅgadeva mentions. Whereas the ancient Mārga Tāla system was based on only five meters, the Deśī Tāla system of the Saṅgītaratnākara includes some 120 tālas, many of them having a large number of aṅgas. The variety of aṅgas has increased to six. Although a few of the tālas can be shown to be creations of the author, there is no doubt that a large number of them were in actual use. In complexity, they may be compared to the intricate poetic meters of classical Sanskrit, lengthy patterns of long and short syllables in a particular order.

Although basic principles of rāga and tāla are the same, there is a definite stylistic cleavage between North and South Indian music of the present day. Scholars disagree as to whether or not these differences have always been pronounced, for there are no strong indications of such a situation in musical treatises until after the 13th century. Today there are important differences in the instruments used, particular rāgas and tālas, the types of ornamentation, musical forms, and other details, although both systems trace their theory back to the Nāṭyaśāstra and Saṅgītaratnākara.

Until recently, North Indian music has been an aristocratic art reserved for the courts and upper levels of society. Even at present the audience for classical music in North India is relatively smaller than in the South. Partly because of the number of princely courts, a variety of different gharānās (schools or styles) evolved. Since improvisation plays such an important role, performing musicians have strongly influenced the direction of musical development. In addition, each geographical region has had its own personality, musically speaking. The finest musicians of the past are known, and several of the foremost performers of the present time, for instance, trace their musical lineage directly to the famous Tān Sen, brilliant singer at the court of the Emperor Akbar.

A North Indian rāga may be expounded in a number of ways. One of the most common is the ālāp, wherein the melodic characteristics are exploited in free rhythm, without words if the soloist is a singer. The characteristic phrases that have been developed over the years bring out the beauty and unique personality of the rāga, emphasize its particular tones, establish their hierarchy of importance, and the appropriate ornaments. The singer gradually extends the range in ever-changing combinations of phrases to create a powerful musical and emotional mood for whichever rāga he has chosen. In the North, the rāgas are associated with definite periods of the day or night, seasons, festivals, or natural phenomena like the monsoon or fire, and are performed only at the proper time. They have also been personified in miniature paintings, and have iconographic associations. Toḍī Rāgiṇī, for example, is usually shown as a lady in a white sari, playing a stringed instrument (bīn), and attended by deer or gazelles that have come to listen.

The rāga is sometimes used in conjunction with a text, and this is gen-

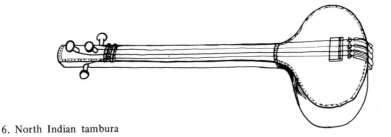

6. North Indian tambura

erally set in a particular tāla, or meter, There are various song forms, the most common being the khyāl, a relatively short set piece used as the basis for improvisation. Other important song forms are the lighter and more erotically inspired thumrīs, and the more difficult dhrupads and dhamārs. Dhrupad singing is an older style than khyāl, and requires highly-trained control of the voice. It is ordinarily accompanied only with the barrel-drum, pakhāvaj. Perhaps because it demands so much concentration on the part of the listener, it is not often heard at present, and there are few performers left. Nevertheless, it remains one of the most beautiful and profound genres of North Indian music.

Recordings: Khyal and Thumri
    a. Khansahib Abdul Karim Khan. Odeon MOAE 144.
    b. Surshri Kesar Bai Kerkar. Odeon (to be released)
    c. Ameer Khan, Ragas Marwa and Darbari Kanada. Odeon MOAE-130.
    d. Bhimsen Joshi, Ragas Malkauns and Maru-Bihag. Odeon MOCE 1029.
Dhrupad
    a. A Musical Anthology of the Orient. India III (Dhrupads). Khansahib, Nasir Moinuddin Dagar and Khansahib Nasir Aminuddin Dagar, Ragas Asaveri and Bhairavi. Pakhavaj solo by Chhatrapati Singh. Barenreiter BM 30 L 2018.
    b. Dagar Brothers, Ragas Darbari Kanada and Adana. Pakhavaj accompaniment by S. V. Patwardhan. Odeon MOAE 135.

Ananda Coomaraswamy, in his essay on Indian music in *The Dance of Shiva*, sums up the attitude Indian musicians have toward their art.

The Indian singer is a poet, and the poet a singer. The dominant subject matter of the songs is human or divine love in all its aspects, or the direct praise of God, and the words are always sincere and passionate. The more essentially the singer is a musician, however, the more the words are regarded merely as the vehicle of the music: in art-song the words are always brief, voicing a mood rather than telling any story, and they are used to support the music with little regard to their own logic—precisely as the representative element in a modern painting merely serves as the basis for an organisation of pure form or color. In the musical form called *alap*—an improvisation on the raga theme, this preponderance of the music is carried so far that only meaningless syllables are used. The voice itself is a musical instrument, and the song is more than the words of the song. This form is especially favored by the Indian virtuoso, who naturally feels a certain contempt for those whose first interest in the song is connected with the words. . . .[5]

The singer is generally supported by the drone instrument tambura, that establishes a constant reference point by sounding the tonic note, usually also the fifth, and sometimes other tones of the rāga as well. The adjustment of small threads between the strings and the flat bridge allows the tambura to produce a strong overtone complex. This means that the singer must control his pitch intonation with formidable accuracy. The other two accompanying instruments are usually a sāraṅgī, a bowed stringed instrument producing a silvery tone because of the large number of sympathetic strings, and the tablā, a set of two small hand drums capable of being played with great virtuosity and of producing delicacy as well as power, speed as well as a wide range of tone color. The higher-pitched tablā is carefully tuned to the tonic drone. Semi-permanent tuning paste and a special arrangement of composite drum-heads enables it to produce a clear, ringing musical tone as one of its many possible sounds. Indian drummers can represent the sounds of their instruments in spoken syllables, and frequently recite them at prodigious speed.

> Recording: The Drums of India. Chatur Lal, tablā, accompanied by Ramnarayan, sarangi. World Pacific WP 1403.

It would not be incorrect to say that the Indian singer may be replaced by an instrumental soloist, for all melodic music for instruments is firmly based in the vocal style and represents an extension of it in terms of range and specific tone color. Stringed instruments, especially plucked lutes, are favored as well as wind instruments of the reed and flute familes.

The principal melodic instruments of Hindustani music are the sitār, sarod, sāraṅgī, śanai and flute. Also used are various types of bīn (vīṇā), sūrbahār, esrāj, dilruba, guitar and violin.

> Recordings: a. Music of India, Ragas and Talas. Ravi Shankar, sitār; Alla Rakha, tabla. Ragas Madhu-Kauns and Jogiya. Dhun and tabla solo. Odeon ALP 1665.

[5] Ananda Coomaraswamy, *The Dance of Shiva*, New York: Noonday Press, 1957, pp. 92, 93.

b. Music of India. Ustad Vilayat Khan, sitar; Ustad Imrat Khan, surbahar; Pandit Shanta Prasad, tabla. Ragas Miya ki Malhar, Miya ki Todi, Pilu (thumri); tabla solo. Odeon ALP 1946

7. North Indian tablā

The sitār is a long-necked lute with a gourd sound chamber. The wide, hollow neck supports moveable curved metal frets that are set for the main tones of the rāga. The sideways pulling of the strings to produce innumerable slides and ornaments is an important part of the instrumental technique. Sometimes the drone strings are plucked in powerful rhythmic patterns during the type of improvisation called jhāla. Sympathetic strings beneath the main playing strings give an added lustral aura to the melody.

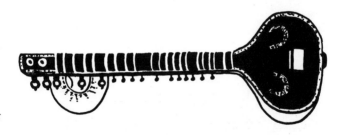

8. Sitār

The sarod is tuned differently from the sitār and has a different family tree. Its tone can be strong and masculine, and it is emphasized when the plectrum is struck against the skin cover of the sounding box. Unlike the sitār, there are no frets; the fingernail slides on the wide steel finger-board to stop the metal strings at the desired position.

Recordings: a. Music of India, Morning and Evening Ragas. Ali Akbar Khan, sarod; Chatur Lal, tabla. Ragas Sindh Bhairavi and Pilu. Angel 35283.
b. The Music of India. Sharan Rani, sarod; Chatur Lal, tabla. Ragas Kausi Kanada and Lalit. Tabla solo. World Pacific WP 1418.

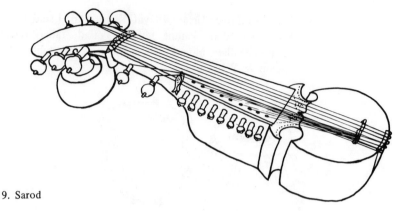

9. Sarod

Because the sārangī has gut strings, it used to be played primarily by the companions of dancing girls and other members of the lower stratum of society. Usually there are three main playing strings, and a large number (perhaps 30 or 40) of sympathetic strings. Some of these emphasize the tonic and fifth, while some are retuned to vibrate with the main tones of the particular rāga being played, as with the sitār, sarod, and other stringed instruments. The thick gut strings of the sārangī are not pressed against the fingerboard but are stopped with the back of the fingernail.

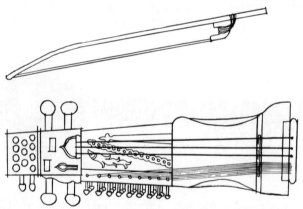

10. Sārangī

Recordings: Inde du nord, rāgas du matin et du soir. Ram Narayan, sarangi; Chatur Lal, tabla. Ragas Shuddh Todi and Marva. Tabla solo. Boite a Musique LD 094.

The classical stringed instrument of North Indian music is the vīṇā, or bīn. It is a fretted stick zither made from a bamboo rod with two large gourd resonators, and is normally accompanied in concert by the classical barrel drum, pakhāvaj. The word vīṇā appears in the Vedas, and was apparently used as a generic term for stringed instruments. However, the pro-

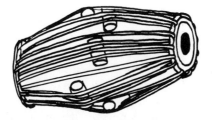

11. Pakhāvaj

totype of the present vīṇā appears first in the 7th century Pallava sculptures at Mahābalipuram, near present-day Madras. Within a century or two, such instruments with fingerboards entirely replaced the harp family, and only

12. Bīn. (copy from C. R. Day, *The Music and Musical Instruments of Southern India and the Deccan*, London: Novello, Ewer, and Co., 1891, Plate 1)

the saung harp of Burma remains to remind us of the harp's importance in the music of ancient India. Unfortunately, there are few players of the bīn today, partly because its sound is small and unsuited to concert performances for large audiences (it is still the preferred instrument of holy men and yogis), partly because it is exceedingly difficult to play in tune. A modern version without frets, the vichitra bīn, is played by sliding an egg-shaped piece of glass along the strings in the manner of the Hawaiian guitar. The guitar itself, played in the same fashion, is gaining in popularity.

Less common stringed instruments include the surbahar, a kind of bass sitār with a very attractive sound, at its best in the slower ālāp section, the esrāj and dilruba, bowed instruments with fretboards similar to the sitār, and the western violin, played sometimes as a solo instrument, sometimes as a replacement for the sāraṅgī.

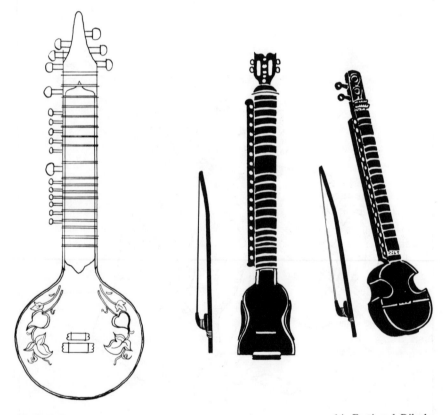

13. Sūrbahār   14. Esrāj and Dilruba

Although instruments of the horn and trumpet type appear in early sculpture, they have never been developed in India, and are only occasionally found as folk or temple instruments today. The main wind instruments have been the bamboo flute and double-reeds of the oboe type. In

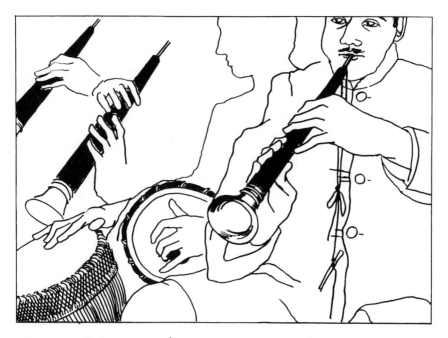

15. Śahnai, Khurdak, and Dugga

North India, the bamboo flute used in classical music is often of very large size, and has a deep and compelling tone quality. Although simple in appearance, it is played with virtuoso technique. It is an especially favored instrument in Bengal. The use of double reed instruments to provide the music for rites of passage is an ancient practice found all over the Middle East, India, Southeast Asia, and even China. An indispensable member of all wedding parties in North India is the small oboe, śahnai, accompanied by the khurdak and dugga, two small drums resembling tablā but archaic in construction and technique, played by one musician. Generally a śahnai party includes at least one secondary melody instrument, and one or two drone players using an instrument like the śahnai but without playing holes. By using the cheeks as a reservoir, the players can breathe independently and emit a continuous stream of air to provide the constant drone required. Although the śahnai is played by many rustic performers, it has in recent years been elevated to the status of a concert instrument. In the hands of a master it is capable of great subtleties of tone, technique, and expression.

Recordings: a. Pannalal Ghosh, flute. Ragas Yaman and Shri. Odeon MOAE-102.
b. Bismillah Khan, Shehnai. Raga Todi and Mishra Thumri. Odeon MOAE-113.

The instrumental forms of music resemble vocal forms for the most part, although an intermediate section between ālāp and composition, the jor, is especially developed instrumentally, particularly by the plucked stringed instruments. The jor has a regular rhythmic pulsation, as opposed to the free rhythm of the ālāp. However, there is no metrical organization of rhythm until the introduction of a composition in a particular tāla. Such an instrumental composition is called a gat. It corresponds to the khyāl in vocal music, and is also accompanied by the tablā.

Improvisation on a composition must follow the exigencies of both the rāga and the tāla. The usual pattern is to begin melodic variations on a portion of the composed melody, which often occupies just one cycle of the tāla. The improvisation gets longer and more and more elaborate until the point where it may occupy several cycles of the tāla. The performer will always return eventually to the composition, or at least a portion of it. Both gat and khyāl usually have a 'lead-in' melody that begins several beats before the first beat of the tala and leads up to it as the most important point in the rhythmic structure. The drummer too will improvise, calling on the hundreds of small set patterns he has learned through long training, rearranging them, modifying them with variation technique, inserting longer and more complex patterns at main divisions in the musical architecture. There is an exchange of improvisation. While the soloist is developing melodic and rhythmic complexities the drummer will keep a relatively simple pattern that outlines the origins of the tāla by contrast of timbre produced with different strokes of the hands and fingers. There is, in fact, a particular orthodox stroke pattern to show the structure of each tāla, called theka. Sometimes the soloist will repeat the composition in its simple original form, at which time the drummer may introduce rhythmically complex improvisation. When both improvise simultaneously in cross-rhythms, the audience listens attentively to see that they both arrive at the end of their patterns on the sam, or first beat of the tāla cycle. When they do, the response is often vocal, for the audience is deeply involved.

The improvisational element that looms so large in Indian classical music gives it a freshness and spontaneity in performance that reflects the mood of the moment. At the same time, the performer works within a tradition of utmost complexity, sophistication, and refinement. He must spend years of training and study in close contact with his guru, or teacher, before he is free to express himself fully within the framework of the rāga and tāla systems. Each rāga is ever open to development. A musician projects himself toward the realization of the musical beauty within a given rāga. Other musicians around him do the same. Others before have done it; those who come after will continue. But no one realizes completely at any one time the infinite possibilities inherent in the ragas, and the success of a particular performance is measured in relative terms. Coomaraswamy again expresses cogently the psychological climate of artistic expression.

... The master musicians of India are always represented as the pupils of a god, or as visiting the heaven-world to learn there the music of the spheres—that is to say, their knowledge springs from a source far within the surface of the empirical activity of the waking consciousness. In this connection it is explained why it is that human art must be studied, and may not be identified with the imitation of our daily behavior. When Shiva expounds the technique of the drama to Bharata—that famous author of the Natya Shastra—he declares that human art must be subject to law, because in man the inner and outer life are still in conflict. Man has not yet found Himself, but all his activity proceeds from a laborious working of the mind, and all his virtue is self-conscious. What we call our life is uncoordinated, and far from the harmony of art, which rises above good and evil. It is otherwise with the gods, whose every gesture immediately reflects the affections of the inner life. Art is an imitation of that perfect spontaneity—the indentity of intuition and expression in those who are of the kingdom of heaven, which is within us. Thus it is that art is nearer to life than any fact can be; and Mr. Yeats has reason when he says that Indian music, though its theory is elaborate and its technique so difficult, is not an art, but life itself.[6]

How have the North Indians attempted to classify their many rāgas? (see figure 16.) By means both poetic and practical. The Saṅgītadarpaṇa of Damodara (c. 1625) expounds a system of six male rāgas, originally pentatonic—Bhairav, Mālkoś, Hindol, Dīpak, Śrī, and Megh—each having a number of wives (rāginīs) and sons (putras). This emphasizes the musical fact of strong main rāgas, showing archaic pentatonic bone structure, with related modes, often more delicate or having specialized character. A more recent classification groups them according to ten basic fret settings (thāṭs) on the sitār. These are not the rāgas themselves, since rāgas might omit tones in ascent or descent, use microtonal inflection or occasional alternate pitches, etc. Nevertheless, the scales of the thāṭs can illustrate some basic tone material of the present North Indian rāga system.

A listing of twenty-five of the most common rāgas (see Fig. 17) will further serve to show the sequential arrangement of the tones. This sequential arrangement is a strong enough factor in the musical phrase to make it impossible to notate most rāgas as a simple scale from lowest to highest. Sometimes tones can be used only in ascending (or descending) phrases. Sometimes there are alternate tones for certain scale degrees (for instance, both $D^\flat$ and $D^\natural$), depending on context. And ornaments always add microtonal inflections that are not shown in the notation. The best way to become acquainted with the rāgas, of course, is through performance or recordings.

Several of the most common North Indian tālas are listed below (see Fig. 18). The aṅgas are classified either as tāli ('beat,' expressed with a hand-

[6] *Ibid.*, pp. 94, 95.

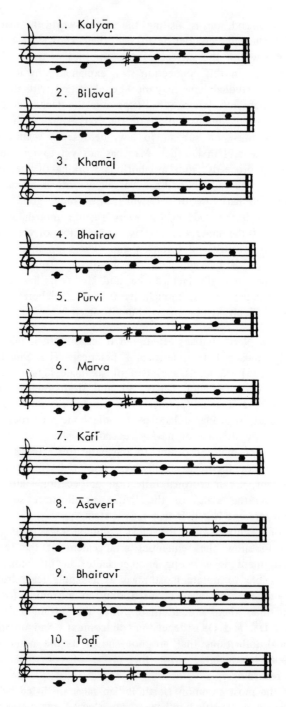

16. Ten Thāts of North Indian
Rāga Classification
(after Bhatkande)

clap), or khālī ('empty,' expressed with a wave). This structure is often reflected in the music by the omission of the lower-pitched left hand drum, or by a peculiar twist or small climax in the musical phrase on the khālī aṅga.

The Hindustani music of the North can be sensuous and more romantic in mood than the South Indian or Carnatic (Karṇātaka) music. There is more dwelling on long held tones, less busy activity. Unlike the Southern music, it tends to increase in speed by definite stages in both the jor and jhāla sections, as well as in the improvisation on the khyāl or gat. In fact, after a certain speed has been reached, it is customary to introduce a new composition appropriate for faster tempo—often in a different tāla. Although principals are the same, and identical names sometimes appear, none of the specific tālas and rāgas of North and South India are alike, except for a handful of direct borrowings.

V.   South Indian Classical Music

South Indian music underwent systematization and change in the 16th and 17th centuries. The important 16th century composer, Purandara Dasa, who renounced his life as a successful businessman to become a saintly poet-musician, is often referred to as the 'Grandfather of Carnatic Music,' and his country Karnātaka (the present Mysore State) gave the style its

When the cultural center shifted from Vijayanagara, the last of the great Hindu empires, to Tanjore, the music developed an elaborate melodic ornamentation and flowered rhythmically to encompass a wonderfully expressive and varied use of musical time under a control that is perhaps unequalled in any other musical culture. Great bhaktas poured out their religious emotion in kṛtis and other musical forms of impressive architectural scope. Three of the most famous composers, Tyāgarāja, Muttusvāmi Dīkṣitar, and Syāma Śāstri, flourished at the same time and were all born in the same little village of Tiruvarur, in Tanjore district.

When their golden era passed in the mid-19th century, the cultural center shifted to Madras city, and their tradition was continued by other composers—lesser lights, perhaps, but creators of important artistic works that are still performed along with those of the 'musical trinity' whose compositions form the main fare of contemporary concert programs. This emergence of the saint-composer as a powerful artistic personality is only one facet of the Carnatic musical scene that distinguishes it from the Hindustani and other important style areas, where fewer composers are remembered and the compositions are usually on a smaller scale.

The present classification of Carnatic rāgas is based on a system of seventy-two melakartas, or seven-tone parent scales, first expounded in 1620 by the theorist Venkatamakhin in an important work, the Caturdaṇdi Prakāsika. In the melakarta scheme, tonic and fifth (sa and pa) are always present. Half of the scales use the perfect fourth (suddha madhyama), the

17. Twenty-five North Indian Rāgas

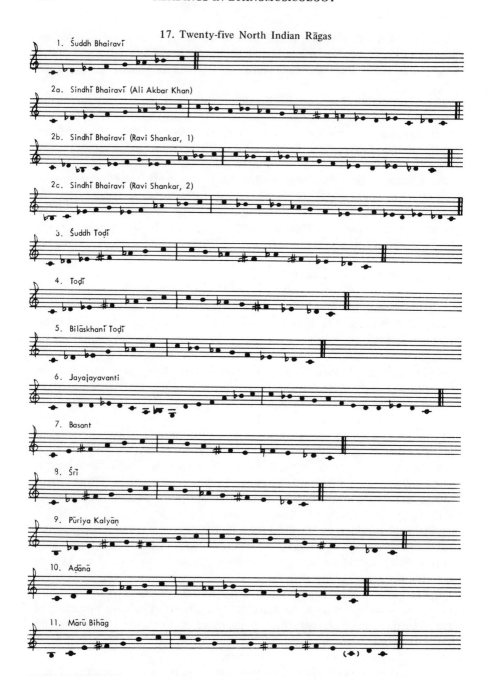

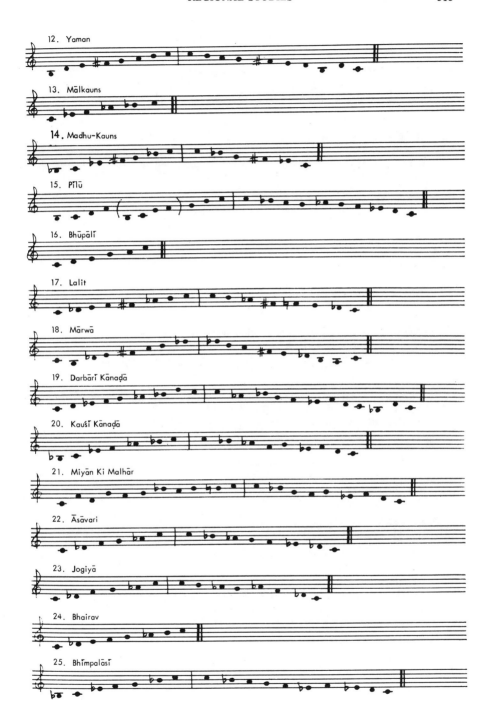

18. Some Typical Ṭhekas for North Indian Tālas

1. **TĪNTĀL:** 16 beats, 4-4-4-4, clap-clap-wave-clap

1	2	3	4	5	6	7	8	9	10	11	12	13	14	15	16
dha	dhin	dhin	dha	dha	dhin	dhin	dha	dha	tin	tin	ta	ta	dhin	dhin	dha
X				2				O				3			

2. **SITĀR KHĀNĪ:** 16 beats, 4-4-4-4, clap-clap-wave-clap

1	2	3	4	5	6	7	8	9	10	11	12	13	14	15	16
dha	gadhin	ᵹg	dha	dha	gadhin	ᵹg	ta	ta	gatin	ᵹg	ta	dha	gadhin	ᵹga	dha
X				2				O				3			

3. **RUPAK TĀL:** 7 beats, 3-2-2, wave-clap-clap

1	2	3	4	5	6	7
tin	tin	na	dhin	na	dhin	na
⊗			2		3	

4. **JHĀPTĀL:** 10 beats, 2-3-2-3, clap-clap-wave-clap

1	2	3	4	5	6	7	8	9	10
dhin	na	dhin	dhin	na	tin	na	dhin	dhin	na
X		2			O		3		

5. **EKTĀL:** 12 beats, 2-2-2-2-2-2, clap-wave-clap-wave-clap-clap

1	2	3	4	5	6	7	8	9	10	11	12
dhin	dhin	dhage	tirakita	tu	na	ka	ta	dhage	tirakita	dhin	na
X		O		2		O		3		4	

6. **CAUTĀL:** 12 beats, 2-2-2-2-2-2, clap-wave-clap-wave-clap-clap

1	2	3	4	5	6	7	8	9	10	11	12
dha	dha	din	ta	kita	dha	din	ta	tita	kata	gadi	gang
X		O		2		O		3		4	

7. **DĀDRA TĀL:** 6 beats, 3-3, clap-wave

1	2	3	4	5	6
dha	dhin	na	dha	tun	na
X			O		

8. **KAHĀRWA TĀL:** 8 beats, 4-4, clap-clap

1	2	3	4	5	6	7	8
dha	ge	na	tin	na	ka	dhin	na
X				2			

9. **DĪPCANDI TĀL:** 14 beats, 3-4-3-4, clap-clap-wave-clap

1	2	3	4	5	6	7	8	9	10	11	12	13	14
dha	dhin	-	dha	ge	tin	-	ta	tin	-	dha	ge	dhin	-
X			2				O			3			

10. **DHAMĀR TĀL:** 14 beats, 5-2-3-4, clap-clap-wave-wave

1	2	3	4	5	6	7	8	9	10	11	12	13	14
ka	dhi	ṭa	dhi	ṭa	dha	-	ga	ti	ṭa	ti	ṭa	ta	-
X					2		O			3			

Taken from the Banaras style of tablajī Panchu Maharaj

last thirty-six use the augmented fourth (prati madhayama). The basic tones used are the twelve of the piano keyboard (or vīṇā fretboard). By mathematical alternation of three possible ris, three gas, three dhas, and three nis (some tones being enharmonic with others), a complete and rationally logical series is completed. As a further systematization, the rāga names were altered—Śankharābhāraṇam became Dhiraśankarābhāraṇam, Kalyāṇi became Mecakalyāṇi, etc.—so that the first two syllables would indicate the numerical position of the mela (source scale) in the scheme of seventy-two. To determine the rank of a mela, one must number the consonantal syllables of the Sanskrit alphabet from 1 through 9, plus 0, and repeat to the end. The numbers of the first two mela syllables are reversed to find the correct position. (Dhira is 9-2, reversed 2-9, thus Dhiraśankarābhāranam is number twenty-nine in the scheme of seventy-two.)

From the practical point of view, the melakarta system does not project faithfully the contemporary musical situation. There are many more rāgas having gapped scales, differing ascent and descent, vakra ('crooked') configuration rather than a simple lowest to highest tone series, or vice versa than there are sampūrna (straight seven-tone) modes. Then too, certain strongly characteristic svaras (called jīva svaras or 'soul tones') give life to the rāga, either by their special ornamentation or melodic stress. Other tones in a given rāga may be generally avoided, creating a melodic poignancy when they do appear. Perhaps the most important single musical hallmark of the rāga, its traditional grouping of the basic note material into characteristic small melodic phrases, is hardly touched upon in the native theory. It is extremely important, however, to remember that the point of view of an Indian theorist is quite different from that of the European, who attempts to describe as faithfully and scientifically as possible a musical situation that has already taken place. In the seventy-two melakarta system, we find a great many ragas grouped under a relatively small number of parent scales. (Śankarābhāraṇam, for instance, may have fifteen or twenty children.) Yet, many interesting possibilities for new and still unused seven-tone scales emerge. Musicians can now turn to the system for inspiration in creating new rāgas, and in this way a number of new configurations, such as Kanakaṅgi (C, D♭, E♭♭, F, G, A♭, B♭♭, C), which assumes special importance as the first scale of the seventy-two, have come to be used by performers.

The present tāla system of Carnatic music, based on seven basic types (sapta tālas), is equally systematic. The seven tāla types are formed from only three aṅgas: anudrutam, one akṣarakāla ('beat'); drutam, two akṣarakālas; and laghu, a variable aṅga of which there are five types (jātis): catuśra (4 akṣarakālas), tiśra (3), miśra (7), khaṇḍa (5), and saṅkīrṇa (9). Since each of the seven main tāla patterns contains at least one laghu, five times seven, or thirty-five tālas comprise the whole scheme. Of these, perhaps half a dozen are in common use, another half dozen are used infrequently, and the remainder make up a reservoir that is now being drawn

19. Twenty-five South Indian Rāga Scales

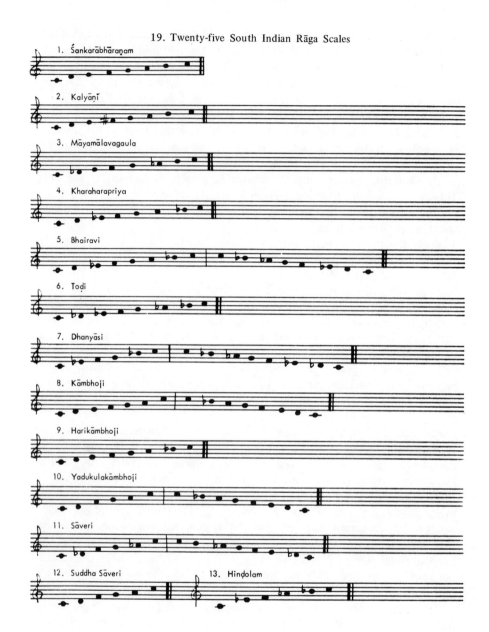

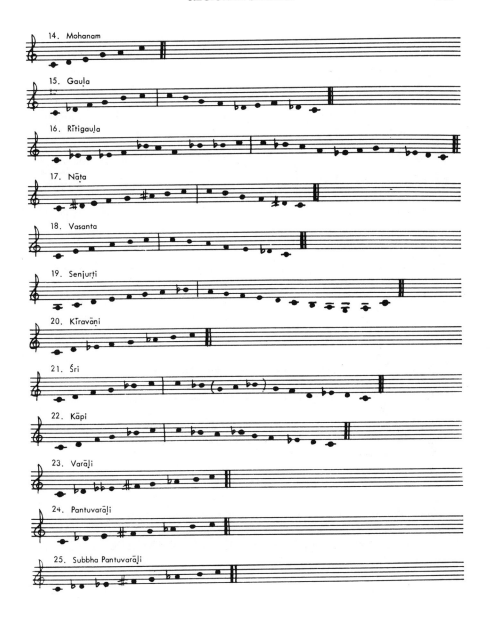

upon in the same way that the theoretical melas of the rāga classification system furnish new basic musical materials for the composer and creative artist-performer.

Laghu Bheda

	Caturaśra 4	Tiśra 3	Miśra 7	Khaṇḍa 5	Saṅkīrṇa 9
1. Dhruva	$I^4 O\ I^4\ I^4$	$I^3 O\ I^3\ I^3$	$I^7 O\ I^7\ I^7$	$I^5 O\ I^5\ I^5$	$I^9 O\ I^9\ I^9$
2. Maṭya	$I^4 O\ I^4$	$I^3 O\ I^3$	$I^7 O\ I^7$	$I^5 O\ I^5$	$I^9 O\ I^9$
3. Rūpaka	$O\ I^4$	$O\ I^3$	$O\ I^7$	$O\ I^5$	$O\ I^9$
4. Tripuṭa	$I^4 OO$	$I^3 OO$	$I^7 OO$	$I^5 OO$	$I^9 OO$
5. Jhampa	$I^4 XO$	$I^3 XO$	$I^7 XO$	$I^5 XO$	$I^9 XO$
6. Aṭa	$I^4 I^4 OO$	$I^3 I^3 OO$	$I^7 I^7 OO$	$I^5 I^5 OO$	$I^9 I^9 OO$
7. Eka	I^4	I^3	I^7	I^5	I^9

X (anudruta) is one akṣara in length, shown by a handclap

O (druta) is two akṣaras in length, shown by a clap and a wave

I (laghu) is a variable anga, 3, 4, 5, 7 or 9 akṣaras in length, indicated by a handclap followed by the appropriate number of finger counts, starting with the little finger

20. The Thirty-Five Tālas

Other tāla systems used in South India are the cāpu tālas, mainly two simple patterns of five beats (2 + 3) and seven beats (3 + 4), the Tirrupugal tālas—intricate metrical patterns determined by the verse structure of a number of hymns (Tirrupugal) by a single 15th century composer, Arunagirinādar, two four-beat patterns (actually different combinations of three beats and a wave) showing North Indian or folk influence—the Désādi and Madhyādi tālas, and occasional use of Deśī tālas of the Saṅgītaratnākara period as a tour de force in a special composition like a Pallavi, an elaborate improvisation built on a short but intricate melody with text.

Fewer musical instruments are used in Carnatic classical music than in the Hindustani tradition. The instrumental style is even closer to the vocal, and there is no such independent instrumental composition as the North Indian gat. Players of the vīṇā, nāgasvāram, flute or violin perform the song literature, and improvise upon it according to the nature of their instruments, but close to vocal style.

21. South Indian Vīṇā

The vīṇā in South India has become a long-necked lute with a large resonating bowl, held across the lap by the seated player. A small gourd-shaped
resonator, now generally made from papier-maché and useful only as a
counter-balance, hangs from the neck. There are four playing strings, and
three drone strings on a special side bridge. The plucking of the drone
strings usually outlines the aṅga structure of the tāla cycle, so with melody,
drone, and the rhythmic skeleton represented the vīṇā becomes the most
nearly self-sufficient of Indian instruments.

> Recording: Classical Indian Music. K. S. Narayanaswami, vina; Narayana
> Menon, vina; Palghat Raghu, mridangam. Spoken intro-
> duction by Yehudi Menuhin. London CM 9282.

Within the past few decades in South India there has been a tendency to
prefer a lower pitch for both vocal and instrumental music than prevailed in
the past. All instruments, therefore, have tended to become larger, and the
nāgasvarām, a powerful reed pipe of the oboe family, is not only more than
twice as long as its relative, the now rare mukhavīṇā (resembling the North
Indian śahnai), but it is capable of great power of tone. With its reed pipe
drone, the attu, accompanying tālam (small time-keeping bell metal cymbals)

22. Nāgasvāram and Tavil

and the dynamic tavil drum, played with a short stick in the left hand and hard cloth and paste 'thimbles' on the fingers of the right hand, the nāgasvāram can produce an ear-splitting sound in a small room. This is a benefit, however, because the sound is highly auspicious and indispensable for weddings, temple ceremonies, and other rites, often held out of doors or in large halls. In concert there are generally two nāgasvarām players and two tavils who alternate and exchange improvisation.

> Recording: Karukurichi Arunachalam, nagasvaram. Odeon (to be released)

The clarinet has gained in popularity as a medium for art music in recent years. The older Albert system instrument is used so that the fingers are in direct contact with the sound holes for the production of slides and other ornaments, as on the unkeyed nāgasavāram. Two styles have developed—one in which the tone is very close to the double-reed sound of the nāgasvāram and the accompaniment is with tavil, and a second in which the tone is closer to the western concept of clarinet sound and the accompaniment is with the barrel drum, mṛdaṅga.

The mṛdaṅga is the rhythmic instrument par excellence of South Indian music, as the vīṇā is the ideal melodic instrument. It is a barrel drum of highly refined construction, with two complex heads consisting of layers of skin of different types and two different kinds of tuning paste, expertly applied. It must be carefully tuned to the tonic drone, and is capable of about fifteen to twenty different timbres and tones depending on the position of the striking hands or fingers. As with other drums, these sounds can be represented by spoken syllables. The performer's function is continuous improvisation based on hundreds of set patterns learned in his long training. He generally performs at least one solo of ten or fiteen minute's length in the concert as well as accompaniment for all compositions and improvisations within the tāla framework. The mṛdaṅgam is the normal accompaniment for voice, vīṇā, flute and violin.

23. Mṛdaṅga

The South Indian flute is generally smaller and higher-pitched than its North Indian counterpart, but like it is made from bamboo.

> Recording: T. Viswanathan, flute. World Pacific (to be released)

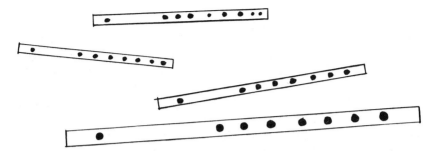

24. North and South Indian Flutes

The western violin adapted for Indian use in the matter of tuning and playing position has been a major accompanying instrument for voice in South India for several decades. It is also heard as a solo instrument and often accompanies flute, clarinet, and sometimes vīṇā. Tuned to the tonic and fifth, it is held between chest and foot, which is not only more comfortable for the musician (who sits cross-legged upon the floor), but also facilitates the many slides and trill-like gamakas that are central to the melodic style. The violin generally answers the soloist during the improvisation, creating a brilliant repartee in the form of a musical dialogue and it doubles and reinforce the melody of the composed portions of the performance. It has probably replaced the vīṇā or other native instruments because of its greater power in the modern concert hall.

Several secondary rhythmic instruments are often found as accompaniments on the South Indian concert platform. The kanjira is a small tambourine with a single jingle. The morsing is an ordinary metal jew's harp. The ghatam is a round and resonant earthen pot of special fired clay played with the fingers and hands. The opening is stopped against the player's bare stomach for changes in timbre. All of these simple instruments produce a variety of tone and complexity of rhythmic pattern that is sure to astonish a foreign listener hearing them for the first time.

The kṛti has been mentioned as the most important musical form in the South. It is generally in three main sections: pallavi, anupallavi, and

25. Morsing, Ghatam, and Kanjira

caraṇam. The text is poetically rich and often deeply philosophical. The composer addresses his deity in fervently emotional terms, beautifully fulfilling the spirit of bhakti. Other important musical forms are the vaṛṇam (a complex style having both words and composed svara passages), the padam and jāvali (florid love songs to the deity which can often be interpreted on the worldly plane as well), the tillana (a highly rhythmic form taken like the padam and jāvali from the repertoire of Bharata Nāṭya, the South Indian classical dance), the Pallavi (a small but intricate composition used as the basis for a grand improvisation), and many other less important musical forms.

On these elaborate forms are raised equally elaborate improvisations, which may be realized in several ways. The ālāpana, improvisation of rāga phrases in free rhythm, outside the tāla and without drum, is of great importance. Occasionally a tānam adds a more regular rhythmic pulsation, although still without tāla and drum. Once a composition has been introduced, two main types of improvisation might be done: neraval, improvisation of new melody in the rāga using a line of the text as the base, and svara kalpaṇa, insertion of improvised passages of svaras (solfeggio), always returning to the composed melody at a certain point in the tāla cycle and at a certain pitch level to link gracefully. The svara kalpaṇa tends to move from shorter to longer and more rhythmically complex patterns, and is usually done in two speeds, first medium and then fast.

Recording: The Sounds of Subbulakshmi. World Pacific WP 1440.

Both Hindustani and Carnatic music require a long and arduous training, the memorization of enormous quantities of musical material through rote teaching, and a close and continuous relationship between student and guru for the transmission of both composed pieces and improvisatory techniques. Whether or not the traditional and formalized methods of teaching can be modified to suit a changing society in which few have the security and time for the single-minded concentration necessary to specialize in one particular aspect of art music is a most important question if the great traditions of Indian music are to continue. Thus far, the new music schools and university departments based on European models seem unlikely to train artists of stature, although they are helping to make musical study available to many who will not be concert artists. Indian music is, however, an art for professionals. As the older generation of artists disappears from the concert platforms one by one with few musicians of equal caliber appearing to take their place, there is cause for concern as to what the future holds for Indian art music.

VI.   Folk, Tribal, and Popular Music

A wide variety of folk and tribal music can be found in India, although at present few studies of note have been carried out, and a mere smattering of recordings have been made. Even these serve to point up the wealth and diversity of material that abound. The Hindu and Muslim villagers are no less musically inclined than their urban counterparts in Madras or Banaras, but Indian writers have tended to look down upon folk music as inferior and uninteresting in comparison to the rāgas of the art music traditions. A wonderful sound picture of the ancient South Indian countryside, including different types of folk songs that might have been heard, is given in the Śilappadikāram as the Buddhist nun Kavundi leads Kovalan and Mādavi on their journey along the banks of the sacred river Kāvēri.

Thus saying, the venerable Kavundi took up her sacred begging-bowl and her netted bag suspended from her shoulders. Holding a pea-cock's feathers in her hand and praying that the pañcamantra might be their guide on the way, Kavundi, unrivalled in the practice of vir-tue, accompanied the other two in their journey.

Though Saturn gets angry, though the (fiery) comet is visible, though Venus of the bright rays travels towards the south (of the sky), no harm is rendered to the Kāvēri which has its source in the windswept heights of the Coorg hills where, to the accompaniment of raging thunder, the seasonal clouds pregnant with rain pour down their blessings; the Kāvēri which dashes along with such diverse hill produce to meet the advancing tide of the wealth-bearing sea. But finding her movement arrested by the barrier—the anicut with its doorway—she noisily leaps beyond it in the sportive mood natural to her first freshes. No sound other than this can be heard. We can hear there neither the sound of the bucket, nor of the water-lift; neither the usually loud pecottah, nor the palm-leaf basket used in irrigation.

In the beautiful forest of lotuses appearing out of ponds in regions surrounded by paddy-fields and sugar-cane could be heard, just as in a battle-field where two monarchs fight, different kinds of sounds pro-duced by the water-fowl, the loud-voiced crane, the red-footed swan, the green-footed heron, wild fowl, the water crow (black heron), fishes, creeping insects, birds and big herons.

Wallowing in the mire, in regions left unploughed, black buffaloes would come out with their unwashed hair and their red eyes, and rub their itching backs upon the straw granary when it gets loose and re-leases the grain stocked within amidst the sheaves of paddy whose rice-corn hangs down like fly whisks made of the fur of the kavari yak. In those places brawny-armed labourers and cultivators would as-semble making a motley of sound.

There was also the sound of (rural) songs sung to (new) tunes by low-caste women in their drunken moods while they looked through their fish-like large eyes and uttered indecent words standing in playful postures and, threw mud upon each other, covering up their broad, bangled shoulders and breasts with mud, having removed the (faded) fragrant flowers from their hair and replaced them with paddy-shoots.

There was also the sound of the benedictory songs (ērmangalam) sung reverently by the ploughmen standing by their ploughshares and seeming to break open the ground which they decorated with garlands made of paddy-stalks, luxuriant arugu, and water-lilies.

There was also heard the muhavai song sung (by the field-labourers) when they drove cattle over the reaped paddy sheaves to thresh the corn; and the cheering applause of those who heard the round-shaped tabor smeared with mud played by proud minstrels who used to produce clear music by their kiṇai.

Having heard these songs in regular succession along the banks of the great rivers, the travellers grew glad in their hearts and did not feel the fatigue of the journey.[7]

Such plentiful folk songs probably bore some resemblance to the classical musical tradition of the time, as they do today; we know that there was a limited amount of borrowing back and forth, just as in Europe. On the other hand there are types of music found with certain castes and tribes that cannot be related at all to the mainstream. The hill tribes of North and South India, as well as a number of other relatively isolated ethnic groups often maintain traditions quite distinct from one another. Some of these appear to reflect ancient and archaic strands of indigenous music. Others bear resemblance to musical styles of Africa, Central Asia, Southeast Asia, even Indonesia and Melanesia. There are many questions to be resolved.

Perhaps the best approach to the folk and tribal music of India, with its bewildering array of styles, instruments and social functions, is through the recordings now available, that are at least suggestive of the scope of the problem and inadequacy of our knowledge. Jacket notes are often the only descriptive information available.

Recordings: a. Columbia World Library of Folk and Primitive Music, Vol. 13: India. Columbia SL 215.

              b. Music from South India, Kerala. Folkways FE 4365.

              c. Au sud de l'Inde. Le Chant du Monde LO-S 8238.

              d. Chants et danses populaires du Bengale. Boite a Musique, LD 076

              e. Folk Music of Kashmir. Folkways FE 4350.

              f. Songs of Assam, Uttar Pradesh and the Andamans. Folkways FE 4380.

              g. Ritual Music of Manipur. Folkways FE 4479.

[7] *The Śilappadikaram, op cit.*, pp. 160-162.

Of all the types of India's music, the "filmi gīt' or popular music is the most ubiquitous. Even the casual tourist on a short visit will hear it on every hand, for it is dispersed through powerful media—primarily films and radio, but also phonograph and jukebox. Bazaar shops and tea stalls blast it into the streets on overloaded loudspeakers; white-collar workers fill the busses and trains with it from pocket transistor radios; college boys and houseboys sing it happily as they bicycle to the day's occupations.

Nearly all Indian films contain a number of popular songs. The movie industry is large, and an army of composers and studio musicians grind out tunes by the hundreds. The vitality content is high, the musical content low—anything that is catchy will do. The melodies may derive from Broadway, Punjabi folk songs, Greek popular music, South American rhythms, in short anywhere. The instruments can be combinations of sitārs, pianos, folk drums, china bowls, French horns, in short anything. The results may be horrifying to musicians, lucrative to tune makers, and soul-satisfying to millions who have never heard an artist of the great tradition expound a midnight rāga for some small gathering of connoisseurs. What will become of this brash newcomer to the musical scene is anyone's guess. It is raw, commercial, sentimental, exasperating, and amazingly lively. It owes something musical to everyone, but allegiance to no one except an awesomely massive public with an awesomely undeveloped musical taste. Still, the public takes its jangling 'filmi gīt' to heart with enthusiasm and joy just as it has taken its music to heart for centuries.

Recording: Modern Motion Picture Music of India. Capital T 10090.

We live at a moment in the history of East meeting West that is both thrilling and frightening. Only now does the world become a 'global village.' The reactions to the accelerated exchange of culture are so many and varied that it is hard to see clearly what is happening on all the fronts, even in such a new and specific area of acculturation as music. What does it mean when a sitār virtuoso can pack Lincoln Center, when rock and roll groups try to imitate the 'rāga sound', when American singers improvise on krtis in strict classical tradition before maharajas?

At least a few points are clear. We find new insight and perhaps new humility by discovering the many ways that music can be made, and the virtuosity with which others have explored such avenues as, for instance, rhythm. If we listen carefully and with the right spirit, we may even discover new interpretations of the human condition, new visions of serenity and beauty. We may find values that have been neglected or lost, and return to our own ways refreshed and wiser. Our awareness of the enormous power to obliterate that has been built up in the western world is certain to be clarified.

What are the difficulties confronting the westerner who wishes to see the soul of India through her music? There are many, but none that cannot be resolved through patience, the willingness to listen and learn, the application of intelligence, and the acceptance of other concepts of time and the role of ego.

What are the dangers in all of this merging and mixing? Again there are many, at least from the point of view that beauty exists and that it is vulnerable. Just as a lotus will die in a frozen lake, what is tender and delicate, the product of centuries of development in Indian music, can be withered in the blast of applause from a crowd intent of the excitement of mere speed. The relationship of performer and audience in India has been traditionally intimate. The artist responds like a sensitive plant to the nature and expectations of his listeners. In fact, the whole esthetic theory of the rasas rests on the presumption that it is the duty of the rasika (he who 'tastes') to understand and study to his fullest ability what it is that the performer is doing. His enjoyment then goes deep, and the communication of mood is at its fullest and most pleasurable. We have to learn to listen for what the performer can say to us, even though it is new, instead of holding to our own preconceived demands. It is then that he will reveal those gifts that are peculiarly Indian—of which there are many.

The rock and roll musician who carries home a new sitār from the oriental imports store is exercizing the same undeniable prerogative as the Indian film composer who throws in a few delicious piano arpeggios for a dash of the exotic in his latest musical extravaganza. But the results in both cases are likely to be dismal without a little care in finding out what others have done and what can be done. Perhaps the rock and roll may sound better if our player knows that one never steps over a sitar because it is considered to have a soul. If he realizes the truly intimate quality of its sound, he is bound to change the course of rock and roll altogether.

What is happening will happen, and although the foregoing is probably germane, it is simply stating something we already know: the Orient can teach us to be patient. There are ample indications that we are about to sit down and look around, look inside, find other ways of perceiving time. No wonder the popularity of Indian music is growing in the West—it requires all of these things! It is an inner landscape of many colors where no two blossoms are the same.

Selected Bibliography

Adiyārkkunallavār, The Śilappadikāram, transl. by V. R. Ramachandra Dikshitar, Madras: Oxford University Press, 1939.

Bharata-Muni, supposed author, Nātyaśāstra, ed. by Manomohan Ghosh, Calcutta: Asiatic Society, Vol. I, 1951, Vol. II, 1961.

Brown, Robert E., The Mṛdanga: A Study of Drumming in South India, University of California at Los Angeles, Ph.D. dissertation, 1965. Ann Arbor: University Microfilms, Inc., 2 vols.

Danielou, Alain, Northern Indian Music, Vol. I, Theory and Technique, London: Christopher Johnson, 1949; Vol. II, The Main Ragas, London: Halcyon Press, 1954.

Day, C. R., *The Music and Musical Instruments of Southern India and the Deccan*, London: Novello, Ewer and Co., 1891.

Fox-Strangeways, A. H., *The Music of Hindostan*, Oxford: Clarendon Press, 1914.

Marcel-Dubois, Claudie, *Les instruments de musique de l'Inde ancienne*, Paris: Presses Universitaires de France, 1941.

Popley, Herbert A., *The Music of India*, Calcutta: Young Men's Christian Association Press, 1921.

Powers, Harold Stone, *The Background of the South Indian Raga-System*, Princeton University, Ph.D. dissertation, 1959. Ann Arbor: University Microfilms, Inc.

Sachs, Curt, *The History of Musical Instruments*, New York: W. W. Norton, 1940.

Sachs, Curt, *The Rise of Music in the Ancient World*, New York: W. W. Norton, 1943.

Sambamoorthy, P., *South Indian Music*, Madras: The Indian Music Publishing House, 1955 (Book I), 1956 (Book II), 1953 (Book III), 1954 (Book IV), 1951 (Book V).

Sārṅgadeva, *Saṅgītaratnākara*, transl. by C. Kunhan Raja, Vol. I, chap 1 (Svara), Madras: The Aydar Library, 1945.

Subba Rao, T. V., *Studies in Indian Music*, Bombay: Asia Publishing House, 1962.

MODERN TRENDS IN GHANA MUSIC

J. H. Nketia

The student of African musical practice in changing Africa is often haunted by a feeling of urgency. He must hasten to collect examples of the variety of musical types cultivated in a given area "before they are lost forever". Wherever he goes, he does not content himself with what he gets in the towns: he visits places where the forces of acculturation are least evident, making a careful selection of the available material in order that he might take back recordings of "authentic" African music for preservation and study.

This feeling is justifiable not only on account of the accelerated pace of change in Africa but also because the dynamic agents of musical change are foreign, powerful and greatly alluring. They have been so in Ghana. The importance of the approach and the methods used, therefore, cannot be disputed even if they appear to be guided by a museum-cultural outlook, for it is only through systematic collection, study and documentation of this material that the evolution of African music can be adequately documented in the future.

But the importance of the work of the student of African music does not lie only in the future. The material can be a source of inspiration to creative musicians within and outside Africa. Far too often modern African musicians look too far afield for such inspiration when there is abundant material waiting at their door-steps. Such collections and studies can have repercussions on present day trends in our musical practice. The African musician who is leading his people towards new goals needs to be thoroughly acquainted with the cultural values of his own society. By disseminating a knowledge of authentic African music, the emerging African may be enabled to appreciate the value of his heritage and build on it for the future.

In studying African music, however, we cannot afford to be completely oblivious to the factors that are affecting it for good or ill, for the African and his culture no longer enjoy the isolation of the past. The presence of change impresses itself on the field worker, however devoted he might be to the cause of indigenous African music. It might arouse his sympathy for the African who is striving to adapt himself to new musical ideas, or it might make him contemptuous of the innovations he meets. The feeling of admiration which the complex rhythms of drums engender in him might turn into disgust at the sight of the guitar or the saxophone. The African tune which fascinates him by its peculiar tonal organization and rhythmic phrasing might be looked down upon by him or at best considered highly amus-

330

ing if it was no longer sung in unison, in strict parallel thirds or organum in fourths and fifths.

In whatever ways we judge these innovations, we cannot ignore the fact that they are the "growing pains" of a new era, a new phase in the evolution of African music which merits some notice, and perhaps sympathetic understanding of the peculiar situation in 'which the African now finds himself. In Ghana, and I believe in other places, new composite musical traditions are emerging from the contact of indigenous African music on the one hand, and on the other, the music imported from Europe and the other side of the Atlantic—musical traditions wedged, as it were, between two cultures, musical traditions embodying the reactions of culture contact, the tendencies to conservatism and change expressing themselves in the rejection, adoption and adaptation of non-African musical forms.

While the composite musical traditions which have already emerged are *transitional* and cannot yet be regarded as *mature* traditions, they are interesting from various points of view. They tend to be identified with new social institutions and their verbal content often gives interesting indications of the values that have come to be accepted or questioned in modern life. They are certainly not faced by any serious threat of decline or neglect by urban and rural communities in Ghana for whom they provide a new form of social music. They are popular and greatly commercialized.[1]

A study of the music of these new traditions might be of theoretical interest. It might enable us to determine more definitely what constitutes the "African approach" to music, or what Hugh Tracey describes as "the African mentality behind the trappings of adopted art forms".[2] It might enable us to see what elements are so vital to the African's approach to music that they get perpetuated in the new traditions, what elements are modified, what elements are left out, and so on. A study of the selection and adaptation taking place in modern music might provide objective tests for our theories or at any rate show how much emphasis should be given to various aspects of African music which we seek to describe. All these presuppose a knowledge of indigenous African music, which I believe must always be our starting point in African musical research.

A study of transitional music might also have useful practical results. It might enable modern musicians to see what they are doing and perhaps do it better. It might even help in establishing a closer bond between the old and the new.

With the foregoing observations in mind, I would now like to draw attention to the transitional forms in Ghana and the way they have been evolving as new traditions in our musical life. I shall limit myself mainly to

[1] See NKETIA, J. H. "The Gramophone and Contemporary African Music in the Gold Coast," *Proceedings of Conference of West African Institute of Social and Economic Research,* 1955.

[2] African Music Society Newsletter, Volume 1 No. 5.

the factors of change and the trends along which the traditions are developing.

In Ghana two new musical traditions have emerged as a result of the forces of acculturation out of which Ghana herself has been born. The first which has developed gradually over the past sixty years or more is fairly well standardized and is popularly known by the English title of High Life, a title which reflects the early attitude of people to it as a new but somewhat insidious form of social music. Though based on gay rhythms of African foundation, it began from the inspiration of Western band music which was admired for its noisy splendour, and later the ballroom at which thoughtful Africans never looked favourably. These incorporated percussion and movement, and suggested a new line for creating a gay type of African music which would be markedly different from the lighter type of traditional music.

Like band music used for parades, the High Life grew up as "street music". Wherever it was played, players and dancers moved slowly along from one end of the street to another. This attracted young people by its novelty and always drew spectators. As street music people danced to it individually and freely as we still do, moving in regular forward or sideways steps, each foot doing two consecutive beats while the body and the hands swayed rhythmically. It was a simple dance and lacked the artistic routine of our traditional dances. It has continued to remain so, though various styles of movement become fashionable from time to time.

When the High Life developed into a standardized item for the ballroom, dancing partners for this particular dance soon became an intolerable formality. The tradition soon grew of partners freely breaking up as they still do in order that they may each "enjoy the rhythm better" in the true African fashion.

The High Life has continued to remain in vogue as a new popular music in modern Ghana. Nowadays its development depends largely on town bands: instrumental dance bands which specialize in music other than the High Life, and vocal dance bands supported by guitar or accordion and percussion. There are over twenty such bands in Accra alone, though they are by no means equally popular.

The growth of High Life bands has not followed the same pattern. Differences will be found according to the educational background of members of the band, their ability to assimilate new ideas, and so on. There are also environmental factors. Musicians in the municipalities are developing along different lines from those in towns and villages. Moreover opportunities for performing and the conditions under which they perform tend to be different.

For urban bands, the setting is frequently the ballroom, the wedding reception, the café or night club. For town musicians the setting is the occasional dance in town or dances in other towns to which they may be invited, while village bands find their setting in the street: Theirs is to perambulate the street with their High Life which often attracts crowds of appreciative dancers who follow them round every corner. All these differences are reflected in the music of the different bands who show varying degrees of polish and discipline. Many bands, particularly vocal bands, compose their own High Life songs. These songs, especially those of popular bands, get quickly known through the radio and the commercial disc.

Different types of High Life music are now being developed. There are two standard forms of Ghanaian creation: the High Life of fast tempo which is the normal one, and the slow High Life popularly referred to as Blues, merely because of its tempo, for it is always blues without the blue notes, and is often different in rhythmical conception.

The association of the High Life with the Ballroom and Western musical instruments has tended to make Western harmonic usages the ideal which many musicians aim at. Already certain chord formations have become characteristic and many musicians go beyond the common chords. A lot of experimentation is going on, but the characteristic song style of the High Life, its basic rhythm and phrase lengths, its percussion and style of dancing have continued to be maintained.

The High Life is essentially vocal music. Even when played by instruments there must always be a vocal interlude. The songs are sung in our language, and are based on a variety of subjects. There are topical songs, songs about individuals, moral songs, songs about death, political songs, and so on. The tunes are often catchy, sentimental or gay but simple enough in outline to be readily grasped by the ordinary man about town.

Although the development of the High Life began along the coast of Southern Ghana, it is today found in the greater part of the country as the one type of African music which is not tribal in idiom, for as far as traditional music is concerned Ghanaians are separated by differences in musical idiom, differences which make it difficult for the Akan to appreciate Ewe music or for the Grunsi to appreciate the music of the Dagbani.

The musical importance of the High Life in Ghana, therefore, is that it is intertribal, and standardized as a song type. It serves as a new type of folk music which may be heard on the lips of the breadseller, the workman as well as the professional musician, a new type of folk music that may be known even to people who are not regular visitors to places of dancing.

The second type of new African music in Ghana emerged much later than the High Life. Unlike the High Life which is oriented to the place of dancing, the second type of tradition is orientated to the concert hall, the Church (as a place for performing music), and educational institutions. The musical types are not as formally standardized as the High Life although they are unmistakable from any other type of Ghana music. They are more serious in outlook, more elaborate in structure and on the whole tend to be less popularly known.

Composers of this type of music look to traditional music for inspiration and sometimes for their song motifs. For their gay, lively pieces, some of them even draw on the High Life form, for the attitude of Ghanaians to the High Life is that it is a new addition to our folk music. Because folk music is their starting point, many of our composers are serious students of Ghana music who collect traditional folk songs, learn to drum and play African musical instruments in order that the new music which they create may reflect quite clearly the African tradition from which they spring.

The father of this tradition is Ephraim Amu who started to re-create traditional music in the 1920's when as a teacher of music he suddenly became alive to the need for studying our music, and for re-creating it so that in time it might replace the Western hymn and serve the new musical needs which have arisen through the adoption of Western institutions. The publication of his original compositions of "Twenty Five African Songs" in 1933 by Sheldon Press set the pattern for a new African music which has been followed by many literate and semi-literate composers ever since. The introduction to the songs consists of 80 progressive "Exercises" in the reading of African rhythm, exercises based on a very close analysis of unilineal rhythms as he then understood them. The notation which he used has continued to be used by other musicians in much the same form or with a few modifications. Besides paving the way for a new type of music, therefore, he has also helped in establishing a tradition of written African music in Ghana.

Ephraim Amu's style and the theoretical considerations which guided his compositions thirty years ago have of course changed a great deal. His later works which are more complex have yet to be published. They are broadcast on the radio and are heard at special concerts. They exhibit the same African features which he and other Ghanaian musicians believe must be maintained: the characteristic African ways of forming rhythms and rhythm patterns, responsorial patterns, tonal and rhythmic correlations between words and melody, and for the area now being served by this new music, the use of two and three part forms, judicious use of thirds where parts break into two, and so on. Ephraim Amu believes, like other Ghanaians, that the African can learn from the West in matters of harmony and counterpoint, provided the characteristic tonal organization of our melodies, cadential patterns, etc. are maintained. This, of course, sets a limitation on the type of harmonies one could use in order to retain the African flavour which is often looked for in these new songs.

Amu's interest is not only in vocal music but also in instrumental African music. At the School of Music of which he is head, drumming is compulsory for all students. He has even succeeded in getting it approved as a subject for certificate examinations in music by Examining Bodies overseas. Many of his past students have taken this examination.

Unlike other musicians who do not mind using foreign instruments, Amu believes in the development of our own instruments. He has continued to develop our end blown flutes—to increase their pitch ranges, vary their sizes, fit them with improved mouth pieces. He makes these instruments himself and writes music for ensembles of them which are played by his music students at the College of Technology. He believes, and I think quite rightly, that the peculiar African charm of the music of our end blown flutes would be lost if we were to abandon our African instrument for the Western flute.

Following Amu other musicians have sought to write new African music for use in Church by church choirs, music for use in schools and music for the concert hall. Not enough music has been written. The question of African hymns for the Church is still an unfulfilled hope of the future. Not all the composers have succeeded in blending African and Western forms, but there is a genuine interest among this group in preserving the folk music tradition and in recreating it for the new forms of social life and the institutions which have emerged through our contact with the West.

In contemporary life, the new traditions that are being created and the old tradition exist side by side along with imported music from Europe and the other side of the Atlantic. All these traditions are contextually distributed in such a way as to make them complementary. Different institutions make use of different musical traditions. The institution of Government still carries under its wings the Western military band and a National Anthem in the idiom of Western music, while the institution of chiefship maintains the African drum orchestra and continues to flourish its traditional fanfares of ivory horns.

Cafés, night clubs, ballrooms make use of varieties of the new Ghana music as well as African derived music, while old style music continues to be used at African ritual and ceremonies.

Whatever may be said about the quality of the new music that is being created or the efforts of musicians to find an answer to the the problem of social change, there can be no doubt of the social importance of the experiments that are being made, experiments which need to be guided if they are to prove worthy of the new African.

CHINESE MUSIC [1]

Laurence Picken

Introduction

In spite of considerable differences between the musical practices of one locality and another, the vast territory of Far Eastern Asia–China, Mongolia, Tibet, Shinjiang,[2] Shikang, Korea, Japan, Indo-China, Siam, Burma, Malaya, Java, Bali, etc.–can be regarded, with respect to its musical culture, as a unit, to be compared and contrasted with India perhaps on the one hand and western Europe on the other. A wave of musical culture seems to have swept over China to the seaboard of the great land-mass of Asia and beyond, so that there survive at the present time, on the periphery, types of orchestras and habits of polyphonic treatment which have vanished almost entirely from the central region.

This interpretation of the total musical picture of the Far East is to a considerable extent explicit in the surveys of Far Eastern music made by Sachs.[3] Though the course of the exposition adopted here has been largely determined

[The text reprinted here is taken from the article "The Music of Far Eastern Asia: 1. China, " *The New Oxford History of Music*.]

[1] Recent accounts of Chinese music are: Kenneth Robinson, 'Chinesische Musik, I. Geschichtliche Entwicklung von der Frühzeit (Shang-Dynastie) bis zum Ende der Han-Zeit (1523 a. Chr. bis 206 p. Chr) (Deutsche Ubs, und Bearb.: Hans Eckardt),' *Die Musik in Geschichte und Gegenwart*, ii (ed. Friedrich Blume) (Kassel und Basel, 1952), columns 1195-1205. This account is based directly on the Chinese sources. H. Eckardt, 'Chinesische Musik, II. Vom Ende der Han-Zeit bis zum Ende der Sui-Zeit (220-618). Der Einbruch westlicher Musik', ibid., columns 1205-7; 'III. Die T'ang-Zeit (618-907). Die Rolle der westländischen (Hu-)Musik. Die Zehn Orchester. Die Musik der Zewi Abteilungen. Akademien und Konservatorien,' ibid., columns 1207-16; P.C. Crossley-Holland, 'Chinese Music,' *Grove's Dictionary of Music and Musicians* (ed. E. Blom), ii (London, 1954), pp. 219-48. Dr. Eckardt's bibliography includes a valuable selection of recent Japanese publications, and materials on central Asian music and East-West musical interchange. Mr. Crossley-Holland's bibliography is virtually complete for works in European languages.

[2] The system of Romanization adopted here is that primarily due to Professor Jaw Yuanrenn of the University of California. Its main feature is that the tones are inherent in the spelling as they are in the spoken word. Knowing the system, the Romanized form can be read in its correct tone, thus reducing ambiguity. Typographically this system has the advantage that it avoids the use of all aspirates, diacritic signs, and superscript numerals. Some familiar words appear in new guise: Jou = Chou[1], Hann = Han[4], Wey = Wei[4], Tarng = T'ang[2], Sonq = Sung[4]; chyn = ch'in[2], pyipar = p'i[2]-p'a[2], shiau = hsiao[1], seh = sê[4]; Symaa Chian = Szu[1]-ma[3], Ch'ien[1], Ju Shii = Chu[1] Hsi[3]. Again, the two types of pitch-pipes, previously written alike as lü, but pronounced in two different tones: lü[3] and lü[4], are differentiated as leu and liuh. A guide to the system will be found in W. Simon, *The New Official Chinese Latin Script, Gwoyeu Romatzyh* (London, 1944).

[3] *The History of Musical Instruments* (New York, 1940); *The Rise of Music in the Ancient World, East and West* (New York, 1943).

by this interpretation, it must not be accepted as more than a working hypothesis.

Prehistory and Ethnology of the Far East

China is to be regarded as a continent apart, turning her back on the rest of Eurasia, more isolated even than India; and it is this geographical setting which has determined the main features of Chinese history.[4] Behind her natural barriers there developed a culture of such integrity that when, in the fourth century, invaders and conquerors came, it was they who were absorbed; and thus it has always been. The Chinese of Tarng times was an entirely different person, ethnically speaking, from the Chinese of Chyn and Hann times, because of this constant absorption of invaders from the north and conquered peoples in the south.[5]

Palaeolithic sites have been found in the Ordos region, and it is known that neolithic civilizations flourished in Mongolia as well as throughout the Yellow River valley. At the time of the development of high civilization at the turn of the third millennium B.C., the Chinese, or rather, the Proto-Chinese, differed from surrounding peoples in the superior organization of their agriculture rather than in physical character. Even at the present time they have linguistic relatives all over the Far East; indeed it is customary to recognize a Sino-Tibetan language-group which includes, on the one hand, Chinese and the various Thai languages of southern China and Indo-China and, on the other, the Tibeto-Burman languages of Tibet and Burma and (in China proper) of the Luoluo and Mosuo peoples of Yunnan and Syhchuan. This group does not by any means embrace all the mongoloid peoples of China, however. Not included in it are the Turco-Mongols of the Gobi Desert, and the Miau and Yau peoples of southern and southwestern China; the linguistic affinities of the two latter are still uncertain.

The invasions of north China in historic times all came from Mongolia or Manchuria, never from Shinjiang (Turkestan); that is to say, the invaders were always barbarians, never bearers of high civilization, such as were the merchants or pilgrims, transmitters of cultural gifts of the highest importance—mathematics, Buddhism, music, etc.—who passed along the Silk Road or the Buddhist Pilgrim route.

This pressure from the north provided an incentive to the progressive sinicization of southern China and perhaps led to constant movement south-wards of earlier offshoots of the mongoloid stock, the Proto-Chinese or, more generally, the palaeomongoloids. Among these one may perhaps include the Proto-Malays. The Japanese are also sometimes grouped with the palaeomongoloids. A number of characters suggest that they are a branch of the mongoloids

---

[4] R. Grousset, *L'Asie orientale des origines au XVe siècle* (Paris, 1946), p. 139.

[5] G. Haloun, 'Die Rekonstruktion der chinesischen Urgeschichte durch die Chinesen,' *Japanisch-Deutche Zeitschrift für Wissenschaft und Technik,* iii (Kobe, 1925), pp. 243-70.

separated off at a very early date; it is known that they are not the original inhabitants of much of the territory they now occupy.

Coming south to Indo-China and Indonesia, it is certain that the present ethnic complexity of this region goes back to prehistoric times. In addition to Negritos, the most ancient inhabitants seem to have included relatives of the present inhabitants of Australia, New Guinea, and Melanesia. A second and later wave of prehistoric immigrants to this region brought the Proto-Malay element, to be found in the present Bataks and Dyaks of the islands, and in the Cham and other vanished peoples of the mainland. These folk are in many respects mongoloid; their ethnological position is uncertain, but they may perhaps be placed at the base of the mongoloid stock. They have a bamboo culture, and this fact may perhaps be important as an indication of affinity with the third wave of immigrants, the brachycephalic mongoloids, who also have to some extent a bamboo culture. These entered across the north-west frontier of Indo-China, and it is possible that they brought with them the first Bronze Age culture to reach Indo-China. As compared with Europe this culture arrived comparatively late.

At the time of the unification of China at the end of the third century B.C., the southern limit of Chinese territory scarcely extended beyond the Yangtz River. Not until Hann times was southern China added to the Chinese domain; but by 111 B.C. Annam, in Indo-China, had been annexed. The Chinese continued to dominate this region during Hann times and from then until the tenth century. As early as the second and third centuries of our era, however, the colonization by the Hindus of Burma, Siam, Indonesia, and the coast of Indo-China, had begun and reached a peak in the fourth and fifth centuries,[6] so that from the earliest times there has been a clash of cultures in this area.

The presence of the Ainu in northern Japan must not be forgotten even in this brief sketch of Far Eastern ethnology. They are not mongoloids and have existed in their present position since before the arrival of the Japanese.

Considering the 'continent' of China, Indo-China, and Indonesia as a whole, evidence points to a constant movement southward of more or less mongoloid peoples. To diffusion in other directions may be ascribed the colonization of the American continent: the Eskimos, and the Indians of North and South America are mongoloids whose affinities with the Pacific area, in the widest sense, is exhibited, among other characters, in their armoury of musical instruments. With the exception of a few instruments of universal occurrence all these (or their close relatives) are to be found exclusively in China, the territory between China and India, the Malay Archipelago, and the Pacific Islands. Of the instruments used by American Indians 50 per cent occur in the Burmese hinterland and adjacent countries.[7]

In the light of this short account of ethnological relationships in the Far East, it is surely not surprising to find a marked uniformity in musical culture over the whole area, particularly with respect to more primitive features. It is known that primitive characteristics of musical culture are often preserved with great

[6]G. Coedès, *Les États hindouisés d'Indochine et d'Indonésie* (Paris, 1948), pp. 36, 81.
[7]Sachs, *The History of Musical Instruments*, p. 203.

tenacity by peoples otherwise at a high cultural level: European folk-song, for example, retains extremely primitive features.[8] The persistence in China proper, in spite of constant contact with other musical cultures (via Turkestan), of the characteristic minor third pentatonic genus, with the fourth as the dominant melodic unit, is the expression in musical terms of that vigour in her autochthonous culture to which, at the beginning of this section, her powers of absorbing conquerors and conquered were ascribed.

The Place of Music in Chinese Civilization

The views on music held by the Chinese in antiquity were remarkable in that its essence was conceived to be not sound but a transcendent power. To a considerable extent this view of the nature of music survives even to this day. The music of the seven-stringed zither (p. 347) tends constantly towards imagined sounds: a vibrato is prolonged long after all audible sound has ceased; the unplucked string, set in motion by a suddenly arrested glissando, produces a sound scarcely audible even to the performer. In the hands of performers of an older generation the instrument tends to be used to suggest, rather than to produce, sounds.

As early as the date of compilation of the *Joulii* (*The Ceremonial of the State of Jou*) in the third century B.C., a system relating musical sounds to the order of the Universe had been worked out. Its elaboration forms part of that scientific systematization of knowledge which took place between the fifth and the third centuries B.C. (the period of the Warring States), after the decay of the feudal system and at a time when the process of fusion to form states[9] had already begun. At a very early date, at least as early as the *Leu Shyh Chuenchiou* (*The Spring and Autumn of Leu Buhwei*), 239 B.C., a theory was devised by which the notes of the Chinese musical world could be derived from a fundamental pitch-pipe by simple arithmetical operations. The orderly generation of sounds from a fundamental by this procedure was equated with other types of order in the Universe: with the four directions, with the categories of substance, with the orderly sequence of the seasons.[10]

> (F) Autumn
> (C) Spring
> (G) Winter
> (D) Summer

This system was extended and worked out in a manner analogous to that of similar systems in India, Islam, ancient Greece, and the Christian Middle Ages.

In an attempt to preserve the harmonious correspondence between their system of sounds and the order of the Universe, the Chinese were early faced

[8] Sachs, *The Rise of Music in the Ancient World*, p.296.
[9] Haloun, op. cit., pp. 243-6.
[10] Sachs, *The Rise of Music*, p. 110.

with the problem of fixing an absolute pitch. The pitch-pipes were not only of standard length but of standard capacity, and it is understandable that the Imperial Bureau of Music became part of the Imperial Bureau of Weights and Measures.

The belief in the power of music to sustain (or if improperly used to destroy) Universal Harmony was but an extension of the belief in the magic power of sounds. As a manifestation of a state of the soul, a single sound had the power of influencing other souls for good or ill. By extension, it could influence objects and all the phenomena of Nature. Symaa Chian (163–85 B.C.) describes two zither tunes of magic power:[11] when the first was played, two groups of eight black cranes appeared at the opening strain; at the second strain, they stretched out their necks and cried, extended their wings and began to dance.

The conditions under which the zither might be played (up to fifty years ago) were originally of magical significance, but gradually their significance was forgotten until they became merely symbolic of the ideal way of life of the *literatus*[12] In Ming times the playing of the zither was forbidden to women (though that did not prevent their playing it), and it was forbidden to perform before any but cultured persons. The fact that the zither became the favourite instrument of Taoist and Buddhist monks meant that it exchanged its more ancient magical associations for those of the monastery, but that it retained at all times the power to command a respectful hearing.

The categories of hieratic and popular music are to be distinguished in most cultures, in antiquity as in recent times, but China is perhaps unique in the extent to which ritual music came to be regarded as an effective regulator of the harmony of the Universe in general and of the State in particular, so that the first duty of the Ruler was to look to the perfect maintenance of tradition in the execution of the music and ritual of the State.

Chinese Musical Instruments

The earliest Chinese documents (*c.* 1300–1050 B.C.) are inscriptions on fragments of bone recording the decisions of the tortoise-bone oracle. A number of these contain characters either certainly or possibly depicting musical instruments, and it has been suggested that they provide evidence for the use of drums struck by a drum-stick, bells on a wooden stand struck by a stick, suspended triangular stones struck by a padded stick, and a horn struck with a stick.[13]

Excavations on the famous Shang sites in the plain of north-east China at Anyang have yielded sonorous stones *(chinq)* (pl. 1 *(b)*) and a globular flute *(shuin)*. The former are L-shaped slabs of calcareous stone which (according to

---

[11]Symaa Chian, *Shyyjih* (17), xxiv, fo. 37 vᵒ. Translated in R.H. van Gulik, *The Lore of the Chinese Lute* (Tokyo, 1940), p. 137.

[12]R.H. van Gulik, op. cit., pp. 134-48.

[13]E.H. Gibson, 'Music and Musical Instruments of Shang,' *Journal of The North China Branch of the Royal Asiatic Society*, lxviii (Shanghai, 1937), pp. 8-18.

the pictographs in bone inscriptions) were hung from a frame and struck with a padded stick. The *shiun* from the Shang site is barrel-shaped and about 2½ inches high, carved with an ogre-mask. Hollow, with an apical blow-hole and five finger-holes in the side, it is said to produce the note-series: *do re mi fa sol*.[14]

In many of the folk-songs and dynastic songs from the Book of Songs *(Shyjing)* often said to have been selected by Confucius, but probably only used by him for purposes of instruction—references to music occur specifically mentioning some of the instruments supposed to be represented in the bone characters or found in Shang sites. According to Sachs's tentative chronology of primitive instruments, flutes with holes, and drums, such as are mentioned in these songs, belong to the middle neolithic stratum; they occur in neolithic sites and are distributed over several continents. The sonorous stones are also included among neolithic instruments. In some songs there are references to bells; these are the Bronze Age counterpart of sonorous stones.

Whistle flutes of clay, with or without finger holes, occur in China as children's toys. In Shikang there is a whistle flute with four finger holes in the form of a frog; and there are specimens with two finger holes from Gueyjou in the form. of a bird. The fact that in each case the whistle has the shape of an animal may well be significant. Such clay whistle flutes are also to be found in central America and may be a legacy from a late neolithic substrate. A bamboo whistle-flute is reported to have been seen in funeral processions fifty years ago.[15]

The Shang were overthrown by the Jou about 1050 B.C., and many songs in the *Shyjing* suggest a considerable increase in the number of instruments used by the Jou (1050–255 B.C.). In addition to sonorous stones and stone-chimes, bells and bell-chimes, their idiophones include the percussion clapper *(chongdwu)* (pl. 4 *(a)* the trough *(juh)* resembling a rice-pounding mortar with pestle; and the tiger *(yeu)*, with a serrated strip of wood along its back, thrice scraped to mark the end of the music. Scrapers (according to Sachs) are idiophones reaching back to the earliest neolithic stratum; there is some evidence that they have a life-giving significance as charms. The Jou armoury of instruments also included chordophones, for the existence of which in Shang times there is no evidence. Thus the first of the songs (in the traditional order) refers to welcoming the noble lady: 'With *chyn* and *seh* we hearten her.' The two instruments referred to are both half-tube zithers (using Sachs's nomenclature) of which the former (or a descendant) is still in use as the classical seven-stringed zither *(chyn)* and the latter *(seh)* survives in a descendant with thirteen brass strings, the *jeng*.[16] New aerophones include the mouth-organ, *sheng* (pl. 1 *(a)*), two cross flutes, *yoh* and *chyr*, a double pipe, *goan*, and the panpipes, *shiau*. Several sorts of drum, including one of earthenware, are mentioned.

From the *Yilii (Rites and Ceremonies)*, edited at the latest in the third

[14]H.G. Creel, *The Birth of China* (New York, 1937), p. 99.

[15]A.C. Moule, 'A List of the Musical and other Sound-Producing Instruments of the Chinese,' *Journal of the North China Branch of the Royal Asiatic Society,* xxxix (1908), pp. 1-160.

[16]Cf. *The History of Music in Sound* (H.M.V.), i, side 1.

century B.C., we have the following description of the distribution of the orchestra at the great archery tournament:

> On the day before the shoot are suspended, for the musicians, to the east of the eastern steps, facing west, the sonorous stones associated with the mouth-organs; south of these are the bells *(jong)* associated with the mouth-organs, and south of these are other bells *(boh)*: all these are arranged in order towards the south. West of the eastern steps a drum is set up; it is beaten from the south. The answering drum *(byi)* is to the east of this; it is struck from the south. To the west of the western steps are the sonorous stones associated with laudatory declamation; they face east. To the south of these are bells *(jong)* and to the south of these are other bells *(boh)*; these are all arranged in order towards the south. To the south of all these a drum is set up; it is struck from the east. To the north of this is the starting drum *byi*. A drum is set up to the east of the western steps, it faces south. In the space between the set-up drums are the bamboos [flutes and mouth organs, presumably]. The hand-drum, *taur* [struck by two buttons on two strings] rests on the western cords supporting the sonorous stones associated with laudatory declamation.[17] (See pl. 1*(b)*.)

The *chyn* probably had but five strings originally, the number being later increased to seven. The *seh* had twenty-six strings of silk-gut. The *jeng*, which survives particularly in southern and south-western China,[18] has thirteen brass strings and seems to be a small version of the *seh*; it is the only one of the half-tube zithers which includes the bamboo determinative in its ideograph. This may perhaps be regarded as support for the theory that it was originally made from an internode of bamboo divided down the middle into two half-cylinders.

The mouth-organ, *sheng*,[19] is always symbolized by a gourd (as the *shiun* is by clay, and the flutes by bamboo) and at some period a gourd formed (and in some places still forms) the wind-chest; among a number of primitive peoples playing the instrument today, however, the wind-chest is made of wood, and in China and Japan it is often made of lacquer. Thirteen or so slender bamboo pipes, differing in length, are arranged so that each opens into the wind-chest by an aperture covered by a free reed of copper. A small hole in the pipe near the reed is stopped at will, so that a sufficient back pressure can be produced for the reed to be set vibrating when the pressure in the wind-chest is raised or lowered by blowing into or sucking the mouth-piece. The reed may be tuned by weighting with wax. The number of pipes has varied considerably in China at

[17] *Yilii*, vii.

[18] R.H. van Gulik, 'Brief Note on the Cheng, the Chinese Small Cither,' *Tòyò Ongaku Kenkyū*, xi (Tokyo, 1951), pp. 10-25.

[19] F.W. Eastlake, 'The "Sho" or Chinese Reed Organ,' *China Review*, xi (Hong Kong, 1882-3, pp. 33-41; L.C. Goodrich, 'The Chinese Shéng and Western Musical Instruments,' *China Magazine*, xvii (New York, 1941) pp. 10, 11, 14; L.M. Traynor and S. Kishibe, 'On the Four Unknown Pipes of the Shō (Mouth Organ) used in Ancient Japanese Court Music,' *Tòyò Ongaku Kenkyū*, ix (Tokyo, 1951), pp. 22-53.

different epochs, and among non-Chinese tribes the number is much less at the present time. They are so arranged that the lower notes can be accompanied by their octave or fourth or fifth. The *tessitura* of the modern Chinese instrument is soprano, but it is very probable that the early forms were of considerably lower pitch. It is known from late Bronze Age figured drums, probably of the fourth century B.C.[20] found in northern Annam[21] that the *sheng* in use at that time closely resembled the large forms found among the tribes-people in southern China at the present day, and accordingly must have had a range approximating to D–d.

Mention must also be made of the *jiun*, a stringed instrument used by the Jou for determining the pitch of bells; it consisted of strings mounted on a resonating table, 7 feet long.

The political unification of China brought about between 250 and 220 B.C. by King Jenq of Chyn *Chyn Shyy Hwangdih)* was followed by the downfall of the unifier's dynasty and the succession to power of the Hann, during whose reign extensive contacts with various nomadic peoples on the north-western frontier of the Chinese empire, as well as with central and western Asia and India, led to the appearance of new musical instruments in Chinese orchestras. Chief of these was the *pyipar*, a short lute. It is reported to have been played on horseback[22] and seems to have been a short-necked instrument with a circular body, four strings, and twelve frets.

Jing Farng, Imperial Secretary in 45 B.C., devised a stringed instrument after the fashion of a *seh*, the *joen*, in function resembling the *jiun* of the Jou, for it was used to fix the sound of the sixty notes into which Jing Farng divided the octave (p.00).

Some of the earliest representations of zithers, stone chimes, *sheng*, vertical flutes, panpipes, and the drum known as *ingguu* occur in the shallow bas-reliefs from Hann times on the walls of the Wuu family tombs in Shandong province.[23] On other Hann reliefs cross-flutes occur. In some of these Hann scenes the *chyn* is shown with but five strings.

By late Wey times, that is, some two centuries after the overthrow of the Chinese empire in the third century A.D. by mercenaries settled on the northern frontier, the *pyipar* begins to appear in bas-reliefs as a four- or five-stringed, pear-shaped, bent-necked lute and may have resembled the *gaku biwa* of the Japanese court orchestra—an instrument over 3 feet in length.

A vertical angular harp also came to China in late Wey times, and representations are to be seen in the frescoes at Duenhwang and on many stelae

---

[20]B. Karlgren, 'The Date of the Early Dong-so'n Culture,' *Bulletin of the Museum of Far Eastern Archaeology*s xiv (Stockholm, 1942, pp. 1-28.

[21]V. Goloubew, 'L'Age du bronze au Tonkin et dans le Nord-Annam,' *Bulletin de l'école française de l'extrême orient*, xxix (Hanoy, 1929), pp. 1-46.

[22]Liou Shi, *Shyhming* (46). See L.E.R. Picken, 'The Origin of the Short Lute,' *Galpin Society Journal*, viii (1955), pp. 32-42.

[23]H.E. Fernald, 'Ancient Chinese Musical Instruments,' *Museum Journal* (Philadelphia, 1936). Reprinted in Hsiao Ch'ien, *A Harp with a Thousands Strings* (London, 1944), pp. 395-440.

of the sixth century A.D.[23] According to size the harp had sixteen to twenty-five strings and is referred to in Chinese texts as *konghour* (pl. 2 *(a)*). It did not establish itself in China as did other instruments originally imported in court orchestras from abroad.

The Shoosooin (Nara, Japan) preserves several Chinese *pyipars* of Tarng date (A.D. 600–900). This was an era of extensive intercourse between China and central Asia. Many new instruments and many types of orchestra were introduced, usually associated with their own dancers, jugglers, or acrobats, characteristically costumed. The size and composition of these orchestras is known from Tarng frescoes in the Thousand Buddha Caves at Duenhwang and from the Tarng histories.

Toy globular flutes with two finger holes occur in Tarng kiln-sites in the neighbourhood of the provincial capital of Syhchuan; some have the form of quasi-human heads. They furnish an instance of the survival as toys of ancient musical instruments whose ritual use has been forgotten.

Relatives of the *pyipar* in use at the present time, and possibly introduced in Tarng times, are the *yuehchyn*, a four-stringed flat lute, the strings of which are said to be tuned in pairs a fifth apart; and the *sanshyan*, a three-stringed flat lute, played with a jade plectrum; the strings are tuned: *do fa do* or *do re la*.

To the same period of importation probably belong the various bowed instruments, of which a considerable variety are in use in China today. Bowed instruments are first mentioned in Persia in the ninth century[24] and a reference to a bowed zither, related to the *jeng*, occurs in a Chinese account of a Khitan orchestra playing at the Chinese court about A.D. 900. An instrument of this kind was in fairly common use in Pekin up to fifty years ago.[25]

Bowed lutes (that is, fiddles) arose at a slightly later date, and all varieties found in China are known collectively as *hwuchyn* ('barbarian' *chyn*), suggesting that the instrument came to China from central Asia. The *ellhwu* is perhaps the commonest form of *hwuchyn*.[26] It has a hexagonal tubular wooden body a few inches long, one end of which is covered with snakeskin, the other end is open; the whole acts as a resonator. The handle is inserted into the body at right angles to its long axis. There are two strings of silk-gut tuned a fifth apart, stopped by the fleshy part of the fingers, and the hair of the bow passes between the strings. The instrument is played with constant vibrato and glissandi and has a veiled tone of great beauty.

It is interesting to note that a dulcimer in use in south China today bears the name of *yangchyn*, the 'foreign' zither. It resembles the Persian dulcimer known as *santir*, but its distribution on the south-eastern seaboard suggests that it reached China from the sea rather than from central Asia.

[24] Sachs, *The History of Musical Instruments*, p. 216.

[25] A.C. Moule, op. cit., p. 120. In relation to a number of points in the history of Chinese instruments see T. Norlind, 'Beiträge zur chinesischen Instrumentengeschichte,' *Svensk Tidskrift för Musikforskning*, xv (1933), pp. 48-83. See also: F.A. Kuttner, 'The Musical Significance of Archaic Chinese Jades of the *Pi*-Disk Type,' *Artibus Asiae*, xvi 1/2 (Ascona, 1953), pp. 25-50.

[26] A *hwuchyn* leads the ensemble in *The History of Music in Sound*, i, side 3 (*b*).

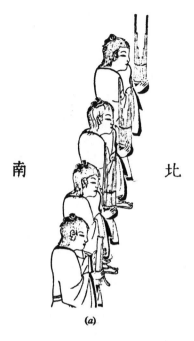

南　　北

(a)

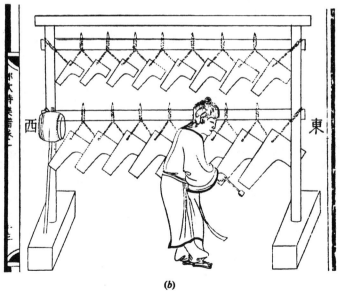

西　　東

(b)

(a) CHINESE PLAYERS OF MOUTH-ORGAN AND
PERCUSSION-CLAPPER

(b) CHINESE SONOROUS STONES AND HAND-DRUM

From Prince Ju Tzayyuh, *The Handbook of Music* (1596)

History of Theory and Notation

The writings of Leu Buhwei from 239 B.C. contain an account of the making of the pitch-pipes by Ling Luen: *ling* means music or musician, *luen* is a rule or to rule.[27] The name and the person were invented in the course of that scientific reconstruction by the Chinese of their own prehistory which occurred in the period of the Warring States. There are no grounds for regarding the passage so often quoted from Leu Buhwei as other than a rationalization; it does not concern a historic figure nor does it include any precise geographical indications—the terms usually translated as place names are in fact general terms for geographical features:

> He [Music Ruler] gathered bamboos in a valley on a mountain pass, taking those grown of uniform bore and thickness, and cut between two nodes; the length of the piece being three inches and nine tenths, he blew it, making this to be the *do* of Yellow Bell [the fundamental of the Chinese system].[28]

At the present time the scale most characteristic of the Far East (as defined at the beginning of this chapter) is pentatonic without semitones, consisting of three whole tones and two minor thirds, the thirds being separated by one or two whole tones. The scale has the form:

do re mi sol la.

The ancient names for this series, as pronounced today, are:

gong shang jeau jyy yeu.

The evidence for the existence of five-note melodies in early Jou times is confined to references to the 'five degrees,' and to the names of the five notes in texts compiled in the third or fourth centuries B.C. The same texts contain references to the seven sounds or the seven 'beginnings,' and it has been supposed that these indicate that a seven-note scale with two semitones was known even in Jou times. The first definition of the notes is that given by Symaa Chian in the second century B.C.

The process by which the lowest note (Yellow Bell) engendered the rest of the notes in the Chinese system is also described in the writings of Leu Buhwei: 'To the three parts of the generator add one part, making the superior generation. From the three parts of the generator reject one part, making the lower generation.'[29] The interpretation of this passage is that the complete note-series (of which the names are also given) was obtained by cutting bamboo

[27] G. Haloun, *Tocharer und Indogermanen* (Lepizig, 1926), pp. 156 ff.
[28] *Leu Shyh Chuenchiou,* v. *Guu Yueh* (61).
[29] *Leu Shyh Chuenchiou,* vi. *Inliuh* (63).

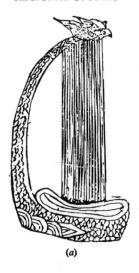

(a)

古怨

泛聲

兮不逮懷後來兮何處屢回顧

世事兮何據手翻覆兮雲雨過金谷兮花謝委塵土

悲佳人兮薄命誰為主豈不猶有春兮妾自傷

土運暮髮將素

歡有窮兮恨無數弦欲絕兮聲苦滿目江山兮淚

沾屨君不見年年汾水上兮惟秋雁飛去

(b)

(a) CHINESE ROC-HEADED VERTICAL HARP WITH 18 STRINGS

From Chern Yang, *Yueh Shu* (13th-14th century)

(b) CHINESE 7-STRINGED ZITHER TABLATURE

From the end of the 12th century

tubes (of the same diameter) to lengths calculated by alternately subtracting and adding one-third of the length of the preceding tube, so that the ratio of the length of any pipe to that of the next in the series was as 3:2 or as 3:4. The notes given by pipes two-thirds of the length of their predecessors in the series were said to belong to the inferior generation; these are the six female *leu*, made (according to legend) from the singing of the female roc. The six remaining notes were said to belong to the superior generation; these are the six male *liuhs* made (according to legend) from the singing of the male roc. Theoretically this procedure yielded a chain of ascending fifths and descending fourths:

and, if arranged in ascending order, the note sequence:

F, F♯, G, G♯, A, A♯, B, C, C♯, D, D♯, E.

The *liuhleu* (the complete note-series) was not a 'chromatic scale,' but an array of all the notes in the Chinese musical firmament of the third century B.C. The process of generation described in the writings of Leu Buhwei presumably provided an approximate theory, satisfying the desire for order of those engaged at that time in systematizing the sum total of human knowledge. Similarly, the two 'whole-tone scales' of the male and female *liuh* (both *leu* and *liuh* are referred to collectively as the twelve *liuh*) were the result of a classification of the series into two groups by origin; there is no evidence that the Chinese musical genius at any time found expression in melodies referable to whole-tone scales.

It is certain that melodies making use of various scales must have existed before the *liuhleu*. The latter provided a theoretical means of deriving an array of notes, any one of which (again in theory) could act as *do* (that is, *gong*) in the five-note series. A pentatonic scale has five loci of modal inversion: that is, the series may begin (and end) on each of the five notes in turn, giving five modes. Each mode takes the name of the note which is *finalis*, which ends melodies in that mode. It is probable that the fact that different melodies were in different modes had been recognized at a very early date, and that transposition of the modes, changing the *liuh* selected as tonic, was practised.

Obviously, variation in the unit of length on which the length of the fundamental pitch-pipe was based at different times must have meant that absolute pitch was never attained. Under the Jou the minimal length of the Yellow Bell pipe is estimated to have been 20 centimetres. Europeans have accepted pitches of F (Amiot), E (Courant), D (van Aalst), E (Mahillon).[30] For convenience the value of F will be adopted here.

The fact that so many of the *liuhleu* bear the name of *jong* (bell) suggests that part of the original note-series may have been a set of bells (like the celestas or kettle-gong chimes in the Balinese orchestra). It is known that by 500 B.C. bells

[30] For references see Bibliography, pp. 482-3.

were cast in sets of six or seven members bearing, in some cases, names similar to those of bells in the *liuhleu* series. It is also possible that the names of the *liuhleu* were originally applied to a note-series differing from the *liuhleu* of Leu Buhwei.

Folk-Song

The scientific study of Chinese folk-music has scarcely begun, for though many collections are now being made, no collector, so far as is known, has as yet made recordings in the field; all depend on the ear. From personal observations made during a brief stay in central China it seems probable that traces of other and older types of scalar structure survive in the folk-music. This is suggested by street-cries collected in Syhchuan and Gueyjou Provinces. The enharmonic tetrachord (a fourth built up from a major third and a minor second) of the Japanese modes *hirazyoosi, kumoizyoosi,* and *iwatozyoosi* is rare in classical Chinese music and *jingshih*; it occurs, however, in the following street-cry:

Ex. 1

Again, chains of thirds, so striking a feature of Western, African, Polynesian, and American Indian music, rarely occur in classical Chinese music, so strong is the tendency for a minor third to form a unit by adding a major second; yet Exs. 2 and 3 (also street-cries) are both expanded triads:

Ex. 2

Ex. 3

Ex. 3 illustrates a primitive stage of the 123 scale[1] (E, F, G, B) in which two superposed thirds form a pentachord and the lower third is filled in (123.5). Ex. 4 is interesting in that the fourths are only acciacaturas:

Ex. 4

One feature of everyday life in China which impresses the stranger is the singing of the coolies; when pulling or carrying loads, they improvise a seemingly

[31]Wang Kwang-chi, 'Uber die chinesische klassische Oper 1530-1860,' *Orient et Occident, Bibliothèque Sino-Internationale* (Geneva, 1934).

continuous chant, which has the function of coordinating activities and maintaining the rate of working at the optimum pace set by the leader. It is in fact an antiphon between leader and gang, in which statement and answer tread so closely on each other's heels that the sound is effectively continuous. Ex. 5 might be sung (to the vowel sound 'ah') by men pulling a loaded cart up hill.

Ex. 5

Ex. 6, on the other hand, might be sung by men trotting with a load slung on poles.

Ex. 6

In such improvised antiphons it is the leader alone who varies his utterance with successive repetitions. The answer frequently overlaps the statement. Sometimes one hears 'shanties' such as the following:

Ex. 7

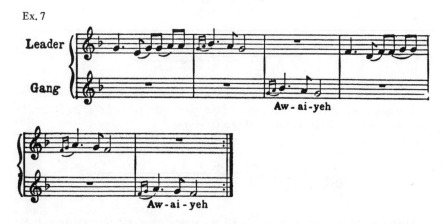

An excellent short collection of popular Chinese songs, many of them folk-songs, has been published by C.H. and S.H. Chen.[33] The collection merits

[32] Sachs, *The Rise of Music in the Ancient World*, p. 123.

praise not only for the notable accuracy of its transcriptions but for the quality of the accompaniments devised by C.H. Chen. In themselves they provide useful material for studying melodic variation and heterophony in Chinese music.

Ex. 8 is a well-known folk-song, sung to different words in different districts.[34] It is a good example of pure pentatonic genus, still characteristic of Chinese melody in spite of the constant infiltration of other genera from central Asia. Another purely pentatonic folk-song is shown in Ex. 9, taken from a setting by Liu Shea-An [*sic*][35]

Ex. 8

Ex. 9

Within the last few years many popular collections of folk-songs from all provinces have been printed in China, transcribed in the numerical notation. Though popular in character, these collections are of the greatest value and already enable us to determine the regions of transition to types of melody resembling those of western Asia.

Buddhist Music

The music of the Buddhist office as practised in Chinese monasteries deserves special attention, since it embodies many features at first sight foreign to the Chinese musical genius. While some of these may well be due to Indian and Tibetan influence, some may echo that more primitive stratum of folk-music

[33]C.H. and S.H. Chen, *The Flower Drum and other Chinese Songs* (New York, 1943). Other folk-tunes are to be found in A.G. Jacobs, *The Chinese-American Song and Game Book* (New York, 1944), and S.M. Graves and M.F. Farley, *Min River Boat Songs* (New York, 1946).

[34]For another version of this tune see Hsiao Shusien, 'La chanson populaire chinoise, *Sinologica*, i (Basel, 1947), pp. 65-86.

[35]Liu Shea-An, *Three Songs* (Tokyo, 1935).

revealed in the street-cries already discussed. In a small monastery in Anshuenn, Gueyjou Province, novices in their teens have been heard chanting the scriptures in thirds (cf. the English and Scandinavian *gymel* of the twelfth century). The range of cantillation was a fourth, and the result could be placed alongside Lachmann's juxtaposition of the German folk-song 'Laterne, Laterne!' and Hornbostel's Macusi Indian melody[36] as an example of the survival in China of tendencies observable in very primitive musical cultures elsewhere. At a funeral in a small country town, Meitarn in Gueyjou Province, Buddhist priests were heard singing, to the accompaniment of cymbals and triangle, a metrical chant of that infectious gaiety so common in India and so rare in China. The aspect of Buddhist music which most merits study, however, is the singing of the office by precentor and novices. The instrumental accompaniment is provided entirely by idiophones and membranophones; the instruments include a large drum, a large bell, a gong, cymbals, a triangle, a small bell, and a wooden fish. The office begins with intoned statements and responses by precentor and novices, with occasional interruptions by single instruments. As the service proceeds the speed of recitation increases, and the precentor no longer waits for the novices to end their response before recommencing; as the overlapping antiphon develops, the frequency of percussive interruptions increases.[37]

Concerning the Taoist office no information is available. Several hymns making use of a notation unlike any other Chinese notation are printed in the Ming *Dawtzanq*. They have not been transcribed.

---

[36]R. Lachmann, 'Musik der außereuropäischen Natur- und Kulturvölker,' *Handbuch der Musikwissenschaft* (Potsdam, 1929), p. 8; quoted by Sachs in *The Rise of Music in the Ancient World*, p. 40.

[37]See also A. Stanley, 'Putoshan,' *Journal of the North China Branch of the Royal Asiatic Society*, xlvi (1915), pp. 1-18.

PRACTICAL APPROACHES TO JAPANESE MUSIC
William P. Malm
Introduction

Japanese music, like the other Japanese fine arts, has gone through several marked stylistic changes. These extend over a period from approximately the seventh century to the present day. During the Nara and Heian periods Buddhist chanting and court orchestral music *(gagaku)* flourished while the Kamakura and Muromachi periods saw the rise of *biwa* lute accompanied narratives and a host of theatricals which culminated in the *noh* drama and its music. The Edo period luxuriated in music for the thirteen stringed *koto* zither, the end-blown *shakuhachi* flute, and the three stringed *shamisen*. The latter became an essential element in the *bunraku* puppet plays and the *kabuki* theatre. In the twentieth century, traditional musicians made several efforts to meet the challenge of western music, with varying degrees of success. Through all these periods of music history certain fundamental Japanese musical characteristics can be found. Their specific applications change with each period as, for example, in the West the concept of many-part (polyphonic) music in the thirteenth century varies vastly from that of the sixteenth, eighteenth, or twentieth centuries. The principles to be discussed have an importance to Japanese music analogous to polyphony in western music. Continuing the analogy, an awareness of the western fondness for several different lines of music sounding simultaneously is certainly one useful guide to understanding western music in general. With such knowledge one could go on to distinguish periods or styles of music in which a more vertical (harmonic) orientation is present such as early classical music, hymns, or modern folk singing, and traditions in which a more horizontal (contrapuntal) orientation dominates as in fugues, twelve tone music, and Dixieland. By this process, ideally, one becomes an "intelligent" music lover. The principles in Japanese music presented below can also be subjected to such a process of refinement. My intent in this article, however, is not to create a new body of Japanese music lovers, but rather to provide guidelines for an intelligent approach to Japan's various music traditions.

Basic Concepts in Japanese Music

The characteristics of Japanese music fall under three general headings; 1) the sound ideal, 2) the structural ideal, and 3) the artistic intent. In actual practice, of course, these three areas are difficult to separate.

THE SOUND IDEAL. A basic concept in most Japanese music is to get the maximum effect from the minimum amount of material. Many times the full technical possibilities of an instrument have not been exploited in order to concentrate the player's and the listener's attention on a deliberately restricted sound spectrum. The *taiko* stick drum of the *noh* and *kabuki* theatres is a good example. It has two cowhide heads stretched over iron rings some twenty inches in diameter and lashed over a barrel-shaped body which is suspended off the floor by a special frame. One could play some brilliant solos on the *taiko* by banging away on its rim and heads, but the Japanese play it only on a small circle of deerskin set in the center of one head. The slightly muffled yet resonant tone that results is a musical equivalent of the *shibui* colors of Japanese fabrics and other materials. It is a brightness showing through a subtle dullness. Since part of art is, by definition, artifice, it is important to realize just how deliberate such effects can be. In the case of this *taiko* sound, one finds that it is capable of still further refinement. When the drum is used in pieces which contain dramatic dances the ropes that lash the skins to the body are tightened so that the pitch of the sound is higher while in more lyrical compositions the pitch is lowered. It is the combination of many such "little" things that creates artistry in the performance of any music, be it by Beethoven or Kineya Rokusaemon, the Sixth.

A restriction of the sound spectrum does not mean a sameness of sound. It means, rather, looking for variety in a microcosmos instead of a macrocosmos. Consider the sound of the thirteen stringed *koto* zither as an example. Its harp-like tone has often appealed to foreigners and, judging from personal experience, the soothing sameness of its sound apparently makes it an ideal background music for "oriental" parties. When one actually studies *koto* music it becomes apparent that its supposedly plain classical melodies are subjected to a large number of subtle variations. The strings of the instrument can be twisted, pushed down, or stroked in a variety of ways, each of which adds its own special color to the tones of the instrument. Of course, to be effective these techniques must in themselves be used with restraint. One can often judge the artistry of a performance by the player's sense of taste in the distribution of such ornamentations.[1]

Another aspect of the Japanese sound ideal is the chamber music approach. While this idea is partially an extension of the maximum effect-minimum material axiom, it has additional connotations. By a chamber music approach I mean that no matter how large the ensemble becomes, the individual instruments are meant to be heard. The antithesis to this is found in the orchestral music approach of the western romantic and impressionistic schools in which the sounds of individual instruments are merged into one massive musical color. The chamber music sound can easily be heard in such ensembles as the western piano trio (piano, violin, and cello) or in Japanese *sankyoku (koto, shakuhachi,* and *shamisen)*. It is my contention, however, that the principle applies as well to the larger Japanese ensembles such as the *gagaku* court orchestra and the *kabuki nagauta* ensemble.[2] In *gagaku* the arpeggios of the pear-shaped *biwa* lute and the court *koto (gaku-so)* are clearly etched against the harmonic matrix of the *sho* mouth organ. The melody played on the *hichiriki* oboe differs slightly from that of the flute and those who have heard the *hichiriki's* tone quality would agree that it would be unlikely to merge with any other sound. The sounds of the interpunctuating drums and gong are also distinct. In the *kabuki* ensemble, the stacatto-like notes of the *shamisen* are clearly separated from the vocal line. In very lyrical sections a bamboo flute is used which tends to merge with the vocal sound, but even in this case the flute's ornamentations help to separate its line from the voice and *shamisen.* When the *noh* flute *(nokan)* is used in *kabuki,* it differs from the voice and *shamisen* parts not only in melody but in tonality. The three drums of the *kabuki* (borrowed along with the *nokan* from the *hayashi* ensemble of the *noh* drama) also present contrasting sounds. Besides the *taiko* stick drum mentioned earlier there is a *ko-tsuzumi* shoulder drum and an *o-tsuzumi* side drum. Though both *tsuzumi* are played with the right hand, their tones are quite different. The *ko-tsuzumi* produces four different sounds, the most characteristic being a deep, trailing "pon." The *tsuzumi* by contrast produces a sharp, hard, cracking sound. Put all these *kabuki* sounds together and you have great variety but little coalescence. This is the essence of the Japanese chamber music sound ideal, distinctness versus coalescence. Such an ideal is not exclusively Japanese. It is found, for example, in most Near Eastern and Indian ensembles as well as in medieval and renaissance Europe performance practice. Nevertheless, it is a useful point of contrast between Japanese music and the western symphonic tradition as well as between Japanese music and the *gamelan* orchestras of Indonesia, similar ensembles in Southeast Asia, and the theatre orchestras of China.

THE STRUCTURAL INTENT. In most music the basic structural unit is the melody. By extending the time span of our structural hearing we are able to recognize phrases, periods, sections, and entire pieces as coherent units. In the last three hundred years of western music there has been a general tendency to hear individual melodies in two parts and entire pieces in rounded or closed forms. The western two part attitude is often expressed in such terms as question and answer, arsis and thesis, or antecedent and consequent. Thus, for example, the first four notes of Beethoven's Fifth Symphony (G G G E flat) require for us a four note answer (F F F D). In addition, we presume that, if this theme is important to the work, it is likely to show up again somewhere near the end of the piece if not earlier. This is what is meant by a rounded approach to form, the feeling that material heard earlier should return.

In addition to being frequently used in art music, binary tunes and rounded forms are also characteristic of most western folk and popular music. In binary tunes like "Clementine," for example, we presume that a line like the one ending ". . . excavating for a mine" must be answered by a line like the one ending ". . . and his daughter, Clementine." As for rounded forms, one has only to think of the AABA form of such old standards as "Sweet Sue," "Blue Moon," or "Smoke Gets in Your Eyes" to realize that the rounded form has long been a way of life in tinpan alley, not to mention the "gay nineties" or Stephen Foster.

In Japanese folk and popular music there are many binary tunes and rounded forms. The two part melodies are also common in art music. There are, however, a very large number of Japanese examples which divide the melody into three parts and use what is called an open form, i.e., a form in which the material first heard does not return later.

Many examples of three part melodies can be found in the vocal music of the *noh* drama called *utaii* or *yokyoku.* For example, the standard 7-5 syllable division of a line such as "Sore kato omou, omo kage no" from the play *Hana gatami* would seem to require a two part division but, when set in the typical eight beat phrase of *noh,* it looks as follows (Gakudo 1922: 135):

$$
|\!\leftarrow\!\!\text{---}\text{---}\text{ JO}\text{---}\text{---}\!\rightarrow\!|\!\leftarrow\!\text{---}\text{ HA }\text{---}\text{---}\text{---}\text{ KYU}\!\rightarrow\!|
$$

$$
\begin{array}{cccccccc}
1 & 2 & 3 & 4 & 5 & 6 & 7 & 8 \\
\end{array}
$$

so——re ka-to——o-mo-u——o-mo ka-ge no——

In *noh* the terms used to describe these divisions are *jo-ha-kyu,* introduction, scattering, and rushing. These divisions are reinforced by the accompanying drummers who tend to place special vocal calls *(kakegoe)* before the third, fifth, and seventh beats. There also tend to be more drum beats played during the rushing *kyu* section just as, in the example above, there are more syllables at that point.

Larger applications of the *jo-ha-kyu* concept can be found by studying an entire *noh* drama for its many sections can be arranged in three large divisions (Tatsuo 1957: 181-200). Actually, the terms *jo-ha-kyu* first appeared in Japan as general divisions in the ancient court dances *(bugaku).* Since that time they have been used to explain both the minute and general meaning of pieces from many genre. The subdivisions of *nagauta shamisen* music, for example, have often been arranged like *noh* music in three parts (Malm 1963: 36, 40, 118). In *gidayu* music from the puppet theatre one can find acts divided into three sections called *kuchi, naka,* and *kiri.*

While some of the applications of a three part form on Japanese music have been artificial twentieth century superimpositions, the very fact that the Japanese musician turns to *jo-ha-kyu* or some equivalent tripartite term when he is forced to explain something shows that it forms part of his basic attitude towards music. It is his "natural" first reaction just as the binary approach is "natural" for the westerner. The term natural has been put in quotes because neither approach is really the result of natural laws. Both are the result of cultural conditioning. Both are valid, but their validity must be judged within their cultural context.[3] One should add that the general Japanese performer, like his western counterpart, is wont to play his part and not intellectualize about its meaning. An understanding of the three part approach in Japanese music, however, may prove useful to the intellectualized western listener.

The reader familiar with western music has perhaps by now evoked the famous three part sonata allegro form of western classical music (exposition, development, and recapitulation) to confound my generalizations. The entire approach of this form to the musical material, however, is totally different from that found in Japan. Indeed, it is very important to realize that one must not listen in Japanese music for returning themes or thematic development, at least, not as they occur in western symphonies and sonatas. There are, of course, Japanese forms in which material is repeated. In court orchestra music *(gagaku)*, for example, melodies are often broken into three or more sections which are repeated in various ways (Harich-Schneider 1953: 49-74). In addition, *koto* variation pieces *(danmono)* display a kind of developmental technique in which a main melodic figure begins each section *(dan)* of the variations while the rest of the material relates to this "theme," some other earlier material, or is an accretion of new ideas which in turn may be varied in a later section.[4] The music of the *noh* flute displays a similar variation and accretion technique.

These various examples not withstanding, the western listener is generally more aware of a seemingly endless wandering in Japanese tunes rather than a repetition of previously heard material. Obviously some new orientation is needed if the ear is to follow the logic that must be there. To find this logic, one should really approach each kind of Japanese music as an individual case capable of a solution unique from other Japanese cases. The discussion that follows, however, will deal with a principle common to many Japanese genre. This is the principle of stereotyped patterns.

Stereotyped patterns are essential to communication, be it music or Morse code. In music they play an important role in the aesthetic enjoyment of a piece because the listener tends to anticipate the coming sounds through familiarity with the patterns of the particular music. This idea is, of course, not uniquely Japanese.[5] Its specific applications in Japanese music, however, can be quite different from those of the West. The drums of the *noh* drama are an excellent example. Their music consists almost entirely of named, stereotyped rhythm patterns, usually oriented to an eight-beat phrase.[6] A practice book for a *noh* drummer (notation is never used on stage) contains only the names of the patterns to be played. It is rather like the lead sheet of a jazz pianist or the figured bass of the Baroque harpsichordist, for in each case a single symbol or term stands for a musical complex. The crucial difference in the analogy is that the western examples both deal with vertical sound complexes called chords while the Japanese example deals with horizontal rhythmic patterns. Nevertheless, the analogy can be carried even further because these rhythmic patterns, like western chords, tend to appear in given orders. Thus, by cultural conditioning, the intelligent listener to *noh* music feels a sense of closure when, for example, the *taiko* pattern *uchikomi* is followed by the pattern *kashira*. It is the same kind of satisfaction a western-trained listener receives from the final chord of an "amen" cadence.

The puppet theatre music, called *gidayu-bushi*, offers a very different approach to stereotyped patterns. One singer and one *shamisen* player carry the full musical and narrative load. Musical research in this field has only just begun, but a preliminary study shows at least two kinds of stereotyped patterns in use. First, there are a set of repertory-wide leitmotives which are clues to emotions, actions, or the character of the puppets. For example, the pattern *naki* (crying) is played high for women's weeping and low for men's. Likewise, the entrance pattern *nori* will vary considerably in its tune depending on the age and sex of the character coming on stage.

The second kind of pattern in *gidayu* serves as a clue to the formal division of the play. If, for instance, in a concert of *gidayu* music the *shamisen* begins a selection with the tune called *sanju*, one knows, even though there is no scenery, that the next section represents a change of scene from the last. If the pattern *okuri* is played the setting is the same and if *sonae* is used the performance is starting at the very beginning of the first scene of a play.[7] There are other patterns which tend to show up only at certain points within sections of the form and thus signal a formal change just as, in western classical music, the return of the first theme in its original key signals the recapitulation in sonata-allegro form. In short, patterns are clues not only to what is happening but also to what might happen next. For example, if the crying pattern *naki* is followed by *shichome* one knows that the end of an aria *(sawari)* is approaching. If narration is to follow immediately after the tears the *shamisen* will play a short phrase that ends in a sudden "wrong note" in relation to the scale in which the previous pattern was played.[8] This leaves the ear suspended, the anticipation unresolved, and leads the listener into the narration smoothly. As yet I have not found a name for this song-to-narration pattern. There are many other such unnamed stereotypes, each of which guides the perceptive listener through some specific aspect of the music. The cumulative effect of all these patterns is a sense of logic in the musical form.

It is important to recall once more that stereotyped melodies are not uniquely Japanese. Renaissance madrigals have their mannerisms, Baroque cantatas and chorale preludes have their doctrine of affections, and romantic operas, particularly Wagner's, have leitmotives. In addition, every music in the world must have specific ways of indicating a stop, a start, or a moment of tension. It is as true for a Mozart symphony as it is for a Piphat orchestral piece from Thailand or a Chinese opera aria. In the study of ethnomusicology one is constantly reminded that the term art, as indicated earlier, is related to artifice and artificiality. The logic of music, while certainly influenced by the physical laws of sound, is basically man-made. The wonder is that we can still call so many pieces divine. Perhaps one of the great appeals of art may be that, as we struggle to find logic in other man-made structures such as history or sociology, the arts show us that man can create something which is both logical and beautiful. In any case, the western listener should approach unfamiliar musics with the expectation of logic, though the base from which this logic starts may be different from that of the music to which he is accustomed.

One of the more complex forms of Japanese musical logic is found in the main music of the *kabuki* theatre, *nagauta*. It combines principles from both the *noh* and *bunraku* traditions as well as adding ideas of its own. The standard *kabuki* ensemble, as mentioned earlier, consists of the *noh hayashi* (three drums and a flute) plus a line of *shamisen* and singers. A bamboo flute *(takebue)* is also used on stage while a whole battery of percussion instruments plus additional flutes and *shamisen* may be used by an off-stage *(geza)* group.[9] In addition, musicians from other genre of *shamisen* music such as *kiyomoto, tokiwazu, gidayu,* or *shinnai* may appear on or off stage. When a kabuki piece is derived from a *noh* play or has an "ancient" atmosphere, the drums make extensive use of the stereotyped rhythm patterns mentioned earlier. In *kabuki* dance pieces there is a greater tendency for the *tsuzumi* drummers to emphasize the rhythm of the *shamisen* in a style of drumming called *chiri-kara* after the menmonics with which their part is learned. In addition, the *kabuki* has created its own stereotyped rhythm patterns to fit the needs of its more exuberant dance style. For example, in *kabuki* music there is a long rhythmic-melodic unit played by the *taiko* and *noh* flute called *sarashi.*[10] It is used specifically for that part of the dance in which two long streamers *(sarashi)* are waved by the dancer in imitation of a folk manner of drying dyed strips of cloth. The interesting aspect of this pattern is that it also is used in other dances in which this choreography does not appear. In such cases it evokes the same mood rather than supporting the same gesture. Thus, rhythm patterns can contribute to the mood and character of a piece as well as articulate its rhythm or its form.

The melodic stereotypes of *nagauta shamisen* music are of four types. First, there are melodies borrowed from other *shamisen* genre, many of which have ceased to exist as independent styles today. These borrowings evoke the mood of these other styles. A second type of borrowing is really a subtype of the first but its use is so specific that it is separated here. This is the so-called forty-eight *ozatsuma-te* derived from the now defunct *ozatsuma-bushi.* These patterns are all named and are used whenever there is a recitative or a moment of *kabuki-* or *noh-* style speaking in the midst of a *nagauta* piece. One need only think of a Mozart opera recitative to realize that the West has a similar stereotyped way of accompanying declamatory *vis à vis* lyrical sections in a vocal piece. *Nagauta* is classified as a more lyrical *(utamono)* than narrative *(katarimono)* genre. Therefore, there are few of the named patterns which stand for specific dramaturgical actions such as were mentioned in *gidayu.* There are, however, subtle reactions to the text in *nagauta* such as the depiction of a hot summer day in *Azuma hakkei* and a slight staggering rhythm whenever the drinking of *saké* wine is mentioned. The fourth type of stereotypes in *nagauta* indicates formal divisions. In *nagauta* they tend to be unnamed though they function just as clearly as the form-indicating patterns of *gidayu.*

One of the problems in approaching *kabuki* music is the fact that it does combine so many different techniques. When the drum rhythms of the *noh* flute shows that its melody is often inextricably linked with the rhythm of the seems to be a kind of chaos. Sometimes the *taiko* rhythm doesn't match up with the *shamisen* and the *noh* flute, as noted earlier, is always in the "wrong key." From what has been said already about *noh* drum rhythms, however, we know that they operate much like chord sequences in western music with their sense of

order and progression to a "tonic" pattern. A study of the *noh* flute shows that
its melody is often inextricably linked with the rhythm of the seemingly
dissident *taiko* drum. Put very simply, there seems to be a unit in *nagauta*
ensemble music which serves neither a basically melodic or rhythmic function.
Instead, it adds color to the music and creates tension against the melodic line
which drives the melody forward to a goal at some cadence point. In western
music these are important functions of the unit called harmony. Harmony plays
no significant role in *nagauta* and this unit of one drum and one flute obviously
cannot play chords. I believe, however, that in lieu of harmony this third unit
can perform harmony's functions. I have called this the dynamic unit, not in the
sense of loud and soft dynamics but in the connotation of dynamism, that
quality in things which gives them their sense of motion and action. Thus, if
western music can be said to have melody, rhythm, and harmony, *nagauta* can
be said to display melody, rhythm, and dynamism.

There are several additional structural intents in Japanese music that will be
mentioned briefly. It has been implied that Japanese melodies tend to be
non-harmonized and ornamented. In addition, they show a very careful use of
melodic tension through notes that require further resolution. This is an
important means of keeping up a purely melodic dynamism when rhythm is not
prominent. All Japanese rhythm is not as metronomic as our earlier discussion
might indicate. In fact, one of the most interesting aspects of Japanese rhythm is
the frequent use of a rather elastic beat. The beginning rhythm of a court
orchestra piece, for example, can best be understood by taking a deep breath
before every fourth beat. The term breath rhythm, in fact, is most useful in
discussing such situations. Likewise, one can seldom tap one's foot to the
rhythm of a *noh* drama except in the dance sections. The great flexibility of *noh*
rhythm is one of the reasons that the drum calls *(kakegoe)* are so important. It
must be remembered that there is never a conductor as such in a Japanese
traditional ensemble. Often there is not even eye contact between the musicians.
The drum calls that startle so many westerners on first hearing are a vital part of
the musical structure as well as distinctive coloristic device. Similar calls are
given by the *shamisen* players in narrative musics to assist the singers in timing
their entrances on each phrase. Understanding the meaning of such calls is
certainly an important step towards the appreciation of this characteristic
device. Understanding the frequent flexibilities in rhythm should also increase
one's enjoyment.

THE ARTISTIC INTENT. So much has been said about stereotyped patterns
that one might think, as some Japanese have said (Eishi 1952: 5-6), that
Japanese music is nothing but a string of stereotyped patterns. When one looks
at specific pieces, however, it is obvious that the arrangement of patterns and
their linking materials are means to a very creative end just as the stereotypes of
various periods of western music history are handled quite differently according
to the individual genius of each composer. Japan has had its compositional
geniuses as well. Most of the names that come down to us from before the

sixteenth century are difficult to verify. A similar situation existed in the study of western music until the flourishing of musicology in this century. After the sixteenth century, the situation clears up in both Japan and the West. Thus one can speak of Japan's great composers such as Yamada Kengyo (1757-1817) in *koto* music, Takemoto Gidayu (1651-1714) in *buraku* music, and Kineya Rokuzaemon, the Tenth (1800-1859) in *nagauta*. Our study of non-western art music has not progressed to the point where we discuss stylistic characteristics of individual composers as we do with Haydn or Mozart, but this is a result of the primitive state of our knowledge of non-western music, not the result of any primitive state in the music itself.

It is true, nevertheless, that the relation of the composer to his creation in Japan differs from that relation in the West. For example, the names attached to *shamisen* pieces are always those of a singer. As far as we can tell at present, the singer creates the vocal line on the basis of a given poem. He is not always the creator the *shamisen* accompaniment. In the puppet theatre, individual singers pride themselves on their special styles and hence adapt previous compositions in the light of their own talents. The *shamisen* player must then make the necessary adjustments in the traditional accompaniment by extending, shortening, or altering specific phrases as necessary. When larger ensembles are involved such as the *nagauta* group in the *kabuki,* other instrumentalists are called in to contribute their part. Thus, some pieces are truly cooperate compositions. While the composer whose name is attached to the piece is the main performer, the drummers, *shamisen* players, and flutists had their part in the creation of the artistic whole. When the music is connected with the theatre it undergoes occasional revisions to suit the requirements of new productions and new actors. In addition, the guild *(ryu)* system in Japanese music tends to encourage variant versions of the same piece. Thus, while there is a standard repertoire, there is not a standard version of each piece except as the standard refers to a specific group of performers. There is no improvisation involved here; rather there is variation. Once a given guild sets the piece they play it the same way every time. The variation comes in the guild interpretation of the piece plus the stylistic penchants of individual singers. Analogous situations can be found in purely instrumental forms by comparing various guild performances of, for example, the *honkyoku* pieces for the *shakuhachi* flute or the *danmono* of the *koto* tradition.

Variation in performances can extend beyond the notes. Many guilds have changed the construction of the instrument and use special playing techniques. Actually, such variations reinforce a very important characteristic of Japanese music which can only be appreciated *in vivo*. In Japan it is not just what you play but how you play it. The correct posture, arm movement, gesture, and facial expression are as important as the correct pitches.

Perhaps the most stable performance tradition is court orchestra music because of its relatively limited repertoire and few number of performing groups. There is little belief that it is played today as it was centuries ago (Garfias 1960: 16), but the tradition has two stabilizing factors which are unusual in Japan:

notation and a fixed pitch system. Since its importation from China in the Nara period, *gagaku* has used individual part books, some of which contained fingerings plus a vocal mnemonic for the instrumental melody.[11] The part books were arranged according to the mode in which the piece was played and the basic pitches upon which these modes were based were derived from pitch pipes of fairly fixed measurement.

Such details are seldom ours to enjoy in the music traditions that followed. The *noh* drama, as shown earlier, gave a fairly accurate picture of its drum accompaniment through the names of the stereotyped patterns being used but the actual performance of these patterns, if we can judge from contemporary practice, varied with the different guilds. Writings on *noh* singing from Zeami on give us many theoretical clues to style including some discussions of pitch and scales, but the form of notation used *(gomaten)* serves only as a reminder of a repertoire already learned. It cannot be sightread. There is considerable variation not only in the various schools of *noh* singing but also in the accompanying drum and flute parts. As with the *kabuki* mentioned earlier, a given performance group will be consistent in its particular version of a specific piece.

There are a few notations of *koto* and other musics from the Edo period but, in general, *koto* and *shamisen* notations remain rare and, when existent, rather vague until the twentieth century. Since that time both traditions have developed rather detailed notations which give clear indications of rhythm, intervals, and instrumental techniques plus the vocal line when it is present. The only inconvenience of these systems is that, again, each instrument and each of the several guilds playing one instrument uses a different system.

It is important to note that while the intervals between notes are set in Japanese notations, the basic pitch (except for *gagaku*) is not. In vocal music, the basic pitch depends entirely on the range of the singer. Instrumental pieces are tuned to the best resonance of a given instrument. An analogous situation in the West is found in vocal music where, for example, one can buy a copy of a Schubert song in any one of several different keys depending on the range of the voice. The difference in the Japanese case is that the notation does not show pitch but rather interval and thus one notation serves for all "keys." One need only tune the instrument to the proper starting pitch. Thus, there is no specific "key" for a given Japanese piece such as the western sonatas in B flat minor or symphonies in A major.

The word key has been put in quotes above because Japanese music is not in the keys of the western major-minor tradition. It has its own scale systems such as the *ryo-ritsu* pair of scales and the *in-yo* pair along with their modal forms.[12] Of course, contemporary Japanese music played on traditional instruments may make use of all tonal systems including an occasional brush with the Schoenbergian twelve-tone rows.

All that has been said above may seem to be somewhat remote from our subheading of the artistic intent. These attitudes towards notation, pitch, and variation, however, are all reflections of the artist's view of his own work. A composer with the idea of self-expression so hallowed in nineteenth century western art music or the concept of the social message popular in the twentieth century would, I believe, view these problems very differently. One has only to think of Beethoven or Verdi raging against the slightest changes in their pieces and the plethora of detail on performance practice which loads every page of late nineteenth century scores. Indeed, certain modern western composers have been dabbling with non-western principles in order to loosen up the tight hold western composers have had on their creations in recent centuries. A good performance of a Japanese piece needs all the accuracy of the performance of a Mozart symphony, but in Japan the model for accuracy is not necessarily that of the original composer. Within the limits of a given school and a given generation the standards of performance are exacting and provide solid ground for an appraisal of a given performance. Other schools or other generations may change the standard in its details. The general outline of the piece as seen in its form, text, and important melodic moments, however, tends to remain constant. The intent of the composer is to provide this framework.

Another aspect of the artistic intent of Japanese music is its tendency to be word-oriented. This is obvious in the great number of vocal forms found in Japan. However, purely instrumental pieces as well tend to be descriptive or to be the evocation of something poetical. This is seen, for example, in the repertoire of the *shakuhachi* where such titles as "The Sound of the Deers" *(shika no tone)* are common. Even the titles of *gagaku* pieces such as "The Barbarians Drinking Wine" *(Konju)* and their frequent use as dance accompaniment give this repertoire a literary tint. The first important exceptions to this literary tendency are the *koto* variation pieces with their abstract forms and titles.

A similar word orientation is found in much of the music of China and may have been part of Japan's Chinese heritage along with so many of her instruments and much of her theory. Indeed, there is always a tendency to lump the Chinese and Japanese musical cultures together since they have the same general roots. The end products of these roots, however, are quite different, though Japanese music in general has more relationship to Chinese music than to other Asian cultures. Again, *gagaku* seems to be the exception when one compares it with the present day instrumental ensembles of Southeast Asia. Its historical roots, however, are also primarily Chinese. Actually the linking of various national musics depends to a large extent on one's point of view. If one chooses to study music as history, the high civilizations of the East and West provide ample written and archaeological material for the construction of chains of influence from one side of the world to the other.[13] If one takes simply the similarity of sound, the patterns of distribution become very different and intriguing.[14] If one takes the basic approaches to music as a guide, as this article has done, inter-cultural linkage becomes more tenuous. Each culture offers its own unique solutions to the aesthetic, creative challenges of art music, but each has to contend with similar problems such as tension and release, unity and variety, and meaningfulness to the members of the culture in which it is created.

Conclusion

Thus, while the actual sounds and some of the principles of Japanese music differ from those of the West, there are in the two musics a surprising number of approaches which serve analogous functions. As we learn more about other oriental traditions it becomes apparent that similar analogies can be made for their musics as well. Perhaps the term "oriental music" is becoming meaningless except in the geographical sense. Of course, there is still the problem of meaningfulness in music. It is primarily the private property of the cultural carrier. Nevertheless, I believe that the cultural outsider can at least learn to recognize the musical logic of a given genre with the proper clues and a musical ear. This can be a pleasurable experience. It also may provide new insights for the listener into the character and structure of the society as a whole. It is the hope of many ethnomusicologists that it can. In any event, the enjoyment of the arts has taken on an international potential. Non-western plastic arts have long been held in esteem. Non-western music may also now join the ranks of the respectful.[15] Music is not a universal language, but its many dialects are wonderful to hear. I hope the approaches listed in this article may prove useful when the reader looks for a meaningful experience in *hogaku,* the traditional music of Japan.

Notes

[1] These differences can be heard by comparing various performances of the piece "Rokudan" on the Miyage Michio record (Nihon Victor JL 7), the Eto Kimio record (World 1428), and the Yuize Shinichi record (Cook 1132). The last is, in my opinion, overdone.

[2] It can also be applied to larger western ensembles such as the orchestra as used by Anton Webern. By the same token, western chamber works can sound orchestral, for example, the Ravel string quartet.

[3] In this context it is interesting to note that the academic discipline concerned with music outside the Euro-American art tradition was first called comparative musicology, but later changed its name to ethnomusicology, the study of music in culture.

[4] This technique can be heard clearly in the recorded piece listed in note 1.

[5] One of the best discussions of anticipation and patterning in the comprehension of music is found in Meyer 1956.

[6] For specific examples, see Malm 1958.

[7] See further *Bunraku* (in Japanese) 1959.

[8] For example, in a passage that has been using the scale A B C   E F , the last notes will be F E D.

[9] The instruments and functions of *geza* music are discussed in Malm 1959.

[10] A transcription of this pattern can be seen in Malm 1963.

[11] This notation can be seen in Malm 1959.

[12] A resumé of Japanese scale systems is found in Peri 1934.

[13] For example, there have been attempts to link the *shamisen* with the *nefer* of ancient Egypt (Tanabe 1963: 13). A study of the movement of music along the East-West trade routes can be seen in Kishibe 1940: 261-304.

[14] For example, the sound of some Okinawan folk songs resembles that of the Tung people of China and also a folk style in Indonesia, while the female singers of Korea produce a sound similar to that found in Southwest Asia and among the gypsies of Spain.

[15] Respect will not come without a struggle. As late as 1960, Maraini said that the Orient could claim equality in everything but science and music (1960: 13). The statement may be more a result of his Italian background than his Japanese insight.

References Cited

Bunraku, 1959, *Bunkazai.* Tokyo.

Garfias, Robert, 1960, "Gradual Modification of the *Gagaku* Tradition." *Ethnomusicology.* IV, January: 16-9.

Harich-Schneider, Eto, 1953, "The Present Condition of Japanese Court Music." *Musical Quarterly.* XXXIX, Jan.: 49-74.

Kikkawa, Eishi, 1952, "*Samisen* and *Samisen* Music." *KBS BULLETIN.* June: 5-6.

Kishibe, Shigeo, 1940, "The Origin of the P'ip'a." *The Transactions of the Asiatic Society of Japan.* December: 261-304.

Malm, William P., 1958, "The Rhythmic Orientation of Two Drums in the Japanese *Noh* Drama." *Ethnomusicology.* II, September: 181-200.

Malm, William P., 1959, *Japanese Music and Musical Instruments.* Tokyo, Tuttle and Company.

Malm, William P., 1963, *Nagauta: The Heart of Kabuki Music.* Tokyo, Tuttle and Company.

Maraini, Fosco, 1960, *Meeting with Japan.* New York, Viking Press.

Meyer, Leonard, 1956, *Emotion and Meaning in Music.* Chicago, University of Chicago Press.

Minawaga, Tatsuo, 1957, "Japanese *Noh* Music." *Journal of the American Musicological Society.* X, Fall: 181-200.

SELECTED AND ANNOTATED BIBLIOGRAPHY

Bibliographies

"Current Bibliography," in nearly every issue of *Ethnomusicology*, Journal of the Society for Ethnomusicology, Wesleyan University Press, Middletown, Conn., (1953-   )

Gillis, Frank and Alan P. Merriam, *Ethnomusicology and Folk Music, An International Bibliography of Dissertations and Theses,* Special Series in Ethnomusicology No. 1, Society for Ethnomusicology, Wesleyan University Press, Middletown, Conn., (1966)

Haywood, Charles, *A Bibliography of North American Folklore and Folksong*, New York, (1951.) Includes North American Indian music.

Kunst, Jaap, *Ethnomusicology*, 3rd ed., The Hague, (1959,) and *Supplement to the Third Edition of Ethnomusicology*, (1960,) Includes discussion of the field and 5,079 bibliographic items and a subject index.

Thieme, Darius, *African Music, A Briefly Annotated Bibliography*, Library of Congress, Reference Dept., Music Division, (1964), 55 pp.

Nettle, Bruno, "Annotated Bibliography," in *Music in Primitive Culture*, Harvard Univ. Press, 1956, 21 pp.

Waterman, Richard A., and William Lichtenwanger, Virginia H. Herrmann, Horace I. Poleman, and Cecil Hobbs, "Bibliography of Asian Musics," in *Notes*, 2nd Series, Vols V-VIII, (1947-51).

Periodicals

African Music, Journal of the African Music Society, Roodepoort (Johannesburg), (1955-   ). Articles, notes, news, book and record reviews.

Anuario (Yearbook, Anuário) Inter-American Institute for Musical Research, Tulane Univ., New Orleans, (1965-   ). Articles in Spanish, Portuguese and English on traditional musicology and ethnomusicology.

Les Colloques de Wégimont, University of Liege, (1957-   ). Proceedings of occasional conferences, emphasis on European folk music.

Ethnomusicology, Journal of the Society for Ethnomusicoloty, Wesleyan Univ., Middletown, Conn., (1953-   ). Articles, bibliography, discography, book and record reviews.

The Folklore and Folk Music Archivist, Archives of Traditional Music, Indiana University, Bloomington, (1958-   ). Articles on archiving methods and descriptions of various archives and their holdings.

Journal of the International Folk Music Society, 35 Princess Court, Queensway, London W 2, (1948-   ). Proceedings of annual conferences, reviews of books and journals.

Special Series in Ethnomusicology, Society for Ethnomusicology, Wesleyan Univ., Middletown, Conn., (1966-   ). Monograph series.

Selected Reports, Institute of Ethnomusicology, Univ. of California, Los Angeles, (1966-   ). Articles by members of the Institute.

Studies in Ethnomusicology, Oak Publications, New York, (1961-   ). Articles in occasional issues. Vol. II appeared in 1965.

General Works

Bose, Fritz, *Musikalische Völkerkunde*, (Freiburg im Breisgau, 1953), Deals with Oriental as well as tribal musics.

Festival of Oriental Music and the Related Arts, (University of California, Los Angeles, 1960). Includes short essays on music of Bali, Java, Japan, India and Persia.

Merriam, Alan P., *The Anthropology of Music*, (Northwestern University Press, 1964). Discusses music as social behavior.

Meyer, Leonard B., *Emotion and Meaning in Music*, (University of Chicago Press, 1956). "Meaning" as defined by the perception of musical patterning.

Nettl, Bruno, *Theory and Method in Ethnomusicology*, Glencoe Free Press, 1964). The bibliographic resources, the methods, the scholars and their theoretical appraoches.

Sachs, Curt, *The Wellsprings of Music*, (Martinus Nijhof, 1962). Speculations on the development of melody, backed by an encyclopedic knowledge of world music.

Regional Studies

AFRICA

Kolinski, Mieczyslaw, "Music," in Melville and Frances Herskovits, *Suriname Folklore*, (New York, 1936). Characterizes West African music and discusses its survival in Suriname.

Kirby, Percival R., *The Musical Instruments of the Native Races of South Africa*, (Oxford Univ. Press, 1934). Extensive survey of instruments among the Bantu, Bushmen and Hottentots, with a commentary on their use and place in these cultures.

Merriam, Alan P., "African Music Reexamined in the Light of New Materials from the Belgian Congo and Ruanda-Urundi," *Zaire*, 7: 245-253 (1953). Criticises the notion of complex drumming as characteristic of all African music and surveys various African musical styles.

Nketia, J. H., *Drumming in Akan Communities of Ghana*, (Univ. of Ghana Press, 1963). Describes in detail the making and playing of drums and their important place in the life of the commmunity.

Tracey, Hugh, *Chopi Musicians*, (London, 1948). The complex interplay between Chopi poets, composers, conductors, dancers, and the orchestral music in which they all have a part.

Waterman, Richard A., "African Influences on American Negro Music," in Sol Tax, ed. *Acculturation in the Americas*, (New York, 1952). Discusses the mingling of African and European musical styles.

AMERICAN INDIAN

Densmore, Frances, *Chippewa Music*, Bulletins 45 and 53 of Bureau of American Ethnology, (Washington, 1910, 1913)

Densmore, Frances, *Teton Sioux Music*, Bulletin 61, same series, 1918. These are outstanding among the 13 major tribal studies she published. Both music and social context are fully treated.

Herzog, George, "A Comparison of Pueblo and Pima Musical Styles," *Journal of American Folklore*, 48: 283-417 (1938). A classic combination of cultural and musical analysis.

Izikowitz, Karl Gustav, *Musical and Other Sound Instruments of the South American Indians*, (Göteborg, 1935). An attempt to reconstruct the history of the instruments through analysis of their construction and geographical distribution.

Kurath, Gertrude, *Iroquois Music and Dance: Ceremonial Arts of Two Seneca Longhouses*, Bureau of American Ethnology, Bulletin 187, (Washington, 1964). Full year's cycle of religious dances treated ethnomusicologically and choreologically.

McAllester, David P., *Enemy Way Music*, Papers, Peabody Museum, Harvard, XLI, No. 3, (Cambridge, 1954). Social and esthetic values of the Navaho Indians as seen in their music and behavior.

Nettl, Bruno, "North American Indian Musical Styles," *Journal of American Folklore*, 67: 44-56; 297-307; 351-368, (1954). A definition of music areas compared with American Indian culture areas.

Roberts, Helen H., and Diamond Jenness, *Songs of the Copper Eskimo*, Report of the Canadian Arctic Expedition 1913-1918, Vol. XIV, (Ottawa, 1925). Discussion of the culture and almost 100 pp. of texts and translations by Jenness, detailed transcriptions and analyses by Roberts.

EUROPE AND AMERICA

Baines, Anthony, *Bagpipes,* (Oxford, 1960). Discussion in depth of form and use of bagpipes and related instruments the world over.

Bronson, Bertrand H., *The Traditional Tunes of the Child Ballads,* Vols. I and II, (Princeton University Press, 1959 & 1962). A painstaking research into the melodies of the English and Scottish ballad texts compiled by Child.

Chase, Gilbert, *A Guide to the Music of Latin America,* Pan American Union (Washington, 1962).

Child, Francis J., *The English and Scottish Popular Ballads,* 5 vols. bound as 3, (New York 1962, originally Boston, 1882-1898). Compendium of texts, intensively compared for European versions.

Courlander, Harold, *Negro Folk Music in U.S.A.,* (Columbia Univ. Press, 1963).

Karpeles, Maude, ed., *Folk Songs of Europe,* (London, 1956).

Kodaly, Zoltan, *Folk Music of Hungary,* (Barrie and Rockliff, 1960).

Kremenliev, Boris, *Bulgarian-Macedonian Folk Music,* (Univ. of California Press, Berkeley, 1952).

Lord, Albert B., *The Singer of Tales,* (Harvard Univ. Press, 1964). Though based on Balkan epics, discussion of poetic composition in oral tradition has wide relevance for other cultures.

Ortiz, Fernando, *Los Instrumentos de la Música Afrocubana,* 4 vol. (Habana, 1952-54). Detailed study of construction and uses of instruments, and their place in the culture.

OCEANIA

Anderson, Johannes C., *Maori Music,* (New Plymouth, N.Z., 1934). Includes observations on Polynesian music in general by early travelers and later scholars.

Burrows, Edwin G., *Native Music of the Tuamotus,* Bishop Museum, Bulletin 109, (Honolulu, 1933). Music of one Polynesian society seen anthropologically and ethnomusicologically.

Christensen, Dieter and Gerd Koch, *Die Musik der Ellice-Inseln,* Music, texts, and social context treated in detail. A 7-inch record containing nine of the songs is included.

Elkin, A. P., and Trevor A. Jones, *Arnhem Land Music,* (Univ. of Sydney, 1953, reprinted from *Oceania,* Vol. XXIV, No. 2, 1953). Songs, texts and dances in North Australia treated in detail in their social and religious context.

Emerson, Nathaniel B., *Unwritten Literature of Hawaii,* Bureau of American Ethnology, Bulletin 38, (Washington, 1909). A discussion of the chants of the hula: dance, texts, instruments, and social milieu.

Roberts, Helen H., *Ancient Hawaiian Music,* Bishop Museum Bulletin 29, (Honolulu, 1926). Extensive discussion of the music and instruments of Hawaiian chants, but without translations of the texts.

THE ORIENT

Berner, Alfred, *Studen zur Arabischen Musik,* (Leipzig, 1937). Tone systems, melodic forms, tuning and use of instruments.

Embree, John F., *Japanese Peasant Songs,* Memoirs of American Folklore Society, Vol. 38, (Richmond, 1944). Detailed discussion of texts and social context but not the music.

Kunst, Jaap, *Music in Java,* 2 vols. (The Hague, 1949). Emphasis is on history, structure and tuning of orchestral instruments.

Levis, John H., *Foundations of Chinese Musical Art,* (Peiping, 1936). Detailed discussion of the development of the music, and analysis of tone systems, notation and composition.

Malm, William P., *Japanese Music and Musical Instruments*, (Rutland and Tokyo, 1959). An extensive introduction to most of the kinds of music, folk and classical.

Malm, William P., *Nagauta, The Heart of Kabuki Music*, (Rutland and Tokyo, 1963). Detailed treatment of the history, content and social function of one genre of Japanese music.

Strangways, A. H. F., *The Music of Hindostan*, (Oxford, 1914). Emphasis on North India, thorough treatment of raga, tala, instruments and the history of Indian music.

Werner, Eric, *The Philosophy and Theory of Music in Judaeo-Arabic Culture*, (Cincinnati, 1941).